T0112568

ABOUT THE AUTHOR

David Ludden is Professor of Political Economy and Globalization in the History Department at New York University. His research concerns histories of development and globalization and *India and South Asia: A Short History* represents one aspect of his effort to foster interdisciplinary research on South Asia and globalization.

INDIA

AND SOUTH ASIA

A Short History

DAVID LUDDEN

ONEWORLD

A Oneworld Book

First published by Oneworld Publications 2002
Reprinted 2005, 2007
This edition published in 2014

Copyright © David Ludden 2002, 2014

The moral right of David Ludden to be identified as
the Author of this work has been asserted by him in accordance
with the Copyright, Designs, and Patents Act 1988.

All rights reserved
Copyright under Berne Convention
A CIP record for this title is available from the British Library

ISBN 978-1-85168-936-1
eBook ISBN 978-1-78074-108-6

Printed and bound in Denmark by Nørhaven

Oneworld Publications
10 Bloomsbury Street
London WC1B 3SR
England

Stay up to date with the latest books,
special offers, and exclusive content from
Oneworld with our monthly newsletter

Sign up on our website
www.oneworld-publications.com

For Mohona Sara Siddiqi

Contents

List of Maps, Tables, and Figures

Preface and Acknowledgements

I finished writing the first edition of this book not long before 11 September 2001, which now seems very long ago. Scholars then rarely thought of Afghanistan as being an integral part of contemporary South Asia, let alone as a theatre of war affecting politics and societies across the region. Few scholars thought of Maoist rebels as being significant in South Asia. Ethnic war seemed endless in Sri Lanka, Hindutva ruled New Delhi, and Pakistan seemed to be a permanent military state. The Maldives were not yet drowning. Climate change did not seem to threaten Bhutan or Bangladesh. Global media, finance, trade, and labour mobility attracted little attention. These are but a few indications of how dramatically the huge part of the world discussed in this book has changed since 2001.

Today, what came to be called 'globalization' during the 1990s has affected everyday life in various ways in every corner of South Asia, and history looks different today, not only because it has more recent chapters, but also because ideas about history have changed. Most notably, history can no longer be contained inside maps of national states. The Country Profiles that concluded the first edition of this book now appear sadly archaic, not only in their factual content but also in their conceptualization. The final chapters of this edition endeavour to weave together national histories with transnational trends that now affect all of the countries in the region.

Every chapter has been revised for this new edition to reflect some of the impact of new scholarship and changing orientations toward history over the very long term. A short text like this can never do justice to the ever-growing wealth of new scholarship which has revealed, for instance, that Indus Valley cultures were much more expansive than was previously known; that ancient, medieval, and early-modern societies were likewise more complex, diverse, and interconnected; and that pre-modern South Asia as a whole was more deeply and broadly connected to wider Eurasian trends, creating many East–West parallels. Scholars have now woven colonial history into post-colonial theory and vastly increased the scale and sophistication of research on gender, the environment, law, under-represented social groups, and many other subjects. I have presented some of this new knowledge in the text and in Selected Readings.

I have continued the old practice of using the names of contemporary political territories, cities, and regions to locate events throughout history. But I now flag the novelty of our current cultural scene by using new place names in the last chapters, notably for cities formerly known as Madras, Bombay, Calcutta, Baroda, and Trivandrum, and for the region formerly known as Orissa. I have used a slightly modified thematic scheme in the book as a whole, which is described in the Introduction. There is now a blog for updates, feedback, and conversations: http://southasiahistory. blogspot.com/. I am grateful to Sapana Gandhi and Sabina Panday for able research assistance.

Some of the original Preface and cover text is no longer accurate, because I have moved from the University of Pennsylvania to New York University, but original Acknowledgements still pertain. I have used ideas and information from many people. I want to thank the following people by name without implicating them in any errors of fact or interpretation that remain in the text. In no particular order, they are: Muzaffar Alam, G. Aloysius, Romila Thapar, Binay Bhushan Chaudhuri, Dharma Kumar, Amiya Kumar Bagchi, Ashok Rudra, Irfan Habib, Neeladri Bhattacharya, Bina Agarwal, Amartya Sen, M. S. S. Pandian, Gail Omvedt, Sheldon Pollock, A. R. Desai, Sanjay Subrahmanyam, Bernard S. Cohn, Sumit Guha, Dina Mahnaz Siddiqi, Sugata Bose, Ayesha Jalal, David Washbrook, Richard Eaton, Gyanendra Pandey, Sandria Freitag, Carol Breckenridge, Nicholas B. Dirks, Christopher Bayly, Christopher Baker, Anand Yang, Michelle Maskiell, Barbara Metcalf, Gyan Prakash, Brian Caton, Robert Nichols, Vivek Bhandari, Sanjay Joshi, and Savita Nair.

Thanks also to David Nelson for his constant bibliographic assistance; and to Jeremie Dufault, Teresa Watts, Linda Oh, Sue Yi, Richard Mo, Anna Cullotti, and Vivek Arora for their help on various phases of this project. Lori Uscher merits special thanks for her detailed reading, perceptive comments, and insightful suggestions. The editorial staff at Oneworld Publications have been steadfast throughout, and I appreciate all their hard work, patience, and encouragement.

Introduction:
Social History and
Political Territory

This survey of history concerns the world region that now includes Afghanistan, Bangladesh, Bhutan, India, the Maldives, Nepal, Pakistan, and Sri Lanka. I follow convention by using politics and state territory to describe geography and chronology, but my central concern is social change, including its economic, political, and cultural dimensions. To introduce the very long-term history of social change in South Asia, I focus on the mobility of people, ideas, and other important elements in social life and on human territorial attachments that give culture and politics spatial form. Each chapter focuses on innovations in each historical period that affect people in everyday life, and condition their production and reproduction of social identities.

Each chapter draws connections between large-scale trends in the wider world and patterns of change in South Asia's many regions and countless localities, where disparate histories unfold and no one set of peoples or places typifies history as a whole. The book pays close attention to spatial diversity, so that rather than telling one single story, it presents a series of strategic simplifications to sketch mosaic contours of history. My goal is to establish a reliable historical starting point for further study, providing a useful framework for organizing an ever-increasing flood of new factual information. My starting point for thinking about the past is rooted emphatically in the present: this book seeks to make history useful in the present, when South Asia, like Asia as a whole, is subject to radical transformation. Global identities are emerging today in South Asia that are as novel, world-making, and trendsetting as anti-colonial national identities were when they hit the streets in South Asia more than a century ago.

Successive chapters trace the invention and reinvention of group definitions, associations, solidarities, and interactions, shaping people's experience, feelings, and thinking about who they are, where they live, where they belong, who belongs with them, who deserves to get what in society, and who and what are foreign, alien, and threatening. In each historical period, we find the picture changing dramatically. Each epoch brings unique forces to bear on the composition of social identity. Social conditions change and vary so much over space and time that the portrayal of South Asia as housing a single civilization characterized by continuity and coherence over millennia appears as an ideological activity rather than an accurate description of historical reality. We see how that ideology works in the last chapters. Spaces and times of history emerge in this book as being diverse, changing configurations of human social conditions, experience, thought, and imagination, where social identities take shape and change fundamentally over space and time, among changing political, cultural, and economic forces, from ancient times to the present.

The book combines ideas from two contrasting approaches to the historical problem of social identity. We cannot solve that problem here, but we can use it to study social change. One approach can be called 'essentialist'. It begins by assuming that people inherit group identity as an attribute, like a genetic trait. Individuals thus have a definite identity when they are born, they share it with all group members, they organize their life around it, and they live with it until they die. Scholars who deploy this approach can thus interpret social activity as an expression of pre-existing group sentiments and mentalities. Historically, they can argue that social groups – defined by nationality, ethnicity, religion, language, race, gender, caste, class, or other traits – express essential group characteristics through the activity of group members, particularly that of leaders who claim to represent group sentiments and interests in public. This approach allows historians to read speeches and texts composed by leaders, and to interpret group activities under their leadership – such as protests, riots, or political movements – as the expression of group feelings and aspirations. Elections and opinion polls are also interpreted in this vein, using phrasing such as 'the nation speaks'.

The other approach can be called 'constructivist'. It begins by assuming that identities are not inherited naturally, like skin colour or body type, but are rather cultural phenomena and products of human agency. Ideas, interactions, and experiences that shape social identity form incoherent packages that are malleable, dispersed, ambiguous, shifting, and contextual, with many possible meanings. Countless combinations and permutations of elements that compose social identity make it unlikely to acquire uniformity over any sizable population or stability over time. Individual decisions about friendship, marriage, migration, and learning challenge inherited social identities with unpredictable preferences. People must work to reproduce identities over time, to propagate identity spatially, to make it feel like a permanent, essential inheritance, and to make some identities feel more important than others for individuals in their social life.

In this constructivist view, social activists of many kinds – in politics, religion, the arts, markets, and other sites – exert social power that shapes group sentiment, experience, and identification, using all available media, in each historical period. Records preserved from the past thus become saturated with markers and expressions of group identity, as we will see with medieval temple inscriptions, and a millennium later, with modern print media. This saturation spreads and deepens as communication media become more pervasive, making identities appear to be natural and permanent, and that appearance becomes a major ideological force in modern times. Nevertheless, identities remain unstable products of social power, contested by social forces pushing and pulling this way and that. Collective action is therefore not an expression of fixed, inherited identities, but rather a mobilization of social power to generate the feeling that people belong to a group endowed with leaders who personify its spirit and pursue its interests.

Both approaches have strengths and weaknesses. Essentialists have as much trouble explaining change as constructivists have explaining continuity. Essentialists have the advantage that most people in fact do seem to believe – and they express their belief in many historical texts – that their identity is essential, authentic, and inherited. Constructivists meanwhile have the advantage that all identities can be shown to have come into being historically under specific conditions and under the influence of documented social forces. History thus needs to combine both approaches, in order to excavate the authentic personal experience of being human and to explain how being human is a complicated social process transforming identities over space and time even as people believe those identities are fixed and inherited.

This book combines both approaches but leans towards constructivism, for it seeks to appreciate the authentic experience of social life inside a very long-term perspective on the shaping and changing of social identities. In this dual perspective, all identities are changing historical phenomena, though change is typically too slow for people to see in their lifetimes. Human agency is always at work. People's diverse situations, values, and decisions make a difference, as they engage in friendships, politics, marriage, migration, learning, religious activity, and other social opportunities to invest cultural capital in their social being. Some elements of personal identity may be cherished assets, serving as social entitlements to be preserved and passed down over generations; while others may be constraints which people feel are imposed, ill-fitting, and ready for change. In their lifetimes, people with various combinations of identity elements make countless personal investments, which add up in populations over time to become a force driving social change that is largely invisible in historical records.

What is most historically visible in available documentation is social action that alters conditions under which people make decisions that affect social identity. Famous leaders get the most credit for generating big changes. Their activity is a convenient marker of change under way, but great transformations of the social world result rather from an accumulation of countless small decisions by ordinary people in everyday life. Leaders are more visible, historically, but invisible investments by their followers are much more important for explaining big changes over time.

The chronological architecture of this book is based on the big changes across epochs which separate social worlds in South Asia that have become sufficiently different from one another to warrant separate histories of their own. Each chapter's geographical framework is appropriate in its own time period, as historical spaces shift with the changing spatial composition of social worlds in South Asia.

Chapter One opens with a brief consideration of the physical landscape shaping South Asian history and the immeasurable span of time that preceded the appearance of written historical records in the first millennium of the Common Era. Archaeology and philology allow us to envision complex social worlds emerging in the Indus Valley and produced by Vedic cultures, both of which were connected extensively to West and Central Asia. The first historically visible transformation of social worlds in South Asia occurred during the millennium after 500 BCE spanning the rise and fall of the imperial Mauryas and Guptas. Ancient records reveal activities and identities in South Asia that were extensively connected to societies around the Silk Road and the Indian Ocean; in that context, imperial civilization emerged along the Indo-Gangetic Plain.

Chapter Two describes a medieval epoch forming a long millennium from the fall of the Guptas to the rise of the imperial Mughals in the sixteenth century, when dense documentation enables us to visualize social life in local settings all across South Asia. We can thus begin to see social change being driven by two interacting social processes. On the one hand, powerful people strove to reproduce their social stature and their material entitlements, over generations, under changing conditions, inside imperial ranks; while, on the other hand, and at the same time, ordinary people also struggled to improve their entitlements and their social stature inside the same imperial ranks. This latter striving often led to smooth social mobility up the ranks, but it also pitted inferiors against superiors in struggles that reshuffled the ranks in various ways. When successful struggles were led by people who sought to change the rules of empire and overthrow old elites, resulting changes in social power relations were catastrophic for the people who were most deeply invested in established privileges, and who produced many historical records to document their plight and disparage those who wrought havoc upon their civilization.

In Chapter Three, we see that after 1500 it becomes more impractical to separate social change in South Asia from histories that travel the globe. From ancient times, South Asia had been an important space in a wider world, forming Asia's vast land bridge between the Silk Road and the Indian Ocean. Before 1700, people in South Asia had focused most of their activity on the inland circuits of mobility that ran overland across West and Central Asia. In that historical space, Delhi became an enduring site of inland military power and political authority. By 1700, increasing wealth and power had been moving for two centuries along sea routes across the Indian Ocean from the Atlantic to the Pacific. This spatial shift towards the sea in the wider world of human mobility accelerated after 1700; it propelled a shift in the spatial balance of power in South Asia, increasing the relative economic and political importance of the seaward side of Asia's land bridge, that is, the coastal regions of South Asia.

A transformation of South Asia's political geography occurred in the eighteenth century, driven both by inland trends in regional states and by the expansion of European power at sea, which together focused epochal struggles for power on the regions around seaports.

This spatial shift of social power to focus more influentially on coastal regions occurred everywhere in the world, and forms a geographical framework for modernity. History in South Asia entered its early-modern phase when its spatial context became more truly global than ever before, focusing on routes around the world both overland and overseas. The creation of a world-embracing space of human history is captured by the French term *mondialisation*, which evokes the long-term historical process of organizing institutions – of trade, politics, culture, law, and social relations – on an ever-expanding spatial scale, eventually to cover the globe. *Mondialisation* can reasonably be said to have begun in ancient Eurasia, in the days of Ashoka Maurya and Alexander the Great. It advanced slowly and steadily over centuries and accelerated mightily with the Mongol military integration of inland Eurasia. It entered its more comprehensive modern phase with Europe's expansion by sea after 1492. The twentieth-century age of air travel launched a new spatial frame for world history in South Asia, which we consider in the final chapter.

Modern world history acquired solid anchorage in South Asia, where early-modern *mondialisation* began in the eastern hemisphere, when South Asian ports and coastal regions became primary destinations for European ships and battlegrounds for European imperialism. South Asia thus acquired a major role in modern world history, which emerged initially from the eighteenth-century regional politics of transition between the Mughal and British Empires.

Chapter Four describes the modern imperial order that emerged under British supremacy in nineteenth-century South Asia. This provides a window on to the world of modern social history that was shaped everywhere by imperial formations of power and authority. All modern societies have emerged in a world of empires. South Asia was a pre-eminent imperial territory, containing three-quarters of the entire population of the British Empire and ninety percent of its non-Europeans. The peoples in South Asia played significant roles in shaping the world of modernity as a whole by sustaining the British Empire, feeding world capitalism, and generating national identities and anti-colonial nationalist movements that displaced imperialism to form the world of national states in the twentieth century.

Chapter Five shows how social change in imperial environments produced one of the most compelling political forces shaping modern world history: anti-colonial nationalism. National forces that would drive twentieth-century politics around the world were fully born in South Asia in the late decades of the nineteenth century, complete with a well-honed theoretical critique of imperial exploitation and replete with organizations designed to press popular demands on imperial elites. In 1905, a national movement in British India produced mass public protests, street politics, violence, political art, and mass support for nationalist demands that imperial elites redirect the flow of wealth in the world of empire to benefit the people of South Asia. In 1920, nationalists launched a movement for independence, challenging the foundations of empire. At the same time, powerful competing demands for territorial authority emerged in specific regions. The mobilization of national aspirations led eventually to national independence, the partition of British India into India and Pakistan, in 1947, and then to the birth of Bangladesh in 1971.

The last three chapters trace the historical production of present-day nationality and nationhood in Afghanistan, Bangladesh, Bhutan, India, the Maldives, Nepal, Pakistan, and Sri Lanka. Chapter Six considers the changing substance of national state territorialism through the period of national state consolidation, from the 1920s into the 1970s. Nineteenth-century imperial authority had produced the possibility of national identities attached to specific territories, which changed dramatically during the imbroglio of imperial and national politics. The substance of national identities changed after 1920, during decades of struggle for independence, and changed again after 1947, as nations became identified with national states, facing numerous challenges and obstacles. Chapter Seven focuses on one major trend in the changing substance of nationality – the rise of identity politics – which has mobilized cultural diversity in many directions and also expanded the national presence of public religion. Chapter Eight focuses on a second major trend, the changing spatial configuration of social and political power that occurs when nationality and nationhood become embedded in the processes of globalization.

The broad conclusion of this book is that social identity is profoundly historical: it is produced in time and in space, in specific periods of history and in particular places. The social identities we embrace today did not exist in earlier times. Even today, national and cultural identities are not experienced in the same way by different kinds of people in different places. We can see this changing reality more clearly when studying history in the long term, but its salience is critical today. Social identities that are currently defined by nationality, ethnicity, caste, religion, and class are very modern constructs, however essential and eternal they may feel. Their political mobilization may evoke ancient traditions, but the politics attached to religions and ethnic identities today are products of the present. Taking a long view of history, we can see that social identities feel most like permanent, essential, natural facts of life when they are embedded in systems of power that organize social experience by saturating everyday life with expressions of group membership and institutional authority. Nations appear to house separate cultures and histories only because social identities have been constructed inside powerful modern state institutions. As we will see, the expansive power of the market economy in the world of nations has tended to aggravate the separation of social identities. Geographical boundaries that define South Asia politically have changed massively over the centuries, but because boundaries are not changing today, national identities appear to be permanent and immutable in present-day perspectives. Historicizing the present reveals that social spaces where identities acquire their form and substance are indeed changing dramatically today, along with the institutions that hold them in place. The study of connections between local, regional, national, and global histories over many centuries provides a useful way to think creatively about social life and the future unfolding in the world around us today.

Inventing Civilization

South Asian history has no one beginning, no one chronology, no single plot or narrative. It is not a singular history, but rather many histories, with indefinite, contested origins and with countless separate trajectories that multiply as we learn more about the past. In recent decades, history's multiplicity, antiquity, and ambiguity have become more complicated as scholars have opened up new perspectives on the past and made new discoveries.

As recently as the 1960s, it seemed to most scholars that South Asian history began at a singular moment in the second millennium BCE, when the oldest-known texts, the Vedas, were composed. A clear, continuous stream of cultural tradition once seemed to flow from Vedic to modern times, allowing modern scholars to dip into ancient texts to savour the original essence of a culture they could still see around them. Culture seemed to grow into a fully developed classical civilization under the ancient empires of the Mauryas (321–181 BCE) and the Guptas (320–520 CE), on the banks of the sacred river Ganga. Classical societies appeared to follow Vedic norms, and to embody sacred traditions recorded in later Sanskrit texts, which prescribe the division of Hindu society into ritual strata, called *varna*, containing ranked social groups called *jati*. Classical tradition seemed to provide a blueprint for caste society down to modern times. After the Gupta Empire collapsed, apparently under the impact of foreign invasions, political fragmentation was seen to have characterized medieval times; but despite a long series of foreign conquests, the clear stream of Hindu tradition seemed to flow on continuously. After the end of the ancient empires, history brought turmoil and social and economic change, but ancient traditions appeared to maintain their integrity, responding and adapting to the challenges of history right down to the present day.

In this traditional formulation, we hear echoes of modern nationalism resounding in the idea that indigenous resistance to foreign invasion spurred the early formation of the ancient empires. It is indeed true that in the wake of victories by Darius, king of Persia, who conquered Sind and Gandhara in the sixth century BCE, and after several early efforts at empire building by rulers along the banks of the Ganga, the Maurya Empire rose at the same time as Alexander the Great entered Punjab from Persia in 327 BCE. But now we can see that modern national identities had projected themselves into the distant past by imagining that Mauryan armies were defending their homeland against foreign invaders from Greece and Persia. This same idea of defensive response was also used to explain the later rise of the Guptas, who finally managed to unify the Ganga basin once again after centuries of conquest by Indo-Greeks, Sakas, Indo-Parthians, and Kushanas, travelling across West and Central Asia and marching down the Hindu Kush into the Indus Valley lowlands. The same idea was used again to show how invading Hunas from Central Asia broke up the Gupta Empire, in the fifth century, when political fragmentation inside India was seen to have prevented imperial unity against the invaders. The same fractious disunity inside India continued to prevent solidarity against many later invaders. In the eighth century, Arabs came by sea to conquer Sind. From the twelfth century onward, invading conquerors included Afghans, Turks, Mongols, Persians, and, finally, Europeans. From 1290 until 1947, Muslims and Christians ruled most of the land of Indic civilization. The British were the last foreign rulers, from 1757 to 1947. Thus it fell to modern nationalism to unify native peoples against foreign threats once and for all.

This grand narrative of history in South Asia – based on the idea of an original, indigenous culture facing foreign invasions – provided the first framework for modern historical studies. It informed national cultures and national identities. It perpetuated the idea that Hindus, Buddhists, Muslims, and Christians each represent distinct civilizations with their own ancient, native territories. Thus it helped to bolster the identification of independent national states, each with their separate domain of world history.

New discoveries and new perspectives now provide many different avenues for exploring South Asia's ancient, medieval, and modern history. We now see that rather than having had one singular origin, South Asia has always included diverse peoples and cultures with different points of departure and distinctive historical trajectories. What once seemed like a single tree of Indic culture rooted in the Vedas, with many branches spreading out over the centuries, has come to look more like a vast forest of many cultures filled with countless trees of various sizes, ages, and types, constantly crossbreeding to fertilize one another. The profusion of cultures also blurs the boundaries of the forest. Cultural boundaries drawn by modern scholars in and around South Asia have come to be seen more as artifacts of modern national cultures than as an accurate reflection of pre-modern conditions. Prehistoric urban sites in the Indus river valley, much older than the Vedas, and many smaller offshoots scattered from Punjab to Gujarat, participated in a vast prehistory of urbanism that spread across southern Eurasia; and they also participated in the indigenous evolution of agropastoral societies in South Asia. Pre-Vedic cultures should not be assigned exclusively to the prehistory of modern South Asia, West Asia, India, or Pakistan: they participate in all of these at the same time. The singers of the Vedas informed cultures in ancient South Asia, and also moved among prehistoric pastoral cultures crisscrossing Central and West Asia. The mingling and fusion of cultures have always occurred in vast open Asian spaces cut up into modern territories by boundaries that divide today's national states.

With all this in view, it becomes obvious that we must now separate the academic study of pre-modern history from the construction of modern identities. We need to separate the study of the distant past from cultural politics in the world of nations. As we will see, pre-modern history does indeed help us to understand the present, but not by its immanent foreshadowing of current conditions, or by its revelation of classical truths to guide modern life; rather by its indication that distinctly modern modes of social existence came into being in the nineteenth and twentieth centuries, setting them apart from medieval and ancient histories. Using ancient and medieval evidence to validate modern boundaries, identities, and cultures obscures more than it reveals about premodern and modern histories alike. Pre-modern South Asia took shape inside spaces of mobility spanning all regions of southern Eurasia. These great open spaces composed South Asia's social world in a fluid, mobile manner, quite unlike today's restrictive national territorialism. The first basic lesson of this book is that travelling back into the distant past reveals cultures, identities, and environments which are as different from ours as their physical surroundings. Landscapes inhabited by pre-modern peoples in

TABLE 1. A CHRONOLOGICAL FRAMEWORK FOR ANTIQUITY

I. Prehistory BCE

To 2500	Stone age, microlithic tool cultures, Mehrgarh.
2500–1500	Harappa and Indus Valley urban culture.

II. Earliest history to 600 BCE

1200–400s	Early Vedas, late Vedas and Brahmanas.
1000s	Iron smelting and tools.
900s	Period of wars recounted in *Mahabharata*.
700s	Formation of *janapada*s and sixteen *mahajanapada*s.

III. Ancient transformation

a. The original states, *circa* 600 to 327 BCE

600s–500s	Rise of states: Kuru, Panchala, Kosala, Magadha.
500s	Persian king Darius occupies Sind and Gandhara; life of Mahavira.
400s	Life of Buddha; composition of *Ramayana* and *Mahabharata*.
327	Alexander the Great enters Punjab.

b. The original empire, 300s–185 BCE

Late 300s	Chandragupta Maurya founds Mauryan Empire; composition of Panini's grammar, possible first version of *Arthasastra*.
268–233	Ashoka Maurya.
185	Last Mauryas; founding of Sunga dynasty in Pataliputra.

c. Imperial competition 250 BCE–250 CE

250 BCE–250	North-west: Indo-Greeks, northern Sakas, Indo-Parthians, Kushanas.
55 BCE–500s	South: Satavahana and Vakataka dynasties in Prastisthana and Vidarbha.
70–409 CE	West: Sakas in Malwa Ujjaini-Rajasthan-Gujarat.

TABLE 1. *CONTINUED*

c. Imperial competition 250 BCE–250 CE (continued)

100 BCE–100	Early Siva and Vishnu worship; Buddhist stupas prominent in north-west, south-east, Sri Lanka; early Sangam literature; composition of Manu's *dharmasastra*, *Bhagavad Gita*.

d. Dynastic territories *circa* 200 BCE–600 CE

320–840s	Ganga basin: Guptas and Pusyaputis.
400s–500s	North-west: southern Hunas.
100 BCE–400	Southern peninsula: Cheras, Cholas, and Pandyas.
200s–500s	Maharashtra: Vakatakas, Kalacuris, and Rashtrakutas.
500s–750s	Karnataka: Chalukyas.
200s BCE–1200s	Sri Lanka: Lambakannas.

South Asia were thinly populated. Small human communities were widely scattered. Much more land was covered by forests filled with wild animals than by farms, villages, towns, and cities. Entering this landscape provides a much-needed critical perspective on the radical novelty of modernity.

LAND AND WATER

Aeons ago in the geological past, a triangle of rocky land broke off from East Africa, drifted north in the Indian Ocean, and crashed into Eurasia. The upheaval produced the Himalayas; its violence still visits the pivotal point of the geological merger, when earthquakes rock regions from Gujarat across the Himalayas to Bangladesh. Merging tectonic plates produced volcanoes that spewed ash across the new peninsula. Monsoon rains washed this fertile black volcanic soil into wide seams along peninsular rivers. Rain and melting ice and snow scoured Himalayan slopes to make the great rivers Indus, Ganga, and Brahmaputra. These rivers washed Himalayan silt across the plains, and even now dump it continuously into the Bengal delta. Silt visible in satellite photos is still washing along the floor of the Indian Ocean as far south

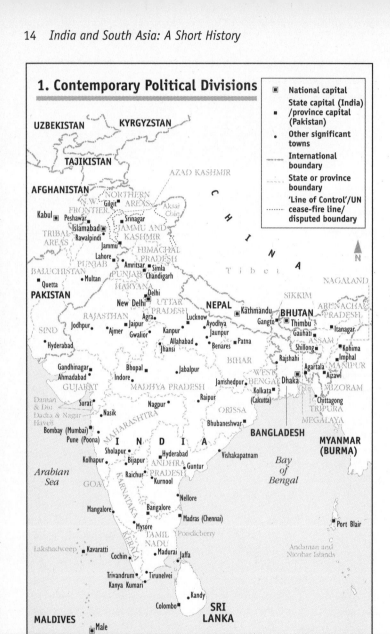

1. Contemporary Political Divisions

■	National capital
▪	State capital (India) /province capital (Pakistan)
•	Other significant towns
	International boundary
	State or province boundary
	'Line of Control'/UN cease-fire line/ disputed boundary

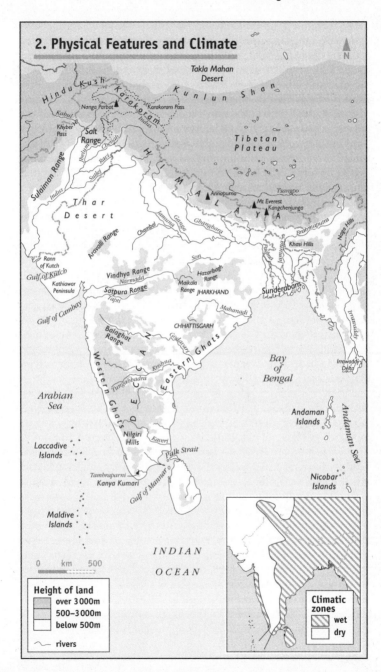

2. Physical Features and Climate

Takla Mahan Desert

Hindu Kush

Karakoram

Kunlun Shan

Nanga Parbat

Karakoram Pass

Kabul

Khyber Pass

Salt Range

Jhelum

Chenab

Indus

Ravi

Sutlej

Tibetan Plateau

Annapurna

Mt Everest

Kangchenjunga

Tsangpo

H I M A L A Y A

Thar Desert

Sulaiman Range

Indus

Aravalli Range

Chambal

Jamuna

Ganges

Ghaghara

Brahmaputra

Nago Hills

Khasi Hills

Rann of Kutch

Gulf of Kutch

Kathiawar Peninsula

Vindhya Range

Narmada

Son

Hazaribagh Range

Maikala Range

JHARKHAND

Sunderbans

Satpura Range

Tapti

CHHATTISGARH

Mahanadi

Gulf of Cambay

Balaghat Range

Godavari

Eastern Ghats

Irrawaddy

D E C C A N

Western Ghats

Krishna

Tungabhadra

Bay of Bengal

Arabian Sea

Andaman Islands

Andaman Sea

Laccadive Islands

Nilgiri Hills

Kaveri

Palk Strait

Tambraparni

Kanya Kumari

Gulf of Mannar

Nicobar Islands

Maldive Islands

INDIAN OCEAN

0   km   500

Height of land

over 3 000m

500–3 000m

below 500m

~ rivers

Climatic zones

wet

dry

as Sri Lanka. Over millennia, flowing silt routinely changed the course of Indo-Gangetic rivers. In deltaic Bengal, the Ganga shifted steadily eastward, and by the eighteenth century the Ganga and Brahmaputra had merged in what is now Bangladesh. Silt constantly forms new islands, called *char*, in the rivers of Bangladesh, as rivers wash land on river banks out to sea.

South Asia's natural environment occupies the south-western edge of monsoon Asia. Embracing the Himalayas and Sri Lanka, it stretches from Afghanistan to Burma between five and forty degrees north latitude. It is hot at midday all year, but temperatures do vary between winter and summer. In the northern plains, winters are quite cold and peak summer heat is brutal. Yet seasons are marked more by rainfall than by temperature. When Central Asia heats up each spring, rising hot dry air draws in wet cooler air from the oceans and generates barometric disparities that spark storms of varying scope and ferocity from Baluchistan to Korea: these rainstorms and their winds are called monsoons.

Rain is always the big weather news in South Asia, and there is little to report from January to June. The dry, unrelenting heat peaks in May. Then the monsoon hits. Its starting date varies, but normally its happy arrival falls at the beginning of June. First, the monsoon rains soak the coast and the east, South Asia's wet half, where rainfall normally exceeds eighty centimetres per year. In Assam, Bangladesh, and the north-east mountains, as much as three metres of monsoon rain can fall in six months. In these wet regions, cyclones and floods normally bring the worst weather news. On the east coast, from Chennai to Chittagong, killer cyclones strike every few years. A 'super-cyclone' hit Odisha in 1999, washing away villages hundreds of miles inland. In Bengal, storms from the sea often combine with flooding. In the eastern Ganga basin and all along the Brahmaputra, severe flooding is a constant threat. In Bangladesh, much of the land floods annually; in the live delta, there is more water than land, and fish are as essential to the diet as the waterways are to transport. The meaning of flooding has changed dramatically over the centuries. In the eighteenth century, seagoing ships were built in the mountains above the Bengal plains and floated out to sea across a hundred miles of flooded forest; but now that same land is full of farms, villages, towns, and cities, including Dhaka, and flooding causes mass death and destruction. People living in the wet coastal regions and islands of South and South-East Asia are today the most vulnerable in the world to rising sea levels, increased flooding, and storm surges caused by global climate change.

The monsoon arrives later in the western, dry half of South Asia, which includes the interior peninsula. Rains start as late as the end of July in Baluchistan and Multan. In dry South Asia the bad-weather news is normally drought, but devastating flash floods do occur when swollen rivers wash suddenly over hard parched land, as they did in Hyderabad, Andhra Pradesh, in 2000, and in the Indus Valley in 2010. The monsoon is very often late and stingy in dry South Asia. All of the interior peninsula and western plains – running north from Gujarat to the Khyber Pass and east from Sind to Malwa and Delhi – remain parched and dusty most of the year. Most rivers are bone dry in the summer. Rainfall rarely measures more than eighty centimetres annually, often less than twenty, and in the Thar Desert, in Rajasthan, less than ten. Desert winds from Rajasthan blow dust storms across Delhi in the late summer.

The very long-term climatic trend seems to be towards increasing aridity. The drying up of the Saraswati River, which once flowed into Rajasthan across eastern Punjab, was a major ecological event in prehistory. Prehistoric Indus Valley cities probably declined in part because they could not get enough water; as did Fatehpur Sikri, the first Mughal fortress capital, built too far west, too far into the desert, in the sixteenth century. Deforestation has been broadly blamed for increasing aridity as well as flooding in South Asia, and current trends in global climate change seem to be amplifying climate extremes, making desertification seem as unstoppable in the long term in dry regions as submersion by the sea seems to be for the coastal plains and islands.

OPEN GEOGRAPHY

Human living environments span a wider range of climatic variation in South Asia than anywhere else in the world at these latitudes. Environments to the west (in the Middle East and Africa) are uniformly dry; and to the east (in South-East Asia and China), uniformly wet. South Asia has both extremes. South Asia's dry half is climatically part of a vast geographical zone that covers western Asia and northern Africa: the natural ground cover is thin scrub forest; nomadic tribes and pastoral economies are historically prominent; millet and wheat are ancient staple grains; irrigation is the key to agrarian wealth; and old oasis towns dot sandy expanses of thinly populated land like port cities. South Asia's wet half is instead climatically part of a humid climatic zone running along the eastern Indian Ocean rim, from Bombay to Sri Lanka and through

Bangladesh and Burma south to Indonesia, where heavy rain, cloudy, humid days, dense tropical jungles, slash-and-burn farming, rice-paddy cultivation, fishing, and seafaring have historically been prominent features of everyday life. People living at high altitudes inhabit other environments altogether, which in the arid west shade off into Central Asia, in the north resemble Tibet more than India, and in the north-east resemble interior South-East Asia much more than Rajasthan or Gujarat. Places along the coast physically resemble coastal Indonesia more than arid inland or high-altitude South Asia.

Spaces defined by historical activity and by networks of interaction shaping everyday life in South Asia have never corresponded to the boundaries of modern states. South Asia has been formed as an open space for movement and communication. To and from its dry half, routes of migration, trade, and resettlement lead to and from Asia's dry west and north, into the arid home of the Silk Road, and running into Africa. Human cultivation of millet and wheat began somewhere along these routes; exactly where is unknown. Recent carbon dates for pollen found in dry lakes in Rajasthan indicate that a period of increasing moisture occurred in Asia's dry zone at the time of the earliest-known grain cultivation in the Middle East, around 7500 BCE; this means that archaeological finds at Mehrgarh and elsewhere may represent the roughly simultaneous origination of dry grain cultivation in South Asia and the Middle East. In the Himalayas, settlers, herders, and migrants move regularly across Tibet, and Tibetan Buddhism is as deeply entrenched in Nepal as Hinduism. Mountains are open terrain connecting Burma, Assam, and Bengal. The earliest evidence of rice cultivation in South Asia is roughly contemporary with evidence from South-East Asia. In the eighteenth century, migrants from Arakan did much of the most arduous new land clearance in southern Bengal. In Shillong, now in India's north-eastern state of Meghalaya, people speak Mon-Khmer, Tibeto-Burman, and Indo-European languages. All the coastal regions are also intimately interconnected: Sinhala and Bangla languages are closely related; southern India has sent many waves of migrants to Sri Lanka; and coast ports have long been their own best trading partners, including those in South-East Asia, where so-called 'Indianization' occurred during the first millennium CE, when merchants from Gujarat arrived routinely in Java. In 1800, fishing ships from many towns along India's east and west coasts brought workers and equipment for digging pearls from the ocean floor in the Gulf of Manaar off the coast of Sri Lanka.

From ancient times, cultural elements of all sorts have moved in all directions. We find Hindu temples and Sanskrit texts in Cambodia and Indonesia. Buddhism flourished more in East and South-East Asia than in its birthplace in northern India. Japanese Buddhists now tour holy sites in India the way Christians visit Jerusalem. Christians and Jews came by sea to settle on the Kerala coast in the early centuries CE. Islam spread across southern Asia by land among inland regions, and by sea among Indian Ocean ports, until the majority of the world's Muslims lived east of Iran. The definitive linguistic components of South Asian languages are spread all across Asia. Examples are endless of vast cultural mobility, mixing, and dispersion.

To understand South Asia, we should think of all of its civilizations as being historically invented as bounded cultural entities. There is no one set of boundaries to assume as definitive containers for history in South Asia. Political boundaries have changed many times. It is most appropriate to study South Asia as a vast open geographical space spreading across southern Eurasia, rather than imagining it to be a world region with one territorial definition.

PREHISTORIC SOCIETIES

Humans have lived in South Asia for half a million years. Relics indicate that the earliest human settlers lived in virtually every ecological niche. They would all have migrated from somewhere else at some point in time, but certain places have been continuously occupied since the eighth millennium BCE, when agro-pastoral settlements were established. Mehrgarh, in central Baluchistan, is now the oldest site where archaeology can show that microlithic tool-using people produced a complex farming society; it is in the dry, mountainous land between the Indus Valley and Afghanistan, where physical remains survive much better than they do in wet lands. From the seventh to the fourth millennium BCE, Mehrgarh underwent indigenous technological development connected to migratory trade with western and central Asia.

Similar sites dating to about 3000 BCE also indicate a cultural complex which has been named after the later Indus Valley site at Harappa; it includes large, solid buildings, pottery, wool and cotton textiles, copperware, seals, and female figurines. Along the Indus Valley, large cities were built by about 2500 BCE at Mohenjo-Daro and Harappa; but five hundred years later, they were being depopulated; and a few centuries later, they were abandoned. As the

Indus Valley cities declined, other smaller sites containing similar cultural material multiplied north and south, in Gujarat and Punjab. Recent findings suggest that Harappan cultural production may have continued into the first millennium BCE, alongside settlements that are distinguished by later archaeological finds of Painted Grey Ware pottery. The famous prehistoric cities along the Indus emerged within a very old, resilient cultural complex that covered a vast area of dry land and river valleys stretching from Afghanistan to Sind, Punjab, and the western Gangetic Plain. This cultural complex was both indigenous to South Asia and enriched by long-distance trade.

If we set out on a tour of South Asia in 2000 BCE, we would certainly begin by admiring its massive Indus Valley cities, with their advanced hydrology and architecture, which required great technical skill and organized construction work. Outside these few cities, however, we would find that most of the scant human population consisted of hunters, gatherers, herders, and farmers, living in small mobile settlements. Wild animals – including elephants, tigers, deer, and buffaloes – outnumbered humans many times over.

Dry, wet, mountain, and coastal climates supported distinctive human communities. In wet regions, dense tropical jungles were naturally well endowed with food supplies for humans, but also with wild animals (notably snakes and tigers) and micro-organisms (notably waterborne parasites) that killed humans. To create stable living environments in tropical settings, people had to clear jungles to create farms, arduous work that had to be done repeatedly because jungle growth is tenacious. Before the advent of iron tools, around 1200 BCE, jungles constantly defeated human efforts to create permanent farming settlements; shifting cultivation was the only agrarian option, and combined with hunting, gathering, and fishing, it provided for an ample human diet. Rice, originally a swamp grass, was first domesticated on temporary fields. Slash-and-burn farming remained the norm long after agrarian societies began to cut, burn, and build permanent fields and settlements to produce expansive landscapes of settled agriculture in the plains. This agrarian transformation of the wet lowlands began in the first millennium BCE.

In dry lands, migratory life typically moved over wider spaces. Where water failed to come to the land, people and animals moved to water. Animal herding and nomadism combined naturally with extensive hunting, warfare, and trade, which developed productive but conflict-ridden synergies with sedentary farming.

Nomads raised animals that farming communities used for manure and ploughing, for edible meat and milk, and for skins, fur, and wool. Nomads engaged in trade and transported craft products and implements among settled communities. Animal-herding pastoral peoples exchanged goods with farmers who provided them with staple grains (millets and wheat), fruits, vegetables, and manufactures, including metal tools and weapons. For grazing their animals, herders often needed water and grass that lay in localities controlled by farmers, whose crops benefited from animal manure. Farmers and herders were also hunters, and their hunting skills were often turned against human competitors seeking land and water. Nomads on horseback became the most powerful warriors, ranging over wide distances.

Agro-pastoral communities combining the skills and resources of herders, farmers, and craftworkers built the homelands that we see scattered in archaeological remains in dry regions from Baluchistan to Punjab and the Deccan. Social mixtures of hunting, gathering, herding, farming, manufacturing, and trade supported prehistoric communities that combined sedentary and migratory ways of life. Archaeological remains from Gujarat in the second millennium BCE indicate that pastoral circuits of animal grazing and nomadic migration ran through sedentary farming communities like thread through beads on a necklace.

Elements of sedentary cultures moved along circuits of migration and trade that connected and sustained an array of small, separate communities. Cultural assemblages thus emerged which were composed of various symbolic and material elements that we see in archaeological evidence. As elements dispersed geographically, they formed distinct cultural areas that changed shape and overlapped. The cultural complex that includes Mehrgarh and Harappa is now the oldest we know. Physical remains indicate that a different but perhaps related Banas culture characterized by white-painted black and red pottery developed in Rajasthan and Malwa in the millennium after 2500 BCE. At the same time, another Malwa culture was spreading south in central India, a Savalda complex formed in Maharashtra, and other areas of settlement marked by distinctive pottery and metal tools developed in the eastern Vindhyas and southern Deccan. Other cultural areas of comparable antiquity are also visible in the southern peninsula which contained megalithic tombs, urns, cists, rock-cut caves, cairns, sarcophagi, and stone tombs that resemble hats called *topi kals*. Especially in the wetter regions, evidence of cultural activity in prehistory returned invisibly to nature, though later evidence indicates many cultural contributions from prehistoric forest dwellers.

In Punjab, a dry region with grasslands watered by five rivers (hence '*panch*' and '*ab*') draining the western Himalayas, one prehistoric culture left no material remains, but some of its ritual texts were preserved orally over the millennia. The culture is called Aryan, and evidence in its texts indicates that it spread slowly south-east, following the course of the Yamuna and Ganga Rivers. Its elite called itself *Arya* (pure) and distinguished themselves sharply from others. Aryans led kin groups organized as nomadic horse-herding tribes. Their ritual texts are called Vedas, composed in Sanskrit. Vedic Sanskrit is recorded only in hymns that were part of Vedic rituals to Aryan gods. To be Aryan apparently meant to belong to the elite among pastoral tribes. Texts that record Aryan culture are not precisely datable, but they seem to begin around 1200 BCE with four collections of Vedic hymns (*Rg*, *Sama*, *Yajur*, and *Artharva*).

Textual evidence indicates that the use of Sanskrit and Vedic rituals spread unevenly across the subsequent millennium. Six hundred years after the first Vedas, ritual texts called Brahmanas and mystical and philosophical Aranyakas and Upanishads describe activity farther and farther east in the Ganga basin. Two epic poems, *Ramayana* and *Mahabharata*, refer to wars among tribes, probably in the first half of the first millennium BCE, in the western Ganga basin; but the epics were composed centuries after the wars they describe and they were added to and revised many times over the centuries that followed. The major ancient grammatical text of the Sanskrit language, Panini's *Astadhyayi* (with a geographical appendix, *Ganapatha*) is datable to the late fourth century BCE by references to contemporary events and personalities. By that time, the corpus of ancient Sanskrit texts had formed a coherent cultural complex, Vedic Brahmanism. In that textual culture, social rituals prescribed that rulers must protect and enforce stratified ranks among four *varna*s: Brahman (priest), Kshatriya (warrior), Vaisya (merchant), and Sudra (worker). Ritual texts also describe the territory of Aryan culture, called Madhyama Dis or Madhya Desh, 'the central country'. By about 500 BCE, Aryan cultural evidence had spread east from Gandhara (in the hills above Punjab, where Panini composed his grammar) and Kurukshetra (near Delhi, where the *Mahabharata* wars occurred) as far to the east as the confluence of the Ganga and Yamuna at Pratisthana/Prayaga (Allahabad). Sanskrit geographical knowledge was much more extensive – Rama, the hero of the *Ramayana*, travelled south across the peninsula and the sea to Lanka (Sri Lanka) to save his wife, Sita, from her captor, Ravana – but as Panini indicates in a detailed list of peoples and places, ancient Sanskrit authors were at home in Punjab, Haryana, and the Ganga-Yamuna Doab. Here, their culture was one among many, though we know much less about others.

ANCIENT TRANSFORMATION

Prehistory shades into history as ancient documentation becomes firmly datable. This begins to occur in the sixth century BCE, during the reign of the Magadha kings in the eastern Ganga basin, when Buddhist texts can be dated along with recorded activity by Achaemenid Greek rulers in Persia and Afghanistan.

During the first thousand years of recorded history in South Asia, an ancient transformation produced entirely new social environments. Prehistoric societies were many but small, and they had no visible institutions. In the sixth century BCE, history's curtain rises on a dramatic scene of political invention as powerful people begin to make powerful states. By 300 BCE, societies along the Ganga basin were part of vast networks of politics, economy, and culture. Settlements stretching from Afghanistan to Bengal were connected to one another by regular flows of ideas and goods running through cities that became central sites for imperial society. By 100 CE, competing imperial armies ranged from Central Asia to Sri Lanka. By 500 CE, complex regions of social change all across South Asia were connected intricately to one another and to the wider world.

The ancient transformation from *circa* 500 BCE to *circa* 500 CE produced a cultural complex that would be called 'classical' in later times. This epochal change is so complex and poorly documented that no single explanation will ever suffice. Clearly, however, iron-making technologies that appear in Vedic times played a productive role. Chopping and digging with iron tools gave new advantages to people who struggled against the forest: they could now burn down trees to make farms and keep new jungle growth away with arduous manual labour. In the Ganga basin, land clearance to make permanent farms spread from west to east and created a new landscape spanning wet and dry regions for the first time. Rice-growing societies in the eastern Ganga basin could sustain larger populations; they also had closer access to iron ores and other minerals in the mountains of Jharkhand. River routes into and out of the mountains provided rapid entry into the Gangetic transport system for people working the uplands north and south of the Ganga. Iron tools increased agricultural output everywhere, but made a much bigger difference in the east, where iron weapons also strengthened warriors. People with iron tools made the boats that travelled the highway of the Ganga, and the carts that plied the roads along the basin.

The first organized state institutions appear in the eastern Ganga basin, fed by major trading routes running along rivers from Bihar to Gujarat and the Hindu Kush. Kautilya's *Arthasastra* indicates that by the start of the Common Era, long-distance trade sustained widely known sites of commodity specialization from Central Asia and Sind to Assam. Horses came from Punjab; pearls from Sind; cotton and sandalwood from Malwa; elephants, stones, and minerals from the southern mountains; cotton and silk from Bengal; and sandalwood from Assam. Cotton, silk, and wool cloth came from many places along the Ganga. Iron and silver came from mines in Jharkhand.

A vast triangle of trade routes connecting Kabul, Gujarat, and Assam became perhaps the largest integrated economic space in the ancient world. By 300 BCE, production and trade in this region was generating enough profit, taxation, tribute, and consumption to sustain a burst of social invention, most visibly along the highway of the Ganga, especially in the east. The first big cities built after the fall of Harappa arose around Pataliputra (now Patna in Bihar). They had a distinctive urban culture, elites, and expressive arts. Social stratification became complex. Initially, social strata were based on elite control of agricultural land and farm labour by lineage elders in territories called *janapada*s and *maha* (great) *janapada*s. These small domains were named after their dominant clans and are described in the epics as well as in Panini's grammar, Buddhist texts, and other sources. Panini indicates that in 300 BCE the *janapada*s were the most prominent political features of the Indo-Gangetic flatlands from Punjab to Bengal. By this time, however, new ruling elite strata and institutions had also appeared where rulers rose above limitations of kinship, forming states. Some of these states are called 'republics' because of power sharing among the ruling lineages inside them; others are called 'kingdoms' because of the supremacy of single rulers. What distinguished the new state territories most of all was the rise of capital cities at strategic military and commercial sites, where elite groups of various kinds concentrated their social activity.

CONSTRUCTING EMPIRE

Chandragupta Maurya was born into this ancient world, near Pataliputra, where, in the sixth century BCE, local Magadha rulers had raised armies to conquer widely and create the first large state. From the obscure Moriya clan, Chandragupta may have owned some land around Magadha before he led Magadha armies to conquer the *janapada*s as far west as Punjab and Sind. In doing so, he crossed a cultural divide. Agro-pastoral warrior lineages living in the western dry regions had superior access to most of the length of ancient trade routes, and their various *janapada*s had embraced Aryan culture as far east as Prayaga (Allahabad). Magadha lay further east on the outer fringe of Aryan cultural influence, and it was here, in the east, that the Buddha composed an alternative ethical system, opposed to Aryan Brahmanism. Magadha armies from the east conquered local competitors and then moved west. Victorious commanders subordinated the *janapada*s under an imperial authority whose primary goal was to maintain its own military strength. This rudimentary imperial scaffolding provided the framework for Chandragupta's ambition.

In the far west, Magadha troops faced Achaemenid Greek armies marching across Persia. As Greek soldiers marched east and Magadha troops marched west, they both knew they were following old routes of long-distance travel, but they did not know that they were creating a new world of politics that would stretch from Greece to Bengal. Routes from Europe to the Orient and from Magadha to Persia met in Punjab: the Indus became the symbolic western border of a region that the Greeks called 'India'. The original division of Asia and Europe, East and West, Orient and Occident, derived from military competition over routes and resources flowing across ancient Eurasia. Ancient empires thus invented cultural boundaries that we still live with today; how these territorial identities came down to the present is a long story that we will follow in the coming chapters.

Chandragupta won wars for Magadha in Sind and may have fought Alexander the Great in Punjab before Alexander's army mutinied to force a Greek retreat down the Indus in 327 BCE. Alexander sailed to Mesopotamia and died in Babylon at the age of thirty-four. Chandragupta marched east, conquered his overlords, and became South Asia's first emperor. He launched his Maurya imperial dynasty by building on Magadha victories to incorporate the *janapada*s in a structure of military command that eventually deployed 9,000 elephants, 30,000 cavalry, 8,000 chariots, and 600,000 infantry on its many battlefields. Supporting its war machine with taxes, troops, provisions, commanders, and victories preoccupied the Maurya state, which sustained an official elite that was the first of its kind. Elite intellectuals writing in Sanskrit composed imperial texts. One legendary figure was Kautilya, known as the original author of the *Arthasastra*, a manual of statecraft and administration, which was not completed until the Gupta age, six hundred years later, forming one of many links between the two ancient dynasties that together produced the imperial substance of what became known as classical civilization.

Mauryan armies conquered widely from 321 until 260 BCE. Chandragupta marched west to the Hindu Kush and Kashmir. His son, Bindusara, turned south to the Deccan. After a four-year war of succession, emperor Ashoka conquered Kalinga, on the Orissa coast, where war exhausted imperial resources. Subduing Kalinga cost 100,000 lives and displaced twice as many people. This suffering apparently stunned Ashoka into embracing Buddhism. The Mauryan elite then invented a new, ethical imperialism. By Ashoka's time, the teachings of Gautama Buddha and Mahavira had defined distinctive strains of cultural activity that we know under the names of Buddhism and Jainism; they shared many elements with Aryan Brahmanism but opposed its sacred division of caste society and established another set of values for rulers, including universal ethical norms that made salvation a moral quest. Rulers could support this righteous vision by becoming great alms-givers for learned monks who preached harmonious moral order and showed the way to enlightenment with their piety and learning. Buddhist righteousness (*dhamma*) became a moral compass for Ashoka's empire. Ashoka used vast winnings from war to support Buddhist monks, ritual centres (stupas), preachers, and schools. Instead of conquering the kingdoms south of Kalinga, Ashoka brought them under his spiritual patronage, supporting Buddhist kings in Sri Lanka and Buddhist centres in Andhra, Karnataka, and the Tamil country. Jain missions also prospered in Ashoka's imperial domain.

Maurya dynastic elites invented imperial culture, including new social identities attached to imperial expansion, integration, and authority. As well as supporting its war machine, the empire constituted an ethical ideology and infrastructure. In addition to commanding armies and gathering wealth for war, generals announced the arrival of good governance wherever they conquered. In addition to collecting tribute, officers established a local presence to keep roads open, adjudicate disputes, and supersede the parochial power of the *janapada*s. Building on the legacy of Magadha and initially travelling the same routes, the Maurya regime protected merchants who were major patrons of Buddhism and Jainism. Empire increased the concentration of wealth at central places of imperial authority. It attracted ambitious lineage leaders and disgruntled local competitors who allied with imperial officers and identified themselves with imperial authority. Imperial culture fostered a new elite cosmopolitanism, which elevated its own people and ideas as it reduced the authority of localities and local leaders. Empire institutionalized 'high' and 'low' culture at the same time.

DESIGNING CIVILIZATION

In new territories of empire and elite formation, Brahmanism, Buddhism, and Jainism represented three solutions to fundamental problems of human existence and political order. Their proponents obtained royal patronage in the circuits of urbane cosmopolitanism. All three became more prominent in dispersed localities on the tracks of imperial expansion. They had much in common, including their vast cosmology and their complex ideas about reincarnation and *karma* (the effect of acts in past lives on future lives). They all emerged in the Ganga basin from the mixing of Aryan culture with other cultures during social change in the first millennium BCE. Their intellectuals shared the creative spirit of the Upanishads, later Vedic texts which depict the sacred powers produced in the fires of Vedic sacrifice as being available to empower human transcendence through spiritual discipline, renunciation, contemplation, and mysticism.

By the later centuries BCE, elements of Aryan ideology had been adapted variously to local conditions by elites in diverse agrarian societies. The Brahmanas codified Vedic ritual in the changing contexts where learned Brahmans embodied and translated Aryan tradition. Newly emerging social elites used Sanskrit texts and Vedic rituals, and learned Brahmans began to elevate themselves above others and to institutionalize ranks of privilege. One hymn from the *Rg Veda* became particularly useful. It describes the origin of the world in the sacrificial dismemberment of the Lord of Being, Prajapati, into four *varna* or human essences: his mouth became the

Brahman priest; his arms became the warrior (Rajanya or Kshatriya); his thighs became the Vaisya (farmer and merchant); and his feet became the Sudra (servant). Ancient landowners, merchants, warriors, army commanders, rulers, kings, and emperors used Brahmanical interpretations of *varna* to raise and validate their social status. Thus many elites became at least partially Aryanized by patronizing Brahman knowledge and rituals. Many aspiring groups collaborated with Brahmans to create a higher status for themselves. Brahmanism allowed kin groups to form caste groups (*jati*) by assigning each kin group to a *varna*. The *dharmasastra* texts defined an emerging Brahmanical order, most famously *The Laws of Manu*, *circa* 100 BCE, which explains in great detail how every marriage mixing *jati*s produces a new *jati* with a specific status in the *varna* ranks, thus providing a recipe for organizing complex, diverse, and changing societies into an ideological scheme in which everyone acquires a ranked position.

Jain and Buddhist philosophies, monks, and patrons opposed the social stratification prescribed by Brahmanism, and the spiritual authority of the Brahmans and Vedic rites. Both schools of thought and spiritual discipline arose east of Prayaga, around Magadha, where Mahavira (born *circa* 550) and Gautama Buddha (born *circa* 480) originally preached. It is reasonable to surmise that both represent restless spiritual aspirations among new elites who challenged Vedic ideas about social rank. Merchants relegated to lower *varna* ranks were clearly influential patrons for Buddhist and Jain monks, who propagated the spiritual power of learning, piety, merit, discipline, and ethical values and rejected the idea that complete spiritual purity is attainable only by Brahmans. Jain and Buddhist paths to liberation are open to everyone.

Supporters of Brahmanism, Buddhism, and Jainism moved along routes of mobility and communication that extended their influence under the Mauryas. Imperial elites circulated among localities and settled to become representatives of imperial authority and high culture. Locally, their elite status could attract patronage from aspiring donors who sought prized intermediary roles in imperial society. People could only appreciate high culture when it was translated into local terms, in the vernacular. Most local religious feelings, practices, and ideas could never attain wide currency; they remained local until they were translated into terms that could travel. A three-tiered cultural hierarchy thus developed. At the top, high culture emerged among imperial elites who communicated with one another across great distances at the apex of political authority. Intermediary elites arose in regions of political power as they translated and mixed imperial and local cultures. But many local cultural elements remained just that, out of imperial circuits of power though incorporated by and subordinated to them. Thus the idea of 'great' and 'little' traditions came into being with the expansion of empire and with efforts by aspiring local elites to lift themselves out of their existing status. The interaction of these three levels of culture became a basic feature of social life. They are visible even today, though the centuries have changed their significance. In ancient times, local cultures were overwhelmingly predominant and very few people had access to high culture and elite traditions. Imperial culture made its impact locally in proportion to the power of its patrons in society.

Buddhism exemplifies high culture on the move in ancient times. It spread widely as the elites sank local roots, travelling from town to town in the ambit of Mauryan power and along routes of mobility running into Central Asia, the southern peninsula, and Sri Lanka. Buddhists always confronted opposition from Jains and Brahmans, and everywhere, patronage from various sources decided the outcome of their competition. Ashoka's patronage indicates that rulers in his day devised ingenious means for turning empire into civilization. Giving financial and moral support to high-culture ideas, practices, and intellectuals enabled rulers to attract literate elites to their service and to bring cosmopolitan cultural activists into localities of ethical empire. At the same time, this strategy enabled conquerors to turn tribute from vanquished local warriors into pious generosity. Religious patronage enhanced political supremacy and imperial authority. Instead of suffering humiliating military defeat, a weaker rival could embrace the imperial ranks by negotiating an acceptable contribution to charitable cultural projects endorsed by the emperor.

Such ingenious cultural politics suffused social struggles for power and rank. For rulers, patronizing religious leaders and institutions became indispensable for gaining local support. In everyday life, religious institutions shaped social identities under imperial patronage. Spiritual leaders became socially prominent as they cultivated patronage and turned wealth into moral authority. In local society, financing cultural institutions and religious activities such as festivals and rituals became an indicator of social status. Social rank thus acquired aesthetic, spiritual forms. The highest-status people were those who participated in imperial rituals and commanded the language and culture of the imperial religion. The lowest-status people were those who spoke only local tongues and worshipped local deities. Social mobility among tiers of culture led local people up the imperial ranks as they embraced elite culture, giving it local roots.

The project of civilizing conquered peoples proceeded within empire as influential people established religious institutions in dispersed local societies. Buddhists and Jains seem to have been most successful among merchants. A Greek king of Punjab, Menander, adopted Buddhism and sought to bring more merchants into his realm. Ashoka made Buddhism a moral compass, which made his realm more attractive for merchants. In Mauryan times, kings, monks, and landed elites on the island of Sri Lanka came together under the banner of *dhamma* to create one of the world's most enduring Buddhist kingdoms. Elsewhere, too, religious institutions became central in cultural politics by bringing disparate groups together in new, more extensive regional communities. Pious donors sanctified their own wealth with spending on festivals, shrines, temples, stupas, or pious education; they used public religious rituals to announce their own beneficence. Religious communities formed as emerging social elites pursued their common interests in stability to forge shared identities with public piety.

Donations to Jains and Buddhists became increasingly popular among merchants who travelled routes protected by Mauryan armies. Merchant wealth flowed into religious centres in market towns where it combined with royal patronage to finance a spiritual realm of public sentiment, which brought together local elites and imperial officers, itinerants and residents, civilians and army commanders, and many other people in various professions. Buddhist and Jain sculpture became public art. Gigantic stone sculptures and buildings embodied the physical presence of spiritual and imperial power. Technologies of artistic beauty became media for the everyday experience of spirituality, transcendence, and political stability. A creative explosion in all the arts was a most remarkable feature of this ancient transformation, a permanent cultural legacy. Mauryan territory was created in its day by awesome armies and dreadful war, but future generations would cherish its beautiful pillars, inscriptions, coins, sculptures, buildings, ceremonies, and texts, particularly later Buddhist writers.

Ancient imperialism created a new kind of social space, an imperial landscape. But all around it, most people lived in agro-pastoral communities and lineages, like those in the *janapada*s, dominated most localities. The geography of the Mauryan Empire resembled a spider with a small dense body and long spindly legs. The highest echelons of imperial society lived in the inner circle composed of the ruler, his immediate family, other relatives, and close allies, who formed a dynastic core. Outside the core, empire travelled stringy routes dotted with armed cities. Outside the palace, in the capital cities, the highest ranks in the imperial elite were held by military commanders whose active loyalty and success in war determined imperial fortunes. Wherever these men failed or rebelled, dynastic power crumbled. In the provincial urban centres of imperial authority, administrators applied official rules, merchants cherished law and order, elites gathered wealth, and pious people received patronage: all these groups carried imperial identities into everyday life.

Imperial society flourished where elites mingled; they were its backbone, its strength was theirs. Kautilya's *Arthasastra* indicates that imperial power was concentrated in its original heartland, in old Magadha, where key institutions seem to have survived for about seven hundred years, down to the age of the Guptas. Here, Mauryan officials ruled local society, but not elsewhere. In provincial towns and cities, officials formed a top layer of royalty; under them, old conquered royal families were not removed, but rather subordinated. In most *janapada*s, the Mauryan Empire consisted of strategic urban sites connected loosely to vast hinterlands through lineages and local elites who were there when the Mauryas arrived and were still in control when they left.

IMPERIAL *BHARAT*

The Mauryas defined an ancient territory called *Bharat*. Marching along old trade routes, the empire acquired the geometrical shape of a tall triangle with a broad base, with its apex in Magadha. One long northern leg ran west up the Ganga, across Punjab, into the Hindu Kush; and one long leg ran south-west from Pataliputra, up the Son river valley, down the Narmada River into Berar, Maharashtra, and Gujarat. The broad base spanned Punjab, the Indus, Rajasthan, Gujarat, and western Maharashtra. The north-western frontier revolved around Gandhara and Kashmir; the south-western frontier around Nasika, now Nasik, in Maharashtra. North of Kashmir and west of the Khyber Pass, Greek dynasties held sway. South of Nasika, the Mauryan presence consisted primarily of diplomatic missions. Buddhist activity was particularly prominent in the east, from Bengal down the Orissa coast to Amaravati, Kanchipuram, Madurai, and Anuradhapura in Sri Lanka.

Buddhism and Jainism continued to expand their influence after the fall of the last Mauryas in 185 BCE. Centuries of imperial competition produced expansive dynasties which broke the Mauryas' dynastic authority and ushered in a new set of rulers based in regions all around the eastern Gangetic heartland of *Bharat* (Table 1). In the first centuries CE, Buddhism travelled with warrior Kushanas across the Silk Road to China, became the state religion in Anuradhapura, and spawned monasteries and literatures in various languages on all its routes of travel. Jainism became a permanent cultural presence in Rajasthan and Gujarat, and on trade routes in the southern peninsula.

In 320 CE, four hundred years after the fall of the Mauryas, a new imperial dynasty arose in their eastern Ganga heartland and proceeded to inscribe ancient *Bharat* with Brahmanical authority. The founder, Chandragupta, apparently renamed himself after Chandragupta Maurya. He began his imperial career by marrying a daughter of the Licchavi clan, which had controlled the Terai uplands between Magadha and Nepal since before Mauryan times and would later go on to form a dynasty in the Kathmandu Valley. With this alliance, he conquered westward along the path of the Mauryas. In the late fourth century, his son, Samudragupta, declared himself *maharaja adhi raja*, 'great king of kings', and boldly recounted his conquests on a pillar in Prayaga (Allahabad) which dates back to the Mauryas. The Allahabad inscription divides Gupta lands into four categories. At the centre is Aryavarta, including all the Ganga plain, Naga domains in Bundelkhand and Malwa, Kota lands around Delhi, and Pundravardhana and Vanga in Bengal. Inside Aryavarta, conquered rulers were said to have been brought under direct Gupta administration. Outside this imperial territory, in the southern regions of Dakshinapatha, twelve conquered kings were left on their thrones. In the mountains, unconquered rulers paid tribute. In the north and west, Kushanas and Mundas offered obeisance, as did Sinhala kings in Sri Lanka.

Aryavarta was imperial territory suffused with Brahmanism. Samudragupta built its military framework by conquering the *janapada*s to replace them with imperial officers. Gupta territory was anchored in armed cities and towns, but also in rituals and holy places, forming a terrestrial order that was also a mythical universe. Aryavarta invoked eternal cosmic authority. Protected by

Gupta armies and patronized by officials at every level, imperial Brahmanism subdued all competitors.

Gupta imperial society spread across the Gangetic lowlands. Its core region was much larger than the Mauryas', extending west to Mathura, and its cultural impact was deeper and more permanent. To consecrate Aryavarta, Samudragupta performed Vedic rituals on a grand scale and pursued a widely publicized policy of donating land to Brahmans, funding temple construction, and financing temple rituals. Not surprisingly, Brahman authors saw the fall of the Guptas in the sixth century CE as the onset of cosmic chaos and degradation, or *Kali Yuga*. Many later generations of Sanskrit authors saw the Gupta era as their golden age. *Bharat* thus acquired a classical culture, defined by Brahmans in Sanskrit. The Gupta core region in Uttar Pradesh still has the highest Brahman population in India, and the most actively Brahmanical politicians.

Brahmanism spread outward from the Gupta core and evolved into a diverse but coherent Hindu cultural complex which travelled with Brahman migrations across South Asia and overseas into South-East Asia. Exactly how this cultural complex spread to influence so many disparate societies is still far from fully understood, partly because most of its huge textual record was produced by its proponents, in Sanskrit and other languages. Clearly, Brahmans and Sanskrit were critical in the production of Hindu societies. When Panini codified Sanskrit, it was already an archaic language; he effectively compiled a codebook for a Brahman secret tongue, a user's guide for Brahman cultural software. Buddhist and Jain authors used Pali, Prakrits, and other vernaculars. Local cults expressed themselves in local vernaculars. The influence of Sanskrit spread with the influence of learned Brahman men who were the only people who could officially know the language of the gods and convey its magic. Elements of Sanskrit – its sounds, words, grammar, and script – could be learnt, used, and enjoyed by anyone, however, so that over time, they entered most languages in southern Asia; and translations out of Sanskrit conveyed its influence into literature more widely still. Until the seventeenth century, when it was partially displaced by Persian as the premier elite imperial language, Sanskrit enjoyed a status comparable to Latin in Europe as an elite language of law, ritual, science, philosophy, literature, and high culture generally.

Patronage for the Brahman literati spread their influence far and wide. The Gupta classical age emerged retrospectively, in Puranic literature. *Purana*s form a large corpus of texts that recount 'oldness' or 'venerability' in genealogies and tales of the misty past, combining myth, folklore, history, and historical fiction. A typical *purana* begins with the creation of the world and narrates a genealogy leading from heavenly gods to earthly kings and saints in some present time that can be mythical but also historical, as it is in the genre of *sthala purana*, which explains how a particular god came to reside in a specific temple. *Purana*s have their mundane, factual counterpart in *prasasti* introductions to inscriptions that record temple donations, land grants, and royal proclamations.

Ashokan edicts and Samudragupta's inscriptions were prototypes for millions of texts carved in stone and etched in metal that begin to appear by Gupta times and proliferate from the sixth to the sixteenth centuries. *Prasasti*s recount genealogies and dynastic chronicles: though they often begin in the heavens in mythical times, they always come down to earth to the moment of the activity announced in the inscription. Like *purana*s, *prasasti*s are typically in Sanskrit, though *purana*s were also composed in vernaculars, and inscriptions introduced by Sanskrit *prasasti*s typically include a vernacular text for the business or contractual portion of the record. *Purana*s and *prasasti*s are two major textual media for evoking relations among gods, rulers, and everyday folk, thus between cosmic and mundane power.

The Guptas invested heavily in Puranic mythology and inscriptional documentation. Later, rulers all over South Asia followed their example to produce inscriptional records in all the major languages, including Arabic and Persian. These texts provide a clear sense of cultural geography. In the accumulation of Puranic texts, Aryavarta became the *desa*, the cultured land of civilization where Prayaga (Allahabad) and Kasi (Varanasi/Benares) were the holiest places in the sacred geography of *Bharat*. The *desa* does not include the high mountains, Indus Valley, Punjab, or western desert. The Puranic *desa* of *Bharat* are Madhya *desa* (the Ganga lowlands), Purva *desa* (Bengal and Assam), and Aparanta *desa* (including Avanti, Malwa, Gujarat, Konkan, and Nasik). Places outside the *desa* were frontiers and peripheries. The western plains, Punjab, high mountains, central mountains, and coast and interior peninsula outside Nasika-Konkana are not called *desa* in *purana*s, but rather *asreya*, *patha*, and *pristha*. This Puranic geography travelled widely with migrating Brahman literati. Sanskrit cosmopolitanism made Aryavarta its cultural heartland. With the spread of Brahman influence in post-Gupta centuries, localities far and wide were named and located in relation to the Gangetic holy lands. Kings as far away as Java and Cambodia traced their genealogies to the Guptas and even to the early Aryans.

REGIONS OF IMPERIAL EXPANSION

The ancient empires in the Ganga basin were surrounded by competitors in other regions whose power increased over the centuries. The Mauryas had faced no serious obstacles in their quest for control of major routes and centres east of the Hindu Kush. But when the last Maurya fell and the Sungas took Pataliputra, in 185 BCE, new empires on Magadha's old western frontier foreshadowed a new kind of future. In the south, in Maharashtra, the Satavahanas (55 BCE–250 CE) conquered the Deccan and the eastern peninsula south to Kanchipuram. In the western plains, the Sakas (70–409) expanded south and west into Gujarat from their capital at Ujjaini in Malwa. In the north-west, the Kushanas (0–250) formed the greatest of the new empires. They came from Central Asia and had twin capitals at Purusapura and Mathura. They conquered Afghanistan and the Ganga basin east to Pataliputra. Their most powerful ruler, Kanishka, also conquered the Sakas and the Satavahanas. Non-Gangetic armies formed a strenuous opposition to Gupta expansion outside Aryavarta. The Hunas, Sakas, and Vakatakas hemmed the Guptas in throughout their reign, and competitors tore their realm to bits when the Hunas rampaged down the Ganga to end the era of Gupta supremacy.

After the Guptas, empires ruling the old imperial heartlands of the Mauryas and the Guptas came from Maharashtra, Gujarat, Rajasthan, Punjab, Afghanistan, and Central Asia, which were markedly different from the Ganga basin as material and cultural environments. Agricultural land was not nearly as rich. Nomadic pastoral lineages were much more numerous, powerful, and prestigious. Elites were less sedentary and land-based; they depended more on trade, herds, and war for wealth; and their military control over routes between Delhi and Kabul and between Allahabad and Cambay provided a permanent strategic advantage in struggles for access to markets in Persia, Central Asia, and Indian Ocean ports. They often patronized Brahmans but they were typically eclectic, less inclined to Vedic ritual, and more respectful of nomadic warriors and itinerant merchants. Buddhism and Jainism flourished in their domains. Even the Satavahanas, who were staunch Hindus, also patronized Buddhists. Jainism remained prominent in Gujarat and Rajasthan. All along the Indian Ocean coast, Zoroastrians, Christians, Arabs, and Jews became well established. The Kushanas descended from the Hsung-nu clans in China; like the Sakas and Hunas, they were aliens in Aryavarta who represented a radical alternative to the Guptas, carrying Buddhism with them along the Silk Road.

When Chinese Buddhists toured India in the fifth and seventh centuries, they found that Buddhism had virtually disappeared in its Gangetic homeland under the imperial force of Brahmanism, though it still thrived in Afghanistan and Central Asia. Outside the Ganga basin, however, cultures flourished across the length and breadth of South Asia that were markedly less Brahmanical. Culturally distinct regimes based outside the Brahmanical strongholds in the Gupta heartland struggled constantly against Gangetic imperialism and for control over *Bharat*.

Aryavarta was one region among others in ancient, medieval, and early-modern times. Outside the geographical confines of imperial *Bharat*, political histories and collective identities flowing from them followed different trajectories. In the south, in the Deccan, in ancient Dakshinapatha, south of the Vindhyas, dynasties of Satavahanas, Vakatakas, Kalacuris, Rashtrakutas, and Yadavas conquered and defined cultural regions in central India; and in the seventeenth century, the Marathas followed suit, as we will see. In the west, in Rajasthan, Gurjara-Pratihara lineages launched five hundred years of military colonization in the ninth century, when Rajput clans conquered all across the Ganga basin, into the Himalayas and central India to form a long-lasting, far-reaching political and cultural force. In the north-west, in the land that straddles Punjab, Kashmir, and Afghanistan, Kushanas and later Turks and Afghans produced imperial spaces that repeatedly encompassed the Ganga basin and laid the historic basis for the sixteenth-century Mughal Empire, whose land ran from Samarkand to Assam.

MEDIEVAL TRANSITIONS

Post-Gupta regimes produced a fundamentally new mosaic of social environments; in recognition of this, historians treat the centuries from *circa* 550 to 1556, spanning the empires of the Guptas and Mughals, as a coherent, though very diverse, medieval epoch. One dominant feature of this epoch is increasingly dense and diverse documentation in dozens of languages, media, and regions. By comparison to earlier times, medieval history is very well documented, and its principal protagonists are better known, because inscriptions, travel accounts, chronicles, literature, and other sources multiply with each passing century. In the first millennium, the most visible characters appear in the texts of inscriptions produced by medieval dynasties. Hundreds of thousands of inscriptions have been located, copied, stored, translated, and studied by scholars, but still have not received the attention they deserve. The medieval millennium needs many more historians.

Epigraphy indicates that royal Gupta lineages were still settling in the western frontiers of Aryavarta in the sixth century, when the empire crumbled. They carried the apparatus of Gupta power, using royal gifts to finance temples and Brahmans; such gifts became a hallmark of medieval royalty. To mark the end of Gupta supremacy, a new Maukhari dynasty made grants in their own name on the western edge of the Gupta heartland, around Kanyakubja (Kanauj), in the Doab (Awadh). Then the Pusyabutis did the same farther west along the Yamuna and in Haryana. In the seventh century, the Pusyabuti king Harsha moved his capital to Kanyakubja and celebrated the event with a land grant to two Brahmans. The grant was to be administered personally by one of his commanders under the official protection of the *janapada*s in his realm. This indicates that the *janapada* lineages were still in power, and that Harsha relied for his authority on the wealth and power of subordinates supported by local community leaders.

Inscriptions announce the formation of more than forty new dynasties in the sixth and seventh centuries, across the length and breadth of South Asia. Typical *prasasti*s include elaborate genealogies that trace dynastic origins to mythical progenitors and sanctify royal domains by harking back to ancient kings. Regional societies become more historically visible in these centuries, and many medieval dynasties laid foundations for long-lasting regional political cultures. The complexity of medieval political geography can be sketched out by locating major dynasties in fifteen modern political regions (see Map 2).

1. Kashmir: Karkotas (620s –850s) and Loharas (900s–1300s) were based in the Vale, around Srinagar.
2. Nepal: Licchavis (400s–700s) and Mallas (900s–1700s) ruled the Kathmandu Valley.
3. Punjab: a contested terrain where Shahis (900s–1100s) built a major medieval domain.
4. Rajasthan: Gurjara-Pratiharas gave way to ruling dynasties of Paramaras (800s–1300s), Cahamanas (900s–1100s), and

Rathors (1200s–1500s), in Ujjaini, Ajayameru (Ajmer), and Jodhpur, respectively.

5. Gujarat: Caulukyas (900s–1200s) were the dominant medieval dynasty.

6. Uttar Pradesh: major dynasties included Hunas (500s); Maukharis (500s) at Kanyakubja and Ayodhya; Pusyabutis (500s–840s), whose most famous ruler was Harsha of Kanauj; Varmas (700s); and Gurjara-Pratiharas (700s–1150s), who spread from Gujarat to Bengal.

7. Madhya Pradesh: Candellas (800s–1300s) spread across a region including Khajurao, Awadh, and Gorakhpur; and Kalacuris (500s–1200s) covered land from Kheda and Ujjaini to Tripuri and Bengal.

8. Maharashtra: divided among Vakatakas (200s–500s) at Vidarbha (Nagpur), Kalacuris (500s–1200s) at Nasik, Rashtrakutas (600s–900s) at Vidarbha, and Yadavas (800s–1300s) at Devagiri.

9. Orissa: Gangas at Kataka Bhuvanesvara (300s–1400s) were the longest-lasting dynasties.

10. Bengal: Palas (750s–1100s) and Senas (100–1200s) defined the medieval epoch.

11. Andhra Pradesh: Eastern Chalukyas ruled from the Krishna-Godavari delta (620s–1000s); Kakatiyas ruled from the interior at Warangal, near Hyderabad (1000s–1300s).

12. Karnataka: Chalukyas (500s–750s) at Vatapi (Badami) gave way to the imperial Hoysalas (1000s–1300s) whose domain stretched to the east and west coasts; and later to the greatest southern empire at Vijayanagar (1336–1672).

13. Tamil Nadu: Pallavas (300s–900s), Cholas (800s–1200s), and Pandyas (600s–1300s) ruled the northern, central, and southern regions of the coast at Kanchipuram, Tanjavur, and Madurai respectively.

14. Kerala: the Cheras and Kulasekaras ruled the region around Trivandrum from the fourth to the twelfth century.

15. Sri Lanka: Lambakanna dynasties ruled from later Mauryan times to the twelfth century.

The original establishment of most of the medieval dynasties appears to represent emerging concentrations of wealth and power among warrior and landowning elites in areas of agricultural expansion. These agrarian regimes were deeply rooted locally but they were often spatially expansive and they were all extensively

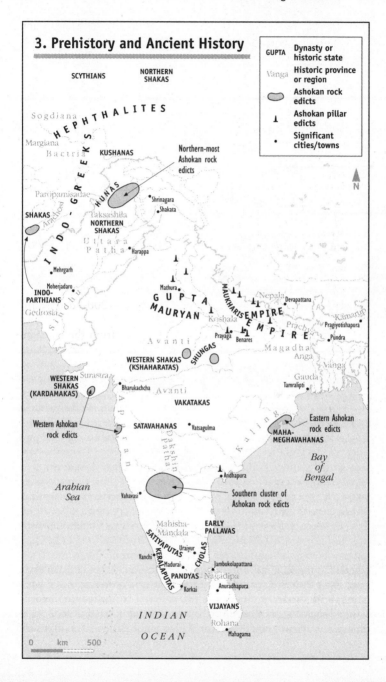

3. Prehistory and Ancient History

GUPTA	Dynasty or historic state
Vanga	Historic province or region
	Ashokan rock edicts
⊥	Ashokan pillar edicts
•	Significant cities/towns

SCYTHIANS

NORTHERN SHAKAS

Sogdiana

HEPHTHALITES

Margiana

Bactria   KUSHANAS

Paropamisadae

Northern-most Ashokan rock edicts

INDO-GREEKS

SHAKAS

Arachosi

HUNAS

•Shrinagara

•Shakata

Taksashila

NORTHERN SHAKAS

Uttara Patha   •Harappa

•Mehrgarh

•Moherjadaro

INDO-PARTHIANS

Gedrosia

⊥ ⊥
•Mathura

⊥

GUPTA

MAURYAN

MAUKHARIS EMPIRE

Nepala •Devapattana

Kamarup

Kosbala

•Pragiyotishapura

Prach

•Prayaga ⊥
•Benares

•Pundra

Avanti

Magadha

Anga

Vanga

WESTERN SHAKAS (KSHAHARATAS)

SHUNGAS

Gauda

•Tamralipti

WESTERN SHAKAS (KARDAMAKAS)

Surastra

•Bharukachcha

Avanti

VAKATAKAS

Western Ashokan rock edicts

SATAVAHANAS

•Vatsagulma

Dakshin Patha

Kaling

Eastern Ashokan rock edicts

MAHA-MEGHAVAHANAS

Bay of Bengal

⊥ •Andhapura

Arabian Sea

•Vahavasi

Southern cluster of Ashokan rock edicts

Mahisha-Mandala

EARLY PALLAVAS

SATIYAPUTAS

•Uraiyur

•Vanchi

CHOLAS

•Madurai

•Jambukolapattana

KERALAPUTAS

PANDYAS   *Nagadipa*

•Korkai

•Anuradhapura

VIJAYANS

Rohana

INDIAN

OCEAN

•Mahagama

N

0   km   500

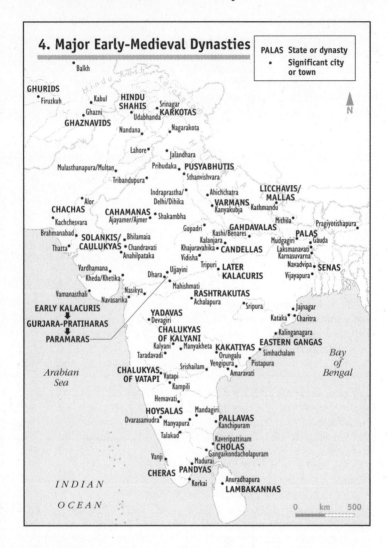

4. Major Early-Medieval Dynasties

PALAS   State or dynasty
•   Significant city or town

Balkh

GHURIDS
Firuzkuh
Kabul   HINDU
SHAHIS   Srinagar
Ghazni   KARKOTAS
GHAZNAVIDS   Udabhanda
Nandana   Nagarakota

Lahore
Jalandhara
Mulasthanapura/Multan   Prihudaka   PUSYABHUTIS
Tribandupura   Sthanvishvara
LICCHAVIS/
MALLAS
Indraprastha/   Ahichchatra
Alor   Delhi/Dihika   VARMANS   Kathmandu
CHACHAS   CAHAMANAS   Shakambha   Kanyakubja   Mithila
Kachchesvara   Ajayamer/Ajmer   Pragiyotishapura
Gopadri   Kashi/Benares   GAHDAVALAS   PALAS
Brahmanabad   SOLANKIS/   Bhilamaia   Kalanjara   Mudgagiri   Gauda
Thatta   CAULUKYAS   Chandravati   Khajuravahika   CANDELLAS   Laksmanavati
Anahilpataka   Vidisha   Karnasuvarna
Vardhamana   Tripuri   LATER   Navadvipa   SENAS
Kheda/Khetika   Dhara   Ujjayini   KALACURIS   Vijayapura
Vamanasthali   Mahishmati
Nasikya   RASHTRAKUTAS
EARLY KALACURIS   Navasarika   Achalapura   Sripura   Jajnagar
Kataka   Charitra
GURJARA-PRATIHARAS   YADAVAS   Kalinganagara
PARAMARAS   Devagiri
CHALUKYAS   EASTERN GANGAS
OF KALYANI   Simhachalam
Kalyani   Manyakheta   KAKATIYAS   *Bay*
Taradavadi   Orungipura   *of*
Srishailam   Vengipura   Pistapura   *Bengal*
Arabian   CHALUKYAS,   Amaravati
Sea   OF VATAPI   Vatapi
Kampili

Hemavati
HOYSALAS   Mandagiri
Dvarasamudra   Manyapura   PALLAVAS
Talakad   Kanchipuram

Kaveripattinam
CHOLAS
Vanji   Gangaikondacholapuram
Madurai
INDIAN   CHERAS   PANDYAS
Korkai   Anuradhapura
OCEAN   LAMBAKANNAS

0   km   500

connected to wide-spreading circuits of trade, culture, and politics.
Each dynasty had a strong territorial identity that was concentrated
in a specific core region, and when military expansion reached its
limit, dynasties retreated into their homeland, unless they were
driven out, which would often be followed by the creation of a new

homeland elsewhere. Over time, compact regional dynasties spread widely and they often produced permanent regional traditions preserved in monuments, literature, mythology, genealogies, and local rights and powers granted by medieval kings.

Many medieval dynasties emerged on routes running to and from ancient *Bharat*. Ancient empires had produced networks of conquest, elite circulation, and cultural communication on long routes of mobility through the Ganga basin. Dispersed urban centres of late antiquity developed around army posts, administrative offices, markets, oases, ports, strategic mountain passes and river crossings, sacred sites, royal courts, lineage headquarters, stupas, monasteries, and other places valued by imperial elites. Habitation and land use had intensified around cities where agro-pastoralism and shifting cultivation spawned permanent farming, manufacturing, and commerce. When political leaders in imperial satellite towns challenged imperial elites for local leadership, vying for local support, new regional polities emerged with political cultures that combined local parochialism and imperial cosmopolitanism.

The Pallava regime at Kanchipuram is a useful example. It emerged from under the canopy of empire thrown across the southern peninsula by the imperial Guptas, Vakatakas and Chalukyas. Pallava kings rose from vassal status to become imperial powers in their own right. Kanchipuram had been a centre of Buddhist learning featured in *Manimekalai*, a Buddhist epic composed in the Tamil language in Gupta times, when Pallavas were Vakataka feudatories. Under the Pallavas, Kanchipuram became a Hindu sacred site and a royal capital; its seaport, Mahaballipuram, was adorned with monumental rock sculpture and temple carvings popularizing the worship of the supreme Hindu gods Siva and Vishnu. The Pallavas' Kanchipuram became a Hindu pilgrimage site and centre for Sanskrit learning, whose temples received endowments from dignitaries and gifts from patrons in localities around the peninsula. On its temple walls, dynastic inscriptions record a Pallava cosmic genealogy and wars of imperial expansion that spawned Pandya and Chola regimes farther south. Ancient imperial authority was slowly transformed in this manner into dozens of new medieval regimes across the expansive frontiers of late antiquity.

Medieval Territory

Ancient South Asia was very thinly populated. Dense forests covered much of the land. Vast expanses of open scrubland separated countless tiny, scattered communities of nomads, shifting cultivators, hunters, gatherers, and settled farmers, who multiplied over the centuries but left few records behind. As we have seen, history's first great transformation occurred in the millennium spanning the Maurya and Gupta Empires. By Gupta times, the ancient landscape held an array of densely populated, complex societies that thrived in fertile lowlands astride major rivers. Their agricultural settlements were still surrounded by dense forest and open scrubland but they were expanding their presence visibly, and two were extensively connected to one another and to places stretching across Eurasia.

By the middle of the first millennium of the Common Era, a second great transformation was under way. It spanned more than eleven centuries from late antiquity to early-modern times, from the sixth through to the seventeenth century. Its early history took off from ancient trends. Its later history helped to launch modernity. This long medieval transformation is first visible in a proliferation of inscriptions carved into stone and etched in metal to document social activity in regions of economic growth and dynastic authority embracing increasingly diverse populations. In this chapter, we consider major innovations in three medieval periods: first, before *circa* 1000 CE, when regional regimes were most intimately connected to ancient empires; then, *circa* 1000–1400, when the rise of the warriors transformed imperial territorialism; and finally, during the late-medieval centuries 1400–1750, when militarism and commercialism combined to formulate early modernity, the subject of Chapter Three.

A MEDIEVAL MILLENNIUM

Like the Pallavas and the Pusyabutis, whom we met at the end of Chapter One, many early-medieval dynasties had ancient mythic genealogies. Like the Guptas, most medieval kings had their homelands in fertile places along river basins. But in medieval societies, people built many more of these fertile places by digging wells, constructing dams, channels, and reservoirs, and lifting water for crops with devices more often powered by bulls in harness. Medieval domains of royalty that emerged in these new fertile places were not mere offshoots of ancient cultures: they were novel formulations of social power that produced new social identities. Their elites had many origins and languages. Inscriptions indicate a virtual revolution in the geographical character of social life in early-medieval times by naming and locating thousands of peoples and places, which seem to come from nowhere, appearing in historical records for the first time.

Medieval social environments evolved over centuries in the context of two long-term economic trends: sedentary farmers increased the productivity of land with more specialized labour and technology, and mobile groups extended transportation and communication by land and sea across southern Eurasia. Already by the seventh century, we can see that long arteries of mobility spanning Eurasia were connected to regional veins in South Asia and to capillaries in growing areas of localized agricultural production. Most new dynasties in the first millennium emerged in places where long trade routes crossed fertile valleys and deltas. In Kashmir, they surrounded Srinagar; and in Nepal, the Kathmandu Valley. In Punjab, they dotted the foothills. They grew along the rivers Ganga, Narmada, Tapti, Sabarmati, Mahanati, Krishna, Godavari, Pennar, Kaveri, Vaigai, and Tambraparni. In the peninsula, they thrived most of all where rivers met the sea. In the flatlands of northern Sri Lanka, they expanded around irrigation reservoirs that received water running down from mountains in the centre of the island.

Any map depicting political geography in medieval times looks kaleidoscopic because the extent of dynastic territories changed very often. But the social environments that developed in medieval domains were based in relatively stable economic areas, and major dynasties had an average lifespan of more than 300 years, compared to 135 and 230 years respectively for the Mauryas and Guptas (Table 2). The secret of their success lay in the central role that dynasties played in building social systems to organize physical and spiritual power. Dynasties helped to organize creative interactions among people involved in mobile and sedentary ways of life, in places where local elites dominated villages and towns that also served itinerant merchants, warriors, craftsmen, and pilgrims. As a result of their success, medieval dynasties became cultural symbols of tradition in territories which would host the formation of many modern social identities.

New forms and constellations of social identity came into being during three long periods of historical innovation. In the early-medieval centuries, until the end of the first millennium, social inventiveness concentrated in compact domains of dynastic authority where kings allied with local elites to direct the course of social change. From the tenth into the fourteenth centuries, warriors with increasingly expansive mobility became prominent agents of change in old medieval territories and in new lands outside them where military regimes developed around hill forts on trade routes and projected their power widely with cavalry and military discipline. After this medieval transition, sultans became the leading political figures, and the greatest sultans ruled the Mughal Empire in the sixteenth century. Like the Maurya and Gupta Empires, the Mughals span the onset of a new epoch which can be usefully called 'early modern'.

Across the long medieval millennium, social environments were being slowly but steadily transformed, providing new kinds of social experience, new settings for socialization in each few generations. Whole new societies emerged in each period. Some ways of life died away as others came into being. Additions of new peoples and new cultural elements also accumulated inside old cultural areas to form more and more complex composites. Overall, people became more identified with the villages, towns, and regions around them. Societies became more complex, more differentiated, and more intricately stratified; the social ranks that defined imperial power and authority became more complex, specialized, diverse, and productive.

EARLY MEDIEVALISM

In the early-medieval centuries, the major changes occurred in places that were not typically big cities like those that anchored ancient empires. Ancient cities were large for their day but were surrounded by open landscapes disconnected from city life; they depended on long-distance lines of support that broke when medieval dynasties carved out regional domains. Early-medieval trade wove dense connections among localities that filled up with farms and markets; and these domains were less dependent on long-distance trade and on wide military operations. These were deeply agrarian dynastic domains, where political power rose on solid foundations in localities integrated into expanding regions of agricultural production. Each medieval domain resembled a grove of banyan trees that hosted various travellers who moved among many groves, enriching them and depending on their sustenance.

Medieval kingdoms arose from the power of social groups in dynastic core regions. Medieval domains were smaller than ancient empires but in aggregate much richer, more powerful, and more productive because medieval dynasties were more intricately involved in regional societies, which were increasing their productive capacities at an unprecedented rate. In this context, dynastic elites enriched themselves with tribute and taxes, amply recorded in inscriptions. They used their wealth on projects of interest to local elites, such as building temples and monasteries, conducting rituals, extending irrigation, supporting learned monks and Brahmans, protecting farms and towns against robbers, defending territory against incursions, and sending armies to bring tribute from other areas. Local elites paid taxes and tribute to sustain their own local powers over land and labour, and they invested jointly with rulers to increase productivity. Local elite involvement in the dynastic order deepened a dynasty's local support and sustained its longevity. All the major medieval dynasties significantly shaped local elite identities, most of which are still visible today.

The organization of political systems differed among regions and changed over time, but documents indicate some general patterns. Most records depict transactions among people with titles in dynastic ranks, and indicate that sovereignty emerged from these transactions rather than being dictated by legal or constitutional rules. Sovereignty consisted of honour and deference expressed in public interactions by people whose activity inscriptions record. Inscriptional transactions were mostly gifts, contracts, and commitments that individuals engaged in to express respect and support for people they recognized as being superiors and subordinates in social ranks of political and cultural authority.

Dynasties grew as rising kings subordinated existing local elites and officially recognized their subaltern status in public ceremonies. Rather than replacing old local rulers in the lower ranks of sovereignty, which threatened all their alliance partners, rising dynasties

TABLE 2. A REGIONAL CHRONOLOGY OF MEDIEVAL DYNASTIES

Location/period	Dynasty	Core and Extent
Andhra Pradesh		
1000s–1300s	Kakatiyas	Warangal–Telangana–Coast
1500s–1600s	Qutb Shahis	Golkonda–Telangana–Coast
Bengal		
750s–1170s	Palas	Gauda–Orissa–Jalandhur
1000s–1200s	Senas	Navadvipa–Vijayapura
1200s–1700s	Ilyas Shahis	Dhaka
1500s	Husain Shahis	Dhaka
1700s	Nawabs	Murshidabad
Ganga River Basin		
500s–840s	Pusyabutis	Sthanisvara (near Delhi)–Ujjaini–Orissa
700s–1150s	Gurjara-Pratiharas	Ujjaini–Gujarat–Punjab–Bengal
800s–1300s	Candellas	Khajurao–Awadh–Gorakpur
996–1118	Ghurids	Afghanistan–Lahore–Sind–Kasi–North Bengal
1000s–1200s	Gahadavalas	Kasi–Kanyakubja–Awadh
1162–1206	Ghaznavids	Lahore–Ghazni–Persia–Central Asia
1206–1526	Delhi Sultanate	Delhi–Afghanistan–Sind–Gujarat–Deccan–Bengal
1527–1707	Mughals	Kabul–Kashmir–Delhi–Gujarat–Assam–Mysore
1540–1555	Sur Shah	Bengal–Punjab
Gujarat		
900s–1200s	Caulukyas	Anahilapataka
1500s	Nizam Shahis	Aurangabad

TABLE 2. *CONTINUED*

Location/period	Dynasty	Core and Extent
Karnataka		
500s–750s	Chalukyas	Vatapi–Narmada–Guntur
1000–1340s	Hoysalas	Dvarasamudram (to both coasts)
1336–1672	Vijayanagar	Raichur Mysore north–both coasts
1500s–1600s	Adl Shahis	Bijapur
1500–1831 (1947)	Udaiyars	Mysore region
Kashmir		
620s–850s	Karkotas	Srinagar–Kabul–Vidisa–Bengal
900s–1300s	Loharas	Srinagar–Kashmir
Kerala		
300s–1100s	Cheras	Kollam–Trivandrum
1700s	Zamorins	Calicut
1700s	Travancore	Trivandrum
Maharashtra		
600s–900s	Rashtrakutas	Vidarbha (Nagpur)–East Coast
800s–1300s	Yadavas	Devagiri
1300s–1500s	Bahmanis	Ahmadnagar
1500s–1600s	Nizam Shahis	Daulatabad (Devagiri)
1600s–1818	Marathas	Pune–Malwa–Nagpur
Nepal		
400s–700s	Licchavis	Kathmandu Valley
900s–1700s	Mallas	Kathmandu Valley
Orissa		
300s–1400s	Gangas	Kataka–Bhuvanesvara
1300s–1500s	Gajapatis	Jajnagar

TABLE 2. *CONTINUED*

Location/period	Dynasty	Core and Extent
Rajasthan		
800s–1300s	Paramaras	Ujjaini–Dhara (Malwa)
900s–1100s	Cahamanas	Ajayameru–Sakambhari
1200–1750 (1948)	Rathors	Jodhpur–Mandur
1300s–1700s (1948)	Sisodiyas	Udaipur–Chitor
Sri Lanka		
200s BCE–1200s	Lambakannas	Anuradhapura–Polunnaruva
1200–1500	Savulus	Kotte–west coast
1700s	Kandy	Kandy–highlands to coasts
Tamil Nadu		
300s–900s	Pallavas	Vengi–Kanchipuram–Tanjavur
600s–1300s	Pandyas	Madurai–Tanjavur–Kanchipuram
800s–1200s	Cholas	Tanjavur–Kanya Kumar–Sri Lanka
1336–1672	Vijayanagar	Vijayanagar–Karnataka–Andhra–Tamil Nadu
1600s	Nayakas	Madurai–Gingi–Tanjavur

strengthened local alliances under their authority by bestowing titles and honours on leaders in the lower ranks. Dynastic lineages competed with one another for supremacy over locals who were often pressed and courted by more than one ruler, and who often recognized more than one sovereign. Multiple sovereignties formed ranked layers as a king (*raja*) became a great king (*maharaja*) or 'king of kings' (*maha-adhi-raja*) by adding the names of more subordinate rulers (*samanta*s) to the list of those who bowed to him. As a result, local people often bowed to a *raja* who bowed to a bigger *raja*, and so on, up the ranks.

Medieval rulers thus typically increased their power not by deepening their direct control over local resources, but rather by extending their domains to cover more localities and by propagating more exalted titles for themselves in ceremonies in more distant places. Royal domains also spread with new agricultural colonization. Although each dynasty concentrated attention on its core territory, it could only grow by spreading its canopy. Expansive dynastic development spawned new small centres of royal authority in new localities more than it created big concentrations of population in major urban centres, which is a logical trend in the sparsely populated medieval landscape, where land was in abundance for making new farms and new village settlements. Such expansion also increased the power of local elites, who organized and controlled the expansion of village agriculture. There were no large state-sponsored schemes of agricultural expansion or colonization recorded anywhere in early-medieval South Asia; the novelty of such activity would be one defining feature of the emerging modernity of the Mughals. Local elites in medieval territory controlled the expansion of farming and thus had their hands most immediately on the resources that medieval dynasties needed in order to thrive.

Political geography as depicted in the inscriptions is composed of localities in which inscriptions appear and record multiple, layered sovereignties overlapping spatially as local elites bow down to dynastic rulers spreading in various directions. Large tracts with no inscriptions surround places with many. Dynastic domains thus resemble archipelagos of inscriptional sites rather than uniform state territories with stable boundaries. Archipelagos overlap as the islands belonging to one king mix with those of another. This motley spatial pattern of sovereignty continued unchallenged until the onset of modern political institutions that began with the Mughals; but even today, unified, uniform national state territories include remnants of motley medieval territorialism, notably Chit Mahals in the borderlands of India and Bangladesh, which derive from the scattered local domains of Cooch Behar.

Most medieval dynasties combined elements of imperialism, regionalism, and localism. Many expanded like empires. All formed regions of competition, overlapping sovereignty, and local support among constituencies. Present-day Tamil Nadu exemplifies the kind of cultural territory formed in various ways in other regions. The most resilient medieval territory, which appears in all the inscriptions, was a small region called a *nadu*, which included a set of related villages, probably connected by kinship and certainly by patriarchal alliances. There were thirty *nadu*s scattered across the land south of Madurai in the Pandya country alone. A medieval *nadu* was a local domain around which were woven extensive networks of personal loyalty, alliance, and fealty. Local domains were defined in wider networks of culture, however, as indicated by the fact that the term *nadu* appears all across overlapping domains of sovereignty that encompassed what is now Tamil Nadu. This weaving together of *nadu* micro-territories began in the sixth century, under the Pallavas, and continued under competing early-medieval dynasties of Cholas, Pandyas, and Cheras, and then later-medieval rulers in Vijayanagar *raya*s, Madurai, and Arcot. All this imperial weaving together of territory produced a broadly shared Tamil language and textual geography of territorial authority, extending into Karnataka, Kerala, Andhra Pradesh, and northern Sri Lanka. All the dynasties that ruled Tamil-speaking people were attached primarily to localities in their own home regions. Inscriptions from Pandya country (around Madurai) treat Chola conquest as a foreign imperial domination, and Chola inscriptions in Tanjavur treat Pandya conquest in the same way. In medieval terms, Chola and Pandya kings ruled separate countries that were defined by personal loyalties rather than by territorial boundaries. Expanding cultural definitions of imperial territorialism are major markers of late-medieval and early-modern transitions.

SPIRITUAL POWERS

Medieval power relations included gods. The cultural milieu included divinity and humanity and drew no sharp line between them: various kinds of beings moved back and forth and lived ambiguously at their conjunction. One Gupta inscription records a royal gift to a local guru who traced his lineage to a god. Royal genealogies typically record celestial ancestors, including the sun and moon. The spirit world was everywhere. Celestial beings brought victory in war and commanded human fates. Spirits of nature caused disease, drought, flood, and fertility for animals, crops, and humans. Visible and invisible powers mingled capriciously. Priests, rulers, mystics, and saints evoked divinity, and gods lived in society. Medieval domains were institutional environments for organizing, deploying, and controlling spiritual powers circulating the universe, inhabiting heaven, earth, and the underworld.

As with politics, also with religion, it is useful to take a bottom-up, locality-first approach to early-medieval history, and trends in Tamil *nadu*s again provide a useful example. In ancient times, before the Common Era, Tamil verse portrayed localities full of spirits. One, called Seyon, was red like the red earth of the hills where he lived. Feared and propitiated, Seyon became the subject of stories that dramatized his power. Personified in ancient Tamil verse, he became a living being with a personality, a human divine. He later acquired various names, one being Murugan; and sometime in the middle of the first millennium, Murugan became a son of Siva, identified with Skanda. Thus an ancient local spirit was gradually transformed by incorporation into *purana*s. The Skanda *Purana* was recreated in the Tamil language by translation from Sanskrit. Other Sanskrit texts were similarly adapted to new settings, most famously the *Ramayana*, whose Tamil version endows Sita's captor, Ravana, with a rather more heroic character than the Sanskrit version. Many *Ramayana*s were composed across the length and breadth of South Asia. Hundreds of local spirits and gods were incorporated into the pantheon where Siva and Vishnu reigned like two great *raja*s complete with their own sprawling, competing clans.

A diverse Hindu cultural complex spread across medieval domains, endowing many localities with common features as localities remained distinctive, with each set of local groups developing its own traditions. Learned Brahmans received gifts of support from rulers and from local elites to organize temples and conduct ceremonies to incorporate local deities, sentiments, and practices into the Puranic pantheon. At the same time, Brahmans rationalized and ritualized the local status hierarchy; they defined local identities in the ritual vocabulary of *varna* and *jati*. Brahmans used high-culture elements from ancient Sanskrit texts to compose locally grounded Hindu ritual domains that multiplied disparately in bits and pieces in the motley medieval manner, filled with ad hoc accommodation.

Brahmans spread Hindu cultural forms in much the same way – and at the same time – as other religious specialists were spreading Jainism, Buddhism, Islam, and Christianity. They travelled extensively. They settled in strategic places under dynastic patronage. They worked with local and regional allies to translate and interpret ideas and rituals into local vernaculars. They merged rustic and cosmopolitan elements. They vied for local elite support. Competing royal patrons backed competing religious specialists, often at the same time. In this lively world of cultural politics, Brahmans defined Hindu orthodoxy in local terms. Their success depended on innovative adaptations to evolving social environments. They were active in two distinct arenas: one was inside the state itself; the other, in local society, particularly in rural society. Brahman rituals and Sanskrit texts became widely influential in medieval dynasties.

The prominence of Sanskrit prose, Puranic deities, and divine genealogy in the *prasasti*s indicates a sweeping royal agreement across South Asia (and in parts of South-East Asia) that Brahmans brought to medieval governance a powerful symbolic technology. Most inscriptions are bilingual documents that symbolize the two-tier cultural space in which medieval dynasties worked. Brahman Sanskrit cosmopolitanism met vernacular languages in the inscriptions. Many early-medieval Sanskrit *prasasti*s report the royal conduct of Vedic rituals, while vernacular texts in many inscriptions record a ruler's financial support for Brahman settlements, Vedic learning, temple building, and temple rituals. There were many ways to sponsor Hindu culture, and they all centred on the temple precincts, where most inscriptions appear and most Hindu identities were initially formed. The spiritual powers of Brahmans mingled with those of gods, who became central figures in medieval life.

GEOGRAPHIES OF RELIGION

Brahmans were among many cultural activists who vied with one another in their deployment of spiritual power, and they all needed mundane local patronage to flourish. Patterns of financial support from ruling dynasties, merchants, and landed elites had a major impact on the changing religious substance of cultural regions.

Buddhism and Islam became most prominent along routes of trade and migration that ran from one end of Asia to the other. In the sixth century, Buddhists received most of the patronage available in Afghanistan, the upper Indus basin, and the Himalayan regions from Kashmir to Nepal; and moving eastward across Central Asia, Buddhists then established themselves firmly in Tibet, China, and Japan. After the eighth century, however, eastward and southern migrations by Arabs and Turks from West and Central Asia shifted religious patronage to Islam in Afghanistan, along the Indus, in Punjab, and in Kashmir. But Buddhist monks had a permanent political base at the hub of Indian Ocean trade in Sri Lanka, and from the eighth century onward, they won state support in regions from Burma into South-East Asia. In Java, early-medieval kings patronized Hindus; but in the ninth century, Buddhists supplanted Hindus at court, though Hindus remained influential in royal circles in Bali, alongside Buddhists. By the tenth century,

Arab traders were expanding their operations in the Indian Ocean. Muslim centres multiplied along the peninsula and on coastal Sri Lanka, and merchant patronage for Islam drew local rulers away from Buddhism in regions around many South-East Asian ports in the later-medieval period.

In Bengal, Buddhists were well established at the start of the medieval period, and the Pala dynasty supported them for four hundred years. But after Hemantasena, a Pala tributary, declared his own independent dynasty, his successor, Vijayasena (1095–1158) defeated the Palas, pushed Sena armies west across Bengal and northern Bihar, patronized Vishnu worship, and expelled Buddhists. Vaishnava Hinduism flourished in Sena domains. The last Sena *raja*, Laksmanasena, patronized the most famous Bengali Vaishnava poet, Jayadeva, who wrote the widely influential devotional poem *Gitagovinda*. In 1206, Laksmanasena was driven out of Bengal by the Turk conqueror Bakhtiyar Khilji, who patronized Islam. After Khilji conquest, there was a general drift of patronage for Islam to the eastern regions of Bengal, where the Senas had not uprooted Buddhists; while Vaishnava Hindus received support from merchants, landowners, and local rulers more in western Bengal, but also in the east. Brahman influence in Bengali society was enhanced from Sena times onward by a distinctly Bengali system of hypergamy, in which high-caste women married Kulin Brahman men who fathered children with multiple wives; this produced a multicaste elite that included merchants, landowners, and administrators which flourished under later-medieval regimes. From Khilji times onward, Muslim converts and migrants populated new agricultural settlements in eastern Bengal, where Vaishnavism in particular, but Hindu temples, arts, poetry, and music in general, also flourished under the patronage of Hindu landlords, merchants, and administrative elites.

Like the multiple sovereignties in medieval domains, multireligious cultures developed in most medieval regions, where patronage sustained diverse religious institutions. Popular rituals and local sentiments often merged and overlapped, crossing the lines of religious tradition, particularly in the spiritual domain of devotional cults that revolved around charismatic individuals.

The Kathmandu Valley was a Buddhist stronghold ruled by Hindu kings. The Buddha had been born in the southern foothills (Terai) of Nepal, where Ashoka inscribed a Maurya column. In Gupta times, Licchavis began their long reign, and claiming Kshatriya status, launched a tradition of sovereignty in which high-caste kings from the

Ganga lowlands maintained supremacy over a mostly Buddhist population. Powerful medieval kings in Tibet made Himalayan passes to the north major arteries of culture, commerce, and politics reaching into China, which brought more and more Buddhists and their patrons into the valley. Kingdoms around Kathmandu became a mixing ground for Hindus from the south and Buddhists from the north, and like the dynasties in Bengal, they made multicultural patronage a permanent tradition.

In the western plains – in Gujarat, Rajasthan, Malwa, and Bundelkhand – medieval Hindu dynasties of Kalacuris, Caulukyas, Paramaras, and Candellas also patronized Jains, who were prominent among merchants. One Caulukya king is said to have become Jain. Hindu and Jain cultural features blended into one another. Jain temple worship and Hindu–Jain marriage became common. In Gujarat – Mohandas Gandhi's homeland – it is difficult to say where Jainism ends and Hinduism begins. Non-violence, the fundamental Jain virtue, became philosophically prominent among Hindus in this region, where patrons for Jainism included archetypal Kshatriya warriors, the great Rajput lineages. Gujarati Bania (merchant) castes made their version of Vaisya culture very Jain, a cultural phenomenon with its origins in the mixed patronage of medieval dynasties.

In the peninsula, medieval worshippers of Siva and Vishnu displaced Buddhism and Jainism from the cultural prominence they had enjoyed in early-medieval times, especially in Madurai and Kanchipuram. Pockets of Jainism remained, however, and all along the peninsular coast, most prominently in Kerala, Hindu kings patronized diverse merchant communities that were essential features of life along the Indian Ocean coast, including Jains, Zoroastrians, Muslims, Christians, and Jews. Arab Muslim settlements received patronage from non-Muslim rulers all along the coast, as they did across the Palk Straits in Sri Lanka.

Inside medieval Hindu cultural environments, trends in popular religion indicate the increasing influence of religious feelings of a distinctly non-Brahman kind that first achieved prominence in temple worship farthest from the original home of classical Brahman orthodoxy. In the far south, from the eighth century onward, non-Brahman cultural activists took the lead in spreading Siva and Vishnu worship in old Dakshinapatha by inventing devotional (*bhakti*) worship that valued emotion above knowledge, discipline, and ritual; by composing vernacular verse in Tamil, not Sanskrit; by promoting female saints and mass participation in deity worship;

by giving devotees a direct relation to god independent of Brahmanical mediation; by making low-caste status respectable in the eyes of god; by making songfests ad hoc sites of worship; by praising poet saints over Brahman gurus; and by creating pilgrimage places rooted in local traditions. *Bhakti* poets produced a new style of emotive, popular cultural politics. Devotionalism made divine frenzy and passion for god a high virtue, and by the tenth century, these energies had been turned against religious competitors. Several texts indicate massacres of Buddhists and Jains. Under Chola kings, worshippers of Siva (Shivites) prospered at the expense of Vishnu worshippers (Vaishnavas), triggering battles among sectarian forces.

Bhakti devotionalism and sectarian competition challenged Brahman elite proponents of Sanskrit religion as it attracted more patronage from ruling dynasties. To cultivate a popular following, many rulers in the south supported Vaishnava (*Alvar*) and Shivite (*Nayanar*) *bhakti* poets. The most celebrated Hindu intellectual of the early-medieval age, Shankaracharya (788–820), made his name during his short life by developing a Sanskrit high-culture rendition of Tamil devotional poetry, reconciling Shivism and Vaishnavism through a non-dualistic *advaita* philosophy that drew on the Upanishads and incorporated elements from Buddhism, travelling from Kerala to Kashmir and back again to establish monastic centres. Shankara helped to absorb and normalize popular devotionalism in elite Brahman high culture.

Populist challenges to the spiritual power of Brahmans were mostly of local importance, but one of major regional stature emerged in the Kannada-speaking interior of the peninsula, where the *bhakti* saint Basava established a sect called the Virashaivas (also called the Lingayats) with a non-Brahman *jangama* priesthood. Virashaivism attracted royal patronage and many adherents from merchant communities and became regionally dominant in northern Karnataka, where Lingayats remain pre-eminent today.

Popular devotionalism attracted passionate believers to temples and pilgrimage sites. This made public patronage increasingly complex and fraught, because sects could provide decisive military and financial support for dynastic contenders. Multiple and layered sovereignties continued among the gods as dynasties gave privileges and funds in various forms – minimally as tax exemptions – simultaneously to various religious institutions and leaders. Popular movements made such support contentious. Rulers had to balance support for their core religious constituency with support for others, which might bring condemnation from allies. Muslim rulers often faced criticism for the patronage they typically gave Hindu groups, following established precedent. Devotees of Vishnu and Siva could be equally unforgiving. As *bhakti* travelled north along Shankara's tracks, competing Hindu sectarians not only wrote devotional poems like Jayadeva's *Gitagovinda*, but also raised armies to fight for sectarian control of pilgrimage sites and temple festivals. In the northern plains, from at least the fifteenth century, armies of Shivite and Vaishnava ascetics fought to protect sectarian wealth against raids from competitors and to capture revenues from popular religious gatherings such as the *kumbh mela* in Hardwar and Prayaga (Allahabad). In the sixteenth century, the Mughal emperor Akbar witnessed a pitched battle between two sects of Shivites, and Akbar's own religious eclecticism reflects an effort to reconcile contentious devotional loyalties through debate and mystical speculation.

IMPERIAL *DHARMA*

New kinds of society came into being as medieval agrarian domains expanded into landscapes inhabited by nomads, hunters, and forest dwellers. Kings, Brahmans, and local landed elites led the drive to extend and protect the moral authority of *dharma*. For kings, peace and prosperity in their domains were definite signs of righteousness, as in Rama's kingdom in the *Ramayana*. Protecting *dharma* enabled royal families and local elites to form ranks of honour and spiritual merit that also disciplined the labour force, co-ordinated economic activities, and secured rights over landed property. Medieval texts on *dharma* do not insist that a king be a Kshatriya, and in much of the subcontinent, medieval *jati* ranks developed without the presence of all four *varna*s. Medieval prescriptive texts, *sastra*s, rather declare that a king's sacred duty – *rajadharma* – is to protect local custom. The *Manusmriti* (*Laws of Manu*) also says that *dharma* includes the sacred right of first possession for people who clear the land for cultivation, even if they had taken the land from hunters and pastoralists, which was typically the case. Kings needed to give grants of farmland to temples and Brahmans to express dynastic support for *dharma*, but they also had to protect local rights to land. Kings, Brahmans, and local landed elites had to work together to realize *dharma*.

Political territory became *dharma*'s abode as ritually ranked kin groups became ranked caste groups (*jati*s). Coercion was certainly involved in the creation of caste societies, but the practice of rank-ing *jati* groups according to *varna* was also attractive for many groups, particularly in the higher social ranks. Caste norms stabi-lized communities, organized production, and sanctified social power. Rituals of caste ranking facilitated family alliances by meas-uring family status. The labour, land, and assets of low-ranking *jati*s came under the control of dominant high-caste families who made strategic alliances with Brahmans and kings. Dominant castes came into control of local communities in dynastic territories. The expan-sion of caste society appears to have been a top-down process that did not typically depend upon everyday coercion. It emerged as an evolving caste hegemony in which the coercive features were hidden by beliefs in *dharma* that became widely accepted as they provided everyone with a place in the social ranks.

The spread of *jati* ranking as a feature of social life seems to have been propelled by ritual alliances among upwardly mobile groups. New dynastic realms were places where the building of ranking systems made good sense. Dynastic lineage leaders and Brahmans were critical protagonists in creating these systems of social difference, status, and power. New societies came to include new social groups, and institutions formed around models of behav-iour, identity, aesthetics, and patronage were codified in Sanskrit texts as these were interpreted locally by Brahmans who sanctified social rank. People moved up in society by supporting and emulating Brahmans. Families rising in social stature hired Brahman genealo-gists and court poets; they patronized Brahmans and temples; they endowed feeding places for holy men and pilgrims; and they staged festivals, fed saints, and variously joined in activities that brought gods, priests, kings, and farmers into communion.

All this occurred as farmers expanded their control over land and labour, and as populations of peasants, nomads, pastoralists, hunters, and forest tribes were slowly finding new social identities. Over many generations, people became high-caste landowners, kings, protectors of *dharma*, Kshatriyas, Vaisyas, Superior Sudras, Inferior Sudras, untouchables, and aliens beyond the pale. Dominant agrarian castes came into being in different regions: Jats, Rajputs, Kunbis, Vellalas, Velamas, Reddys, Kapus, Nayars, and many others. In this long process, ancient identities were lost. In ancient times, the Hoysala kings' ancestors were Melapas, hill chiefs in the Soseyur forests. Udaiyar and Yadava dynasties descended from herders. Tevar kings descended from Marava and Kallar hunters. Gurjaras and Rajputs had once been pastoral nomads. Places, too, acquired new identities as they became known by the names of dynasties and local groups in control. Land became ethnically marked by traditions of group control. Dominant castes identified with dynastic territories that became their homelands. The only people who could be equally 'at home' in all the lands of *dharma* were Brahmans. Even today, Brahmans have high status in every part of Hindu society, but all other high castes have regional identities according to territories of traditional residence and stature; these territories are in turn identified with their historically dominant caste groups.

Activity that dramatized emerging social identities appears in temple inscriptions. Rituals performed by Brahmans using Sanskrit liturgies brought cosmic spiritual powers down to earth to sanctify a caste social order. Temples were divine sites for enacting social rank among worshippers who protected *dharma* and financed rituals; and the rituals brought a variety of local, regional, and imperial gods together. Though medieval societies witnessed many kinds of rituals, by all kinds of spiritualists and officiates from all kinds of social backgrounds in all manner of locations, which brought rain, secured crops, drove away disease, delivered healthy babies and bolstered dynasties, medieval inscriptions only treat rituals conducted by Brahman priests for Siva, Vishnu, and their Puranic relatives. Temples to these great sovereign gods served as towering sacred landmarks, monuments to political power.

The Hindu temple as a sacred and architectural complex emerged in full form in the later Gupta period. Its elaboration and spread from the sixth to the fourteenth centuries provide a glorious medieval architectural legacy, from Mahaballipuram to Khajuraho. The absorption of local deities, rituals, symbols, and spirituality into Puranic literature and related myth, folklore, and artistic representation constituted Hindu worship by enhancing the cultural potency of local deities, devotees, and patrons. Local cults were woven into Puranic traditions and temple rituals as local communities came under royal authority. The greatness of the gods enhanced the glamour of royal patrons. Rich centres of temple worship combined many of the technical skills – controlled by Brahmans – that were needed to develop agrarian territories, from architecture and engineering to law and financial management. Building a great temple attracted Brahmans and established a theatre of royal grandeur. Great kings built great temples and supported many learned Brahmans. The distribution and content of temples and inscriptions thus maps medieval social geography. Lands rich with inscriptions are concentrated in eastern and central Uttar Pradesh, West Bengal, Gujarat, western Maharashtra, and along the coastal plains. Where we do not find many medieval temple inscriptions – in Punjab, in Jat territories in the western Ganga plains, and in most mountainous regions – we can surmise that Brahman influence was small and cultures less Hinduized in medieval times.

Social identities emerged around temples as people and gods lived together. Gifts by kings, landed elites, merchants, and others to Brahmans and temples increased the spiritual stature of the donor. Inscriptions are contracts and advertisements. The more popular a temple became – the more praised in song and more attractive for pilgrims – the greater became the value of its patronage and the number of people whose identity attached to it. Rising *bhakti* devotionalism enhanced the virtue, volume, and commercial value of pilgrimage, as it increased temple donations and investments. Donations became increasingly popular as a means and marker of social mobility as temples became commercial centres, meeting places for landowners and employers, and manufacturing centres. Increasing participation in temple rituals made them more effective sites for social ranking, as temple honours were distributed according to rank and all worshippers were positioned in ranked proximity to the deity. Rulers came first. Rich donors appeared in the order of the ranked values of their temple endowments. Popular *bhakti* movements made sovereign gods ever more central in everyday social life, even for the poorest people who did all the hardest manual labour, who were prohibited from ever setting foot in the temple, whose exclusion marked them as people of the lowest social rank. Some powerful *bhakti* saints came from the lowest of the low, whose devotion was so strong that gods came out of the temples to return their love.

People joined temple society by giving to gods and Brahmans; gifts that increased the status of donors, executors of the grant, by extension increased the status of extended kin groups. Over time, kinship circles formed around lineages and clans that fed gods and Brahmans, and these kin groups formed high-status, non-Brahman elite *jati*s, elevated above others in ritual and society. Brahmans reaped major benefits. In the open spaces of Rashtrakuta power, one inscription records a gift of 8000 measures of land to 1000 Brahmans, and 4000 measures to a single Brahman. In each specific context, an inscription of this kind appears to mark an effort by a non-Brahman power block to enhance its status and that of its local allies.

Such gambits were not without risk. A small but significant set of inscriptions records local opposition to Brahman settlements, collection of taxes, and claims on local resources. The authority of Hindu kingship spread slowly – often violently – into the vast spaces that lay outside its reach in the early-medieval centuries. In many instances, land grants appear to mark frontiers of royal power, and here resistance might be expected. Even where local society did accept the ritual and social status of Brahmans, fierce competitive struggles might flare up over land grants. In the ninth century, local conflicts of this kind accompanied new Brahman settlements on the Tamil coast. In the Rashtrakuta realm, inscriptions warn that violence and curses will be heaped upon opponents of Brahman land grants, and texts proclaim that people who murder Brahmans will be punished harshly, which implies that such murders did occur.

THE RISE OF THE WARRIORS

Many violent conflicts are recorded as features of political practice during ancient and early-medieval times. One typical ninth-century royal inscription brags that Candellas reduced to submission 'wild tribes of Bhillas, Sabaras and Pulindas'. Conquering enemies and tribes preoccupied most dynastic genealogies. Valorous killing and death pervade literature and folklore. The ancient poems *Mahabharata* and *Ramayana* popularized epic war. Ancient and medieval hero stones memorialized local warriors and widow martyrs who became deified as *sati* by immolating themselves on their husband's funeral pyre. Ancient Tamil poets praised kings' bloody deeds. Buddhist tales depict the gore of graveyards, cremation grounds, and battlefields to convey life's suffering and impermanence.

Organized warfare became a civilizing force under the Mauryas and the Guptas. Medieval kings fought to define ranks of *raja*s and *samanta*s as they conquered nomads and forest people, 'wild tribes' outside the world of *dharma*. Tribal societies outside *dharma* occupied most of the land around villages and towns. Subduing tribes, expelling unruly elements, protecting farms against nomads, and assimilating tribal groups into caste society, all required organized violence. The steady absorption of tribal peoples into complex agrarian societies helps to explain the increasing prominence of animal deities and blood sacrifice in Hindu worship, which were missing in Vedic rituals and ancient Brahmanism. Medieval dynasties had a basic commitment to the expansion of permanent field cultivation; this required constant fighting on the frontiers of farming. Violent conflicts among sedentary farmers, pastoral nomads, shifting cultivators, hunters, warriors, and forest dwellers indicate that many groups opposed the rule of *dharma*. But many pastoral and tribal peoples were also assimilated; their proportion of the agrarian population was particularly high in the western plains, central mountains, Punjab, western Gangetic basin, and the interior peninsula. In these regions, assimilated and unassimilated tribal groups retained substantial political power. Rajput rulers recognized Bhil chiefs as their allies, and Bhils acquired a central role in some Rajput coronation ceremonies.

Farming communities expanded agriculture in medieval domains by pushing pastoral nomads and forest cultivators away; but at the same time, herders, hunters, nomads, and other peoples entered expanding agrarian societies, becoming labourers, farmers, craft producers, animal breeders and keepers, transporters, dairy producers, soldiers, traders, warriors, sorcerers, and kings. Agricultural territories included more diverse populations, not only different kinds of farmers – including peasants, landlords, and landless workers – but also non-farming groups who were essential for farming: artisans, cattle herders, hunters, transporters, traders, collectors of forest produce, well-diggers, priests, engineers, architects, healers, astrologers, and warriors. Many of these people were newly embraced by the rule of *dharma*. Without them, economies could not expand; their incorporation was an important social project.

In this context, warriors expanded their influence. Various factors promoted the rise of warrior power, and one was certainly the increasing number of people with specialized military skills living in agrarian societies. Warriors with nomadic roots often became military specialists, most prominently in Rajasthan and the surrounding regions, where warrior dynasties emerged from the Gurjara-Pratihara clans that conquered most of the Ganga basin after the eighth century.

By the tenth century, professional military cadres became features of dynastic power generally, and old dynasties used large armies to accumulate wealth outside core territories that could no longer sustain their acquisitive ruling classes. The Cholas exemplify this trend. In the tenth century, the Chola dynasty boasted a vast administrative apparatus and huge temples in the Kaveri delta, and Chola pioneers were moving up the Kaveri to build new domains on the slopes below Mysore. Chola armies then campaigned across the peninsula from Andhra and northern Karnataka to Kanya Kumari, and Kerala; they crossed the Palk Straits to fight in Sri Lanka. They conquered the Pandyas, made themselves a new ruling elite, and brought Brahmans and service castes to work for them. Chola expansion spawned new dynasties among competitors. Warriors pushed out of coastal Andhra by the Cholas established a new Kakatiya dynasty at Warangal in the interior uplands. Kakatiyas built irrigation tanks that were marvels of the age. Similar dynastic inventions occurred in the Mysore region, where Chola pressure combined with Chalukya expansion in the Deccan to generate a new Hoysala dynasty, whose temple sculptures record the professional prominence of the Hoysala armed cavalry sporting Arabian horses.

When Chola imperial expansion reached its limit, the weight of dynastic power shifted from the coast into the interior uplands, where warrior nomads and pastoralists were transformed over centuries into warrior–peasant alliances on farming frontiers. New centres of dynastic power arose in Karnataka, Andhra, and Maharashtra, where local warriors faced enemies who galloped along routes across Malwa, Rajasthan, Afghanistan, and Central Asia. Late-medieval militarism in the Deccan – based in Khandesh, Berar, Maharashtra, Andhra, and Karnataka – had its social origins on the land with ancient histories. Dynasties emerged from the mobilization of warriors inside and around farming communities, where peasants struggled with and came from pastoral, hunting, and mountain societies. Earlier dynasties were more pastoral, and later dynasties more agrarian: standing to fight became part of farming. In the Deccan, where drought was common, running off to war in the hot, dry season came naturally. All the dominant agrarian castes that came into being in the medieval Deccan included both soldiers and field cultivators.

By contrast, in Rajasthan, a single dominant warrior group evolved, called Rajput (from *Rajaputra* – sons of kings): they rarely engaged in farming, even to supervise farm labour, because farming was literally beneath them; farming was for their peasant subjects. In the ninth century, separate clans of Rajput Cahamanas (Chauhans), Paramaras (Pawars), Guhilas (Sisodias), and Caulukyas (Solankis) were splitting off from sprawling Gurjara-Pratihara clans, whose distant ancestors were pastoralists and who formed an imperial dynasty that spread across Rajasthan, Malwa, and the Ganga basin. In later centuries, separate Rajput lineages spread out across the plains and adjacent mountains, settling in fortresses, and ruling over peasants. Rajput nobles endowed temples and employed Brahmans, but their devotion to war, clan, and supremacy over peasants were the true measures of Rajput *dharma*. They attracted allies and imitators as they made themselves a model of *rajadharma*, ideal Kshatriyas.

Rajput cultural influence spread widely among allies, competitors, and imitators. The genealogies that constituted the valorous record of a Rajput ancestry became coveted assets among aspiring rulers who multiplied east of Rajasthan until, in the eighteenth century, a cultural Rajputization of tribal kingdoms occurred across the mountains of central and eastern India. Rajput supremacy also stimulated the rise of warrior Jat peasant clans in the western frontiers of old *Bharat* – in Rajasthan, the western Ganga basin, and Punjab – where Rajputs and Jats built fortified villages and hilltop forts, sometimes allied with one another, but most often at odds.

The third population of warriors who propelled the medieval transition during three centuries after 1000 CE consisted of huge clans of Turk, Afghan, and Mongol horse nomads, who dominated warrior society in the uplands north-west of the Indus, Punjab, and Rajasthan, in Afghanistan, Persia, and Central Asia. They became the dominant military force in the lowlands, after the tenth century, when Paramaras held Malwa; Cahamanas fought for northern Rajasthan and routes across the Indo-Gangetic watershed; Hindu Shahis fought Rajputs from their base in Punjab; and Sultan Mahmud assumed power in Ghazni, in Afghanistan.

Mahmud of Ghazni's father, Sabuktigin, fought Hindu Shahis in Punjab to acquire tribute to support his wars in Afghanistan and Persia. A deeply clannish Turk leader, he professed Islam – as Timur would do, centuries later – primarily to make strategic alliances. Mahmud succeeded his father in 997 and extended his patrimonial ambition in all directions. He conquered Afghanistan and Persia, he obtained the title *Yamin al-Daula* (Right Hand of the State) from the Caliph, and he took tribute from local rulers in seventeen raids across the Indus basin. Mahmud defeated Hindu Sahis in 1018; then he sacked Mathura and Kanyakubja; and, in 1026, he sacked the pilgrimage centre of Somanatha, on the coast of the Saurashtra peninsula in Gujarat. His deeds became literally legendary. They were memorialized, often fancifully, by generations of admirers and detractors who bestowed upon him everlasting fame for his pillage, plunder, and the murder of heretics and infidels, including Muslims and non-Muslims. He became symbolic in cultural politics. In the fourteenth century, two Sunni authors, Barani and Isami – writing in Delhi and in the Deccan Bahmani kingdom respectively – praised Mahmud as an ideal Muslim ruler because he persecuted rival Muslim sects of Shias and Ismailis as well as non-believers.

Mahmud of Ghazni also used some of his wealth to support Al-Biruni, the master geographer, who lived in Lahore in the 1040s and compiled a brilliant geography of medieval India using material provided by his Ghaznavi patrons. Al-Biruni had come from Persia and travelled trade routes documented for centuries by Arab geographers whose knowledge had guided Mahmud's expansion to the west and his raids to the east and south. Al-Biruni's geography locates places all across the Indo-Ganga basin and along the Indian Ocean coast, most importantly, Gujarat and Sind, where merchants brought horse traders from Arabia, competing with horse traders from Ghazni. It is likely that Mahmud's raids in Gujarat were in part directed at his compatriots' commercial competitors. Rich Indian merchants in Ghazni would have been able to provide Mahmud with intelligence on the most lucrative sites for military assault. By Mahmud's time, the Indus and Ganga river basins were, like Rajasthan and Gujarat, part of the trading world of Central Asia; and Mahmud brought them into Central Asian politics as well.

From the twelfth to the fourteenth centuries, armies from Central Asia engulfed South Asia's northern plains. Between the time of Al-Biruni's geographical tract (1048) and the travels of Marco Polo (1271–95) and Ibn Batuta (1325–54), the inland routes of mobility in southern Eurasia became a continuous terrain of dynastic competition that ran from Qum in Persia to Samarkand in Central Asia, to Delhi, Surat, and Dhaka. At the same time, the Indian Ocean became an integrated commercial system. South Asia became a land of wealth and trade connecting the Silk Road and the Indian Ocean.

THE LATER-MEDIEVAL TRANSITION

At the same time, trends in Sri Lanka took a dramatically different turn, as the island was becoming a hub of Indian Ocean trade. Tamils had migrated and settled on the island since ancient times. Their settlements had mingled among those of the Sinhalas. Eleventh-century Chola conquests appear to have aggravated local conflicts that already undermined the operation of irrigation systems on which the population depended. Irrigation may also have reached a physical limit; malaria may have become prevalent. After 1200, the ancient irrigation system collapsed, the agrarian economy lost its foundation, the Sinhala population moved south-west to the coast around Colombo, Tamil kingdoms arose in the far north, and malarial lands spread between Tamil and Sinhala regions.

In the first several centuries of the second millennium CE, the contours of political geography shifted substantially. In Sri Lanka, virtually the whole population shifted to the coast, the coastal trade flourished, and for thirty years after Cheng Ho's fleet landed in 1430, Chinese emperors collected tribute from rulers in Sri Lanka. Another centre of imperial power that would prevail in modern times also emerged in Delhi. The Delhi Sultanate had its origins in victories by Mahmud of Ghazni's rival, Muhammad Ghuri, who sacked Ghazni in 1151, and then expelled the Ghaznavids to Punjab in 1157. Muhammad Ghuri marched into the Indus basin to uproot the Ghaznavids in 1186. On the way, his armies conquered Multan (1175), Sind (1182), Peshawar, and Lahore (1186). In 1190, he occupied Bhatinda, in Rajasthan, which triggered battles with the Rajput Prithviraja Chauhan, whom he finally defeated in 1192. Having broken the Rajput hold on western routes to the Ganga basin, the Ghurid armies marched eastward until Bakhtiyar Khilji finally defeated Laksmanasena in Bengal in 1200. Muhammad Ghuri died in 1206. His trusted Mamluk (ex-slave) general, Qutb ud din Aibak, governor of Delhi, declared independence. His dynasty was the first in a series that became known as the Delhi Sultanate. Later, Ghurid and Ghaznavid efforts to bring Delhi back into their fold were finally repulsed by the Delhi sultan Iltutmish in 1211–36.

The Delhi Sultanate became an epoch-making Indian dynasty by repelling the Mongols, who were unstoppable elsewhere in Asia. Genghis Khan (born 1150s or 1160s, died 1227) unified Mongol tribes to produce the largest political territory ever known to that time. His grandson, Batu Khan, commanded Mongol armies assigned to conquer Europe in 1237. Batu Khan conquered Bulgaria, Moscow, Kiev, Hungary, and Poland, forcing local rulers to pay tribute to the Golden Horde. Another grandson, Kublai Khan, conquered northern China and became the Yuan emperor in 1271. His armies finally defeated the southern Sung in 1279, and his dynasty ruled until 1368. Across Eurasia, a Mongol postal system and a road network extended from China to Turkestan, Persia, and Russia, fostering overland trade that brought gunpowder, the compass, and printing to Europe from China. Along these routes, Marco Polo travelled from Venice to China and back. But the Mongols could not conquer India. Mongol horsemen grazed in Punjab for some years and raided Lahore, Multan, and Sind. One son of the Delhi sultan Balban, Muhammad, governor of Sind, died fighting Mongols in 1285. Having failed time and again to conquer the armies of the Delhi sultans, the Mongols withdrew from the Indus basin to concentrate their powers elsewhere, with spectacular success.

Turk warriors related by marriage to Mongols did, however, succeed in India. Timur was born at Kesh, near Samarkand, in a short-lived Mongol successor state, the Chaghatai Khanate of Trans-Oxiana. The man called Tamerlane by Europeans became the governor of the Chaghatai district and then vizier to its Khan. In 1370, he usurped the Khan's power and made himself Amir. He professed Islam but slaughtered people of all religions in the disciplined manner of a Mongol warrior. By 1387, he had conquered Persia and Afghanistan, and in 1398, he swept into India. He took Multan on the way to Delhi, and there he put its sultans to flight and destroyed their citadel. He then conquered the Ganga basin and put the governor of Multan on the Delhi throne on his way back to Afghanistan. His victories had killed the imperial authority of the Delhi Sultanate, which broke into satellite sultanates and survived as a regional power until its territory was conquered in 1526 by Babur, the founder of a Mughal dynasty. Babur claimed descent from both Timur and Genghis Khan. His conquest of Delhi and the Ganga basin was the penultimate step in the rise of warrior power in South Asia. As we will see, his grandson, Akbar, took the final step in the sixteenth century by establishing the Mughal Empire.

A transition that began at the end of the first millennium separates early- and late-medieval history. In early-medieval times, internal developments inside core regions of dynastic authority played the leading role in changing local societies. By 1200, this was no longer true. Warriors from distant homelands became prominent in localities everywhere. The rise of the warriors had begun with imperial Gurjara-Pratiharas and Cholas. Warrior ascendancy over agrarian elites had spread far and wide before Mahmud of Ghazni arrived on the scene. Ghaznavids and their successors institutionalized professional warrior imperialism; and they also marked a shift in the regional origins and cultural composition of military overlords. Rajputs were Kshatriyas who patronized Brahmans and worshipped Puranic deities, and one of their responses to their new military competition was to seek followers for a new Rama cult to support their cause. Their enemies were

Turks, Afghans, and Mongols from Central Asia, some of whom, like Mahmud of Ghazni, praised war in the name of Islam.

Central Asian warriors became supreme during South Asia's medieval transition by deploying swift-horse cavalry skilled in firing arrows at full gallop, volley after volley; by raising vast armies dedicated to siege and open-field combat, undeterred by local alliance building; and by organizing cavalry well supplied with saddles, stirrups, and the latest weapons, running rapidly over long distances, staying on the move to subsist on the fruits of conquest. Turk and Afghan tribes supplied the best men for this kind of warfare, as well as ethnic solidarity for discipline and social support. Central Asian steppe grasslands and herds provided horses at low prices. Routes across Mongol domains provided superior military technology. In 1200, dynasties east and south of the Hindu Kush relied on horses that came from Afghanistan by land and from Arabia by sea; they rarely fought on horses; they rarely fought to the death; and they rarely built strong forts; all of this put them at a disadvantage.

Before 1200, India had served Central Asian warriors as a rich place to raid in order to finance Central Asian wars. Ghaznavids, Ghurids, Mongols, and Timur all looked at India in this way. Trade routes across Punjab were easy targets, and Multan was a jewel en route to Gujarat. The Ganga basin was a huge source of wealth for the taking. The Delhi Sultanate's defeat of the Mongols changed the political environment, however, because it marked a domestication of Central Asian sultans inside India, where they had rich territory to defend and where they became part of a changing political culture.

Mongols thus had many indirect effects on the South Asia regions that they never saw. Warriors such as Qutb ud din Aibak were trained in Mongol warrior skills and used them to defend their domains against Mongols. Mongols pushed Turk and Afghan tribes out of Central Asia to settle in the Indian lowlands. The Delhi Sultanate brought Mongol technologies into the project of building dynasties that could thrive under later-medieval conditions. Migrant warriors from Central Asia continued to conquer in the Indian lowlands in the wake of the Mongols, because they had better access than local rivals to trade routes in the Central Asian interior that carried the latest military technology. Babur is a dramatic example: in the sixteenth century, he used matchlocks and cannon against the last Delhi Sultans, who held fast to honourable but by then archaic methods of steppe warfare.

MOBILITY AND CULTURAL MIXING

Mongol expansion accelerated migration into India. Warriors, scholars, mystics, merchants, artists, artisans, peasants, and workers followed ancient trade routes and new opportunities that opened up in the new domains of Indian sultans. Migrants walked and rode down the Hindu Kush; they travelled from town to town, across Punjab, down the Ganga basin into Bengal, down the Indus into Sind and Gujarat, across the Vindhyas, into the Deccan, and down the coast. From Bengal and other sites along the coast, some continued overseas. They moved and resettled to find work, education, patronage, influence, adventure, and better living. They travelled these routes for five centuries, never in large numbers compared to the resident population, but as newcomers they settled where others had settled before, and their accumulation, natural increase, and local influence changed societies all across South Asia for ever. This was one of the world's most significant long-term migratory flows.

South Asia was a land of wealth and opportunity. Among the overland migrants who came into India primarily from the southern regions of Central and West Asia, two social categories can be usefully distinguished. Leading the way, warriors organized fighters, military suppliers, and service providers on ethnic lines in groups defined by tribe, clan, and lineage, mostly Turks and Afghans. Even these groups were multi-ethnic, but groups in the second, non-military category were even more so. Migrants in both categories coming from Persia increased over time, especially after 1556, when Persian literati came into the service of the Mughal Empire and the centre of gravity of Persian culture shifted into South Asia. Most immigrants were Muslim non-combatants. They generated multicultural centres of social change, mostly in and around urban centres. They greatly accelerated urbanization. Historical documentation also increased with waves of immigration, often as a consequence of patronage by sultans. Most new documentation pertains to the sultans' activities and interests, rather than to those of ordinary immigrants. Al Biruni's *Kitab ta'rikh al-Hind*, a descriptive account of India in 1030 CE, begins the new age of documentation and carries a feeling of discovery and exploration. New architectural documentation begins in 1311, with Alauddin Khilji's Alai Darwaza in Delhi, a massive gateway that makes a solid Muslim cultural statement. We know much more about sultans, however, than about Al Biruni's Lahore or about the people who passed through the Alai Darwaza.

From the thirteenth to the sixteenth centuries, Turk and Afghan warriors pushed old medieval dynasties into subordinate positions and carved out independent domains for themselves. They formed a new, culturally distinct ruling class, poised above old dynastic clans and village elites. Thus the new dynasties added layers to the multilayered sovereignties of medieval history. As before, losers in war fled to fight elsewhere. As during Chola expansion, chain reactions ensued. Conquered Rajputs overcame local rulers in the western Himalayas and Punjab hills, who climbed to fight in higher valleys. As they arrived in Nepal, Yaksha Malla (1429–82) divided his kingdom among his three sons, who ruled Kathmandu, Patan, and Bhaktpur (all now inside the city of Kathmandu); and each son had to fight Kshatriyas who had fled defeat in the plains. Fighters from north India also moved south, where, in the fourteenth century, two brothers Bukka built a new dynasty at Vijayanagar on the southern edge of Turk and Afghan expansion. Telugu and Kannada warriors fled Bahmani sultans in the Deccan to conquer Tamils farther south and form new dynastic enclaves on the south-east coast.

Centuries of competitive interaction imbued military rulers with many common traits. Subordination, alliance building, emulation, and learning brought cultural borrowing, diffusion, and amalgamation. In new dynastic domains, a new kind of cultural complex emerged that gave rulers many options, one of which was to define Hindu and Muslim religious sects in opposition to one another; but they more typically engaged in multicultural patronage. In later-medieval societies, the spirit and practice of Hindu *bhakti* mingled with Muslim *sufi* mysticism around saintly exemplars of spiritual power and in music, poetry, and eclectic divine experience. Spiritual guides, teachers, mystics, poets, festivities, and sacrificial offerings attracted people who worshipped at temples and mosques. Turkish, Afghan, Persian, and regional Hindu aesthetic and engineering motifs mingled in the arts, in fortresses and palaces, and within consumer taste. The regalia of royalty formed a symbolic language of honour that was spoken by rulers of all religions, who recognized one another's authority and engaged in common rituals of rank. *Raja*s and sultans fought, taxed, invested, administered, and transacted with one another using the same lexicon and technologies, learning from one another. Vijayanagar provides a good example of such mingling. Its Rayas faced deadly enemies in the Bijapur sultans, who eventually destroyed Vijayanagar; but the Rayas themselves became Hindu sultans and their techniques of power closely resembled those of the Bijapur sultans. Nayakas in the south and Rajputs in the north likewise assumed the mixed character of Hindu sultans.

FORT CITIES

At the heart of each new dynastic territory, capitals needed serious fortification. Big stone forts arose in rapid succession on major arteries of mobility running east–west in the northern plains and north–south in the peninsula: at Kota (1264), Bijapur (1325), Vijayanagar (1336), Gulbarga (1347), Jaunpur (1359), Hisar (1361), Ahmedabad (1413), Jodhpur (1465), Ludhiana (1481), Ahmadnagar (1494), Udaipur (1500), and Agra (1506). In this context, Delhi began its long career as an imperial capital, strategically astride routes down the Ganga and into Malwa and the Deccan. The fort remained the central site of political power for six centuries.

The new dynastic capitals were often not located in the most fertile agricultural tracts or in old medieval centres in riverine lowlands, but rather in uplands on dry ground in strategic sites along routes of communication, march, and supply. As new dynastic domains grew richer, forts became fortified cities with palaces, large open courtyards, gardens, fountains, garrisons, stables, markets, mosques, temples, shrines, and servants' quarters. The architectural elaboration of fortified space became big business; it produced a new kind of urban landscape. Even the elegant Taj Mahal is encased in fortifications. Inside a typical fort, we find palace glamour as well as stables and barracks; we see a self-contained, armed city, most of whose elements came from far away. Permanent armies drawing specialist soldiers and supplies from extensive networks of trade and migration sustained these new urban centres. No new dynasty of any significance rested on resources from its capital's immediate hinterland; and to this extent, they were all imperial, however small.

Political geography no longer focused as much on agrarian core regions; rather, it focused on forts strung along routes of conquest and areas of supply around them, forming networks of economic integration. A typical sultan's domain consisted of a series of fortified sites, each with an army that lived on taxes from its surrounding land. Dynasties expanded when more fort commanders bowed down to one sultan, and fragmented when commanders became independent, as they often did. The two great imperial success stories were the Delhi Sultans, whose five dynastic lineages embraced a shifting collection of subordinate rulers for three hundred years, from 1206 to 1526; and the Mughals, whose one lineage controlled a much larger, more tightly integrated territory of military command for about half that long, from Akbar's coronation in 1556 to Aurangzeb's death in 1707.

Urbanism reached new heights under military regimes that promoted vast physical and social mobility. Armies protected trade routes and sultans built strategic roads. The army provided the surest route to upward mobility, which always required extensive travel. In 1595, Abu Fazl's treatise on Akbar's reign, *A'in-i Akbari*, suggests that the military may have employed (directly and indirectly) almost a quarter of the imperial population. Many men travelled long distances to fight. It became standard practice for peasants to leave the Bhojpuri region, on the border of Bihar and Uttar Pradesh, after the harvest each year, to fight as far away as the Deccan, to collect wages and booty, and then return home to plant the next crop. Short-distance seasonal military migration became an integral feature of peasant subsistence in the Deccan. Dynasties expanded as warriors migrated to its periphery to fight, settle, and attract new waves of military migration, pressing on peasants by disrupting farm operations and forcing villagers to feed armies. Life on the move became a very common social experience: seasonal migrants, people fleeing war and drought, army suppliers and camp followers, artisans moving to find work and peasants looking for new land, traders, nomads, shifting cultivators, hunters, herders, and transporters and other people on the move for at least part of each year may have comprised half the total population of the major dynastic domains in the seventeenth and eighteenth centuries.

All this mobility increased commerce in many ways, as we will see. But the most notable single innovation of this period was fort-city urbanism, which concentrated goods and services and systems of commercial supply and demand around a large number of specific sites of dynastic wealth and power. The war machine produced a new economic geography. Armies at home and on the move needed diverse goods and services, from horses to weapons to food, rugs, jewellery, art, and entertainment. Rulers accumulated cash and credit to pay troops and buy war materiel. Getting cash to support war required rulers to supply virtual military cities moving across the land for months at a time, filled with all sorts of army personnel, suppliers, retainers, and allied service groups. To maintain his supremacy, a sultan needed cash to finance his wide-ranging display of military power. Financial support became harder to find during seasons of drought and dynastic distress; and as a result, bankers and merchants became powerful in politics as they also became influential in urban society and culture.

New taxes supported later-medieval dynastic regimes. The Delhi Sultans instituted the first tax system designed to sustain an imperial military by making land grants to its officers, which were called *iqta*, as among Ottoman Turks. The old practice of granting land to Brahmans and temples was now extended to the military, by sultans who granted tax territory to commanders who then used the proceeds to support their army and themselves. Taxes paid to local authorities ascended the chain of military command. In practice, most taxes were spent in regions where they were raised on things needed to support the military and administration, which in turn fuelled the growth and concentration of wealth in urban centres.

COMMERCIALISM

Ibn Batuta travelled the new Asian world that emerged in the Mongols' wake. Born in Tangier, Morocco, he left in 1325, travelling overland to Mecca, across Persia, and via Samarkand to Delhi. He lived at the sultan's court in Delhi for eight years and served the sultan as emissary to China. He returned from China by sea via Sumatra, Sri Lanka, Kerala, Goa, and Gujarat before heading back to Morocco. His astute observations often concern commercial conditions. In Turkestan, he found that 'horses . . . are very numerous and the price of them is negligible'. He found Bengal to be 'a vast country, abounding in rice and nowhere in the world have I seen any land where prices are lower than there'. On the road from Goa to Quilon, he wrote, 'I have never seen a safer road than this, for they put to death anyone who steals a single nut, and if any fruit falls no one picks it up but the owner'.

Though much older early-medieval inscriptions do indicate substantial commercial activity, including long-distance trade by major merchant communities, late-medieval documents show that commerce expanded dramatically after 1200. As Ibn Batuta writes, specialized commodities were produced in abundance in particular regions, and rulers protected traders' activities. In addition, his route itself – like that of Marco Polo a century before – indicates that trade across Asia travelled wide circuits of mobility that included the Indian Ocean and the South China Sea. South Asia was a huge land bridge between Central Asia and the southern seas.

A web of long and short trade routes in the Indian Ocean were attached to the coast at numerous strategic sites, typically where river routes inland met the sea. Long routes between China and Europe had touched South Asia since ancient times, meeting coastal routes inland from Gujarat to Bengal. The east coast and Sri Lanka were equally active: in the first century CE, Tamil poets describe the beach as a place of longing, where women pine for men who have gone out to sea. Fisherfolk and coastal traders plied the western seas in Harappan times. Gujarat was a lively port centre in Mauryan times, and eighteenth-century Armenian merchants who brought wool shawls and rugs to Europe from Kashmir and Turkestan travelled through Gujarat and Punjab. Early-medieval Geniza records in Cairo describe voyages to Gujarat and Malabar. For many sea-going merchants from the Mediterranean, Cochin was India's port of entry. Communities of Christian, Muslim, and Jewish traders from the west settled in early-medieval Kerala, where Hindu rulers depended on them to increase dynastic wealth. Ibn Batuta observed that 'most of the merchants from Fars [Persia] and Yemen disembark' at Mangalore, where 'pepper and ginger are exceedingly abundant'. In 1357, John of Marignola, Pope Benedict XII's emissary to China, called Quilon 'the most famous city in the whole of India, where all the pepper in the world grows'. Europeans began building fort-city ports on the west coast when Vasco da Gama arrived in Malabar in 1498.

The sea-coast and overseas connections became increasingly important for people living in the inland interior. Sri Lanka is an extreme but telling example. After the Sinhala population abandoned its old northern homeland and resettled on the south-west coast around Colombo and Galle, the main source of dynastic wealth shifted from agriculture to sea trade. Spices from the mountains were the major exports; above all, cinnamon and pepper. Spices became royal monopolies. Kings contracted with overseas merchants, set prices, and turned profits into royal revenue. Arabs became the major overseas merchant settlers along the coast. Sri Lankan kings and their contemporaries around the Indian Ocean encouraged sea traders to settle in their territory and competed with one another to attract merchants. In 1283, the Sinhala Bhuvanaika Bahu I sent an embassy to the Mamluk sultan of Egypt to make a commercial agreement.

Everywhere in South Asia, warriors needed horses, and many were imported by sea. Exports became more important as farmers pushed agriculture into the interior uplands, where more diverse productive localities entered trading systems strung along rivers leading to and from the sea. Upland forests sent spices, timber, honey, fruits, elephants, and other valuable commodities to the coast in return for rice, meat, tools, and other goods that travelled the coastal trade routes. In this context, farmers began specializing in growing cotton that thrived in black volcanic soil. By 1500, cotton and silk textile manufacturing, trade, and consumption involved many specialists: growers, spinners, weavers, dyers, transporters, bankers, wholesalers, and retailers. Consumers of cloth were concentrated initially in urban centres, where urban traders, bankers, wholesalers, and weavers became critical links in complex chains of commercial transactions that expanded the scale of manufacturing and stretched along the coast and out to sea.

EMERGING IDENTITIES

Along the coast and inland, new societies were being born and old ones were changing. The most dramatic events occurred in hundreds of urban sites, large and small, strung along routes between Central Asia and the Indian Ocean. Records come to us in new kinds of documentation. In the late-medieval centuries, pen-and-ink manuscripts slowly surpassed carved inscriptions as historical documents. Inscriptions and other older sources such as architecture and oral texts also reflect a shift in the substance of texts, however, which indicates an important feature of social change. Individuals become more visible and prominent in historical sources.

Individual identities appear more clearly and elaborately in records of the second millennium CE. Famous individuals acquire larger roles. Authors such as Ibn Batuta and Abul Fazl left historians rich accounts inscribed with personal experience. Like other authors, they had patrons who wanted to see their name in lights. Rulers commissioned dynastic chronicles. Courtiers wrote biographies and hagiographies. Writing history became part of cultural politics. The brightest stars in later-medieval history are individuals we can usefully denote with the word 'sultan'. It was an actual title for many rulers, but generically it conveys a kind of personal identity that came to be shared by many people of importance. The sultan became an ideal type, or cultural model, for patriarchs wielding power in society.

What did it mean to be a sultan? In the Qur'an, this Arabic word connotes a man with spiritual power. Mahmud of Ghazni was the first man to be styled 'sultan' by contemporaries, which indicates his success in cultivating admirers. The title seems to have been popular first among Turks. Seljuq dynasties ruling Palestine and Persia in Mahmud's day were the first to use it routinely, and later, Ottoman Turks made it famous in Europe. When the Caliph began conferring the title, it spread quickly among Muslim rulers and changed along the way. In a fourteenth-century chronicle of Firuz Shah Tughluq's reign in Delhi, Ziauddin Barani said that: 'History is the knowledge of the annals and traditions of prophets, caliphs, sultans, and great men of religion and government'. By this time, sultans had exalted company.

Sultans took various titles that indicate ethnic origins and cultural affiliations, in addition to marking personal status. The greatest sultans in South Asia were the Mughal emperors, who, though part Turk through Babur and Timur, adopted Persian imperial culture and took the Persian title *Padshah* to lift themselves symbolically above Turks, Afghans, and other sultans. Hindu *raja*s never used the title but many styled themselves, their court cultures, and their symbols of sovereignty in the manner of sultans.

Whatever his title, a sultan was a man of personal greatness, not only as an army commander but as a spiritual and moral being. A man of civilization, his wars were civilizing, by definition, though what this meant varied and changed. A sultan's grandeur emerged from the work of the people around him. Putting halos on sultans was a job for poets, scholars (imams and *ulema*), architects, chroniclers, biographers, spiritual guides (Sufis), and Friday prayer leaders at the *jama masjid*, the great congregational mosque essential in any domain. For Hindu sultans, the job fell to Brahmans, priests, genealogists, myth makers, dramatists, singers, temple builders, and festival organizers. Skilled service providers and cultural activists competed for the honour of glorifying sultans, and in doing so advanced their own careers and spiritual stature at the same time.

Public debate, drama, and glamour surrounded sultans and formed their legacy. Mahmud of Ghazni became his own publicist. To impress the Caliph, he surely exaggerated his damage to Somanatha, where local accounts do not describe temple destruction of the sort that he claimed to have wrought. Three hundred years later, chronicles by Barani and Isami depicted Mahmud as an ideal ruler and as the founder of Muslim rule in India, both inaccurate claims; and clearly these two poets were using Mahmud's fictive image for their local political purposes. They were probably engaged in debates about patronage, which were often intense around sultans.

Should the sultan support leaders of various religions, promote his Sufi guides over others, persecute non-Muslims and 'deviant' Muslims like Ahmadis and Ismailis, patronize Hindu temples, ally with Christians, or tax Muslims and non-Muslims at the same rate? Such questions became matters of recorded public dispute among the intelligentsia who advised sultans among the conflicting pressures of dynastic politics. For Mahmud, looting Hindu pilgrims (which he did) was clearly not as laudable as breaking the Somanatha temple idol (which he probably did not do), so it was the latter deed that preoccupied contemporary and later publicists seeking allies among like-minded militarists. In the sixteenth century, Akbar took the opposite tack. He made a virtue of marriages with Hindu Rajput families and brightened his halo by patronizing leaders of various religious groups. His great-grandson, Aurangzeb, turned in the opposite direction. He imposed the *jizya* tax on non-Muslims. He encouraged anti-Hindu feelings among Muslim allies who fought Marathas, who in turn fostered anti-Muslim feelings among their Hindu allies. In all these cases and many more, sultans cultivated appropriate support from religious experts.

The sultan's personality thus emerged from the work of the experts and allies around him who crafted his opinions, policies, and public aura. He cultivated people who might secure his success; his power depended on their power. The social construction of a sultan was an extensive project with many participants. Early sultans such as Mahmud of Ghazni relied entirely on kin and close ethnic allies, but as the political landscape became more complex, imperial personalities became epic dramas, most of all for the great Mughals.

Sufis of the Chisti order were one of the organized groups of cultural activists who enabled the greatest sultans to overshadow others. Its founder, Khwaja Miun-ud-din Chisti, lived in Ajmer, where he died in 1236. His tomb remains one of the holiest Muslim sites in Asia. When Akbar built his vast red sandstone fort city at Fatehpur Sikri (between 1565 and 1589) – abandoned for lack of water, two decades later – he put a lovely marble tomb for Shaikh Salim Chisti in its *jama masjid* (central mosque). Imperial visits to Ajmer to venerate Khwaja Miun-ud-din Chisti became a Mughal ritual, recorded and illustrated in the *Padshahnama*. Chisti influence was more than spiritual, moreover, because Chisti followers had serious clout. For example, in 1400, Chisti leaders (sheikhs) in Bengal objected to the local sultan's patronizing of Brahmans and his allowing non-Muslims to hold high office, and they appealed to the sultan at Jaunpur to back them in their struggle. Their strategy seems to have worked, because the Bengal sultan increased patronage for local Chistis, though he did not abandon multicultural patronage.

The sultan's body, speech, piety, personal habits, hobbies, family, household, ancestors, wives, sons, and in-laws formed the core of his public identity; they appear in public gossip, art, lore, song, and chronicle. His public *darbar* dramatized the sultan's power, as he received court guests, ambassadors, supplicants, allies, and payers of taxes and tribute. The institution of the *darbar* evolved over time. Its early Central Asian home was a regal tent on the battlefield; in later centuries, it acquired architectural grandeur, as at the Mughal fort cities in Fatehpur Sikri, Agra, and Delhi, whose *darbar* halls are massive stages for the emperor's performance of his power. Many *darbar*s incorporated Hindu and Muslim traditions of display and drama. We have a detailed rendering of *darbar* scenes in eighteenth-century paintings that now accompany the seventeenth-century *Padshahnama*, the chronicle of the third Mughal emperor, Shah Jahan. These illustrations show hanging rugs that recall the *darbar*'s nomadic heritage, and each and every person depicted in the paintings had a specific rank at court and relation to the emperor.

The *darbar* became a place for expressing in public all the personal identities that were being defined in politics and in society in relation to sultans. To spread that imperial construction of identity throughout his realm, a sultan took his *darbar* wherever he went. The *darbar* spent much of its social life on the move, especially in battle. The ruler's travelling court became an enduring cultural phenomenon: down to the present day, touring administrators, tax collectors, judges, media stars, and politicians enact the social power relations that revolve around them in public displays of rank, gift giving, honour, and praise, like touring sultans.

A sultan's retinue, regalia, and family symbolized his greatness. Sultans were sticklers for etiquette and protocol, lest subordinates exceed their station. The sultan had to have the biggest, richest, and most elaborate and valuable things visible on his person, to dramatize his ascendancy. Vijayanagar Rayas styled themselves 'Lords of the Eastern and Western Oceans' by adorning their bodies with precious commodities from overseas trade, specifically perfumes and costly items such as Chinese silk and porcelain. The sultan's home was a larger version of his own body and evoked his powers to accumulate, command, control, and define wealth, value, and taste. These grandiose habits of consumption became an enduring fact of political life, down to the present day, and were a stimulant to the elaborate economic systems of finance and production to supply the needs of the court and all its satellite grandees.

Domestic dramas also enhanced the sultan's greatness, above all, marriage. Weddings were great events of political life because marriage was the most secure means for creating alliances. In the *Padshahnama*, warfare and weddings are depicted most elaborately. Even the Mughal Empire was at base a family affair. In the inner secret precincts of the palace, family members vied for influence and engaged in the intrigues that often culminated in wars of succession, when relatives might kill one another, as they did in the epic *Mahabharata*. At home, the sultan's honour rested on the stainless virtue of his mother, wives, daughters, and sisters. Sequestered women of the palace lived behind a curtain, *pardah*; women in seclusion, *pardahnasheen*, became the sultan's virtue. Practices of female seclusion spread among the elites, who modelled themselves on the sultans, Hindu and Muslim alike. In this and many other respects, Rajput *raja*s became model Kshatriyas who were also model sultans.

MEDIEVAL TO EARLY MODERN

In the sixteenth century, the rise of the Mughal Empire marks an epochal change comparable to the rise of the Mauryas and Guptas. Its dynastic founder, Babur, bears comparison with the two ancient Chandraguptas. His empire arose, like theirs, from the work of previous empire builders, in his case, the Delhi sultans, and more specifically, the last Lodi dynasty. Like them, he had more famous successors, and made his mark as a military commander. His imperial legacy is equally impressive and hard to explain. Like the ancient imperialists, the Mughals did more than conquer and dominate: they invented an imperial society that took its strength from many sources and continued to expand its influence long after its emperors became unable to compel submission any longer. All of these empires opened new epochs. The greatest medieval empire of the Mughals spans the wide threshold of early-modern times.

Babur was a Chagatai Turk who fled his patrimonial lands near Samarkand to escape Uzbek armies. He followed opportunity into the Ganga basin, where he used Uzbek-style fast-horse phalanx cavalry equipped with muskets and cannon to sweep away the opposition. In 1526, he had conquered sultans from Punjab to Bengal. But his opposition survived. Thirteen years later, an Afghan soldier who had fought for the Lodis and for Babur, and who styled himself Sur Shah to dramatize his Persian education (at Jaunpur), declared a new dynasty in Bengal and Bihar. Sur Shah's armies then beat Babur's son, Humayan, back to Afghanistan, where Humayan raised his own son, Akbar. The Sur dynasty did not survive the Shah's death, though its lasting impact included administrative innovations and a trunk road from Bengal to Punjab. Soon after Sur Shah died, Humayan conquered Delhi, in 1555. He died there by accident. His twelve-year-old-son, Akbar, then ascended his throne under his regent, Bairam Khan. Akbar was crowned in 1556, as Bairam Khan conquered strategic fortress cities at Lahore, Delhi, Agra, and Jaunpur. Bairam Khan had also conquered Malwa and Rajasthan before he was ousted as regent and assassinated.

Akbar ruled for fifty years (1556–1605). He continued to conquer to the end. His armies surpassed all before in their size, funding, leadership, technology, and success. At his death, Akbar's domains stretched from Kabul, Kashmir, and Punjab to Gujarat, Bengal, and Assam; and they were still increasing in the south and up into the mountains on all sides: His mantle passed in wars of succession to his victorious son, Jahangir (1605–27), then to his grandson, Shah Jahan (1627–58), and to his great-grandson, Aurangzeb (1658–1707), whose death was followed by imperial fragmentation, though the dynasty survived until 1858 when it was finally ended by the British, as we will see in Chapter Four.

The secret of Mughal success was that each emperor deployed many armies under his own supreme authority. Mughal armies fought in many places simultaneously and kept winning against the opposition that rose constantly against them. Previous imperial sultans had used commanders such as Sur Shah to win victories, only to lose their loyalty when commanders were strong enough to strike out on their own to declare a new dynasty. Mughal commanders had to be individually strong, mobile, well equipped, and decisive, but they also had to remain loyal in order for the empire to survive. Centralizing power over commanders might keep them loyal for a time, but it would also weaken their ability to respond quickly and decisively to local challenges and opportunities, because transportation and communication were slow and expensive. Too much central control would spark disloyalty among the most ambitious and powerful commanders. The Mughal emperors succeeded because and only as long as they sustained the personal loyalty of nobles who controlled decisive military force. To maintain the precarious balance of noble autonomy and loyalty, imperial wealth had to increase.

The empire needed to expand to survive. Expansion provided opportunities for individually powerful military commanders who entered imperial service to enrich themselves, their kin, clients, retainers, and heirs. The inheritability of a commander's imperial assets posed the single biggest organizational problem because, if imperial assets became a commander's private patrimony, his dependence on the emperor declined, and if loyalty to the emperor prevented passing one's patrimony to one's sons, rebellion would be the only way to insure patrimonial inheritance. An expanding empire produced new opportunities for ambitious sons who would thus not need to rely for their fortune on their inherited patrimony. A commander's imperial assets would thus not need to be hereditary, allowing emperors to reallocate appointments and resources among warrior nobles. Expanding imperial resources provided incentives for loyalty in each generation. Penalties for disloyalty were effective when loyalty paid sure dividends.

In the context of vast military expansion, Akbar built a centralized Mughal system of rules, regulations, symbols, and landmarks that defined imperial territory in a more standardized form than had ever existed before. Using the methods of the Lodis and Sur Shah, Akbar divided his territories into administrative units independent of existing local usage. Groups of villages formed *parganas*, then *sarkars*, and finally *subahs*, which correspond roughly in size to townships, districts, and provinces. The *subah* of Bengal, for instance, contained 19 *sarkars* containing over 600 *parganas*. This naming of territories in standard imperial terms had important symbolic as well as practical effects. Standardizing territorial nomenclature identified all people, however important they were locally, with imperial places, and it located all places inside an imperial hierarchy. It thus imposed an ideology of imperial rank on social identities in all regions of the empire. Imperial standardization progressed further with the distribution of Mughal titles, coinage, weights, measures, road names, town names, property rights, taxes, and government functions, such as post and police, and within criminal and civil law. Terminologies of governance formed a vocabulary of political order that crossed boundaries among languages and regions. Akbar introduced a silver currency that set the standard for all imperial payments and receipts. Coins from Mughal mints made the emperor's face a monetary symbol of value.

Mughal state receipts came primarily from taxes on cultivated land duly measured in standard units, its output ascertained in cadastral surveys. Tax liabilities marked the relations between officials and subjects. A person who was initially responsible for paying the land tax was called a *zamindar*, literally, 'one who has land'. The *zamindar*s were actually revenue intermediaries who stood between Mughal officials and local communities, which allocated local tax obligations among themselves. Beneath the ranks of *zamindar*s, localism reigned. Imperial standardization began above the *zamindar* in his *pargana*. In 1596, a record of assets and assignments in Mughal territory was compiled in Abu Fazl's *A'in-i Akbari*, which is the first-ever standardized compilation of data on administrative and economic conditions to cover territory from Punjab to Malwa, Gujarat, and Bengal.

Imperial wealth increased with the value of land, which made expanding cultivation an imperial project. The total area under cultivation in the Ganga basin and Bengal increased 60 percent from Akbar's coronation to Aurangzeb's death. The most dramatic change occurred in eastern Bengal, where Mughal troops cut down jungles to promote farming, and in 1666, one grant (*sanad*) gave 166 acres of jungle to support a single mosque. Nobles made 288 grants of tax-free land in the Chittagong region to support mosques and shrines, in the style of temple grants in medieval inscriptions and with much the same effect: Islam suffused new agrarian societies in the cleared jungles of eastern Bengal. The men given grants were local leaders who became land-clearance entrepreneurs. They contracted with *zamindar*s to finance cultivation; *zamindar*s advanced funds to peasant farmers and received crops and labour in return.

A NEW IMPERIAL SOCIETY

Many elements that would constitute modern social environments began to appear in the sixteenth century, and for this reason, we can aptly refer to the period *circa* 1550–1850 as being 'early modern'. In expanding agrarian regions, urbanism increased dramatically. In 1595, the *A'in-i Akbari* mentions 180 large cities and 2837 towns. Hierarchies of rank to mark central places in systems of state authority emerge clearly in Mughal times. Large cities held the highest officers of state; smaller cities had lesser officers; and so on down the line, creating official distinctions between imperial core and periphery. The Mughal heartland lay in old imperial *Bharat*, but expanded more powerfully and uniformly north across Punjab in Kashmir, west across the Indus basin, east in Bengal, and south across Malwa, incorporating most of the area of today's Madhya Pradesh. Mughal appointees and institutions expanded still farther south in the eighteenth century, as the centralization of empire weakened. The Mughal Empire thus unified more of South Asia, and Mughal bureaucracy and geography shaped the identities of people and places more widely than any previous regime. A new imperial society emerged, more expansive and inclusive than any before it, more focused on urban elites in the biggest cities.

The bureaucracy recorded in the *A'in-i Akbari* rested on personal loyalty to the emperor among the nobles who held the empire together. The nobility was the backbone of imperial society, commanding armies financed with taxes. The emperor had the biggest army under his private command, but he could not defeat a substantial alliance of great nobles. Warriors with independent means initially became nobles (*amirs*) by being assigned a rank or dignity (*mansab*) including a salary or income from their assigned territory. In 1590, Akbar revised the system to remunerate nobles in proportion to the number of men and horses under their command, which explicitly tied imperial rank to noble military assets. The plan was to create an elite corps of commanders who maintained the dignity of their aristocratic warrior status with service and loyalty to the emperor.

Assignments of all *mansabs* to *mansabdars* officially came at the emperor's discretion, as did appointments of provincial governors, *subahdars*. Such officers were meant to (and routinely did) circulate among the provinces; this in theory prevented them from establishing independent regional bases of political support. In practice, however, all assignments and appointments were political decisions that took into account a noble's independent power. The risk of collusion against the emperor always remained, because an *amir's* troops were loyal to him personally. Troops came from their commander's ethnic group and formed kinship and patronage ties with him. Provincial *zamindars*, bankers, and other resourceful people could also be expected to side with *amirs* or *subahdars*, who were both typically *mansabdars* with their own armies. Keeping the empire together required a Mughal emperor to use his own personal power to engage in the politics of alliance building and opposition breaking, so as to keep his nobles under his supreme authority. Each Mughal war of succession ended with wars that demonstrated which of Akbar's aspiring descendants had bested his rivals in attracting the most powerful allies from among the nobility.

Family alliances built the empire. Akbar's most fundamental alliance was with Rajput *rajas*. He invited them to join high ranks in his nobility. His alliances with them put his empire on a firm footing, in the normal fashion, through marriage. We will consider such family systems of patriarchal alliance in more detail below, when we also see that Akbar spent considerable energy trying to balance the influence of various ethnic family groups who comprised his imperial nobility, Rajputs among them. Eventually, all but one major Rajput clan married into the Mughal dynasty.

Family disputes inside the dynasty generated wars of succession whose outcome hinged on the shifting loyalties of the nobility. Prince Salim, whose mother was a Rajput, rebelled against his father, gathered nobles around him, and had his name read as emperor at Friday prayers in the Allahabad *jama masjid*, in 1602, three years before his father's death. His rebellion failed, but he nonetheless succeeded Akbar to become Emperor Jahangir, after he defeated his own rebel son, Khusrau, whom he blinded and committed to life in prison. When Khusrau died in 1622, Jahangir's other son, Khurram, also rebelled unsuccessfully. He was not killed or imprisoned, but rather exiled to fight in the Deccan. He returned to Agra surrounded by great nobles, five years later, after his father's death, to become Shah Jahan, the great Mughal patron of the arts. Shah Jahan commissioned the *Padshahnama* in 1647, and built the jewel-bedecked Peacock Throne, the Taj Mahal, and a new capital city in Delhi, which he renamed after himself as Shahjahanabad. When Shah Jahan fell ill in 1639, his eldest son, Dara Shukoh, and his youngest son, Aurangzeb, began fighting for the throne. Twenty years later, Aurangzeb finally won and began his long reign as the last great Mughal.

Aurangzeb died in 1707, at eighty-nine, still at war with Maratha rebels in the Deccan, whom we will meet shortly. Within a few years of Aurangzeb's death, the power balance between the emperor and his nobles had shifted noticeably. The nobles gained the upper hand. Rebellions in the provinces could not be quelled. By 1725, the Bengal *subah* was effectively independent, and others followed. The value of Mughal authority throughout imperial society is indicated by the fact that regions of the empire, such as Bengal, retained their official status as imperial provinces long after the Mughal emperors had lost the power to subordinate forcefully their regional rulers.

Regions of Mughal authority lasted longer than the empire itself. As we will see in Chapter Four, until 1802 even the British used Mughal titles and engaged in rituals of respect for the Mughal emperor. This resilient authority came from the fact that regions had changed fundamentally as political territories under Mughal supremacy. The process of change combined elements drawn from many sources. Most importantly, an imperial society imbued with Indo-Persian culture had emerged in all the Mughal regions. This imperial society not only survived but continued to flourish and spread after Aurangzeb's death.

Mughal imperial society combined personnel as well as material and cultural elements drawn widely from circuits of mobility in southern Asia. Its military features included Mongol and Turk military techniques and technologies that were already widespread when Babur began his career. Babur added Uzbek cavalry and the artillery, muskets, and infantry that circulated around regions of Ottoman expansion. New fighting skills, strategies, and equipment arrived with each wave of migrants from Central Asia, and also from Europe after Vasco da Gama arrived in 1498. Military innovations from all over Eurasia arrived in Delhi and in regions along the coast with increasing regularity. Turkish influence was also important in revenue administration, beginning with Timur's adaptation of *iqta* assignments of land to support military commanders, which the Ottoman and the Delhi Sultans adapted. Under the Mughals, Persian influence became prominent, as Akbar recruited Persian administrators, judges, Sufis, artists, and others to expand, stabilize, and refine his empire. Even so, Mughal administration was eclectic. The *mansabdari* system was a combination of Mongol ideas about warrior dignity, Turkish techniques for allocating taxes to military commanders, Persian bureaucratic formalities that separated military, tax, and legal authority, and regional routines of elite control in localities.

Multilayered sovereignties thus continued to thrive under the Mughals' bureaucratic standardization. Elaborate Persian imperial institutions unified a Mughal polity that also danced to the tune of personal loyalties embedded in regions where centuries of cultural mixing had produced new societies. Imperial elites broadly organized by Indo-Persian institutions that spread under Mughal authority became leading figures in these societies. Their identities developed in mixtures of ethnic and religious loyalties inside their regions. Their influence and livelihoods were organized under the umbrella of Mughal supremacy.

Imperial society long outlasted the great emperors because Mughal power strengthened regional elites who were also imperial subordinates, so that when they became independent, in the eighteenth century, many retained their imperial identities, and all drew upon strength that was a legacy of Mughal power. We consider regional histories in the next chapter, but now we need to stress that in all Mughal regions, the imperial system absorbed not only great warriors, *raja*s, and landlords, but also locally dominant caste groups. Royal endowments to temples and Brahmans continued, mostly in the form of tax-free grants of land carried over from earlier dynasties. Brahmans continued to be prominent landowners and state officials. Mughals applied old medieval principles by strengthening subordinate rulers (*samanta*s), as Indo-Persian imperial culture gave multilayered sovereignties a new legitimacy derived from a supreme emperor. In his famous 1665 *farman*, Aurangzeb echoed a basic dictum in the *Manusmriti* by declaring that, 'whoever turns [wasteland] into cultivable land should be recognized as the (owner) *malik* and should not be deprived [of land]'. Local landed elites obtained entitlements to village sovereignty from the highest authority.

Among regional elites, the Persian language provided a common lexicon for politics, administration, and law. Persian literati received vast patronage under the Mughals. Persian immigrants became a privileged elite in Mughal ethnic politics; they formed a cultural elite in and around the courts of the emperor and his nobles. Persian poetry and prose filled the Mughal court and also petitions, tax accounts, and writing by and for the nobility. A Persian cultural elite developed first in the imperial cities – Lahore, Delhi, Agra, Allahabad, and Jaunpur – and then in regional capitals such as Lucknow, Dhaka, and Hyderabad. In Mughal territories from Afghanistan to Bengal, emerging languages, Urdu and Hindustani, combined elements from Sanskrit, Arabic, Persian, and local dialects. Upward mobility in imperial society came with linguistic admixtures of Persian. In Indo-Persian cultural settings, using more Persian made one's language elite and cosmopolitan; and less Persian, more local and parochial.

Indo-Persian cultural forms and vocabularies derived from Mughal authority spread well beyond the empire's official reach in many vernacular forms. One example is the word *sarkar*, which came to mean 'government' in vernacular speech, and hence became a title, an honorific, a place name, and a respectful greeting. As people attached the honorific *sarkar* to personal names and used it to give respect, it came to be part of family identities and hence a family name. Many titles became family names: notably Shah, Chaudhuri, Zamindar, and Talukdar. Mughal terms thus travelled throughout imperial society into society at large with the exertion of military, administrative, and judicial authority by local officers whose status rose when they were adorned with imperial titles.

By 1700, the ideas, rituals, lexicon, and routines for ordering interactions among leaders of society who sustained Mughal power had informed the creation of new cultural territories. As we will see in Chapter Three, regions had different histories, but in all regions touched in any way by Mughal authority – which only excludes Sri Lanka – regional versions of Indo-Persian political culture informed elite social identity. The idea that a single supreme emperor was an all-powerful authority became widespread. This idea drew strength from ancient and early-medieval ideas about imperial supremacy. The authority of the emperor, and hence *sarkar*, was therefore not merely coercive; it was moral, aesthetic, legal, and spiritual, and did not depend on everyday exertions of force. The idea that there exists an all-powerful emperor who validates all the ranks of all the officials who work in his name, and of all the people who receive entitlements from those officials down to the smallest village, became a pervasive feature of everyday life. Like the Persian language, Indo-Persian political culture was most elaborately developed in the Mughal heartland, in the Indus and Ganga basins. But it spread in many vernaculars to the far corners of Mughal expansion and beyond; even eventually to the southernmost tip of the Indian peninsula, where no Mughal emperor ever set foot, where Mughal authority arrived only in the 1750s with armies dispatched by a governor (Nawab) at Arcot, near Madras, who had never bowed to any Mughal.

Indo-Persian political culture underlay the imperial standardization of political order in regions of multilayered sovereignty, subordinating all the sultans, *raja*s, communities, and institutions to one supreme *sarkar*. This political order made room for everyone. It demanded that everyone pay something to the *sarkar* to receive a rank. Local tax and tribute payments went up the ranks of imperial society; they constituted the ritual enactment of respect for authority by each individual, who thereby obtained a position of respect. Taxpayers paid officials in return for entitlements to land and other assets, including rights to receive payments from others below them in the ranks. Local communities paid taxes through headmen who obtained official recognition as community leaders by serving as an imperial intermediary, sending taxes up the ranks. Imperial supremacy confirmed multilayered sovereignty as every member of imperial society enjoyed a specific rank by paying respect to superiors. Official ranks – each with their own duties, symbols, powers, and

responsibilities – defined the normative structure of *sarkar* authority. Everyone in society had a rank, from top to bottom. Payments
went up the ranks; entitlements came down. People of higher and
lower rank exchanged gestures of submission and beneficence in
rituals of mutual self-definition. Everyone's official entitlement to
land, office, or social status carried the symbolic authority of the
emperor. At the apex of authority, the emperor authorized all the
ranks. *Sarkar* authority became the glue holding together interde-
pendent individual and group entitlements in social formations of
imperial inequity.

Public display of subservience dramatized one's personal rank
below one's superiors, which in turn gave all the ranks under the
emperor superiority over inferiors below them. In this cultural context, the institution of the public *darbar* spread among people of
rank at every level. The cultural model of the sultan spread among
people at all levels as they aspired to demonstrate the superiority of
their personal position in society. Ritualized subordination defined
the ranks of authority in multilayered systems of sovereignty and
entitlement. Thus *darbari* culture spread far and wide as every man
endowed with a piece of sovereignty held his own *darbar* to receive
those below him who came to pay respect and tribute. Elaborate
public dramas and literary productions of praise, flattery, and devotion became the media for elevating men whose glory secured the
authority of subordinates. Conversely, conferring honours on
underlings defined sovereignty at every level. Subordinates retained
their power by recognizing a superior who conferred honour on
those below, in return for ritual recognition and political support.
Layers of sovereignty became elaborately graded with Persian
bureaucratic formality. Gradations in the imperial ranks became
units of measure for social mobility in everyday life.

FORMING ETHNICITY

Social groups were officially named as collective entities whose representatives received honour, rank, and entitlement in imperial
society. These groups were thus officially inscribed with collective
social identities, which attached to everyone in them. Akbar perhaps deserves credit for inventing imperial strategies of ethnic balancing. His minions kept accounts of which groups received which
honours and ranks. He was particularly concerned to counterbalance Turks and Afghans, who initially dominated his imperial
service, whose ethnic loyalties made them suspect; to offset their

power, he recruited Rajputs, Persians, and Indian Muslims into the nobility. Strategies were also devised for dividing ethnic groups by pitting leaders against one another in competitions for rank, to reduce their ability to mobilize clans against imperial armies, as Akbar did, for instance, among armed Paxtun tribes controlling regions around the Hindu Kush.

The *Padshahnama* shows that among the 443 'intermediate *mansabdars*' – a rank that swelled to include more nobles as the empire expanded – Iranis (Persians) comprised 28 percent, Turanis (Turks) 23 percent, Rajputs 16 percent, Indian Muslims 15 percent, Afghans 6 percent, and Marathas 2 percent. This suggests that about 72 percent were Muslims, strategically divided by ethnicity. At lower imperial ranks, locally dominant caste groups were counterbalanced by foreigners and immigrants when possible; this was most critical in the Mughal heartland, where the *A'in-i Akbari* shows that ten *pargana*s of *sarkar* Delhi were held respectively by *zamindar*s of different ethnic groups of Muslims and Hindus: Tonwars, Shaiksadahs, Rajputs, Gujars, Jats, Brahmans, Ahirs, and Afghans. Afghans received the greatest proportion of tax-free support for mosques and shrines in Delhi, indicating their recruitment into the area by Mughal authorities; but locally powerful Rajputs and Jats clearly had the stronger military position. Rajputs were left in command of two major hill forts, reflecting their independence and loyalty to the emperor.

In local societies, imperial ranks entered older systems of social ranking and inflected their development. As we have seen, Hindu societies that evolved as upwardly mobile groups used *dharma* to sanctify a ritual ranking of castes (*jati*s) in the *varna* idiom, which put priests and warriors on top and merchants and peasants below. Many different local Hindu ranking systems evolved in dynastic realms where rulers defined *jati* ranks, from the top down; and expanding agrarian societies filled out the *jati* ranks, from the bottom up. In Mughal times, social change outstripped the regulatory capacity of Hindu ranking institutions, and sultans, *raja*s, and state officials conferred honours that redefined social ranks outside the ritual complex of Hindu temple life. The *darbar*s of great men surpassed temples as ritual sites for acquiring honours that marked social mobility.

Several long-term trends thus in effect secularized the ranks of Hindu societies. Social differentiation and assimilation had produced too many roles and ranks for *dharma* to manage. Elite and ordinary weavers, for example, occupied various *varna* ranks.

Kayasthas, an elite non-Brahman clerical *jati*, had no clear *varna* status. A huge population of poor, landless workers had fallen out of the bottom of *varna* ranks into a catch-all category of 'outcaste' or 'untouchable'. Many *jati*s – like the large *jati* of palmyra palm-tree cultivators called Shanars in the southern Tamil country, whom we will meet again later – lived on the margins of Hindu communities and were not allowed into the sacred temple precincts, but they were also essential in everyday economic activity, where they maintained an ambiguous *varna* standing. The majority of Hindus lived in a world of human interactions that included but surpassed *dharma*. Urbanization and migration allowed new arrivals in many places to claim a higher-caste rank than they had enjoyed at birth. For example, when Saurashtra weavers moved from Gujarat to Madurai in the seventeenth century, they claimed to be Brahmans and their claim received support from local *raja*s, which confirmed their status. Many revisionist *dharmasastra*s rationalized countless post hoc adjustments of caste standing confirmed by state authorities.

Hindu societies also included important non-Hindus, so that in the widening expanse of Mughal domains, *varna* became a kind rule-of-thumb guide to social standing. All the later-medieval political regimes were multicultural. Rajputs raised their rank by marrying the Mughal nobility, forming Hindu–Muslim family ties. Shivaji Bhonsle, the founder of a staunchly Hindu Maratha empire, launched his career by serving Deccan sultans whose honours enabled him to rise in the ranks. Eighteenth-century Tamil Hindu Nayakas married Sinhala Buddhist kings at Kandy to create a Hindu–Buddhist regime. All the armies in Mughal and post-Mughal times included various cultural groups. Business families engaged in financial dealings across cultural lines that, by 1650, included many religions and sects of Jains, Bohras, Sunnis, Ahmadiyas, Baniyas, Khatris, Arabs, Chettiyars, Armenians, Jews, Dutch, English, and others. People shifted among subcultural sites with increasing regularity, blurring their boundaries. Christian and Muslim converts typically kept their old *jati* identities. Buddhists in Sri Lanka maintained caste ranks. Tribal groups who became Hindus kept many elements of tribal culture, including marriage practices and rituals.

All the cultural mixing of later-medieval centuries made social ranking on Brahmanical lines, as in the *Manusmriti*, one component part of a multicultural scene where people attained rank in various ways and *sarkar* became a powerful arbiter of social status. Activities that determined social rank blurred cultural boundaries defined by religion, and strictly Hindu ranking systems became inadequate to the task of establishing social status, even among the most observant Hindus. In all regions and vernaculars of Indo-Persian culture, wealthy warriors, priests, merchants, and *zamindar*s occupied the upper social ranks, regardless of religion. And regardless of religion, poor people of all occupations (manual workers, nomads, herders, fisherfolk, forest dwellers, and such) lived in the bottom ranks. Middling peasants, artisans, shopkeepers, and others struggled up the ranks in between. People acquired social standing by obtaining honours in public rituals, which grew in number and variety. *Raja*s, sultans, priests, gurus, Sufis, and monks conferred honours. Businesses, farming communities, urban centres, and families offered opportunities for honour. Financial wealth became an overriding status marker: poor Brahmans had to accept patronage from rich Sudra landowners and Vaisya merchants as well as from mighty *raja*s and sultans.

Increasing commercialism made markets as well as armies lively sites for upward mobility; both became more so in the eighteenth century. But strategic marriage alliances remained a basic technique for raising one's social standing. Marriages among families involved in the political project of maintaining and improving their social rank created new social groups which combined attributes of social class and ethnicity. Rajputs provide good examples: when Rajput families allied with Mughals, they entered into an imperial ruling class and also increased their status as leaders of Rajputs. Their Kshatriya aura never lost its *varna* glow, but its social influence increased in proportion to Rajput success in a politics of social mobility that escaped the confines of *varna*. The status of Rajput became that of a regional ruler under Mughal authority and the conduct of *jati* marriages took on implications outside that of *jati* rank.

Others *jati*s also blurred into collections of status-marked ethnic groups in Indo-Persian cultural ranks that crossed religious lines. This marks another feature of early modernity emerging under the Mughals, when a modern style of government standardization begins with Akbar, and the imperial monetary system turned Mughal India into an integrated economy. The spread of Mughal authority gave India a lasting political identity in an expanding world of seafaring mobility where Europeans sought Indian products and brought India into a trading system that spanned the Atlantic and Pacific. Textual evidence indicates a transition to modern forms of social description and social order: the *A'in-i Akbari*, like early nineteenth-century English census tracts, enumerates caste (*jati*) groups alongside other groups that are defined not by *varna* but rather by language, religion, occupation, and native place.

The term *jati* thus came to connote a South Asian style of multicultural ethnic identity and could denote virtually any type, category, or group of people with similar characteristics who tended to intermarry, live together, engage in similar customs, worship alike, dress alike, eat similar food, speak alike, and respect group leaders. Diverse kinds of groups such as Iranians, Brahmans, Christians, Armenians, Biharis, and Firangis (Europeans) became labelled as *jati*s. The term 'caste' came to mean an ethnic group with a ranked position in social relations. From the Portuguese *casta*, caste takes no account of *varna* but does encode rank among status groups. When Akbar engaged in ethnic politics, he explicitly balanced Afghans, Persians, Turks, Rajputs, Indian Muslims, Jats and other *jati*s, because in his cultural scene, any honour bestowed on any individual always carried implications for the entire group to which that person belonged. In cultural regions of ethnic ranking that emerged from the Mughal Empire, regional and local rulers played ethnic politics among 'castes' that included Buddhists, Muslims, Jains, Christians, and other non-Hindus, who did not use *varna* categories, but did engage in the similar strategies of social ranking which eased mobility and communication across cultural boundaries. Poor Muslim peasants in East Bengal and poor Muslim workers in all the Gangetic cities ranked low among the local Hindus. Rich Muslim nobles and *zamindar*s ranked high in society and received due respect from Hindu elites. As a result of this cultural mixing and diversity, 'caste' became a flexible term with distinct connotations in each distinctive region of early modernity.

THREE

Early-Modern Regions

The eighteenth century is a bridge to modern times. Elements that would characterize modern social environments in South Asia appear during Akbar's reign (1556–1605), but multiply and become more prominent after Aurangzeb's (1658–1707). By 1700, Indo-Persian elites began to resemble modern officials. The Mughal imperial system of rules, roles, and ranks made government (*sarkar*) more bureaucratic. The imperial financial and monetary system began to resemble a modern economy. And yet, in a world of layered sovereignties and shifting alliances, Mughal officials and their successors held very personal powers that made government work. They had their own armies. Their *sarkar* focused on the *darbar*, complete with supplicants bowing down. Family politics held regimes together and tore them apart. Imperial succession required fratricidal war. This Mughal combination of bureaucracy, *darbar*, and family politics would suffuse modernity in South Asia, where today many bureaucrats live like little sultans and kinship pervades political institutions at every level.

Politically, sharp discontinuities separated the eighteenth century from Mughal times, however, as geographical patterns of ethnic association, political order, and regional culture began to build the scaffolding of modern territorialism. Old identities perished to make new ones. The old Indo-Persian elites had come into being inside an ever-expanding empire, but the force maintaining their imperial stature died with Aurangzeb in 1707. Maratha armies reversed Mughal expansion. The loyalty of the nobility wasted away. Rulers in the provinces became independent. Rebels multiplied among *raja*s and *zamindar*s. Layers of empire came unglued. New regional regimes centralized power and administration, defining outlines of modern state territories. By the end of the eighteenth century, old-fashioned Indo-Persian elites lingered in regional capitals, steeped in the grandeur of Shahjahanabad, but the rising power of the British in Madras and Calcutta had formed a new social landscape of imperial power and opportunity.

Geographies of belonging kept changing with the times. In the century after Aurangzeb's death, new regional identities came into being. New maps of social experience informed people's attachments to cultural territories and ethnic landscapes. By 1800, a new kind of empire, powered by mobility at sea, expanding inland from the coast, invented a totally new spatial orientation for the formation of imperial power and authority. In the 1760s, the English East India Company ruled Bengal and Bihar from its capital in Calcutta, officially under the authority of the Mughal emperor. In 1802, the Company conquered Delhi and took the emperor under their protection. A new imperial age had begun.

British imperialism eventually incorporated South Asia into a world of modern empires spanning the globe. This new worldmaking process is captured nicely by the French term *mondialisation*. At the same time, however, the British Empire in South Asia was very South Asian. Like earlier imperial powers, going back to the ancient Chandraguptas, the British built on the work of others, and they relied on allies. They expanded from existing core regions of economic development. Their military campaigns travelled established trade routes, which fed imperial expansion. They relied on ethnic solidarity in core institutions, notably the army. They first came to power in the peripheries of old empires. To sustain their expansion, they formed alliances with aspiring families in areas of contested authority. Their empire also gave rise to an imperial society whose influence would be much greater and longer-lasting than their empire itself, which had a familiar life span – a bit less than two centuries.

We still live in the wake of British imperial history. Many scholars see it as the prime mover of modernity in South Asia. We might consider the British Empire instead, however, as part of a constellation of historical trends, large and small, rather than their primary cause. We have taken that perspective on the Maurya, Gupta, and Mughal Empires, and laying its groundwork for British imperialism is the main goal of this chapter. Early-modern regional histories indicate that changes were under way in South Asia quite independently of British imperialism, which would accumulate to form modern social environments. The British depended on developments already in progress in regions of South Asia for success in their worldwide imperial adventure. In this chapter, we begin by exploring eighteenth- and early-nineteenth-century trends that carried medievalism into modernity; then we trace the process of British imperial expansion, which forced all the regions into a distinctively modern imperial geography.

ETHNIC TERRITORY

By the eighteenth century, ethnic social identities were formed in overlapping idioms of religion, language, caste, class, and occupation, and were typically attached to named places – villages, towns, and regions – separated from and often ranked in relation to one another. Residential segregation was the norm for ethnic groups. Within regions, groups that made competing claims to the same social rank typically occupied different places; they separated territories from one another in the manner of dynastic lineages. Competing business groups concentrated in their own market towns and bazaars; European merchants did this in the same way as Arab, Bohra, Balija and Chettiyar merchants. Dominant landed *jati*s controlled their own territories: Jats, Rajputs, Bhumihars, Kunbis, Vellalas, Velamas, Reddys, Kapus, Kammas, Nayars, Maravas, and countless others. Sectarian religious groups were also often concentrated in specific territories.

Inside territories, ranked divisions among segregated groups held each in a proper place. The *darbar* was the dramatic site where every individual occupied their place in rituals to mark their respective rank. In towns and villages, groups of different rank typically lived in separate quarters. This segregation encouraged group solidarity and reinforced group identity. It gave new migrants to any place a clear sense of where they belonged, and immediate access to local social support. It also discouraged mingling, intermarriage, and inter-dining with people deemed inappropriate. It facilitated the policing of group divisions. It gave each group their own space, unpolluted by others; and it made the exclusion of low-ranking people and outsiders from otherwise open public places that effectively belonged to local elites – most critically, temples, but also roads, wells, and tanks – a natural feature of social environments.

As groups occupied and controlled places and gave them their identity, group leaders represented specific groups to *sarkar* (government authority) in ranks of layered sovereignty. Spaces of residence, large and small, thus became culturally bounded territorial 'home' lands with their own languages, literatures, popular cultures, pilgrimage sites, and histories of dynastic authority. Cultural regions became more coherent as political territories from later-medieval times, when regional territorialism began to focus more sharply on fort cities and networks of exchange and power around them. In the fourteenth century, Warangal, Golkonda, and Vijayanagar defined an Andhra *desa* that included most of the Krishna–Godavari river basins, an emerging Telugu country. To the south, along the coast, a Tamil-language region began to emerge under Vijayanagar that included old dynastic domains of Pallavas, Cholas, and Pandyas. To the west, in the upper Godavari basin, an evolving Marathi region revolved first around Devagiri and then Ahmadnagar, Aurangabad, Junnar, and Pune. Telugu, Marathi, and Tamil regions all bordered a Kannada region that took shape when Hoysalas built their capital at Dwarasamudra, named after its irrigation tank (in Sanskrit, *samudra*), poised above the Mysore plateau and upper Kaveri basin. Bengal began to assume its full modern deltaic form under the Delhi Sultans, but the Mughals made Dhaka and Chittagong urban centres defining the eastern frontiers of an expanding Bengali-language region.

Bundelkhand is a good example of a region defined historically by ethnic patterns of residence, migration, and power relations. It stretched from Malwa and the eastern edge of Rajasthan across the hilly uplands south of the Ganga plains. Senior Rajput lineages had begun to conquer these parts by the tenth century, becoming *raja*s who flourished under the Mughals; and they were still expanding eastward in the early nineteenth century, driven in part by Marathas in Malwa. Beneath the senior Rajput ranks, lesser lineage brethren called *thakur*s formed the ranks of *zamindar*s. Each lineage ruled over a specific local community composed of major subordinate farming castes: Lodhis, Kurmis, Kachhis, Ahirs, and Gujars. Among the farmers, Kurmis rose up in the political ranks, but Ahir families formed family ties with Rajputs and enjoyed special patronage. Individual villages were composed of several settlement clusters linked to one another across Bundelkhand by intermarriage, by landowner-ship, and by labour migration. Under the Mughals, Bundelkhand became known officially as the land of Bundela Rajputs.

As senior lineages and larger, wealthier Rajput clans settled on the eastern frontiers of Bundelkhand, subordinate Thakurs became more independent in western regions of earlier Rajput colonization. Thus Bundelkhand was effectively partitioned horizontally by competing Rajput clans, as well as vertically by power relations among ranked ethnic (*jati*) groups in its constituent localities. After Aurangzeb's death, Bundela Rajputs renounced Mughal authority. They fought against subordination by Maratha armies marching north from Maharashtra and the Company's army of Indian sepoys marching west from Bengal. In 1857, many Bundelas rebelled against the Company Raj, but Rajputs in the east and west could never combine forces.

Likewise in many other regions, ethnic territories formed in Mughal times became more politically prominent when the Mughal's imperial canopy collapsed. We will look at these political histories in more detail below. In some regions, such as Bundelkhand, a single dominant ethnic group spread across diverse localities and became supreme. By contrast, in the Ganga lowlands, from Awadh to Bihar, combinations of Muslims, Brahmans, Bhumihars, Rajputs, Kayasthas, and Banias formed a multi-ethnic *zamindar* ruling class under which farming castes – mostly Ahirs, Kurmis, and Koeris – lorded over landless workers, notably Chamars and Bhuinyas. A third pattern emerged in regions where groups formed ethnic mini-polities, as in the central mountains, where tribal warrior chiefs emulated Rajputs; and also in the Tamil country, where Kallars, Nayakas, and Maravars formed *jati* mini-kingdoms. Later Mughals and their successors typically endowed new rulers with titles to confirm their status and bring them into alliances. As it had been for Akbar, the ethnic politics of territorialism remained a basic feature of imperial order as regional elites appropriated Mughal authority.

Exclusion, marginality, and poverty attached to people and places at the lower end of the imperial ranks. Excluding outsiders and low-ranking people from sacred precincts maintained ritual purity. As we have seen, early-medieval *bhakti* poets struggled against exclusion to reach god. Most low-status poor people worshipped at their own folksy places, while the rich and powerful lavished gifts on exalted gods in beautiful buildings. In Tamil country, Shanars who tapped palmyra palms were excluded from high-caste villages, so they settled outside on poor land to grow palm trees and millet, the poor people's grain, in dry, sandy soil. In Bundelkhand, Ahirs were likewise excluded from Rajput villages and lived in their own settlements along rivers and in ravines, where forests gave them access to land for farming and grazing. The dominance of dominant groups was expressed in the richness of their farms. The lowliest, landless workers were the untouchable low castes who worked for landed families but moved to and from their fields and their separate, defined settlements at a respectful distance, lest they pollute their betters by physical proximity.

FAMILY AND PATRIARCHY

Families created ethnic territory. Families built dynasties and empires. Families made sultans great. Families passed rights and entitlements down the generations. Kin groups joined together to clear land, build fields, dig wells, cultivate, and make war. Communities formed around collections of kin. Marriage networks connected villages, towns, and regions. In villages and empires alike, family suffused all institutions of social entitlement. On the Tamil coast, for instance, the word *pangu*, meaning 'share', came to refer both to an individual's share in family property and to a family's share of village assets, so that *pangali* referred to relatives and also to shareholding families in a community. The term *kulam* referred to a household, lineage, clan, and local caste group (*jati*). On the frontiers of Bengali agrarian expansion, lineage groups (*gushti*) and their power relations organized entire regions of political authority. The term *jati* came to mean 'nation'. Among Muslims, special honours attach to family descent from The Prophet and his companions. Spiritual descent groups (*silsila*) connect Sufis over generations. Villages and whole regions in many parts of Asia are populated by people related by kinship in various ways.

Patriarchs became lynchpins of group identity who mediated transactions among identity groups of all kinds. Clan heads among tribal groups, merchant guild leaders, caste headmen, nomadic chiefs, and warriors from virtually any background could ally with one another with the mutual recognition of their respective patriarchal authority. Heads of households and heads of state could negotiate as patriarchs because they could rely on one another to command labour and allegiance, assets and loyalty, from kinsfolk. Patriarchy sustained trust, confidence, and stability in transactions that relied upon personal promises and pledges, whether for loans, contracts, or taxes paid in return for entitlements to land. Patrimonial entitlements defined property rights. Rulers and financiers took payments of taxes and tribute that constituted ranks of patriarchal entitlement. Family heads thus held property under state protection. Rituals of taxation, *dharma*, *darbar*, markets, and conquest sustained patriarchal patrimony. Genealogies that began with founding patriarchs produced legitimate authority for the headmen of prominent families, community leaders, village elders, and family heads.

The rise of the warriors enhanced the power of patriarchs. Ghaznavids, Ghurids, Khiljis, Tughluqs, Yadavas, Caulukyas, Paramaras, Sisodias, Rajputs, and countless other warrior groups had much in common in this respect. They rallied around family and made alliances by marriage. They conquered farming groups to rule and protect them. They lived in fortress towns and formed an elite stratum ranked above farmers. They forged alliances among families, lineages, and clans. Their families followed strategies of political hypergamy, in which daughters married up the status ranks and sons married down the ranks. Subalterns among warrior clans were junior patriarchs in the ranks of lineages and dynasties. A son born to a lineage inherited a family position that provided a specific set of options for the ranking of his own family. Alliances gave subaltern families leverage in struggles to maintain and improve their position. Becoming a subordinate ruler raised a subordinate family's rank in relation to peers and competitors. Accumulating subordinate patriarchs under one's own authority defined a king and an emperor.

Among the great warrior clans, families married their daughters up the ranks to express her father's subordination and his pursuit of upward mobility; and they married sons down the ranks to express his father's superiority and confirm the acquisition of a subordinate ally. Polygamy further expanded opportunities for subordinate alliance building, as women became hostages to fortune and some became the mothers of kings. In these settings, *pardah* and *sati* became auspicious expressions of female purity, piety, devotion, and heroism. Strength and sacrifice sustained one another. In political institutions formed by competitive alliances among warrior patriarchs, subordination was a moment of power in which all alliances were built upon measurable inequalities of rank. Dominance rested upon extensive alliances with subalterns whose movement up the ranks often meant challenging superiors in war. War and marriage, militarism and family ties, rank and alliance, negotiation and resistance – all together formed patriarchal power in the warrior clans.

When Rajputs and Mughals married, they wedded two traditions of patriarchal power with commonalities that formed a coherent logic of ranking, competition, and alliance. Mughals became apical agents and icons of ranking for all patriarchs below. In Indo-Persian culture, mosque, temple, or church could mark communities of sentiment; and sacred genealogies could be reckoned from Rome, Palestine, Arabia, or Aryavarta, because patriarchal power superseded and encompassed the ideology of *dharma*. No religion constrained a sultan's power to confer titles of rank on subordinates. A sultan's status arose from rituals of conquest and entitlement whose authority went back to the days of the Gurjara-Pratiharas; and eventually, as we will see, officers of the English East India Company became aspiring sultans of Christian imperialism.

Thus the increasing number of Muslims in positions of dynastic power in South Asia after 1200 CE should never be confused or conflated with the political ascendancy of Islam. Ethnicity, patriarchy, and militarism ruled more than religion in the land of great warriors, and the Indo-Persian imperial system set itself apart from all its predecessors by making rituals and conditions of imperial entitlement more secular than ever before. Imperial entitlements and patriarchal ranking entered family strategies at many levels of society. Patrimonial entitlements came to rest on personal recognition by a superior patriarch under the authority of the emperor. In families, occupational groups, sectarian organizations, and caste and tribal societies, an officially recognized headman had to attain his status – at a price – in rituals of state. The courtly *darbar* became the stage for dramas that defined the ranks of all the patriarchs. Superiors granted honours, titles, and entitlements to those below. Inferiors paid tribute, taxes, service, and allegiance to those above. At the lowest echelons, peasant patriarchs paid for titles to land and for authority over landless workers.

Akbar's imperial strategies accentuated the ethnic politics of patriarchy. Rustic patriarchs rose to become dynastic contenders as emerging social identities based on language, religion, and region informed dynastic projects among Rajputs, Marathas, Jats, Rohillas, Durranis, Paxtuns, Baluchis, Sikhs, and, at the lower registers, among the likes of Kunbis, Reddys, Maravas, and Kallars.

Shivaji was the most successful upstart warrior of Mughal times. He built a kingdom, spawned an empire, and became a legendary icon for ethnic solidarity in modern Maharashtra. In the 1670s he founded a Maratha kingdom along the base of the Western Ghats, beginning with a small revenue (*jagir*) territory inherited from his father, who obtained it by serving the Ahmadnagar sultan. Shivaji continued his father's project of constructing a multi-caste Maratha fighting force of warriors and farmers. His military victories enabled him to acquire official titles and assignments of tax revenue from other Deccan sultans. His armies fought Mughals with swift cavalry attacks, and when pursued, fled to home villages in the mountains. Maratha victories stymied Mughal southern expansion and eventually exhausted Mughal resources, helping to bring the empire to an end. A patriotic guerrilla ethos and militant Hindu identity suffused early Maratha struggles and defined Maratha territory. Over generations, during a long process of competitive alliance building, conquest, and institution building, Maratha warriors became deeply involved in the enforcement of Maratha *dharma*, including codes of family rank and female behaviour. Marathas built their empire in alliance with Brahman traditionalists, who became increasingly powerful in Maratha domains and eventually became supreme under the Peshwas. In the eighteenth century, Maratha power grew in all directions, thwarted British expansion until 1818, and fashioned Shivaji into the perfect Hindu ruler. In retrospect, however, we can see that Muslim sultans and Mughal ranks nurtured Maratha leadership, and that Shivaji became a semi-deified patriarchal icon for Maratha identity by combining militaristic patriarchy with ethnicity, language, and religion.

By the eighteenth century, patriarchy took different forms in different regions, according to spatial patterns of kinship practices that are still visible today. In regions where social life was not influenced significantly by great warrior lineages – on the fringes of Mughal power, in the north-eastern mountains, the southern peninsula, Sri Lanka, and Nepal – marriage customs tend to elaborate local family ties, enhancing local identities. Women typically marry in or near their natal village. Marriage to kin is preferred. Female seclusion (*pardah*) is rare and rates of female participation in higher education and wage labour are normal. Women commonly work in public in fields, in shops, and in offices. Unmarried women often walk the streets and use public transport alone or with friends, both male and female. By contrast, in regions ruled by great warrior clans – in the heartlands of Mughal power across Afghanistan, Pakistan, Punjab, Rajasthan, Uttar Pradesh, Bihar, and east across Bangladesh – extensive marriage networks are typical and the regional rank of families is critical. Marriage is normally forbidden within villages and to close kin. Families prefer women to marry at some distance from the natal village, and more so in high-status families. *Pardah* is widely practised, and as a result, women's participation in education and wage labour is low. A woman's place is definitely at home, where her virtue is the family honour. It is thus less common to see women working in public or travelling without male kin. A number of regions mix the elements of these two opposite patterns: in the central mountains, Maharashtra, and West Bengal.

SPATIAL PERSPECTIVES

The repeated reproduction of dominant empires in the Ganga basin has produced a strong consensus among authors from ancient times to the present that this region is the heartland of South Asia. *Purana*s broadcast the pre-eminence of Aryavarta far and wide, and the *A'in-i Akbari* essentially describes an expansion of *Bharat*. As we will see, nineteenth-century nationalists also made *Bharat* India's heartland. But we have already seen that the Gangetic empires provide only one spatial frame for history. Other imperial regions are also important. Turks and Afghans followed Kushanas along the Silk Road to conquer the Ganga basin and beyond. Imperial Rajputs anchored Mughal expansion. When Aurangzeb died, as Marathas conquered in all directions, the Deccan and southern peninsula remained unconquered by the Gangetic empires, along with Nepal, Assam, the eastern mountain jungles, and Sri Lanka. Coastal regions from East Africa to South-East Asia formed a separate geography of territorial anchors for trade and migration along the sea coasts, whose influence travelled up the river valleys inland; these coastal territories would also provide anchorage for European power in Asia.

Gangetic elite culture nevertheless produced a worldview that travelled across regional borderlands to affect ways of seeing the world everywhere in South Asia. From ancient to early-modern times, Gangetic ideas and forms of power spread from north to south, upriver from the lowlands and across the shifting Ganga delta into eastern Bengal. Elites composed imperial cultures in many vernaculars with admixtures of Sanskrit and Persian to spread Gangetic culture into ever-expanding frontiers. Elites all around South Asia thus came to view spaces inhabited by Gangetic elites – which in Mughal times came to include the western inland expanse of the Muslim world – as the heartland of civilization, whose culture had been transplanted in many fertile places. Jungles, mountains, deserts, and all kinds of unruly peoples remained to be civilized. Oceans were another world altogether.

The unimaginably distant overseas origins of Europeans who arrived in growing numbers after 1498 marked them as novelties, like the Arabs and Christians who had been coming ashore for centuries with no serious impact on the Sanskrit and Persian literati, for whom the sea remained outer space. Elite Hindus avoided the pollution that came with sailing 'dark waters' (*kala pani*; a phrase that resonates with ancient Greek), and sultans in South Asia did not have navies (unlike the Ottomans). Ocean crossing was for merchants who lived normal lives ashore under Indo-Persian imperial authority, and for pious Muslim pilgrims to Mecca. The idea that imperial authority might spread inland from overseas was simply unthinkable.

In the landlocked Indo-Persian worldview, its arrival from overseas makes British imperial power indisputably alien. Spatial history provides another perspective, however. Maurya imperialists had expanded from a core region in the eastern Ganga basin that became best qualified to sustain imperial expansion because of natural endowments and earlier political innovations. The Guptas expanded from the same region as it became still more dynamic economically and better connected to western regions on routes linking the Indian Ocean and the Silk Road. Medieval dynasties arose in places previously outside the pale that became cultured and productive when Gupta-era technologies spread and Brahmans settled in riverine sites of agricultural expansion on trade routes. Later-medieval upstart empires also expanded from places outside the medieval heartlands. Hoysalas, Kakatiyas, Candellas, Ghaznavids, and most dramatically, Mughals launched their empires from places that became strategic when warriors took control of valuable resources and technologies. Superior access to routes around the Silk Road had fed empires from ancient times. Outer spaces had often provided strategic sites for imperial innovation. Aryavarta remained eternally fixed in cultural space, but the homelands of empires in South Asia had moved many times.

Geography thus changed dramatically over the centuries, as outer spaces became internal frontiers and then valued regions of imperial order. Mughal territory incorporated many outer spaces to become larger and more integrated, expansive and connected to wider worlds than any imperial predecessor. Its wider world also expanded beyond the medieval Old World of Afro-Eurasia to include the Americas and the seven seas. Ancient, medieval, and early-modern societies in South Asia thus inhabited very different kinds of spaces. Their worlds were very different. In many respects, Mughal imperial territory resembled its contemporaries in Eurasia more than Maurya or Gupta territories. Early-modern states had produced more extractive, standardized systems of resource control inside expanding circuits of mobility. In South Asia, major circuits had always connected the Silk Road with the Indian Ocean, and these circuits still dominated Mughal politics. But circuits of mobility at sea had also come ashore to become valuable inner spaces enriching Mughal territory. As the Mughal canopy collapsed, commercial economies around seaports enriched Mughal successor states. In that context, Europeans followed classical imperial pathways, expanding from imperial peripheries to capture the capital. East India Company armies, dispatched from Calcutta, conquered westward to reunite *Bharat* and then expand its imperial reach beyond all previous limits. In 1911, in a great symbolic act of imperial continuity, King George V and Queen Mary held a grand *darbar* to inaugurate their capital in New Delhi. By then, the British Indian Empire had subordinated more of South Asia to Gangetic authority than any previous regime. In that respect, and in many others, as we will see, British India was the most Indian of all empires.

In 1800, this outcome was anything but inevitable. Regional rulers had strong independent positions. Marathas had conquered north into Punjab, south into Tamil Nadu, and east into Orissa and Bengal. As in the medieval centuries, new ruling powers emerged in strategic places where their military drew strength from economic expansion. Eighteenth-century regional economies revolved around urban centres that flourished under the Mughals, where Indo-Persian elites were often prominent: in Dhaka, Calcutta, Lucknow, Delhi, Agra, Lahore, Multan, Surat, Ahmedabad, Bombay, Pune, Bangalore, Hyderabad, Madras, Cochin, and Trivandrum. The most expansive regional economies generated wealth at the intersection of inland and overseas trade. Strategic access to the sea became a growing source of political strength, not only for the English East India Company, but for all their competitors. The Europeans' decisive advantage was control of the sea.

The eighteenth century thus inverted Sanskrit and Indo-Persian maps. Warriors attacked Delhi from Afghanistan, Iran, Maharashtra, and Bengal. Regional kings in Punjab and tribal chiefs in the hills conquered lowland territories and expelled the nobility. Foreigners were everywhere. This explains why the eighteenth century was understood by historians until quite recently as a time of chaos and decline: for imperial elites, whose texts provide influential documentation, it was a time of cultural degradation, economic upheaval, and political turmoil, like the mythical *Kali Yuga*.

Inside new regional regimes, the scene appears quite the opposite. The eighteenth century was a time of florescence for emerging elites in Punjab, Afghanistan, Nepal, Maharashtra, Assam, Andhra Pradesh, Karnataka, Kerala, Bengal, Gujarat, Tamil Nadu, and elsewhere. Coastal regions achieved unprecedented political importance. Societies along the coast had always embraced the sea, and now they boasted more overseas connections and mixed populations than ever before. The market value of the coastal trade and long-distance overseas trade boosted the value of agricultural output and of many goods and services. The cloth-manufacturing sector benefited most of all. By 1750, most cotton cloth in world

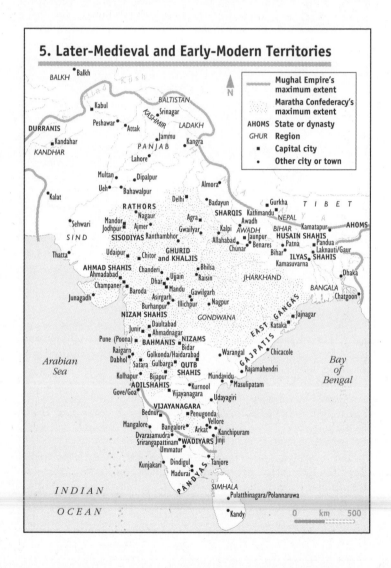

5. Later-Medieval and Early-Modern Territories

Legend:
- Mughal Empire's maximum extent
- Maratha Confederacy's maximum extent
- AHOMS State or dynasty
- GHUR Region
- ■ Capital city
- • Other city or town

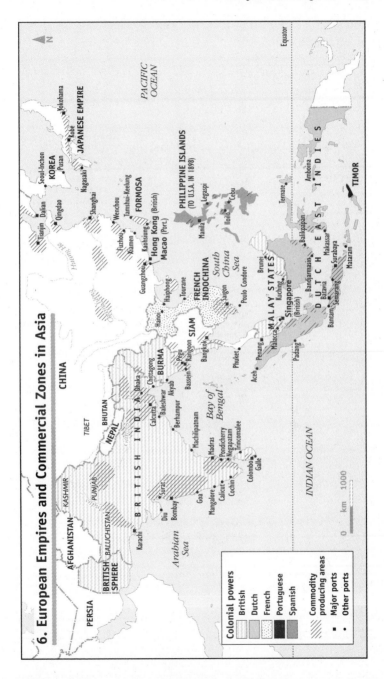

6. European Empires and Commercial Zones in Asia

Colonial powers

- British
- Dutch
- French
- Portuguese
- Spanish

Commodity producing areas

- ■ Major ports
- • Other ports

TABLE 3. A CHRONOLOGICAL FRAMEWORK FOR THE EIGHTEENTH CENTURY

I. Mughal disintegration and regional dynasties

1704	Bengal	Murshid Quli Khan Nawab, 1704–25. Murshidabad, 1706.
1707	Mughals	Aurangzeb dies in the Deccan.
1708	Rajputs	Independent of Mughals.
1709	Afghanistan	Nadir Shah and Ahmad Khan Abdali conquer Herat, Kabul, Punjab.
1713	Hyderabad	Nizam Asaf Jah independent of Mughals.
1714	Agra	Jats begin building state.
1720	Assam	The Ahom expand along Brahmaputra and into the southern mountains.
1724	Hyderabad	Asaf Jah conquers Khandesh and Berar.
1725	Marathas	Mughals concede right to taxes in Gujarat.
1730	Bhutan	Vassal of Tibet and China, becomes independent.
1733	Bengal	Independent from Mughals.

II. Maratha and Durrani expansion

1740	Tamil Nadu	Arcot Nawab under Nizam. Maratha invasions.
1740	Travancore	Marthanda Varma begins unification.
1742	Marathas	Bhonsles control Nagpur Chhattisgarh.
1745	Marathas	Raid Bengal 1742–51.
1746	Marathas	Malwa ceded by Mughals in 1738, confirmed 1746.
1747	Afghanistan	United by Ahmad Khan Abdali under Durrani dynasty.
1747	Mughals	Durranis conquer Delhi. Mughals under Awadh protectorship.
1752	Marathas	Conquer Orissa.
1752	Punjab	Afghan province.
1757	Marathas	Occupy Ahmadabad, end Mughal rule in Gujarat.
1761	Marathas	Defeated at Panipat by Durranis. End of imperial phase.

TABLE 3. *CONTINUED*

III. Regional reorientations

1740	Tamil Nadu	War of Austrian Succession battles between French and British.
1753	Andhra	Coastal region ceded to French, then to British in 1766.
1757	Bengal	Company becomes *zamindar* of 24 *pargana*s after victory at Plassey.
1763	Agra	Jats fall to Sindhia and then to British.
1763	Mysore	Haidar Ali coup. Expansion under son, Tipu Sultan.
1765	Bengal	British Nawabi of Bengal and Bihar.
1765	Nepal	Company force expelled from Terai by Gurkhas.
1766	Sri Lanka	Dutch wars with Kandy from 1736 extend territory all around coast.
1766	Hyderabad	Coast ceded to British as Northern Circars, Madras Presidency.
1768	Nepal	Gurkhas conquer Kathmandu Valley under Prithvi Naryan Shah.
1770	Bengal	Famine kills huge population under East India Company rule.

IV. British expansion

1772	Rohillas	Independent until 1792, then protectorate of Awadh.
1773	Awadh	Native state under British.
1773	Cooch Behar	Native state under British.
1790	Nepal	Gurkhas conquer Garhwal and Kumaun, ceded to British in 1815.
1791	Cochin	Native state under British.
1792	Bengal	Permanent settlement, Lord Cornwallis.
1792	Nepal	Commercial treaty with British.
1792	Malabar	Ceded with Kanara to British by Tipu Sultan.
1793	Laccadives	Conquered by British.

TABLE 3. *CONTINUED*

IV. British expansion (continued)

1794	Benares	Conquered by British.
1795	Travancore	Native state under British.
1796	Sri Lanka	British conquer Dutch.
1798	Hyderabad	Native state under British.
1798	Orissa	Native state of Jaipur under British.
1798	Punjab	Ranjit Singh appointed Afghan governor, forges Sikh kingdom.
1799	Mysore	British conquer Tipu Sultan. Make Udaiyars native-state rulers.
1799	Mysore	Substantial territory ceded to Madras Presidency.

markets came from Gujarat, Maharashtra, Bengal, and the Carnatic (south-eastern peninsula). Merchants, weavers, and rulers in the cloth-exporting regions became more politically powerful. It was an age of creative regionalism within a new world economy, whose trajectories we will follow in later chapters.

RESHAPING TERRITORIALISM

Aurangzeb died fighting Marathas. After his death, his empire weakened with every year. One by one, Mughal *subah*s became independent. Regional elites built new states using technologies, ideas, and personnel that were circulating in the eighteenth-century world economy. In their growing capital cities, regional rulers increased taxation, dynastic wealth, and incentives for political activism. Authors wrote more literature in regional languages. Cults, sects, pilgrimage centres, and cultural activists bolstered assertive regional identities. Most new state elites pursued aggressive policies of administrative centralization. Political transactions became more intensely embroiled in commodity and financial markets. In Bengal, Gujarat, Punjab, the Carnatic, Sri Lanka, Maharashtra, Nepal, and the Ganga basin, businessmen invested simultaneously in trade and in politics. Politics merged with business. Warriors sold their coercive labour service to rulers, who fought to garner tax revenues which they transmitted to treasuries through financial speculators who commanded armies of their own. Official profiteering became customary. The century after Aurangzeb's death was the heyday of entrepreneurial warriors and financier adventurers. Armies were everywhere. Military employment boomed along with commercialism. Social mobility accelerated among people who could grab land and economic opportunities. Struggles for territory settled into civil routines for a few decades, here and there, but rampant armed conflict challenged any status quo. Every eighteenth-century region has its own separate history; each and every one is critically important for the history of modern territorialism.

Marathas

The Mughals had conquered three of the old regions of imperial expansion: Afghanistan, Rajasthan, and the Ganga plains. The Deccan eluded them, as it had the Guptas, the Gurjara-Pratiharas, and the Delhi Sultans. Marathas did not join Mughal imperial society in the manner of Rajputs, Turks, Afghans, and Persians, although Mughal institutions did spread across the Deccan. Maratha warriors simultaneously participated in and also rejected the Mughal imperial system. They came from peasant stock and from pastoral clans recruited by Deccan sultans to balance the influence of Muslim ethnic groups. Marathas came from a Marathi-speaking countryside where Vaishnava peasants and *bhakti* poet saints resented Mughal nobles who patronized non-Marathi Muslim urban-elite allies more than temples, Brahmans, and Hindu pilgrimage centres.

Under the Mughal imperial umbrella, Maharashtra's agrarian economy was expanding along with trade running north, south, and overseas. Village farming elites prospered as cotton thriving in the black soil flowed into weaving centres that fed textile markets both inland and overseas. Commercial agriculture sustained Maratha warrior-peasant chiefs, *deshmukh*s, who expanded their local power by capturing groups of villages numbering between a few dozen and over one hundred. On this agrarian political base, they raised funds and arms for war.

During Shivaji's lifetime (1627–80), the Marathas developed a distinctive style of warfare using small bands of swift horsemen. Maratha armies resembled those of Afghan warriors who often defeated much larger Mughal armies, lumbering across the countryside like cities without forts to protect them. During the long reign of

Shahuji (1682–1749) – the grandson of Shambuji (1657–89), Shivaji's successor – from 1708 to 1749, Maratha armies conquered in all directions. Shahuji supervised the invention of a Maratha imperial society, which had features that serve to illuminate trends in other eighteenth-century social environments.

1. Maratha military force emerged from an armed peasantry whose local power resisted centralized authority. *Deshmukh*s often changed sides in battles between Mughals and Marathas, seeking their own advantage and showing the primacy of local loyalties.
2. Maratha expansion provided many routes of social mobility, not only for fighting peasants but also for Brahmans who filled Maratha posts, led armies, and became politically powerful, especially one Brahman lineage which formed a new ethnic elite, Chitpavans. During Shahuji's reign, the post of Peshwa, managing fiscal administration, became a Chitpavan monopoly that was increasingly powerful. Brahman power increased with the scale of Maratha armies, territory, and revenues, and with the deepening local penetration of Maratha administration. After Shahu's death, the twenty-year-old Balaji Bajirao (1700–61) became Peshwa, assumed ruling power (1720–61), and formed a Maratha Peshwa dynasty.
3. Carefully graded ranks of accountants, financiers, and record keepers, almost all Brahmans, produced a vast historical archive of correspondence penned on paper in a cursive scribal script called Modi, which circulated among officers in villages, towns, and the capital, Pune. These documents record an intricate system of local controls and regional finance, monitored by Peshwas.
4. Peshwa administration became more bureaucratic than the Mughals'. Many of its technical innovations were later adapted by the British, including methods of tax assessment, accounting, census taking, and legal regulation.
5. Maratha administration also included social controls at the village level, where state officials served as local judges to enforce caste rules and patriarchal authority. Imperial Brahmanism enabled high-caste landowners to punish challenges to their local authority in the name of Hindu orthodoxy.
6. A Maratha empire spread across Rajasthan, central India and beyond, but it always remained firmly rooted in its Maratha homeland. Maratha ethnic patriotism made Maratha imperialism culturally parochial.

Maratha social and political identity stood in sharp contrast to Rajputs, which helps to explain the Maratha rejection of Mughal supremacy. Like Rajputs, Shivaji and his father served Muslim sultans. Like Rajputs, Marathas were staunchly Hindu and could generate religious fervour against Muslim enemies. But territorial ambition among Rajputs and Marathas always opposed one another. Maratha *dharma* resisted Rajput *dharma*. Rajputs thrived by conquering farming communities; they looked down on farmers, as did peers among Mughal nobility. Their extravagant consumption, rituals of rank, and patriarchal grandeur formed a cultural model for rulers that Marathas rejected. Marathas came from the lower echelons of imperial society, from dominant farming and agro-pastoral communities which had sustained rustic Deccan warrior lineages from ancient times.

In this respect, Marathas more closely resemble Jats, who also formed military units under the Mughals, conquered widely after Aurangzeb's death, ousted noble overlords (often Rajputs), and formed a new ruling class in a homeland that they invented with their political ascendancy. Like Marathas, Jats combined expansive regional state building with deepening ethnic dominance in farming communities, and with expanding local control among dominant agrarian patriarchs over farmland, forests, and landless workers.

Jats

Jats are a huge, diverse ethnic group spread all across the western plains and Punjab. In British India, Jats formed about 20 percent of the population in Punjab; about 10 percent in Baluchistan, Rajasthan, and around Delhi; and about three percent in Sind and Uttar Pradesh. In Mughal times, most Jats in the Indus basin became Muslims. To the east, in Punjab, a new devotional sect (*panth*) developed, led by Guru Nanak (1469–1538), who preached a new path to enlightenment for people he called Sikhs, 'learners'. Guru Nanak said, 'There is no Hindu and no Muslim'. By this he meant that neither designation pertained among true learners of the path to god, that is, among Sikhs. With this in view, scholars often say that Sikhism combined Hindu *bhakti* and Muslim *sufi* traditions, and like these, it also elevated sacred individuals whose divine words comprise sacred texts. But Guru Nanak's vision was also unique. It was firmly attached to the language and culture of agrarian Punjab.

Nine Gurus succeeded Guru Nanak before conflict with the Mughals led to the execution of two Gurus. In the wake of this event, in 1699, Gobind Rai, who became Guru Gobind Singh (1666–1708), founded the *khalsa*, an armed force whose men took the surname Singh (lion) and women, Kaur (lioness), declared himself the last Guru, and made the *khalsa* a leading Sikh institution. His armies were chased out of Punjab, but after he died in exile in Maharashtra, his successor, Banda Singh (1670–1716), led the *khalsa* into full-scale military competition with all rivals for control of Punjab.

In the decades that followed, Punjab became a battlefield for armies from the west, south, and east. In Afghanistan, Ahmad Shah Durrani (1722–73) built a new Afghan dynasty on the rubble of the Mughals' vast imperial power. His armies conquered from the Amu Darya to the Indian Ocean and from Khorasan across Kashmir, Punjab, and Sind. In 1757, he plundered Delhi, Agra, and Mathura, and married a daughter of the Mughal Muhammad Shah (1702–48), whose reign in Delhi (1719–48) became known for its patronage of the arts. Ahmad Shah Durrani's son, Timur (1748–95), became viceroy in Punjab and married the daughter of another later Mughal ruler, Alamgir II (1699–1759). Timur was driven out of Punjab in the following year by Sikhs, Mughals, and Marathas. In 1759 and 1761, Ahmad Shah Durrani expelled Marathas from Punjab and demolished a Maratha army at Panipat, near Delhi. Sikh armies then organized clan sectarian groups, called *misl*s, to collect protection money and taxes to fight Afghan rule; they took Punjab from Ahmad Shah by stages in the 1760s.

The future founder of an expansive Sikh kingdom, Ranjit Singh (1780–1839), was born in Punjab, where Afghans again held sway against competing Sikh *misl*s. He became chief of the Sukerchakia clan; inherited control of Gujranwala; made two strategic marriage alliances; became the leader of a Sikh clan confederacy; and finally seized Lahore, the old Mughal capital, in 1799. All this he achieved before he was twenty. The Afghan Shah Zaman (1770–1844) appointed him governor of Lahore, and in 1801, Ranjit Singh proclaimed himself Maharaja of Punjab. He minted coins bearing the image of the Sikh Gurus and his army captured Amritsar, a major commercial centre and sacred Sikh city. To build his kingdom, he dispatched armies that included Sikhs, Muslims, and Hindus, almost all Jats, to defeat Sikh *misl*s and Paxtun warrior clans across Punjab and into the mountains, including Kashmir.

South of Punjab, Hindu Jats around Agra and Mathura carved out new territories for themselves around village strongholds. Their eighteenth-century regime expanded well beyond what became the

Jat princely state of Bharatpur under British rule. Rajput clans had long controlled this region. Jat armies ousted the Mughals in 1722 when Bharatpur became independent: its most ambitious ruler, Suraj Mal (1707–63), plundered Delhi in 1753 and seized Agra in 1761. Jat power in this and surrounding regions remained ensconced in fortified village settlements, where warrior peasants defended their independence well into the nineteenth century.

Afghanistan

Punjab remained part of a political region extending from Delhi across Afghanistan to Persia until Sikhs allied with the English East India Company finally drove out Durrani armies in 1837. Persians dominated much of this region until the mid-eighteenth century. In 1738, Nadir Shah (1688–1747) – from a Turkic family, and founder of the Afsharid dynasty in Iran, whose military prowess some praise by calling him 'the Persian Napoleon' – conquered all across Afghanistan and Punjab to sack Delhi. In 1751, allied Paxtun warrior clans under Ahmad Shah Durrani conquered the territory that became Afghanistan, and also Pakistan, as well as the Khorasan and Kohistan Provinces of Iran, along with Punjab and Delhi. He defeated Marathas in 1761 at the Battle of Panipat, to mark the high point of Durrani power. This dynasty is credited with having established the territorial basis of modern Afghanistan with powerful Paxtun alliances which it could not prevent from fragmenting into warring factions. Afghan armies descended into Punjab for the last time in 1837, when Sikh armies allied with the East India Company drove them out, launching Company wars to conquer Punjab and then decades of British campaigns to conquer Afghanistan, in what became known as The Great Game, an imperial competition pitting Britain against Russia, which we will consider in later chapters.

Rajputs

Marathas, Afghans, Sikhs, and Jats pushed the great Rajput clans back into Rajasthan, where they consolidated their power around fortified capital cities. A Maratha Scindia dynasty conquered the old Rajput region of Malwa. Here and elsewhere in regions of Rajput warrior settlement – in Bundelkhand, in Himalayan valleys, and localities across the Ganga basin – Rajputs remained local lords, ruling domains varying in size from one to several hundred farming villages.

Bengal

From Delhi east across the densely populated regions of the Ganga and Brahmaputra lowlands, there were no rustic clans of warriors to dismantle Mughal imperial society as they did in the dry lands west, north-west, and south of the Mughal heartland. Rather, as Mughal power declined, old nobles and aspiring Indo-Persian elites used their attachments to Mughal authority to build new states. In the process, *mansabdar*s, *zamindar*s, and *raja*s as well as many upstarts engaged in shifting alliances and competition. Lucknow, Benares, and Murshidabad became the major capitals for new political systems that emerged after Aurangzeb's death, in the Awadh region of the Ganga-Yamuna Doab, in the eastern Ganga valley, and in Bengal respectively.

Bengal indicates a general pattern among Mughal successor states. When Murshid Quli Khan became the head Mughal revenue officer (*diwan*) in 1704, he moved his capital from Dhaka west to a new city that he named after himself, Murshidabad, on the banks of the Hughli, north of Calcutta, where he had better access to trade moving on the Ganga between Delhi and the Bay of Bengal. Major merchants and bankers on this route transmitted Mughal revenues to Delhi; the *diwan* invited them to live in his capital, which became a showpiece of art and architecture. As Mughal power weakened, he retained more Mughal revenue for himself. It became easier to prevaricate, to avoid sending taxes to Delhi, while also maintaining the ritual appearance of loyalty. Investing in his territory and making alliances with elites in Bengal took precedence over sending taxes to distant emperors. Wealth increased among Bengal's landed elites and merchants, whose donations to temples increased. Increasing temple construction and state wealth brought more employment for elite Brahmans and Kayastha literati and administrators. Bankers, merchants, *zamindar*s, and armed land-revenue collectors and financial speculators became more politically prominent. In this context, the English East India Company played the politics of competitive military alliances and captured the office of *diwan* with a tricky military victory at Plassey, in 1757. In 1761, the East India Company became the Mughal Governor, the Nawab of Bengal.

Gangetic uplands

Weakening Mughal power was not displaced by strong and stable regional regimes everywhere in the Ganga basin, as it was in Bengal,

Awadh, and Benares. In the uplands, away from big cities and rivers, many local chiefs became independent. Old *zamindar*s and local chiefs and *raja*s became rulers of the hills from Punjab and Rohilkhand in the west to Gorakhpur, Assam, Sylhet, and Chittagong in the east. In all these mountain regions, forestation was thick. Agricultural expansion was being driven by forceful frontier warriors and financiers who acquired *zamindar* titles by paying taxes that were in practice merely tribute. Their payments were grudging. Independence gave the frontier *zamindar*s new opportunities for expansion that triggered conflict among them. In these militarized agrarian societies, armed struggles for land went hand in hand with tax payments to secure titles to land against claims by competitors. Land-tax revenues from groups struggling for rights to land fed the treasuries of the regional states that wielded the biggest armies.

In the west, Rohilla Afghan horse traders who had settled on routes in the uplands north of Awadh created their own kingdom. When Rohilkhand was attacked by Marathas, its sultan went to Awadh Nawab (the Mughal governor, now independent) for protection; he relinquished autonomy to keep his Rohilla ethnic territory intact. Similarly, in localities around Ayodhya, Gorakhpur, Gaya, and across the northern and southern uplands of eastern Uttar Pradesh and Bihar, high-caste *zamindar*s, mostly Rajputs and Bhumihar Brahmans, extended their sway as autonomous rulers and frontier subordinates of the Raja of Benares and his competitors.

Frontier expansion by *zamindar*s threatened tribal groups who farmed forests at higher altitudes. In response, many tribal groups produced new political territories. One of the oldest and best known is Cooch Behar, which lies below Bhutan. Today it is part of West Bengal and its forests still house rhinoceros and tigers. It was once an outpost of medieval Kamarupa kings in Assam, and it is populated primarily by the Koch group of the Bodo people, who are spread across Assam and Bengal and speak a Tibeto-Burman vernacular language. Cooch Behar was conquered by a Koch warrior in the sixteenth century. His son paid tribute to the Mughals and extended his territory east into Assam and south into Rangpur (in Bengal). As Mughals declined, regional competitors expanded, including Ahom rulers in Assam. In 1772, Bhutan invaded Cooch Behar and the *raja* sought help from the British. East India Company soldiers forced out the Bhutanese and the Company's Governor General, Warren Hastings, negotiated a truce mediated by the

Tashi Lama in Tibet. The Raja of Cooch Behar then became a vassal of the English, paying them half his annual revenue. Royal titles embellished since Mughal times eventually enabled the ruling family, all their kin, and eventually the entire population of Cooch Behar to assume the name Rajbansi (meaning, 'of royal blood'), thus attaining the *varna* status of Kshatriya.

The north-east

Meanwhile, Ahom rulers who had controlled the Brahmaputra Valley for centuries and were expanding their territory downriver found themselves caught between imperial armies expanding west from Burma and east from Bengal under the English East India Company in Bengal. They sought Company support against the Burmese and fell under Company control as the Company's wars with Burma gave the English control of Assam in 1826.

All the mountain territories east and north-east of Bengal were contested between the imperial English and the Burmese. All these territories had local rulers who, as with the Ahom and the Koch, represented ethnically coherent, though often very small, populations of people who worked in forests and on farmlands on the upland and high mountain fringes of medieval dynasties, the Mughal regime, and its successors in Bengal.

Other mountain regions

Many tribal groups in the mountains of central India and in the high valleys from Baluchistan to the Hindu Kush and across the Himalayas to Sikkim, Nagaland, and Burma formed new political territories as they confronted expanding lowland states and frontier *zamindar*s. In central India, Maratha conquests accelerated a counter 'Rajputization' of tribal ruling groups who crowned *raja*s and *maharaja*s with Rajput lineages.

Bhutan and Sikkim

In the Himalayas, Bhutan became a new political territory in the eighteenth century when a Tibetan Buddhist monk, Sheptoon La-Pha crowned himself Dharma Raja and his successors consolidated their power over the peoples living on steep slopes around their forts. Their Drukpa sect of Tibetan Buddhism became a ruling monastic order.

Sikkim was established in 1642, when Phuntsog Namgyal became *chogyal*, a ruler who, like the Dharma Raja, combined administrative and religious powers. The new state rested on the strength of Bhutias, who began to come from Tibet in the fourteenth century and settled among Lepchas, who had previously assimilated Naong, Chang, Mon, and other tribes. Armies from Sikkim fought for land across the mountains down to the low-lying slopes, and in the process, lost land to an expansive Nepal, which sent many migrants into Sikkim, further complicating ethnic political relations.

Nepal

Nepal became imperial territory under Prithvi Narayan Shah, who brought many small mountain ethnic territories under a centralized military administration based in the Kathmandu Valley. Prithvi Narayan was born in the 1720s into the Shah ruling family of the Gurkha kingdom, and at the age of twenty-two, became king of Gurkha. At forty-nine, he led his armies east across the mountains to conquer the three Malla kingdoms of Kathmandu, Patan, and Bhadgaon. Then, from his new capital in Kathmandu, he sent his armies out to annex the Tarai, Kumaon, Garhwal, Simla, Sikkim, and parts of Tibet. He died aged fifty-two in 1772, but by then he had extended Nepal from Punjab to Sikkim. His regime resembled a Rajput domain ruled by a Kshatriya ruling class, and in the nineteenth century, Nepal officially became a Hindu state, when the Ranas made the caste system law.

Some general patterns

South Asia's eighteenth-century turbulence produced many disparate regional trajectories, but also followed several broad trends. Inside, on the frontiers, and outside Mughal territory, horizontal competition among new regimes fostered battles over assets that they all needed in order to survive and expand. Rising elites sought by various means to establish order in their new domains. Solid state regimes emerged when rulers could subordinate local warriors, defend their borders, and enforce laws to strengthen their social foundations. They often used religious elites, sanctions, and institutions to consolidate power, as did Rajputs, Marathas, Sikhs, Ranas, and kings in Bhutan and Sikkim.

Many eighteenth-century political innovations were financed by expanding commercial production in urban centres and in the countryside that fed treasuries and private accounts at the same time, and which supported new states and rebels alike. Private capital and royal authority needed and used one another in many ways, because war depended on revenues drawn from taxes and tribute. Virtually all new royal personalities modelled themselves on great sultans and demanded a steady flow of elite commodities into the capital cities to display their grandeur on their person and in their homes, *darbar*s, and forts. Markets in arms and official entitlements thrived alongside markets in cloth, jewellery, ornaments, and architectural finery. Militarism and commercialism expanded together.

The peninsula

All these trends epitomized the eighteenth-century landscape south and east of Maharashtra, where three new states fought the Marathas, based respectively in Telugu, Kannada, and Malayalam language regions.

At Hyderabad, a Mughal governor, Nizam-al-Mulk (1671–1748), established himself in territory taken by the Mughals from the Sultan of Golkonda. The Nizam's military fended off Marathas along the border between Telugu and Marathi regions. In Telugu country, elite cadres of warrior *zamindar*s took firm control of the countryside, where villages were dominated by warrior-peasant elites whose genealogies ran back to the Kakatiya kings.

Based in Mysore, the Udaiyar dynasty fought along southern Maratha frontiers to capture land acquired by Aurangzeb when he conquered Bijapur. The Udaiyars built a powerful military force commanded by Deccan Muslim generals, whose leader, Haidar Ali, usurped the throne in 1763. Haidar Ali and his son, Tipu Sultan, built a military regime that stretched from sea to sea across the peninsula, fulfilling the dream of Vijayanagar Rayas to command ports on both coasts. Tipu Sultan subdued the warrior-peasants, and his revenue bureaucracy reached a level of centralized sophistication that rivalled the Marathas'.

In Kerala, the Travancore Raja Marthanda Varma ruled for three decades (1729–58) with a large standing army; he subordinated the old Nayar landed elite which had dominated earlier regimes, and fortified his northern borders. His financial fortunes rested on Syrian Christians whose landed and commercial interests became politically dominant, and on revenues from licences for trade in pepper and other valuable commodities under his royal monopoly.

His successor, Rama Varma, ruled for another forty years (1758–98) and further strengthened Travancore along the same lines against Haidar Ali and Tipu Sultan.

On the east coast, Tamil-speaking areas were held in disparate mini-kingdoms, some ruled by Nayaka descendants of Vijayanagar governors, others by small *raja*s and *palaiyakkar* (Poligar) chiefs in ethnic territories dominated by their caste fellows, mostly Maravas, Kallars, and Nayakas. In the old Chola imperial heartland, Tanjavur, in the Kaveri river delta, Shivaji's cousin Serfoji built a Maratha dynasty that lasted throughout the eighteenth century. Its elite culture combined Maratha, Telugu, and Tamil Brahman influence, and like other Marathas, it used royal authority to regulate local social ranks: in the 1790s, the Tanjavur Maratha *raja* commissioned the first-ever compilation of Sanskrit texts dedicated solely to the codification of *dharma* for women, the *Stridharmapadati*.

In Arcot, near Madras, a dynasty of Nawabs descended from Mughal governors used an army composed primarily of migrant mercenaries to collect tribute and revenues far and wide, under a mythical mantle of Mughal authority. The Arcot Nawab dispatched armies commanded by profiteering revenue-collectors who formed the first system of revenue collection that ever stretched along the coast from the far north to the far south of the Tamil country. But the Nawab's ambition surpassed his assets. By 1770, he depended militarily and financially on loans from English East India Company merchants. To repay the Company, he granted the English a revenue territory, a *jagir*, in the Chinglepet district around Madras. He became a shaky but useful Company ally whose power depended increasingly on English finance and military force.

Sri Lanka

In 1592, a Sinhalese kingdom was established at Kandy in the central highlands, and it struggled for survival against threats from Europeans and Sinhalese landed nobility. After 1658, the Dutch controlled Colombo and other coastal districts, restricting Kandy's access to the sea. To maintain themselves, Kandyan kings sought allies among the armed coastal merchants who bought spices from the highlands to ship overseas, and protection from Dutch and English companies. Kandyan elites enhanced their cultural authority by lavishly patronizing Buddhist monks and monasteries with land grants and official status. To raise their status above their aristocracy, they sought marriage alliances with Tamil Nayakas on the main-land. The major ruling Nayaka lineages did not oblige, but other Nayaka families sent daughters along with their brothers and cous-ins to Kandy to bolster the Kandyan lineage and strengthen its mil-itary. In 1707, Tamil Nayakas inherited the throne in a matrilineal succession, and they continued to recruit Nayaka families from the mainland to bolster their own position. Fierce Nayaka efforts to centralize administration turned monks and landed aristocrats into rebels who, in 1760, dethroned the Nayakas, after which the Dutch took the Kandyan kings under their protection.

EUROPEANS ON THE COAST

Sri Lanka was the first region substantially controlled by Europeans, and it became a microcosm of European imperial his-tory in South Asia. After 1498, Portuguese soldiers conquered a dozen ports on the Indian peninsula and Sri Lanka, where they built coastal fortress enclaves facing the sea. Portugal remained the dominant European power in the Indian Ocean throughout the sixteenth century, when Portuguese captains also controlled the western Sri Lanka coast. They lost their position to the Dutch in 1707, and by 1818, Portugal retained only a few settlements in South Asia, including Goa, south of Bombay, which was then sur-rounded by British India. Goa has thrived ever since as a coastal society mixing Iberian and Konkani cultures. Portuguese legacies in Sri Lanka survive today in family names and in the prevalence of Catholicism.

The Spanish monarchs who ruled Portugal from 1580 to 1640 fought to exclude the Dutch from trade in what they called 'the East Indies'. Dutch merchants fought back and combined to form the United East India Company in 1602. More commercially oriented than the Portuguese, the Dutch Company concentrated on monop-olizing Asian spice supplies for world markets. Under Governors General Anthony van Diemen (1636–45) and Joan Maetsuyker (1653–78), the Dutch took Malacca (1641) and coastal Sri Lanka ports (1658) from the Portuguese, and they used troops, finance, and command of the sea to dominate rulers in the surrounding regions. In Sri Lanka, they assisted the Kandyan kings against the Portuguese to gain bases for expansion. By 1707, they controlled Sri Lanka's spice exports. In Java, they assisted contenders for the throne in Mataram in 1674 and 1704, receiving territory in return. By 1755 they controlled most of Java. Mataram was a small dependency, weaker even than Kandy. These same Dutch policies had less success in Sumatra, which the Netherlands finally conquered in the nineteenth century along with other territories that became modern Indonesia.

In its Asian territories, the Dutch Company initially used existing structures of tax authority to collect tax revenues to finance their trade in Asia and their exports to Europe. The Dutch used monopolies, sea power, loans, and military attacks to pressure local rulers into using their royal monopolies to supply only Dutch ships with cloves, nutmeg, and mace. Coercive power thus fed Dutch exports. Tribute and taxation, paid in kind, forced native growers to sell their produce to the Dutch at set prices. After 1800, the Culture System of forced cultivation through taxation in kind gave the Dutch in Indonesia a powerful position in world sugar markets.

The Dutch loomed over Kandy until 1796, as Dutch administration covered much of the lowlands. The Company divided its territories around Colombo, Galle, and Jaffna into provinces (*dissavani*) and districts (*korales*) in the manner of Kandyan administration. Each *dissavani* was ruled by a *dissava*, who was a Dutch officer, with loyal Sinhalese or Tamil officers under him. The landlocked Kandyan kingdom remained under its own kings. In Dutch territories, Dutch judges brought Sinhala and Tamil elites to assist in determining local customs, and they began to codify customary law. In 1707, the Thesawalamai codified customs among Jaffna Hindus. Muslim law was applied with the help of Muslim leaders. Dutch law was applied in the cities and along the coast, particularly among Christians. The Dutch thereby followed a traditionalist trend that characterized many eighteenth-century states and brought religious elites into official prominence in regimes from Sri Lanka to Nepal.

Eighteenth-century English and French merchant companies competed with the Dutch in Asian waters. The English finally uprooted the Dutch from Sri Lanka during the wars that followed the French revolution, when European armies and navies fought overseas as well as in Europe. These wars became a watershed in the history of South Asia.

We have already seen that, by 1792, the English East India Company controlled the collection of state revenue in territories around forts in Madras and Calcutta, most extensively in Bengal and Bihar. From the start of the Napoleonic wars, however, the Company pursued a more aggressive imperial policy to enhance English fortunes. At the same time, Britain's military became a leading sector in national finance. Annual British state expenditures doubled and tripled in times of war in the 1740s, 1750s, 1770s, and from 1792 to 1815. Between 1781 and 1815, 60 percent of the state budget sustained the military. British public debt rose to finance military expansion, and taxes raised to repay the public debt also provided finance capital for industrial investment. Debt payments rose from 36 percent of public expenditure from 1781 to 1815 to 53 percent in the years 1816 to 1850. In 1750, fewer than 75,000 men typically fought in battles in Europe, but Napoleon led armies of a quarter to half a million men. The British military overseas surpassed all European rivals. When the English East India Company became *diwan* of Bengal in 1761, Company troops numbered 18,000. By 1793, they numbered 90,000. By 1800, they had topped 102,000, and by 1820, they were nearly 230,000. They were mostly Indian sepoys (from the Persian, *sipahi*, 'army' or 'cavalry', also used in Ottoman Turkish), because in 1830 there were only 36,409 'whites' in the King's and Company's armies in India.

In the eighteenth century, European wars became world wars, as European imperial competition changed the political map in South Asia. One indicative personality in the English imperial transition was Charles Cornwallis (1738–1805), whose armies lost to allied French and American troops in Yorktown, in Virginia, in 1781; who became Governor General of British India, in Calcutta, in 1786; and who then led East India Company troops to victory against Tipu Sultan at Seringapatam, in Mysore, in 1792. European struggles quickly affected South Asia: in 1795, when France seized Amsterdam, the Rhine valley, and the Pyrenees, the English responded by taking Sri Lanka from the Dutch.

Initially, the British government did not plan to keep the island they called Ceylon, but reports from the field soon convinced Parliament of Ceylon's commercial value; it became a Crown Colony in 1802. Its administration then moved from Madras to Colombo, out of the hands of the East India Company, and a treaty with the Kandyan king made Britain his protector. English merchants soon complained that Kandy impeded their commerce and demanded roads from the west to the east coast, across the highlands, so the British used internal dissent in Kandy as a reason to conquer the kingdom, in 1815, with help from rebel nobles. Britain promised to maintain rights and privileges enjoyed by the landed nobles and Buddhist monks, but soon reversed this policy, which triggered rebellion, in 1818. Crushing the rebellion enabled the British Crown to bring Kandy under a central Ceylon administration. In 1833, government codes were formalized. English became Sri Lanka's official language of government and education.

BRITISH IMPERIALISM

British power followed a trajectory similar to the Dutch, and the British used Dutch techniques, later in time, with more spectacular results. British ascendancy falls into five phases that begin roughly in 1600, 1740, 1792, 1820, and 1848. In each phase, the shape and substance of 'British India' changed dramatically.

Phase 1

In 1600, knights and merchants of the City of London formed the East India Company, and Queen Elizabeth I granted its royal monopoly charter. The Company failed to weaken Dutch control of spice supplies but succeeded in establishing fortified trading centres, called 'factories', along the Indian coast; these flourished in the same up-and-down manner as other commercial operations, like those of the French, Dutch, and older merchant communities who worked under the authority of the Mughals and their contemporaries. The leading English factories were in Calcutta, Madras, and Bombay, strategic sites along the coast in regions undergoing turbulent political change in Aurangzeb's day, when Elihu Yale (1649–1721) went to India. Yale was a man of his day. Born in Boston and raised in England, he joined the Company in 1670, rose quickly in the ranks, and became Governor at Fort St George in Madras in 1687. There he made a fortune by dubious means, which violated Company rules and led to his dismissal in 1692, and enabled him to return to London, seven years later, a very rich man. In 1718, Cotton Mather convinced him to provide an endowment for Saybrook College, in Connecticut, which then became Yale University.

After Aurangzeb's death, the English East India Company's operations in India, like those of other Europeans, became more militaristic. But a dramatic change occurred only in 1744, during the War of Austrian Succession (1740–8), when English and French ships arrived in India with military officers and troops, announcing that the English and French were at war.

The French had been active in India since 1664, when Jean-Baptiste Colbert (1619–83) formed the French Company of the East Indies with his personal wealth, under Louis XIV, to reduce

French payments to the Dutch for Asian commodities. Colbert's main concern was for national finance, but French wealth by this time also required colonial markets protected by a strong navy, not only in the Atlantic and the Americas, where France struggled with Spain and Britain, but also in Asia. The French wanted Madagascar but acquired Mauritius instead as a base in the Indian Ocean. Their leading settlement in India was Pondicherry, south of Madras. By 1800, it too was surrounded by British India, and it remains today a distinctive coastal society, mixing French and Tamil culture.

Phase 2

Marquis Joseph-François Dupleix (1697–1763) was the French Governor General in India when the War of Austrian Succession in Europe sparked conflict between the French and English on the Carnatic coast, based in Pondicherry and Madras respectively. The entire coast then fell under the Mughal authority of the Nizam of Hyderabad, whose subordinate in the south, Anwaruddin Muhammed Khan (1672–1749), Nawab at Arcot, forbade the French and English to fight in his dominions. Obeying the Nawab, they fought at sea. When the French prevailed, the First Carnatic War (1744–8) came to an end with a struggle for control of Madras, which the Nawab claimed as a prize but a French force of merely four hundred men wrested from him in a short battle which had major consequences, for it convinced Dupleix that a small, disciplined, well-armed and well-supplied French force could defeat local Indian armies.

Dupleix's conclusion made the Second Carnatic War (1749–54) a turning point in history. The war began, like so many others, with a succession dispute. When Nizam-al-Mulk died in 1748, he named his grandson Muzaffar Jang (*circa* 1700–51) the Nizam in Hyderabad. Emperor Muhammad Shah (1702–48) confirmed this succession, which was then contested by Nizam-al-Mulk's second son, Nasir Jang (1712–48). When Nasir Jang took control of Hyderabad, Muzaffar Jang went searching for allies. The British supported Nasir Jang and the French supported Muzaffar Jang, while they also backed opposing claimants to the Nawab's throne at Arcot, where the British backed the son of one Nawab, Mohammad Ali, against the French, who backed a son-in-law of another Nawab, Chanda Sahib. Dupleix's negotiations with Chanda Sahib are described in detail in *The Diary of Ananda Ranga Pillai*, a uniquely rich personal account of Dupleix's Pondicherry, composed by his Tamil bilingual assistant (*dubash*). But this time, Dupleix lost his gamble. Mohammad Ali won the contest, and he favoured his English backers with a sizable share of his tax revenues.

This episode launched a scramble for native allies by English and French officers, which heated up again during the Seven Years' War (1756–63), as it also did in the Americas. A long series of many-sided struggles ensued, pitting the French and English in shifting alliances with native contenders, rulers, and financiers. Dupleix secured an alliance with the Hyderabad Nizam and gained influence in Mysore, to make the French more powerful in the peninsula for several decades. But the English had their eyes on Bengal. Their big break came in 1756, when the Mughal governor, Nawab Siraj-ud-daula (1733–57), sought to limit English fortifications in Calcutta. The English refused. This brought the Nawab's armies down from Murshidabad, and during this conflict, English prisoners suffocated in what became known as the 'Black Hole of Calcutta'. War in the East now appeared sensationally in the English press as a struggle for English survival, not only against the vile French, but also against Indian barbarians.

The English war against France now also included Indian enemies, but in India, the Company was in charge, not Parliament or the King. The English government supplied troops, diplomatic authority, and military funding, but could not control Company decisions in Indian theatres of war that were fully six months by sea from London. The English war machine in India was effectively controlled by adventurous Company entrepreneurs, men like Elihu Yale, who multiplied in number after he got rich in Madras. Unlike the French and Dutch companies, which were managed closely by their governments, the English East India Company depended for its financial strength on private London investors whose sons and representatives sailed in Company ships and worked under Company authority but who made deals and fortunes for themselves inside and outside of the loose strictures of Company discipline. In the 1750s, such men obtained armies.

In 1757, one of these men, Colonel Robert Clive (1725–74), sailed from Madras to Calcutta with a shipload of troops. In Calcutta, he formed an alliance with two bankers, Jagat Seth and Omichand, who arranged for one of the Nawab's ambitious generals, Mir Jaffar (1691–1765), to withdraw from the field when Clive's troops faced Siraj-ud-daula's army at the battle of Plassey. The trick worked. The Company won. Mir Jaffar became Nawab and Clive received three million pounds sterling in the Company's name, half paid in cash by Jagat Seth and half pledged by the new Nawab in revenue assignments around Calcutta.

A few years later, another Bengal Nawab, Mir Qasim, strove again to restrain the English military build-up; and this time, the Nawab enlisted support from the Mughal emperor and the Awadh Nawab. In 1765, when Company troops prevailed against this alliance at Buxar, the Company became the Nawab of Bengal. In 1770, famine ravaged Bengal as Company revenue speculators reaped huge profits. By this time, the Company's territorial ambition had begun to take on a more definite shape. The Marathas' northern imperial expansion had been checked by Afghan armies at Panipat; regional rulers in the peninsula formed alliances with British and French imperial contenders; and the English East India Company substantially controlled the revenues of the Arcot Nawab. An English East India Company empire was growing. This provoked debates in Parliament, where the fabled English Nabobs were excoriated as men who made private fortunes with English public funds. Adam Smith's *The Wealth of Nations* appeared in 1776 and launched a searing critique of government monopolies granted to chartered companies.

Adam Smith also established that commercial expansion was the secret of national wealth. To finance expanding circuits of trade in Asia, the English, like the French and Dutch companies, conquered in Asia to get taxes officially paid to Asian rulers to finance European exports of Asian products to Europe in European ships to benefit European investors and consumers. Using local taxes to finance their Asian trade solved a problem that all European merchants faced: Asian goods had insatiable markets in the West, but Asian consumers had little need to buy anything from Europeans. Sending silver from Europe to pay for Asian goods was unpalatable in Europe, and other solutions to constant shortages of working capital for European trade in Asia emerged early on. European merchants first learnt to buy cheap and sell dear in Asian markets to increase their working capital to finance shiploads heading back to Europe. As in other areas of overseas enterprise, the Dutch pioneered this strategy. English merchants then used their greater freedom to manoeuvre outside Company controls to generate much more local finance from Indian bankers and revenue collectors. Loans given and received by individual Company merchants became the Company's financial backbone.

Europeans also used military power to force local exports onto European ships by compelling local merchants and rulers to sell export commodities to Europeans. This lowered purchase prices and increased supplies. Again, in this the Dutch were pioneers. The English could not dislodge the Dutch from their domineering position in the Asian spice markets, so the English moved instead into Indian textile exports. Cloth added much more value to merchant capital than spices, and European ships soon carried almost all Indian textile exports into the world economy. By 1750, factories in India were fortified warehouses for storing, sorting, ordering, and shipping cloth produced in the coastal interior, where cotton became thread and thread became cloth in native networks of finance and brokerage.

The European wars in Asia added more ways in which to accumulate merchant capital. Europeans financed political competition in the interior to garner the revenues of regional rulers. The English hired out Company sepoys who came from local military labour markets and were trained and armed in European style. The Company also hired out English troops and sold arms, technical advice, and training. Where they or their subordinate allies conquered, they acquired taxes to invest in export trades.

Creative businessmen therefore used militarism to finance the flow of Asian commodities into world trade without relying on commodity sales in Asia or on financial outflows from Europe. Military solutions to financial problems became ever more attractive and lucrative as the size and reputation of European armies grew in Asia. Sea power became a military as well as a commercial asset, because Europeans could choke any sea trade that financed inland enemies, while no native ruler could cut European military supply lines at sea. With bases on the coast in India, opportunities opened wide in the Indian interior, where their rivalry with the Dutch and the French initially drove English expansion. As the English East India Company acquired revenue territory, its adventurous merchants provoked further expansion by extending their financial operations and using military power to increase their control over commercial assets in the interior. By 1780, the Nawab of Arcot, for example, was so deeply in debt to Englishmen that all his land revenues effectively belonged to Company merchants. Native cloth merchants and weavers near the coast soon came under pressure to move their operations into English territory (to lower supply costs for the English) and to deal only with the English on English terms. The Company's everyday commercial operations became more coercive as its territory increased. In Bengal, land-revenue contractors, called 'farmers', used force to collect taxes during the famine in the 1770s which may have killed half the population.

Phase 3

In 1792, France declared war against the enemies of their revolution. The English in South Asia then became truly imperial. By that time, Company armies of sepoys and British troops, based in Bombay, Madras, and Bengal, fought Marathas and rulers in Hyderabad, Mysore, Awadh, and along the Carnatic coast. The English Company held revenue territories not only in Bengal and Bihar but also in the Carnatic, ceded by the Nizam, Peshwas, Tanjavur Raja, and Tipu Sultan. In the 1780s, Governor General Warren Hastings defended Company wars in India against critics in England who complained about the cost and misuse of government troops. He was the last protector of the English Nabobs in India. His parliamentary opponents prevailed and he was forced to resign. He faced corruption charges and parliamentary impeachment. In 1784, Pitt's India Act brought Company adventurers to heel. It gave supreme control of Company affairs to a Board of Control, run by cabinet ministers, making the Company a semi-autonomous government body. The Act decried territorial expansion but the Board quickly appointed a military man, Lord Cornwallis, to be British India's first Governor General. Cornwallis arrived in Bengal as commander-in-chief with war on his mind.

In 1792, Cornwallis led troops against Tipu Sultan, who was then the Company's single most powerful opponent, vilified in London as a barbarous tyrant. Tipu fell at Seringapatam and was finally killed in 1799. Company imperial expansion accelerated. Richard Wellesley (1760–1842) became Governor General in 1798, and England's military aristocracy effectively took charge of Company arms in India, which quadrupled in size from the 1770s to the 1790s and then doubled again before 1820. Company armies with larger contingents of British troops and more advanced English technology conquered Delhi (1803), Nepali forces (1816), Maratha Gaekwads, Scindias, Peshwas, and Bhonsles (1818), and Kandy (1818). Nepal retained its independence within reduced borders that are still in place today. In the Company's Indian empire, similar treaties with so called 'native states' (also called 'princely states') established friendly monarchies in Cooch Behar (1773), Cochin (1791), Jaipur (1794), Travancore (1795), Hyderabad (1798), Mysore (1799), Rampur (1801), Orissa and Cuttack (1804), Pudukkottai (1806), Kohlapur (1812), Cis-Sutlej Hill States (1815), Bastar (1818), Southern Maratha *jagir*s (1819), the Central India Agency (1819), Kutch and Gujarat Gaikwad territories (1807–20) and Rajasthan (1818), where only Ajmer and Mewar became directly administered British territory.

In 1813, Parliament renewed the Company's charter but ended its trading monopoly and opened British India to private merchants and missionaries. As British power increased in India, so did direct control over Indian affairs by Crown and Parliament, as Company autonomy declined. Powerful citizen lobbies in London demanded that Parliament provide all British citizens free access to British territory everywhere. By 1820, the Company ruled large territories in South Asia for the expansion of British national activity. British citizens could now operate in India under Crown protection in Company territories called Presidencies, with their capitals at Bombay, Calcutta, and Madras.

Phase 4

The opening of British India for British national enterprise energized a new phase of British expansion, which entailed deeper British penetration into layers of sovereignty as well as into business networks in South Asia. British merchants pushed Indian business families out of the export trades. Profiting from sales, supplies, and transport of South Asian export commodities in world markets became English imperial business. Protective tariffs in England kept out Indian textiles, protecting English textile manufacturers from Indian competition. The British economy engaged in a strategy of import substitution by producing English-made cloth to meet domestic demand stimulated by a century of Indian cloth imports. Indian exports shifted under this imperial economic pressure to concentrate on primary products such as raw cotton, which fed English textile mills to lower production costs. English exporters of English cloth thus obtained open markets in India for selling English cloth at low tariffs subsidized by Indian taxpayers.

The business of empire expanded its profitability further in the 1820s when the Company's silver rupee became imperial currency and state policy increased its value in relation to Indian commodities to increase the value of remittances from India to London. Land taxes in British India increased under stricter enforcement. Commodity prices in British India fell steadily for the next thirty years, cheapening Indian exports for merchants who sold them in Europe and increasing the real burden of taxes paid in cash by landowners in India. As commodity prices fell, taxpayers had to sell more commodities to raise cash to pay taxes. Coercion by tax collectors and complaints against Company officials increased. Meanwhile, forced cultivation of opium for sale in China and of indigo for export to England expanded in British Bengal. When indigo prices crashed in London, Bengal and Bihar peasants lost money for rent and so lost their land. Many peasant taxpayers had their land sold at government auctions for failure to pay taxes. Government assigned forested land to English investors who built coffee and tea plantations in the hills of Sri Lanka, southern India, Bengal, and Assam.

In 1833, Parliament ended the Company's trading licence, which made the Company purely an arm of British administration, though British India remained in Company hands. At the same time, English became the official language of law and administration, displacing Persian, so that English education became a key to social mobility in imperial society. Indian labour also became an imperial asset, when Britain abolished slavery in 1833, and petitions from English Caribbean planters came to London demanding that government send indentured workers from Calcutta to keep the sugar plantations running in the West Indies.

The integration of the world economy was moving ahead at a faster pace when plans to finance railways in India with Indian taxes came onto the drawing board. Once again, expanding commercial networks and world trade entailed deeper control of Indian resources, and in this respect, native-state rulers remained a source of imperial limitation, as Kandy had been before 1818. Efforts therefore accelerated to bring native rulers under stricter British authority. In 1831, the government of Madras took control of the Raja of Mysore's territory, which was returned to the Raja's successors fifty years later. Other native rulers were even less fortunate; treaties with native states such as Kandy were abrogated and more land was brought thereby into British India. Military efforts were accelerated to bring hill peoples under British control, most strikingly in the north-east, where Naga, Lushan, Garo, Shan, Khasi, Chakma, and Mizo chiefs were all attacked.

Phase 5

In the hills and elsewhere, the final phase of British conquest began in 1848, when Lord Dalhousie conquered the Sikh kingdom and open The Great Game of imperial competition with Russia in Central Asia, where Bukhara and Samarkand fell to Russian troops in 1863 and 1868. When Dalhousie arrived in Calcutta, Britain was also on the offensive in China. British fleets launched the first Opium War (1839–42) in response to the Ch'ing emperor's efforts to stop English sales of opium from India in China. Impediments to 'free trade' by native rulers in Asia became a legitimate basis in Western policy circles for direct military intervention. In 1839, when the governor of Canton seized British opium and drunken British sailors killed a Chinese villager, the British refused to hand over the accused, launched a war, and soon prevailed, forcing the first of a long series of unequal treaties in 1842 at Nanking, which gave Britain a huge indemnity, five ports for British trade, and rights of extraterritoriality whereby British citizens in China would be tried by British courts. Other Western countries quickly obtained the same privileges, and in the second Opium War (1856–60) the French joined the British to force Beijing to open more ports and allow Westerners free travel in the interior.

Dalhousie abrogated more native-state treaties in India, claiming that rulers obstructed British activity, failed to meet financial obligations, or upset law and order. British intentions to rescind the property rights of *zamindar*s in Awadh upon its resumption stoked a vast rebellion that began with a mutiny among Company sepoys around Delhi, in 1857. The rebellion spread among old warrior elites from Haryana across Bundelkhand into central India. Some rebels fled to the Red Fort in Delhi and secured support from the last Mughal ruler. Others held Lucknow against repeated assaults. Warriors in the uplands south of the Ganga carved out rebel states. It took two years for British troops to crush rebels on all fronts. The cruelty of conquest and punishments were extreme. In the aftermath, the Crown dethroned the Mughal and replaced the Company Raj with direct British Crown rule. Queen Victoria then officially ruled British India through her Viceroy.

The age of high imperialism thus began in Asia long before European governments convened in Berlin to launch the scramble for Africa in the 1880s, by which time British India was the keystone of a global British Empire. British wars to conquer Burma began in 1852. Rangoon fell in 1862, and upper Burma in 1886. Battles for Kachin territories on the Burma border lasted from 1884 into the 1930s. India's north-eastern hill states were conquered between 1859 and 1893; Bhutan and Sikkim were taken in 1865 and 1890 respectively. British troops conquered Baluchistan in 1877, 1889, and 1896; invaded Tibet in 1903; and invaded Afghanistan from 1878 until 1891 to establish the political basis of a protectorate legalized in treaties between 1907 and 1919.

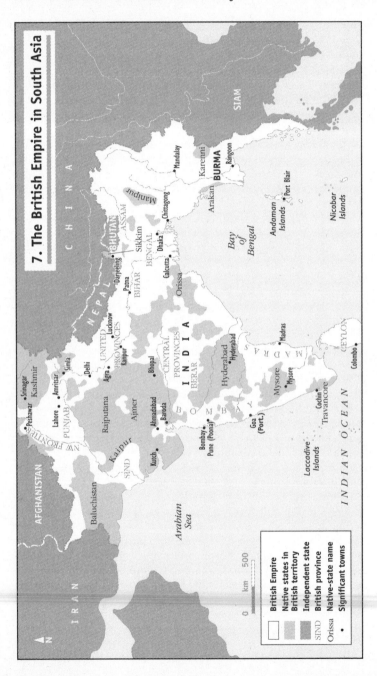

7. The British Empire in South Asia

CHINA

SIAM

BURMA

• Mandalay

Karenni
• Rangoon

Arakan

Andaman
Islands
• Port Blair

Nicobar
Islands

Chittagong

Manipur

ASSAM

BHUTAN

Sikkim

• Darjeeling

NEPAL

BENGAL

Dhaka •

Bay of
Bengal

Patna •
• Lucknow   BIHAR
• Kanpur

Calcutta •

UNITED
PROVINCES

Orissa

• Agra

• Peshawar
• Srinagar
Kashmir
• Simla
• Amritsar
• Delhi

• Lahore

PUNJAB

INDIA

Bhopal •

CENTRAL
PROVINCES

BERAR

Hyderabad •

Hyderabad

• Madras

CEYLON
• Colombo

NW FRONTIER

Rajputana

• Ajmer

Jaipur

Baroda •

Mysore
• Mysore

M A D R A S

AFGHANISTAN

• Ahmadabad

B O M B A Y

Kutch

SIND

Cochin •
Travancore

Goa
(Port.)

IRAN

Baluchistan

Bombay •
Pune (Poona) •

Laccadive
Islands

Arabian
Sea

INDIAN OCEAN

N

0   km   500

British Empire
Native states in
British territory
Independent state
British province
SIND   Native-state name
•   Significant towns

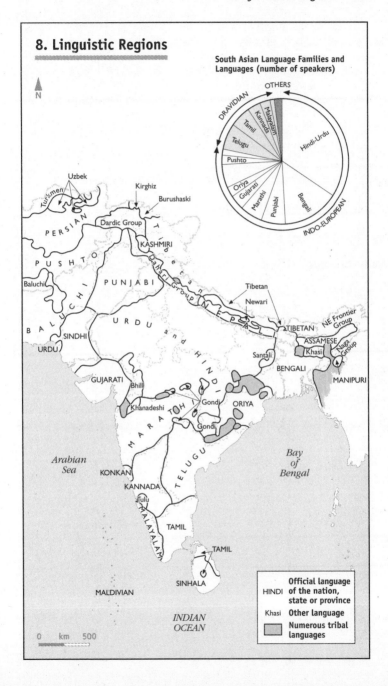

8. Linguistic Regions

South Asian Language Families and Languages (number of speakers)

OTHERS

DRAVIDIAN — Malayalam, Kannada, Tamil, Telugu, Pushto

Hindi-Urdu

Oriya, Gujarati, Marathi, Punjabi, Bengali

INDO-EUROPEAN

N

Turkmen
Uzbek
Kirghiz
Burushaski
PERSIAN
Dardic Group
KASHMIRI
PUSHTO
Baluchi
PUNJABI
Tibetan Group
NEPALI
Tibetan
Newari
TIBETAN
NE Frontier Group
ASSAMESE
Naga Group
BALUCHI
URDU and HINDI
SINDHI
Santali
Khasi
MANIPURI
URDU
BENGALI
GUJARATI
Bhili
Khanadeshi
Gondi
ORIYA
MARATHI
Gondi
Arabian Sea
KONKAN
TELUGU
Bay of Bengal
KANNADA
Tulu
MALAYALAM
TAMIL
TAMIL
SINHALA
MALDIVIAN
INDIAN OCEAN

0 km 500

HINDI Official language of the nation, state or province

Khasi Other language

Numerous tribal languages

The mountains north of Assam (now the Indian state of Arunachal Pradesh) came under British control in 1914, though they do not appear in the 1931 census, and like other high mountain areas, were more pacified and occupied by the military than ruled by British civil administration. During World War I, British India was still expanding into the mountains bordering China, Russia, and Iran. After the war, conquest in South Asia ended as the empire reached its full extent with acquisition of territories from Germany and the Ottoman sultans.

FOUR

Imperial Modernity

All modern societies have taken shape in a world of empires. For many centuries, South Asia provided a land bridge for imperial histories spanning the Silk Road and the Indian Ocean, and in modern times, it provided strategic anchorage for the seaborne articulation of imperial histories spanning Europe and Asia. In the nineteenth century, South Asia's imperial history enriched the world of modernity by sustaining British global expansion, feeding the capitalist world economy, and mobilizing national identities and anti-colonial nationalism, whose evolution in Asia and Africa would displace Western imperialism in the twentieth century.

British imperialism thus provides a useful chronology for modernity in South Asia. In 1800, the English East India Company had ruled Bengal for forty years – Bengal was the first Asian frontier of European colonialism – but elsewhere, the Company then only held scattered bits of territory, and Englishmen had little importance outside Calcutta. By 1820, after British victories over Tipu Sultan, the Dutch, Gurkhas, Napoleon, Kandy, Marathas, and others, British power stood pre-eminent in South Asia and globally. In the 1820s, the Company tightened its grip on the Ganga basin and Bengal, Madras, and Bombay Presidencies. In 1833, English became India's imperial language. The conquest of Punjab in 1848 and the quelling of the 1857 rebellion in northern India solidified the empire. In 1876, Queen Victoria (1819–1901) became Empress. Her later years were the heyday of empire, when the British expanded into Burma, Afghanistan, and Persia, and also, from their base in India, into China, Africa, and the Middle East. Imperial expansion only ended with the acquisition of territories from the Ottoman and Austro-Hungarian Empires at the Treaty of Versailles, in 1919, after British victories secured by Indian troops in World War I.

The war sapped the vitality of all European empires, and their heyday ended at Versailles. In 1918, Joseph Schumpeter (a leading economist who became the Austrian Minister of Finance) had called imperialism an 'heirloom of the absolute monarchical state', an 'atavism' created by rude capitalists and the archaic nobility. Western empires dissolved over the next four decades under international criticism, financial distress, and assaults from nationalists, though diehards like Winston Churchill remained, vowing never to give up India, even on the eve of independence. After 1920, nationalists took centre stage in the creation of a new world order that would cover the planet with national states after 1945.

This chapter explores the making of modern imperial societies. South Asia contained three-quarters of Britain's non-European imperial subjects, and ninety percent lived around the Indian Ocean. Our goal now is to understand how imperial modernity shaped social identities that would participate in the production of nationalities, nationalism, and national territorialism in this vast southern region of Asia. The following chapters follow histories of nationality down to the present day.

ORGANIZING THE RANKS

British imperial power initially depended, like all its predecessors, on alliances with *raja*s, sultans, businessmen, landlords, and many other elites all over South Asia. Major military alliances were most critical, such as with the Nizam of Hyderabad, who supported the Company against the Marathas. At the same time, however, wars against Napoleon stoked British enthusiasm for imperial wars in India, which became a national passion after the horrific sensation produced in the British press by the great rebellion in 1857 provoked an official British commitment to empire in Asia which had been missing during decades of Company imperialism. The resulting concentration of military force in British hands, and the progressive elimination of military competitors for imperial authority after 1820, enabled the British to establish a civilian imperial government, empowered by Crown and Parliament to send armies to crush opposition to its authority both inside and outside imperial territorial boundaries set by conquest and by treaty, measured by surveyors and recorded on maps.

The project of building the empire was a multicultural affair. It involved various kinds of people, in many disparate social locations, who participated for many different reasons. During the decades after 1820, an elite corps of British imperialists gained increasingly autonomous power over all their allies in all regions of South Asia. Allies, most notably native-state rulers, and all loyal imperial subjects, however important, became definitively subordinate in the imperial ranks. The British elites aggressively forced the creation, shaped the contours, and dictated the terms of an expansive imperial society whose modernity appears most obviously in the disarming of the general population and in the construction of a legal and bureaucratic order that provided an official framework for imperial politics.

As long as the Company remained in power, bureaucratic centralization faced obstacles posed by the entrenched interests of Company officials and their local allies. But even under the Company, strenuous efforts were made to subordinate all of the old layers of sovereignty in regions under direct British administration. After 1820, governance in British provinces became visibly more bureaucratic and its administration more centralized. This trend accelerated rapidly after 1858, under Crown rule, when the heyday of bureaucratic institution building coincided with the heyday of British imperialism, from 1870 to 1920. In these more modern decades, printed records supplanted penned foolscap manuscripts in the imperial archives. Administrative and legal tomes published imperial rules and regulations. Surveyors mapped all of the British dominions. Comprehensive census operations counted and sorted the population by ethnic group, sect, gender, age, and location. Official annual reports published statistical data on every aspect of economic and political activity. By 1880, a reader in London could sit in the British Library and read everything that any British official ever needed to know about Britain's Asiatic possessions.

At the pinnacle of empire, in London, the Board of Control and Parliament supervised the Company Raj until 1857, after which elected British governments ruled British India under the Crown. The Colonial Office managed the rest of the empire, including Ceylon. In India, the head of state was the Governor General in Calcutta (before 1858), and then the Viceroy in Calcutta and Delhi. Ceylon was managed as a single colonial territory under the Governor in Colombo, but India was divided into many administrative territories with varying degrees of subordinate autonomy. Though London designed British India's government, regional governors and rulers in native states retained substantial independent authority. British provinces and Presidencies controlled critical areas of policy and budget allocation, notably education, agriculture, and public works.

The imperial bureaucracy in British India was organized around the Indian Civil Service (ICS), which was centrally trained and dispatched to high posts in central government and in the provinces. The ICS became the 'iron frame' of British rule, an elite administrative corps for conducting the imperial state's everyday business down to the local (district) level. Law courts and legal administration developed separately in each province and were brought under a centralized framework of legal procedure. In each province and at the capital in Calcutta (and after 1911, New Delhi) British heads of state wrote the laws of empire under London's authority; and each also had an official Council to advise them. These advisory councils had considerable influence as legislative bodies in the provinces. Their autonomy declined as the Company Raj gave way to Crown rule, but their role and visibility then expanded because state administration and activists in civil society developed a common interest in bringing people with social influence into the official process of law-making.

The imperialist military mentality remained prominent in civil administration from the beginning to the end of the empire. Strictures on activity in civil society enforced early on inside British settlements were expanded to cover all territories under British rule. Police searched out dissidents and repressed perceived threats to law and order. The native press was monitored; censorship ensued when sedition was suspected. Even popular plays lampooning the British were banned, though enforcement was difficult outside the major urban centres. At the same time, the administration sought to expand the scope of local elite representation in government, and local elites demanded increasing representation. Despite official resistance, legal petitioners and popular protestors made their impact on provincial law-making from the very beginning.

Nationalists sought to expand civil representation. As we will see, a major agitation in 1905 led to the formation of legislative councils in 1911, and their powers and electoral base were expanded in 1920 and in 1935, again in response to popular agitation and legal petitioning. This series of constitutional reforms gave increasing powers to regional Legislative Assemblies but left the Imperial Council as mostly ceremonial. The division of authority between London's appointees and elected legislators and ministries became the central issue for political activists; eliminating London's control altogether became a nationalist demand in 1920.

In the lowest tiers of government, in district headquarter towns, District Collectors were ICS men who led the local administration; they were the most senior officers most people ever saw. In 1881, local self-government acts established district and local boards of dignitaries in cities, towns, and district subdivisions to advise the Collectors and to raise funds to undertake projects such as road building, sanitation construction, and education. Increasing authority over the everyday work of government thus devolved onto elective institutions in regional capitals and in local administration, but authority over the imperial system and direct control of the military, external affairs, monetary policy, and Civil Service remained in London.

Imperial modernity organized social change around cities, towns, and villages. Central places and all their hinterlands had acquired official status ranks in Mughal times, when the stature of an officer and of elites rose with the stature of their location. Moving up the ranks in imperial society meant moving up from lower- to higher-status places to join their social circles and imbibe their cultural character, in language, clothing, adornments, arts, and aesthetics. Imperial geography extended to Britain after 1760, when circulating at the highest imperial ranks began to mean rubbing shoulders with English high society. In the ranks below metropolitan London, cosmopolitan capital cities in British India and the native states, and district towns and villages in British territory, provided spaces for social identity and social mobility, leaving people in forests, deserts, high mountains, and jungles on distant status peripheries, as they had been for centuries.

London was the metropolitan core of what became a global empire in the nineteenth century, and around it, imperial careers also emerged in major economic centres such as Lancashire and Manchester, and in the centres of education, that is, Oxford and Cambridge. In the early imperial years, aristocrats such as Lord Cornwallis filled the highest ranks, and having suffered the loss of the American colonies, he worked the imperial system during wars with France to favour his status peers as well as India's conservative elites, including *zamindar* landlords. By 1820, however, middle-class men with small-business ties, utilitarian ideas, and Protestant passions began to top the imperial ranks; men such as Thomas Munro, who became Governor of Madras in 1820, and joined an official generation that launched policy reforms to open India more widely to English national interests, which meant for them primarily middle-class businessmen and missionaries.

After 1858, British politicians, bureaucrats, diplomats, and industrialists presided over high imperialism; men such as Lord George Curzon, who was Viceroy from 1896 to 1910, and who sought to manage the empire for the Crown and for big business in the days when the Union Jack flew on every continent. In his day, however, the empire had competitors: France, Germany, Russia, and America. Nationalist critics of empire had also emerged in Ireland, India, and England. Indian educated elites circulated routinely through London, expanding the ranks of nationalism. Curzon, the great imperial bureaucrat, became thus the first in a long line of defensive British imperialists fighting opponents on many fronts. As imperial opponents increased over the decades, and the circulation of imperial subjects through metropolitan London grew, Curzon's successors became weaker and weaker.

South Asia's cities formed Asian cosmopolitan ranks of political power, legal authority, economic wealth, and social status. Calcutta was the greatest cosmopolitan capital until 1911, when New Delhi became the capital of British India, though Calcutta kept its cosmopolitan social and cultural status for many decades after. Colombo maintained a high rank as the capital of a colony, and Bombay and Madras occupied somewhat lower but still significant ranks as provincial capitals and major port cities. Lahore, Karachi, and Rangoon joined the ranks of major provincial capitals in the nineteenth century, with commercial capital concentrating particularly in the port cities of Karachi and Rangoon. Smaller cities like Bangalore, Ahmedabad, and Allahabad increased their stature with industrialization. Bombay became the supreme capitalist capital of British India, and as such one of the richest cities in Asia, rising steadily in the imperial ranks, in fact, right up to the present day.

These cosmopolitan cities housed urban elites literate in the English vernacular languages who were most influential in the articulation of imperial modernity in their regions. All of these large regional cities were focal points for social change that followed from regional trends in earlier times, and also from British imperial innovations. In these cities, cosmopolitan groups drawing from old and new cultural resources led the regional political systems that would most visibly shape national identities and nationalist politics.

Small provincial cities and local towns formed the lower tiers in the imperial central place hierarchy. These were focal points for most everyday social, political, economic, and cultural activities; they were centres of regional and local authority in earlier times; and they were major sites for literacy and public communication in vernacular languages. At these lower levels, the leaders of the new imperial system forced their influence into existing political environments where their authority took hold among existing social groups and power relations. The loyalties and aspirations of elites at this local level formed the bedrock of imperial politics. Disruption at this level very typically followed the efforts of imperial authority to increase local taxation and control over natural resources, such as forests. Over time, the numerical preponderance, upward mobility, and alliances with higher authorities of elites in these lower imperial echelons gave them increasing influence. Mobilizing the masses could only work at this level, whether for rebellions, law and order, gang labour, national agitation, or voting. As we will see, the influence of leaders at this level grew rapidly after national independence.

One simple way to indicate the cultural content of social identities in this imperial urban hierarchy is to note that as we go down the urban ranks, white complexions and English speakers decline dramatically. Fair complexions and imperial language proficiency were cultural markers of social rank among Brahmans and Indo-Persian elites, and the British further entrenched this imperial aesthetic. Urban ranks corresponded to cultural ranks in the imperial order in many other ways as well, so that empire looked very different at each level. The top ranks were all British, and the bottom ranks were all non-British, everywhere in the empire, all across Asia and Africa, so that South Asia provided a window into imperial social formations more generally. The most intense cultural mixing of social ranks occurred in the cosmopolitan centres, which became the homeland of national politics mixing powers, aspirations, and identities from above and below.

CAPITALISM

We have seen that everyday life in South Asia already included substantial commercial activity before the Europeans arrived. Way back in the fourteenth century, Ibn Batuta had recorded commerce on all the routes he travelled, and at the end of the sixteenth century, the *A'in-i Akbari* made special mention of commercial activities that sustained imperial taxation. In the eighteenth century, the revenues of the East India Company in Bengal came from agrarian economies where countless farmers sold commodities in local markets. In 1806, when Thomas Munro went to collect revenues in Rayalaseema, a dry region in the interior peninsula, far from any

TABLE 4. A CHRONOLOGY OF BRITISH EMPIRE IN SOUTH ASIA

I. Early Company expansion beyond Bengal

1801	Tamil Nadu	Carnatic Poligars conquered. Madras Presidency formed.
1801	Rampur	Native state established in former Rohilkhand.
1802	Marathas	Peshwa cede first territory to British; other Marathas, 1802–5.
1803	Mughals	British conquer and make Delhi a dependency.
1804	Orissa	Mountain native states established: Cuttack Mehals, etc.
1804	Rohillas	Absorbed by Awadh.
1806	Pudukkottai	Native state in Madras Presidency.
1812	Kolhapur	Native state in Bombay Presidency.

II. Imperial expansion after Waterloo

1815	Nepal	Garhwal and Kumaun ceded to British.
1815	Sri Lanka	Kandy last addition to Ceylon as British Crown Colony.
1816	Punjab	Cis-Sutlej and Sikh become states under the Company.
1817	Marathas	Gaikwads cede Cutch Kathiawar as native states to British.
1818	Marathas	Conquered by British to form bulk of Bombay Presidency.
1818	Marathas	Bhonsle Nagpur and Bastar native states (resumed in 1840s).
1818	Marathas	Holkar.
1818	Marathas	Sindhia Malwa becomes native state.
1818	Rajputs	Native states: Mewar, Jodhpur, Jaisalmere, Bikaner, Jaipur.
1820	Madras	Thomas Munro is Governor of Madras to 1824; Ryotwari system established.

TABLE 4. *CONTINUED*

III. Consolidation and further expansion

1833   Charter Act. Company's trade abolished. Abolition of slavery.

1835   Macaulay's Minute on Education. English becomes official language.

1838   British invade Afghanistan. Great Game begins. First Afghan War to 1842.

1846   Kashmir made native state.

1848   Annexation of Punjab. Lord Dalhousie is Governor General to 1856.

1853   Dalhousie's railway plan. First railway opened. Telegraph from Calcutta to Agra.

1857   The Great Rebellion, Foundation of Calcutta, Bombay, and Madras Universities.

IV. The first decades of Crown rule

1858   India under the Crown: Queen's Proclamation.

1861   Indian Councils Act. High Courts Act. Indian Penal Code introduced. First Indian Census. Lord Mayo commissions W. W. Hunter's *The Indian Musalmans: Are They Bound in Conscience to Rebel Against the Queen?* (London, 1871).

1867   Deoband school founded by Muhammad 'Abid Husayn.

1868   Punjab and Oudh Tenancy Acts.

1869   Opening of the Suez Canal. Lord Mayo Viceroy to 1872.

         Jotirao Phule publishes attack on Brahmanism, *Priestcraft Exposed*.

1875   Arya Samaj founded by Swami Dayananda.

         Muhammadan Anglo-Oriental College at Aligarh founded by Syed Ahmad Khan.

1876   Queen Victoria becomes Empress of India.

1877   Deccan Famine.

TABLE 4. *CONTINUED*

V. Imperial heyday and early nationalism

1879	Dadabhai Naoroji publishes *The Poverty of India*.
1880	Famine Commission Report. Famine Codes. Lord Ripon Viceroy to 1884.
1881	First Factory Act.
1882	*Ananda Math* by Bankim Chandra Chatterjee. Swami Dayananda founds first Cow Protection Society.
1883	Singh Sabha opens the Khalsa Press in Lahore. Ilbert Bill controversy.
1884	Local Government Acts.
1885	Indian National Congress founded. Bengal Tenancy Act.
1886	The Sikh reformist *Khalsa Akhbar* begins publication under Ditt Singh.
1887	Tata's Empress cotton mill at Nagpur.
1893	Vivekananda at Parliament of Religions at Chicago. B. G. Tilak popularizes Ganesh festival. Cow protection riots in Uttar Pradesh.
1895	B. G. Tilak revives Shivaji festival.
1896	Plague and famine in India, to 1900.
1897	Kahn Singh Nabha publishes *Ham Hindu Nahin*.
1899	Lord Curzon Viceroy to 1905.
1900	North-West Frontier Province created. Punjab Land Alienation Act. Urdu Protection Society founded in Uttar Pradesh.
1904	Universities Act. Co-operative Societies Act. Archaeological Department.

port or major commercial centre, he reported that the locals were as much a 'nation of shopkeepers' as the Scots. One of his reports is most instructive:

> Almost every ryot [tax-paying peasant] has an account with a bazaar-man and a balance against himself. This account

often runs through 2 or 3 generations and is rarely paid off entirely. It usually 'originates in small advances by the bazaar-man who probably gives seventy or eighty rupees and takes a bond for a hundred with interest at 2.5% monthly (or 30% annually). The ryot in return makes payment in grain, cotton and other articles, which are usually valued against him and he receives occasionally from the bazaar-man small sums for the discharge of his Kists [instalments] . . . [In case of default] the creditor has only to produce [before the local court] a bond; an order for distraint usually follows and the ryot is at once stripped of his cattle, grain and implements of husbandry and will most likely never again rise above the rank of common labourer.

Though comprehensive statistics on rural commerce and debt were not available in Munro's day, British tax collectors relied on commercial proceeds from local trades to satisfy tax demands. Many rural areas contained complex economies; they were certainly not, as later conventional wisdom would have it, environments of simple rustic subsistence. In Munro's out-of-the-way Rayalaseema, landowning farm families (21 percent) were well outnumbered by the combined total of craftworkers (19 percent), merchants (12 percent), and soldiers (10 percent).

Local commercialism supported English East India Company operations, first along the coast of the Indian Ocean. Their own personal resources made English merchants more independent than their European rivals; they identified less than French or Dutch merchants with their home government and relied heavily on local collaborators. By the mid-eighteenth century, financing for Company operations came mostly from Indian family firms that, like the Company, did business across cultures and made money inside markets that included all kinds of goods, services, and taxes. Eighteenth-century taxes fed trade and banking, which in turn provided state revenues; and locally, in agrarian societies, people who controlled land, labour, and capital faced mounting tax pressure from eighteenth-century rulers in the context of expanding markets for agricultural commodities. Some proportion of debt incurred by Munro's Rayalaseema peasants would have gone to pay taxes to secure land rights. No tax payments, no land rights; no commercial finance, no taxes. In eighteenth-century South Asia, circular connections among military powers, local entitlements, and commercial activities were ubiquitous.

As the English East India Company began to build an empire by using military force to raise finance capital to buy goods to ship overseas, it turned the existing circular connections among political powers, local entitlements, finance, and trade into an imperial bonanza. The Company's military force made it the ultimate guarantor of land rights in conquered regions; and in return for granting land rights, it took more taxation than any previous regime. Struggles then ensued between the British government and the Company to centralize the accumulation of taxes in the central treasury. By enriching the treasury, the Company and government could use taxes to secure funding from bankers and investors who would speculate on future cash returns from further conquest. The British government also incurred public debt from bankers who simultaneously financed British industry and war. Industry produced superior weapons for still further conquest. A new circularity was born: war-taxation-entitlements-trade-industrialization. This new circuit of capital accumulation became the bedrock of imperial capitalism with an ever more global reach.

During the wars with Napoleon, British public debt swelled and the scrutiny of state budgets increased. In 1823, the budget became a matter of public record. Cutting the cost of government and raising new revenue to pay state creditors became the order of the day. Political pressure in London forced higher tax collections in South Asia to pay not only Company investors but also the British treasury and private bankers. At the same time, English business sought profits in territories of British expansion, backed by British supremacy at sea. Reflecting public concern in Britain, Parliament sought ways to pursue national profits in the empire. Political support in London for old monopoly companies declined steadily after the publication of Adam Smith's *The Wealth of Nations* (1776). Pitt's India Act of 1784 marked the first step in the replacement of Company privilege by imperial nationalism. In each subsequent Company charter renewal, the autonomy of the Company declined: in 1793, it came under strict state supervision; in 1805, it lost Ceylon; in 1813, it lost its monopoly; in 1833, it lost its business; and in 1858, it died.

Already by 1793, British national interests had been expressed in public debates about the best way to manage Britain's 'Asiatic possessions'. Since the early eighteenth century, prohibitions against selling Indian cloth in England had protected Lancashire against Indian weavers who made better cloth more cheaply; but after 1815, tariffs also killed re-exports from London of Indian cloth.

Imperial tariff policies enabled Lancashire exporters to sell British textiles to India virtually duty-free; and British exporters began to undersell Indian-made cloth inside India. At the same time, India and Ceylon were then targeted to supply English industry and English as well as American consumers. Opium grown by peasants to pay their tax bills in Bengal and Bihar supplied English merchants who sold opium in China and bought Chinese tea and porcelain to sell in Western markets. At home in London, tea from China was sweetened with sugar produced by slaves on British plantations in the West Indies.

After 1820, the tax bureaucracy steadily increased the centralized accumulation of tax revenues. To this end, old layers of sovereignty needed to be eliminated because at each level in the old tax system, people in authority who passed tax payments up the ranks kept a portion for themselves, as a financial benefit and a symbol of their personal power. Thus in the tax systems that the British inherited, each individual of rank and each headman of a community kept a portion of tax proceeds that British administrators strove to acquire. The old system gave all the intermediaries in the tax system a personal interest in increasing total tax collections, but also left them with independent discretionary powers and room to negotiate with superiors for tax relief and leniency in tax collections. Eliminating their leverage became the battle cry for British bureaucrats and politically ambitious administrators such as Thomas Munro, who sought to transmit more tax revenues direct to the central treasury and also claimed (falsely, as it turned out) that eliminating tax middlemen would lower the tax burden for ordinary peasants.

Under orders from London, the Company tried to turn all tax collectors into salaried bureaucrats, and to make taxpayers fear the state's power to seize land for failure to pay taxes. This imperial project paid for military expansion and repaid English financiers handsomely. Because the monies involved in the British Empire globally had to move across vast distances separating very different monetary systems, policymakers tried to keep the relative value of currency in England high compared to others to favour bankers in England. Policymakers also tried to keep the value of the Indian rupee and the English pound favourable for English importers, exporters, and investors in South Asia, a complicated and ultimately impossible agenda. The Bank of England always came first.

Opening South Asia to British investment proved difficult. The year 1813 marked a beginning, when Parliament broke the Company's monopoly, but the project proceeded slowly because of the cost and risk of ventures in unknown territory so far from home. By the 1820s, British nationals had succeeded, however, in cutting Indian businessmen out of the old multicultural commercial partnerships, as established British exporters based in India gathered in national prerogatives and took control of the overseas trade. As we have seen, the reduction of Kandy followed cries for a more integrated transportation system in British Ceylon, but British plantation investments still remained low for another twenty years. The empire was initially more successful in helping to integrate British business operations globally. When the 1833 abolition of slavery in British territories produced a crying need among British West Indian planters for cheap labour to replace the freed slaves, imperial officers arranged to send annual shiploads of indentured Bihari workers from Calcutta to work on Caribbean plantations.

More ambitious imperial plans began in the 1840s, when policymakers in London launched ideas for developing new ports and a railway system in South Asia to lower the cost of overseas exports, quicken military operations, increase revenue, and subsidize British investments. Also in the 1840s, Arthur Cotton argued successfully that crop production could be advanced by state irrigation investments that would pay for themselves with higher taxes on more productive land. Modern state-led economic development was being born.

British textile barons led the way. In the 1840s, Parliament met to consider ways of improving supplies of raw cotton to Lancashire mills. The Maratha interior districts of Bombay Presidency attracted special attention, along with Egypt. Measures were sought to expand cotton exports from these regions to counterbalance Britain's dependence on the American South. The railway would help to solve the problem, but even before it was built, when the American Civil War began, Egypt and India filled a void in cotton supplies created by the Union blockade of Confederate ports.

The imperial transition to industrial capitalism consumed the decades 1840 to 1880. In 1853, Governor General Dalhousie announced the plan to build an Indian railway with state contracts that guaranteed private companies a minimum five percent return, funded by tax revenues; and to secure that return, government kept control of railway construction and management. In the 1870s, the Government of India obtained authority to raise loans for productive purposes, and large irrigation projects began, following earlier success in raising revenues from smaller projects. These projects were all government endeavours using private contractors, and their benefits also accrued to owners of irrigated land. Huge projects opened up arid land formerly used by pastoral nomads in Punjab, who were displaced to implement vast farming operations in the Punjab Canal Colonies, where government land allocations went primarily to Sikhs and Hindu Jat families serving the imperial military. State support for private capital accumulation became a mainstay of the Raj: it benefited British capitalists, Indian landed interests, financiers at all levels, and merchants in commodity markets in South Asia and overseas, all at once.

By 1880, regions of specialized production for world markets had emerged in South Asia. Ceylon was plantation country. Coffee plantations had expanded from 50,000 to 80,000 thousand acres between 1847 and 1857, and peasant farms devoted another 48,000 acres to coffee exports. Despite difficulties raising capital in the 1860s, coffee acreage expanded another 35,000 acres before 1871. But in the 1880s, leaf disease killed coffee, which was rapidly replaced by tea, rubber, cocoanut, and cinchona. Ceylon and India replaced China as the major suppliers of English tea. A supreme plantation crop, tea required heavy investments in cultivation and machinery, which drove out peasant producers and favoured British capitalists who controlled the export markets and consumer access in Europe.

Labour supplies posed the major production constraint for Ceylon tea planters, and the solution was found in the institution of (eventually permanent) labour migration from southern Tamil districts in British India. British plantations in the Malay peninsula also depended on Tamil workers, who settled there in large numbers. British Burma and East Africa also developed within circuits of capital accumulation anchored in India. In Burma, Tamil Chettiyar bankers became the prime financiers for agricultural development in the Irrawaddy River delta, which generated huge exports of rice for world markets, including India, where urban growth rapidly expanded demand for imported rice. In East and South Africa, merchants from Gujarat and emigrant workers from Bombay, Calcutta, and Madras provided both labour and capital for railway construction and urban centres to anchor the imperial economy. Between 1896 and 1928, 75 percent of emigrants from Indian ports went to Ceylon and Malaya; 10 percent to Africa; nine percent to the Caribbean; and the remaining six percent to Fiji and Mauritius.

The Maratha Deccan became cotton country with its black volcanic 'cotton soil'. Following the Civil War boom, cotton farmers incurred such serious debt to finance cotton production that when prices dropped in 1876, riots broke out pitting farmers against non-Maratha bankers, especially Marwaris from Rajasthan. In the same year, cotton duties were abolished in England to further cheapen supplies from India, and a year later, the biggest famine ever recorded struck the Deccan cotton-growing districts. Half the population also died in the dry districts of Rayalaseema, in Madras Presidency. The coincidence of laissez-faire economic policy, imperial expansion, and famine sharpened government attention to capital investment in agriculture. In 1869, Lord Mayo reflected the imperial mindset by saying, '. . . every measure for the improvement of the land enhances the value of the property of the State'. He went on to say, 'The duties which in England are performed by a good landlord fall in India, in a great measure, upon the government. Speaking generally, the only Indian landlord who can command the requisite knowledge is the State.'

In the 1880s, annual government publications indicate South Asia's massive importance as supplier for the capitalist world economy. By 1914, almost all the goods arriving at ports consisted of primary products for overseas export: cotton, wheat, rice, coal, coke, jute, hides and skins, tea, ores, and wool; gunny bags were the only manufacture. Most cotton came to Bombay from Maratha country, and to Madras from southern Tamil country. All tea came to Calcutta and Colombo from British-owned hill plantations in north-east India (Assam and Darjeeling) and around Kandy. By far the most rice came to Rangoon from deltaic Burma. Wheat came primarily from fields under state irrigation in Punjab (60 percent) and the western United Provinces (Uttar Pradesh; 26 percent). Oilseeds came to Bombay from Hyderabad territory (Andhra Pradesh), the Central Provinces (Madhya Pradesh), and Bombay Presidency (Maharashtra). Coal, coke, and ores came from mines around Jharkhand into Calcutta and Bombay, where they stoked local industry as well as exports. Eastern Bengal (Bangladesh) produced almost all the world's jute, which went to Scotland and to Calcutta, where jute cloth output surpassed Dundee by 1908.

Between 1880 and 1914, low prices prevailed in Europe and America as prices kept rising in South Asia. This encouraged investments in South Asia by firms producing for domestic and world markets, rather than primarily for markets in the West. This spurred the government on to raise and spend more in India, resulting in the Local Self-Government Act and a massive expansion of government irrigation from 1880 to 1900. The result was a new spatial pattern of capital accumulation, as imported industrial machinery was domesticated in regions of factory production in British India.

In 1853, the first Indian cotton mill appeared in Bombay. The Factory Act (1881) imposed new rules of operation on Indian factories that were intended to reduce the advantages that Indian capitalists enjoyed over British competitors by virtue of low-cost labour and raw materials in India. In 1887, J. N. Tata's Empress Mill rose at Nagpur, in the heart of Maratha Deccan cotton country. The Tatas became India's greatest industrial dynasty. Tata Iron and Steel Works at Jamshedpur consumed increasing supplies of ore and coal, which by the 1920s rivalled exports from Calcutta. By 1914, India was the world's fourth-largest industrial cotton textile producer: cotton mills numbered 271 and employed 260,000 people, 42 percent in Bombay city, 26 percent elsewhere in Bombay Presidency (mostly Nagpur), and 32 percent elsewhere in British India, at major railway junctures. Coal, iron, steel, jute, and other industries developed at the same time, producing specialized regional concentrations of heavy-industrial production around Bombay, Ahmedabad, Nagpur, Kanpur, Calcutta, Jamshedpur, and Madras. Jute mills around Calcutta multiplied from one to sixty-four, between 1854 and 1914; the number of looms and scale of employment increased twice as fast.

World War I further stimulated industrial policies to make India less dependent on imports; and the Great Depression (1929–33) again boosted incentives for industrial growth by reducing the price of farm output relative to manufacturers. As a result, industrial output in India grew steadily from 1913 to 1938, and was 58 percent higher at the end of the Depression than at the start of World War I; compared to slower and more uneven rates of growth in the UK and Germany. By contrast, plantations languished from the early 1900s to the 1940s. The partial exception was rubber, which benefited from war booms.

By 1920, South Asia had complex, diversified, national economies – dominated by agriculture, but including a large public sector, major industries, and expanding capital looking for growth – where investors large and small were concerned that state policies supported increasing capital accumulation in a changing world economy. Native states and non-British firms participated in this trend. The Mysore government built the high Sivasamudram dam at the headwaters of the Kaveri River, and in 1902 installed an electric generator built by General Electric using techniques and equipment pioneered at Niagara Falls. Bangalore was the first South Asian city lighted with electricity. In 1921, a third of India's industrial production was driven by electricity, and Mysore had a higher proportion of electrified industry (33 percent) than the British Presidencies of Madras (13 percent) and Bengal (22 percent).

As South Asia's internally differentiated regions were collectively and individually integrated into the world economy by networks of investment, migration, communication, and cultural activity, London was losing ground as a world economic power. Economically, South Asia revolved less and less tightly around its imperial metropolis. British India became a land of opportunity for global investors. In 1914, the American consul in Bombay, Henry Baker, called India 'one of the few large countries of the world where there is an "open door" for the trade of all countries'. In 1914, the UK provided almost two-thirds of British India's imports and received one quarter of its exports; by 1926, these figures had fallen to one half and one fifth respectively. In 1926, trade with the UK (including all imports, exports, and re-exports) averaged one third of total trade for South Asia's five major ports (Calcutta, Bombay, Madras, Karachi, and Rangoon). Just over half of total trade was with Europe. Bombay and Rangoon did 43 percent of their overseas business with Asia and the Middle East, and Calcutta did a quarter with America.

The movement of people also expanded and diversified. The Suez Canal, undersea telegraph cables, larger and faster steamers, and eventually telephones and aircraft cheapened world travel and communication. Transnational migration increased and more British families came to South Asia, but few stayed for long: new immigrants averaged half the British resident population between 1891 and 1911. In 1911, British citizens formed 62 percent of Europeans in British India, and 54 percent in native states and agencies. Four times more immigrants came from Asia than from Europe: seven out of ten came overland from Nepal (54 percent) and Afghanistan (16 percent). In 1911, Nepalis entering British India (280,248) exceeded the British resident population by 50 percent, and Asian immigrants altogether numbered three times the British population in India. By 1921, emigration far exceeded immigration: a modern diaspora was under way. Emigration was regionally particular. From 1896 to 1928, 83 percent of 1,206,000 emigrants left British India from Madras (a port that accounted for only 10 percent of total overseas trade), and they mostly went to work in Ceylon (54 percent) and Malaya (39 percent). Bombay emigrants went mostly to East and South Africa; Calcutta emigrants to Fiji and the West Indies.

By 1920, British citizens still controlled the highest echelons of South Asia's economy, but the process of capital accumulation in South Asia that sustained the rise of British imperialism escaped British control. South Asia's economy became more independently established in a world of national economies. A turning point came during World War I. Before the war, London's political position in South Asia seemed supreme. After the war, Britain's power declined visibly in relation to other imperial nations and to social forces in South Asia, where politicians worked to gain control of the national political economy.

SOCIAL FORCES

As the ranks of imperial governance and its centres of economic order evolved in the nineteenth century, networks of mobility connecting cities, towns, and villages built scaffolding for the development of modern regions. The imperial central place hierarchy outlined a spatial design for politics, economics, culture, and social life. At the apex of empire, metropolitans looked out on a world where the sun never set on Western power. In cosmopolitan cities in Asia and Africa, East and West mingled most intensely, and nations were born. At the foundation of empire in rustic towns and villages, where almost everyone lived, imperial society spoke in local languages, and nations took life among the masses.

Metropolitans

Most people in Britain may have thought the empire ran by remote control. It was rarely in the news, except in times of war, famine, or plague, when public pressure perked up to get normality re-established. Reassuring news came in reports of imperial *darbar*s and world exhibitions that dramatized the global richness of Pax Britannica. At most, ten percent of families in the United Kingdom would have had contact with British territory in South Asia. Though some English elites cared intensely about empire, most did not, and they kept national interests close to home. When British eyes looked abroad, they looked primarily to white, temperate climes in Europe, to Canada, Australia, and South Africa. Empire was a profession for bureaucrats in the India Office and Colonial Office, for the military, for diplomats, for Crown appointees in positions abroad, and for office workers, businessmen, academics, missionaries, doctors, engineers, and others working for various periods of time overseas on British projects. Empire was a part-time concern for politicians. Few others in Britain cared or did much about it.

And few British citizens involved in empire ever spent much time in Asia. The tropics were sometimes fun to visit, but rarely desirable for living. South Asia was too hot, dirty, crowded, distant, and alien to attract many British citizens. At the peak of their numerical strength, in 1911, British residents in British India numbered 185,434, under one percent of Britain's population and about six one-hundredths of one percent (0.06 percent) of British India's population. These small numbers lived mostly in securely segregated British enclaves, doing their jobs and maintaining English-style households and communities, trying to live as comfortably as possible until they could go home, hopefully better off than when they arrived.

Cosmopolitans

British territories in Asia were much too large and complex to be ruled from Britain. In 1871, British India had 256 million people, while England, Scotland, and Wales together had 32 million. By 1947, India was ten times bigger than Britain with over 400 million people. Travel time between London and Calcutta fell from six months to six weeks to three weeks in the nineteenth century; and undersea cable links made the telegraph a critical tool for government and business. Though resident Britons in South Asia increased after 1860, faster travel and communication also cheapened remote-control governance. Connecting global empire with imperial territories in Asia was work primarily for cosmopolitans living in the big capital cities, where most resident metropolitans lived.

Great cities in South Asia dramatized the Raj with monumental buildings, ethnically segregated residential quarters, and grand public events. Their businesses, bureaucrats, lawyers, doctors, soldiers, educators, engineers, journalists, and other professionals made empire work. In 1911, seven cities – Calcutta, Madras, Bombay, Hyderabad, Lucknow, Delhi, and Benares – each had many more residents than the total number of British citizens in British India. Calcutta and Bombay stood out: in 1921, they both held over one million people. Madras was half their size, and Delhi, half again, about the size of Colombo with fewer than half a million people. Outside the biggest cities, scores of lower-tier centres along the railways contained most of the remainder of the empire's assets and ninety-five percent of South Asia's urban population, which still amounted to only ten percent of the total population in 1921. The vast majority of people in South Asia lived in rural settings, where few British officials ever set foot, where imperial power lived in hundreds of small cities and large towns.

Empire grew around the big cities. Capital cities were core sites for investment and central nodes for transport and communication. Even today, international travellers typically arrive in South Asia by landing in one of the great cities of the Raj. The imperial transportation system laid the template for all modern central-place infrastructures. After independence, cities maintained the advantages they enjoyed under the British, so that nineteenth-century central places remain central today. Old cosmopolitan cities remain pre-eminent, though Karachi, Delhi, and Dhaka surged ahead after independence to join Calcutta and Bombay in the list of the world's biggest cities. The Mughal legacy also remained: old Mughal cities held half the population of the twenty-five biggest cities in British India. Most places that were physically remote and politically marginal under the Mughals remained remote and marginal under the British, and still do today, scattered among mountains and in poor, dry regions stretching from Baluchistan to Burma and throughout central India into Odisha, Bihar, and the Deccan.

English became South Asia's cosmopolitan language in 1833, when it became the official imperial language for British India and Ceylon. Learning to read and write English fuelled social mobility everywhere in imperial society, and English-educated people concentrated in the major cities. In 1911, Delhi and Calcutta together had more residents enumerated in the census as being literate in English than there were British citizens in all of South Asia. English schools boomed with funding from various sources. Official data in the 1920s indicate that ninety-seven percent of all schools in British India were privately funded, though more than half of these received some government aid and more than a third were managed by local or district boards that were established by government in the 1880s. Endowing schools became a cultural enterprise, like endowing a temple or a mosque. Many aspiring social groups founded English schools. Government concentrated funding on colleges and universities, and most South Asian governments continued this practice after independence.

Literacy in general and English literacy in particular became the hallmark of social status and mobility. The seven million students reportedly in school in the 1911 census comprised about two percent of the Indian population. Overall literacy then probably did not exceed the official figure of six percent; and less than ten percent of these literate people were officially counted as being literate in English, about one half of one percent of the total population.

English literacy was concentrated in cities in British territory. The 1911 census shows much smaller proportions of English literates in the native states than in British provinces. In Calcutta, one third of the total population was reportedly literate in 1911, and forty-four percent of these were counted as being literate in English. Similar high overall literacy rates appear for Dhaka, Bangalore, Benares, and Delhi. Though Madras, Bombay, and Hyderabad had more typically low overall literacy rates, they shared high big-city figures for the percentage of literates who were literate in English, ranging from 22 percent in Bangalore to 48 percent in Madras. In 1911, Calcutta surpassed all cities with an English-literate population of 127,234, which was half again as many as Delhi (80,947) and five times as many as Madras and Bombay combined (25,628). The stature of the capital cities of British India is clearly reflected in the size of their English-literate populations.

Other important features of imperial society also appear in the 1911 census, and one to which we will return below needs to be underlined here. Official documents describing imperial South Asia employ a very particular kind of empirical framework, which had a major influence on how people in society viewed their own identities and those of people around them. Census returns divided the population into religious groups, separating Hindus, Muslims, and Christians; they also divided Hindus on the lines of *varna* classification. Though literacy among urban elites in general was high compared to all other groups, statistics on literacy in the census do not reveal the social identity of most literate ethnic or caste groups: they only allow us to analyse literacy by social categories that are used in the census.

One census group stands out most notably for its literacy: Brahmans. All Brahmans in British India combined to form about six percent of the 1911 population; as an official census category they had exceptionally high rates of literacy: 40 percent in Bengal and Madras Presidencies and in some native states, such as Baroda; and 30 percent in Bombay Presidency and among Kashmiri Pandits. English literacy was also more common among literate Brahmans. In Madras and Bengal Presidencies, more than 25 percent of all literate Brahmans were literate in English; the figure hovers around 20 percent in Bombay, Kashmir, Baroda, and Mysore territories. Brahman stature in imperial society is reflected in high English literacy.

Though English literates were the most prominent members of imperial society, they numbered less than one percent of the total population in the early twentieth century. Most were men from high-status social groups, many were Brahmans, and they mostly lived in big cities. Most literate people who participated in public life read and wrote instead in other languages. Only 15 percent of all the books officially recorded as being published in British India in the 1920s were in English. The proportion of vernacular books was highest in Punjab (94 percent) and in the United Provinces (90 percent), but it was still above 80 percent in Madras, Bengal, and Bombay Presidencies. Regional languages were the most prominent vehicles for communication for participants in imperial society.

People who participated most visibly in public life in the cosmopolitan cities pursued various occupations and professions. Most were civilians. English literates may have comprised about one quarter of the one percent of the population that was employed in the armed forces and public administration. The army built the empire, but civilians maintained and controlled it. In 1911, British India's standing army was very expensive to maintain in its far-flung posts, but also quite small by per capita measures compared to European armies, with one soldier for every one thousand people, a quarter the ratio in Britain itself and one tenth that in Germany. Government in British India, though powerful, was small in size compared to Western Europe, with about three working state officials for every one thousand people.

The empire's ability to concentrate power and wealth in government hands remained limited. From beginning to end, the empire was organized to deliver benefits to private interests; thus the vast majority of people in imperial society worked outside government. In the 1920s, British India's state income was five percent of British India's national income, compared to 19 percent in the UK and 29 percent in Japan; while per capita government revenue in British India was less than one pound sterling, compared to twenty-four pounds in the UK, and five in Japan. By such measures, the imperial government seems small compared to its charge. Only its military budget was large, because it included expenses for imperial wars fought in China, Africa, and the Middle East. Civilian interests kept state revenues down: British businesses kept tariffs down, Indian business kept the income tax down, and landowners kept land taxes from rising even in nominal terms, which drove them down in real value amid steady inflation from 1860 to 1929. After 1880, nationalists worked to drive down imperial taxation still further and shift state expenditure away from the bloated military and into civilian hands.

Agrarian interests

Cosmopolitan cities and regional networks around them provided most personnel for imperial governance and organized its everyday operations. The imperial administration consisted of a tiny London elite, plus small British enclaves in South Asia, and soldiers, police, and bureaucrats in South Asia among whom English-educated, non-British elites were most prominent: all of these people added up to less than two percent of the total population of several hundred million people living in South Asia in the early twentieth century.

Honours, entitlements, and powers conferred, confirmed, authorized, and protected by the imperial state defined the vast majority of imperial society. In this respect, the modern British empire was like earlier empires, but its scope was much wider and its influence much deeper. Modern empire disarmed the population and protected the state from internal military challenges. The legal system arrogated to empire the universal ownership of all land, justified by the British interpretation of rights enjoyed by the Mughal emperors under what they called Oriental Despotism. The imperial state's legal status as supreme landlord – referred to in the quotation from Lord Mayo on p. 150 – allowed officials to assign entitlements to property everywhere; it gave bureaucrats vast legal authority over resources that everyone needed in everyday life. The imperial state retained as public property all the land that it did not assign to private owners. This included all rural and urban residential sites and also roads, rivers, reservoirs, forests, deserts, and any other land that private owners did not buy from the state with taxes.

The small imperial bureaucracy thus had vast legal power. Officials used it to benefit politically important private interests. They gave forest land to English investors in plantations. They gave tracts of new farmland to Sikh military veterans in agricultural colonies favoured with Punjab government irrigation. They took managerial control of huge tracts of 'reserved' forest under the Forest Department. In some mountain regions, forests comprised most of the land, which became available to loggers, miners, and others operating under government contract. Virtually all 'public land' thus allocated had been previously occupied by pastoral nomads, hunters, and forest dwellers, who were summarily displaced.

In farming villages, private-property rights were conferred on individuals in return for tax payments; and as farmers expanded the area under private landownership, they pushed into forested areas. The expansion of private and public control over forest and open scrubland pushed aside nomadic and shifting populations which lost rights to land they had maintained for centuries. Among these groups, there were many fighters who had flourished in the eighteenth century who were now classified as 'criminal castes and tribes'. Most social groups who had lived migratory lives for count-less generations – fighting, hunting, and shifting cultivation from one place to another – became suspect; many were placed under intrusive police surveillance and subjected to various 'rehabilita-tion' programmes intended to make them docile sedentary citizens of modern society. To prevent mass rebellion in predominantly hill-tribe areas in the north-west and north-east, separate tribal territories were carved out for administrative management.

The modern property system and administrative structure pro-duced a more all-inclusive order of entitlements than ever before. As a result, imperial society grew beyond all previous bounds to embrace local landed groups as well as urban elites. But it still left a vast population of landless workers and poor people outside the imperial system of entitlements disenfranchised, dependent on their ability to gain support from influential groups. Their struggles to gain support and establish legal rights to resources became increas-ingly prominent in modern politics.

All property entitlements were legalized and managed in sepa-rate regions of imperial governance. All the regions were legally and administratively incorporated into an imperial scheme where cos-mopolitan bureaucrats only manned the higher echelons. Regions also retained their own legal systems, their own administrative rules and procedures, and their own distinctive elites, including many features inherited from earlier ages. Most people in imperial society lived in places where civilians carrying government authority were not officials but rather people with entitlements authorized, protected, taxed, and regulated by government. Most of these people knew little or no English, lived outside big cities, and did not identify personally with the British or even with government. They lived their lives within old environments of social identity and social experience. They constituted the vast majority of imperial society. They were ordinary people whose lives and livelihoods were necessarily bound up with imperial governance despite their social distance from English elites and cultural exclusion from the cosmopolitan spotlight.

The grandest of the regional elites did actually enter the imperial spotlight, on special occasions. They were native-state dynasties established by treaties during the century of British conquest. Aggressive imperial expansion put many native-state rulers in a harsh light and deposed a good number. All the old ruling families fell under increasing bureaucratic control and surveillance. But the major dynasties remained powerful in their regions. Dynastic families, allies, and subordinates retained substantial control over 40 percent of the land area of British India and 20 percent of its population. The native states held 94 million people in 1947. The largest of these, Hyderabad, had twice the population of Ireland and Scotland combined. Kashmir was the size of France. Mysore, Travancore, Sikkim, and Rajasthan states were also like small countries. Indirect rule through native monarchs allowed the empire to tap resources in the native states, while giving the old elites a solid stake in the imperial system. As in centuries past, subordinate regional rulers held fast to honours which defined their nobility. In 1903, when King Edward VII became Emperor at a Delhi *darbar*, and again in 1911, when a second Delhi *darbar* marked the transfer of the capital, India's 'native princes' marched in the ceremonial ranks to display their honoured place in imperial society.

Also dating back to the century of conquest, Zamindar landlordism defined local agrarian elites in Bengal, Bihar, the United Provinces of Agra and Oudh (Uttar Pradesh), and in scattered regions in the peninsula, Punjab, the North-West Frontier, and central India. As we have seen, the term *zamindar* goes back to Mughal times, when it designated the lowest layer of sovereignty. The English East India Company granted the title to taxpayers who became private owners of landed estates called Zamindaris. Some new Zamindars were old *raja*s. Many descended from eighteenth-century revenue speculators and military adventurers. Others came from rich farming families and elite tribal lineages. Their tenants numbered from dozens to many thousands, and under imperial law, all had to pay rent to Zamindars to retain rights to their land. Zamindari tenants thus became permanent underlings in the political structure of imperial society. As the Company's hunger for revenue and its passion for bureaucracy grew, it squeezed many

Zamindars for more taxes, and shifted their policies in newly acquired territories towards 'settlements' for land revenue with peasants in local communities. But the folly of trying to eliminate the Zamindars from the local ranks of imperial society in lands along the Ganga basin became clear when the effort helped to ignite the vast 1857 rebellion, after which huge new landed estates were signed over to super-rich Zamindars, called Talukdars, in Awadh (Oudh).

The character of Zamindari landlordism changed significantly in the nineteenth century. In 1793, Lord Cornwallis had given Zamindars full powers to set their own rents and define tenures on their estates in the Permanent Settlement with Zamindars in Bengal and Bihar. At the same time, he had fixed Zamindar tax rates in perpetuity, to stabilize state revenues, to give landlords unrestricted rights to increasing rental income, and thus to secure Zamindar loyalty. In the early nineteenth century, however, the Company's rigorous annual cash tax demands crushed many Zamindars and caused a large turnover of Zamindar estates, which provoked complaints against the Company's ill-treatment of the agrarian aristocracy. Even so, for every Zamindar who defaulted on taxes and lost his land, another came forward to buy the land, producing a circulation of Zamindar families rather than a secular decline of the Zamindar class.

When the Company died, the Zamindars lost support. Though they collectively wielded tremendous local power, and though their wealth increased with the value of their land, their legal and economic position as landlords weakened. The government supported their rights but changed the rules of entitlement, abandoning permanent tax rates for periodic reassessments when this was legally possible. New government irrigation often benefited Zamindars, but wealthy tenants invested much more heavily in land, a trend which the government encouraged by enacting tenancy reforms after 1870 that circumscribed the Zamindars' power to define conditions of tenancy. Bankers providing Zamindars with credit absorbed more and more of their rental income.

By 1900, the Zamindars had lost the power to prevent the police from pursuing suspects onto their estates, and they had to abide by new laws that favoured tenants. Many estates had been reorganized by the managerial bureaucracy of the state's Court of Wards. Squeezed by rising tenant resistance and by government restrictions, many Zamindars lost the power to collect rents. They secured their wealth by financing tenant investments and investing their own rental income in non-agricultural ventures in cities and towns. Zamindar rental and banking incomes moved into urban education, business, and the professions. In many towns and small cities, Zamindar families and employees became leaders of society. In the countryside, Zamindars remained powerful elites, and many old Zamindar families remain so today, despite the abolition of most Zamindar tenures in the 1960s.

The shift in government policies away from Zamindari land-tax settlements began in Madras in the early 1800s and reached a milestone in 1813, when Thomas Munro convinced Parliament to authorize a Ryotwari settlement instead with individual farmers in Madras Presidency. Thus, after 1813, the ranks of imperial society extended further down the social scale into the landowning peasantry, as London sought to increase tax revenue and to spread private-property rights more widely than the Zamindari system allowed. In London, Munro convinced Parliament that alien Muslim sultans had imposed Zamindari landlordism in southern India, and that private peasant property in land was the authentic, ancient form of entitlement everywhere in village India. Charles Metcalfe captured the new official view of rural tradition most memorably in 1830:

> The village communities are little republics, having nearly everything they want within themselves, and almost independent of any foreign relations. They seem to last where nothing else lasts. Dynasty after dynasty tumbles down; revolution succeeds to revolution; Hindoo, Patan, Mogul, Mahratta, Sik, English are all masters in turn; but the village communities remain the same . . . If a country remain for a series of years the scene of continued pillage and massacre, so that villages cannot be inhabited, the scattered villagers nevertheless return whenever the power of peaceable possession revives. A generation may pass away, but the succeeding generation will return. The sons will take the place of their fathers; the same site for the village, the same position for the houses, the same lands, will be occupied by the descendants of those who were driven out when the village was depopulated . . .

Following on this official revelation – which was a very far cry from historical reality but served the empire well – government henceforth settled for land revenue primarily with village landowners, either individually or collectively, first in Madras and Bombay Presidencies, and later in Punjab and central India. As a result, in those regions the Zamindar middlemen between the state and farmers were eliminated. Ryotwari settlements with individual Ryots and Mahalwari settlements with villages (*mahals*) vastly increased the population of local patriarchs with official status in the empire.

The rising social status and aspirations of village landowners and Zamindari tenants became a significant political force, particularly in regions where commercial farming produced farming families with assets to invest in the land. Wherever tenant farmers were most active commercially, they had the most success in raising legal challenges to Zamindar rights over their land. Munro had been right to argue that Ryotwari landowners would pay the state handsomely for private-property rights, and they paid higher per capita taxes than all other landowners. But Ryotwari landowners also proved adept at preventing tax rates from rising in proportion to the increasing value of their land. During the inflationary decades 1870 to 1929, when commercial agriculture expanded most dramatically, real tax rates declined as incomes grew among landed families who invested in wells, bulls, and agricultural finance.

The imperial system of land rights was anchored in existing social relations of rank and power in rural society. Its imposition provoked agrarian conflicts with long-term, wide-ranging political effects. All of these conflicts emerged in contexts that were shaped by old ethnic and social formations as well as by the new imperial order. Many conflicts emerged during the transition to new regional systems of agrarian entitlement. The most dramatic example is the 1857 rebellion, which spread widely in the regions around Lucknow and Agra and in nearby Bundelkhand, where old warrior clans fought to prevent the Company from reducing their rural stature. Some families lost out in the process; others won, but overall, formerly dominant social groups, including Rajputs and Thakurs in Bundelkhand, re-established their dominance on new legal grounds under the British.

Struggles between the groups that held official entitlements and those that did not became enduring features of agrarian politics. In each region, tenant struggles evolved in their own social context. Each region had its own collection of politically privileged groups, its own cultural profile of social rank and conflict, its own ethnic flavour.

- Uttar Pradesh and Bihar had the highest percentage of Brahmans at every level in agrarian society. Today, Uttar Pradesh contains roughly forty percent of all Brahmans living in India. The great Zamindars and Talukdars of Uttar Pradesh and Bihar included Brahmans, Muslims, Rajputs, and Bhumihars. Their most prominent tenants were Goala (Ahir), Kurmi, Yadavs, and Lodhis – almost all Hindus. As we will see, the political progress of tenants in this region would include substantial recourse to idioms of Hindu devotionalism and caste status.

- In western Uttar Pradesh, Rajasthan, Punjab, Sind, the North-West Frontier Provinces, Malwa, and the Central Provinces, the various Brahman, Jat, Rajput, Maratha, Sikh, and Muslim landowners each had their own tracts. The spatial pattern of separation among Sikh, Muslim, and Hindu Jats would have particular importance for the infusion of religion into agrarian politics in twentieth-century Punjab. This same general pattern of ethnic group and lineage control of agrarian territory held true in Afghanistan and Nepal.

- In Bengal, the urbane *bhadralok* (respectable people) came substantially from the families of high-caste Hindu Zamindars and their retainers. Zamindar tenant farmers and labourers were low-caste Hindus and Muslims. Three major tenant castes dominated localities in nineteenth-century West Bengal: Sadgop, Kaibartta, and Aguri. These groups had colonized their territories before Permanent Settlement, and in the twentieth century, their power was challenged by upwardly mobile caste groups (Mayra, Chasadhoba, Jogi, Namasudra, and Pod). Menial workers in the homes and factories of Calcutta were largely low-caste Hindus and poor Muslims from Bihar. Almost all Zamindari tenants in the eastern districts of Bengal were Muslims, and most of their landlords were Hindus. All of these ethnic distinctions in Bengal would take on political forms in the twentieth century.

- In Assam, prominent Ahom, Koch, Kalita, and Rajbangshi families controlled territories that received waves of immigrant Bengal peasants looking for land. Conflicts between indigenous peoples and foreign colonists would separate the hill farmers, lowland farmers, plantation owners, and Bengali peasants into competing ethnic factions in the twentieth century.

- In other regions, locally dominant landed castes – Gujarati Kunbis, Maratha Kunbis, Malayali Nayars, Telugu Kammas, Kapus, and Reddys; Kannadiga Vokkaligas, Lingayats, and Boyas; and Tamil Vanniyas, Vellalas, Kallars, and Maravars – controlled their own territories and lorded over low-caste workers and poor peasants. All of these groups became locally dominant as the modern political system evolved. This same general pattern of village-based authority by dominant castes also held true in Ceylon.

- In native states, dynasties and their allies formed ethnic elites, some very small, such as the Muslim dynasty in Hyderabad and the Hindu regime in Kashmir. The ethnic-minority status of the Hyderabad and Kashmir dynasties led them to enact landlord policies that favoured small ruling cliques and caused widespread resentment among tenants whose struggles for land rights became opposition to the dynasty. Both states witnessed severe violence as their native-state dynasties ended in 1947.

Power relations between landlords and tenants changed over time, in part because regional state officials played an increasingly prominent role in enforcing and revising land laws, in response to demands from tenants who were expanding commercial crop production. The main issue pitting tenants against landlords was who had rights to new wealth from the land. When tenants did the work to increase farm production, they fought hard for rights to keep the proceeds. Struggles among farmers, financiers, and landowners embroiled state officials who necessarily took sides in disputes.

Some struggles became violent and turned against the imperial state when it backed the landlords blindly against powerfully organized tenants. One telling case comes from Malabar in northern Kerala. The region had been conquered by Tipu Sultan and then absorbed into Madras Presidency after Tipu's final defeat in 1799. A rapid shift in social power relations then occurred as British administrators reinstalled Brahman (Namboodri) and high-caste Nair *jenmi* landlords who had declined in power or been expelled under Tipu's regime. The autonomy that Mappillai Muslim farmers had enjoyed under Tipu Sultan was then dramatically erased by the British. Mappillai farmers became Muslim tenants whose interests opposed Hindu landlords backed up by the British, whose mistake was to imagine that authentic local tradition had been prescribed by Hindu law. We consider the origin of this imperial mindset in the next section of this chapter.

As a result of British land policy, mosques in Malabar became centres for sermons against landlords and moneylenders that also targeted police and British administrators who enforced demands on tenants by landlords and moneylenders. Twenty-two local

Mappillai revolts occurred between 1836 and 1854; more broke out between 1882 and 1885 and in 1896; and several more erupted before 1919. Altogether, these revolts involved only a few hundred activists; but they left a lasting impression. They inspired heroic folklore with bold attacks on temples and police stations and with their fearless self-martyrdom as *shahids* destined for heaven. The Madras government compiled hundreds of pages of reports on these 'Moplah outbreaks', filled with contemptuous awe for the Mappillai *shahids*. Madras officials wrote thousands of pages on Malabar land tenures in an effort to address tenant problems without disturbing the landlords. Yet nothing much was done in practice except to increase the power of the police.

A large number of agrarian conflicts over entitlements to land arose in areas where farmers were rapidly pushing intensive agriculture into jungles, swamps, and mountains during the nineteenth century. Such regions were numerous in and around Bengal. In 1800, observers guessed that only about one third of cultivable land in the huge expanse of Bengal Presidency was being farmed. By 1900, farms had filled all of the lowlands and were moving into Assam and into the hills on all sides of the deltaic tract, from Chhotanagpur and Orissa to Sylhet and Chittagong.

Conflicts during this rapid transformation of the agrarian landscape were of two major kinds, both etched in ethnic tones. One pitted settled farming communities and landlords against tribal communities practising shifting cultivation, called *jhum*. Conflicts of this kind occurred across all of the mountainous lands from Gujarat to Bastar. The biggest outburst of violence involved a large, diverse group of forest cultivators, the Santhals, who had for centuries farmed the uplands on the fringes of settled villages in the eastern Ganga basin and in the adjacent regions. Santhals interacted regularly with farming communities in the lowlands. They cleared land in the jungle with fire and axe, making the extension of perennial farm cultivation much easier for the lowland farmers. Before the nineteenth century, it appears that Santhal groups did not participate in rituals of rank in agrarian states, however, so they did not obtain official entitlements to land based upon ranked subordination in official hierarchies. Like other tribal groups, they maintained their separate social structures and hierarchies, their own rituals of rank.

In the nineteenth century, as revenue-paying farmers and Zamindars moved into *jhum* lands to expand agriculture, Santhals were steadily pushed deeper into the forest. By 1850, they had moved out of districts in Orissa, Chhotanagpur, Bihar, and Bengal, following skirmishes with Zamindar farmers in 1811, 1820, and 1830. In 1823, large Santhal settlements formed under official state protection ringed the Rajmahal Hills in the Daman-i-Koh, 'the skirt of the hills', where, by the 1840s, 83,000 Santhals lived in government territory, legally free of Zamindar control. Santhal leaders sought to establish a permanent homeland here, away from constant meddling by foreign moneylenders and Company officials. Under the full moon on 30 June 1855, ten thousand Santhals are said to have heard a young leader named Siddhu declare his vision from god that Daman must be 'cleared of all outsiders, that moneylenders and policemen be immediately slaughtered, and that Superintendent Pontet be also slain'. In the ensuing war, Company troops and Zamindars massacred Santhals and their low-caste peasant allies.

Mundas around Ranchi and many other smaller groups also waged similar wars to create independent territories in the nineteenth century. None succeeded, but their legacies still live today in the politics of autonomy in the new Indian state of Jharkhand, 'the land of jungles', and in the mountain jungles of Maoist rebellions in Odisha, Bastar, and elsewhere, which we will consider in Chapter Seven. As the Santhals were driven back from the moving Zamindar borders, the state instituted tribal territories to segregate the forest peoples. In the mountains of the north-east and north-west, this official policy of separate 'tribal area' administration created the territorial basis for separate national identities in Nagaland, Manipur and Mizoram (in India), the Chittagong Hill Tracts (Bangladesh), and the North-West Frontier Province (Pakistan). As farmers pushed from Bengal into Assam, conflicts among farmers and plains tribes also occurred. All these uplands of lowland agrarian expansion remain zones of conflict today.

Nineteenth-century conflicts between Zamindars and tenants also evolved inside the framework of imperial property law. In Zamindar territory, farming was primarily the work of peasant families and of superior tenants who combined labour and finance to create new farmland and to expand commercial production. Zamindars had many ways to exert power over tenants – legal and otherwise – but cultivation always entailed two distinct moments of power: the physical activity of farming and the political extension of Zamindari property rights over new production. By extending and intensifying cultivation, tenants made claims to property that Zamindars also claimed. Collecting rent from tenants was always a political activity that, season after season, reinscribed ranks of inequity into rural society. Struggles over rights to farm land could allow tenants to entrench their legal position, as they increased the value of their own land, resisted Zamindar claims to rent, or bought tenures.

Legal activity thus formed a basic feature of agrarian politics in Bengal and Bihar from the 1760s onward. The comparative strengths of tenants in different Zamindari territories are indicated by their relative success in getting rights recorded and payments acknowledged in receipts. In Bihar, tenants were relatively weak. The Zamindars remained supreme; but in Bengal, the relatively open frontier of agricultural expansion strained Zamindar power. Zamindars always met resistance when they endeavoured to extend their rights over new cultivation, and where open land for peasant colonization was most abundant, Zamindars faced the most difficult challenge. In such areas, a rent-seeking Zamindar might most profitably acquire new revenues by allowing effective ownership to devolve into stratified farming communities in which money lenders and larger tenants established superior rights over farming families. This was typical in Bengal, particularly in the east, north, and south.

Acts of the Bengal government revised the terms of Zamindar property law in 1819, 1822, 1859, 1865, 1869, 1876, 1884, 1885, 1886, and 1894. At every step, pressure from tenants pushed reform. In 1859, the Bengal government insisted for the first time that tenant rights be recorded, which gave tenants new leverage. In 1873, a district judge's ruling encouraged a group in Yusufshahi to form an Agrarian League to defend tenants in Pabna District against additional rent claims, 'illegal cesses' (*abwab*s), and threats to their occupancy rights. The League led demonstrations in town to raise support for their cause. Their activity evoked critical reactions from Zamindar supporters in Calcutta. But Pabna landlords who fought the League impoverished themselves in court, and the number of perpetual leases jumped from 627 to 1633 in the years between 1873 and 1877. This was the beginning of a long movement among Bengal tenants to secure tenures, lower rents, and restrict Zamindar power. Tenant activists and Zamindar allies occupied opposing positions in legal battles that became political positions in regional and national politics in the twentieth century.

Producing Nationality

National identities evolved within modern imperial societies and became a defining feature of modern life. So entrenched are national identities today that they seem to be natural or even eternal, but in most of the world they came into being as a result of historical innovations during the nineteenth century. In South Asia, social change began to take definitively national political forms in Queen Victoria's later years, in the last decades of the nineteenth century.

Nationality became a new kind of collective identity in the old regions of South Asia, such that each made their own distinctive impact on its substance and meaning. Regions had their own vernacular languages, literatures, religious institutions, and cultural legacies. The British Empire embraced all the regions, but in doing so enhanced their distinctiveness. Regions developed their own imperial institutions, urban hierarchies, bureaucracies, and legal and educational systems. Print media, schools, and public activity standardized distinctive regional languages. In official publications such as the census, each region acquired a standard list of caste, ethnic, and religious groups, so that each region attained a distinctive social profile, codified and enumerated in the census every decade after 1871.

Even inside British India, the administration never homogenized all its official statistics the way national states have done since 1950. Each provincial volume of the imperial census has its distinctive features, most of all in the social categories that describe its population. Imperial statistics did not embrace all of the native states until the 1930s. Each regional government printed its own manual of administration. Beginning with legislation that established local governments in the 1880s, political institutions developed distinctively in each region. All the regions had their own style and substance of cultural politics. Their activists, artists, and scholars worked to recuperate and reinterpret distinctive regional traditions; they developed new literary genres; and they engaged in projects of social uplift and reform – all in regional idioms. Imperial modernity gave old regions new life in the world of nations.

INVENTING NATIVE SOCIETY

Regional identities spawned national identities as cosmopolitan elites developed shared ideas about native society. The intellectual substance of national identity emerged initially in descriptions of native society by influential authors in cosmopolitan centres who stood as representatives of the native population and became exemplars of national identity.

The empire's cultural hierarchy had the most profound impact on the identity of the cosmopolitans who invested native society with their own modern meanings. For the British, the most essential division in imperial society was that which separated the 0.06 percent of the population who were British from the 99.94 percent who were not. The 99.94 percent became 'natives'. Marking and reinforcing this ranked cultural division flattered and strengthened the race- and class-conscious ethnic British, whose small numerical force needed all the help it could get. Making British officials seem all powerful was a cultural project that resembled the painting of halos on sultans and imagining the Mughal emperor as being omnipotent. The British, unlike the past imperial order, were no longer composed of shifting ethnic and military alliances, filled with layered sovereignties: empire now officially consigned all its subjects alike to the imperial status of unarmed civilians. The whole population that ranked beneath the British 0.06 percent thus officially comprised a subordinate native society living under British authority.

The intellectual activity that defined the cultural substance of this native society began in the early days of British rule. Initially, East India Company governance rested on the legal premise that the Company ruled India on Indian principles. Native authority legitimated early British legislation and judicial decisions; and the Mughal emperor himself authorized the Company Raj in Bengal. After 1820, British ideas became dominant, but they still needed native authority to secure their legitimacy. Property law needed to be justified with precedents and principles from old texts and old regimes. Personal law needed to be anchored in native codes and practices. In the eighteenth century, therefore, Company officials began their quest to secure indigenous codes and cultural authorities to guide their law-making. Indo-Persian scholars of Arabic, Persian, and Sanskrit stepped forward to provide the needed information. Based on that information, Company lawmakers and judges divided imperial society into legal 'communities' defined by religious law, which seemed to the British to govern South Asia as it did Christian Europe. Sacred texts therefore attained legal authority. Religious texts and experts became part of government policymaking and public debate. In Company courts, native tradition became religious tradition as this was defined by learned elites who controlled sacred texts in classical languages.

The politics of law-making thus included legal reasoning based on the authority of native tradition. Defining tradition became an integral feature of imperial governance. For example, when English missionaries pressured the Company to outlaw *sati* – the immolation of a widow on her husband's funeral pyre – their proposed legislation banning *sati* produced opposition from local groups who claimed *sati* had religious sanction. When the legislation was finally passed in 1829, it rested on the official authority of the Chief Pandit (Hindu religious expert) who was employed by the Calcutta Supreme Court and who opined in 1817 that *sati* was not sanctioned in the officially recognized Sanskrit legal texts (*dharmasastras*). Similarly, Company courts initially followed orthodox Brahman opinion in Calcutta to declare that a remarried widow did not have a wife's legal right to inherit property. But after extended debates and public efforts by social reformers to reinterpret tradition, widow remarriage was legally recognized in 1856. Beginning in the early nineteenth century, social reform movements led by cosmopolitan intellectuals strove to change social practices through innovations in religious interpretation that also facilitated reformist legislation.

After 1858, under Crown rule, there was no further need for courts to consult official Pandits and Maulvis (Muslim legal experts), as Company judges had done, because basic principles for legal judgments had already been firmly established for Hindu and Muslim law respectively. But legislation that touched religious sensibilities still sparked controversy. For example, proposals to legislate a minimum 'age of consent' for a girl's marriage provoked conflicting interpretations of authoritative texts. Many such disputes produced reports and petitions to courts and legislators, because people in countless groups had disputes about marriage, inheritance, and ritual practices. Common law recognized tradition as authoritative. What tradition actually was in reality became a subject for debates recorded and propagated in newspapers, tracts, and at public meetings. An official archive composed of authorized official knowledge about native tradition informed the composition of imperial law on all civil matters. Official studies of traditional practices gave rise to the modern discipline of ethnography, as official texts on administration and law came to include detailed information on cultural traditions among 'castes and tribes', filling official ethnographic compendia for each region.

Government needed native authority to determine what native tradition should be. This made native experts prominent public figures in cosmopolitan circles, where interpreting native tradition became a professional activity for public intellectuals. In these same intellectual circles, learned members of urban society were simultaneously interpreting old traditions, working to understand the changing world around them, and striving to improve that world in their own light. Cosmopolitan disputes about tradition reflected changing social and cultural conditions even as disputants portrayed tradition as being fixed and unchanging. Imperial legal and administrative practices thus provoked endless public disputes about the substance and legitimacy of native tradition. Through this process of imperial disputation, modernity constructed native religious tradition as the hoary and ancient, but also debatable and unstable, inheritance of native cultures.

Metropolitan and cosmopolitan public cultures thus developed a distinctively modern discourse about native society, based on rhetorical and analytical oppositions between change and stability, reform and orthodoxy, Europe and Asia, and modernity and tradition. These oppositions became ingrained in intellectual life and in cultural politics, with many contradictory twists and turns. Traditionalists sought to protect what they claimed to be ancient rights. Modernists fought for what they imagined to be universal rights. Reformers worked to reinterpret and change tradition on what they saw as modern lines. Meanwhile, out in the local courts, district towns and villages, in the lower imperial ranks where most people lived, disputants fought for new rights and entitlements based on ancient tradition as their enemies used sacred texts to fight against innovations in law and social practice.

LANGUAGE AND CLASSIFICATION

Cosmopolitan activists who were literate in English turned their ideas of native society into a vision of the Indian nation as they spoke to one another and to imperial officials as leading native authorities. Three of their activities were most influential: (1) defining tradition, (2) reforming society, and (3) influencing government. All these activities required cultural authority. Old elites were most prominent early on, but as societies changed, authority shifted into various professional niches, particularly in higher education and legal chambers. All these activities were also contentious; they fostered debate and conflict that became more and more vocal and visible in civil society. All these activities preoccupied a wide variety of people inside and outside cosmopolitan settings. Many people engaged in all three. But they were distinctive and they became professional specializations. Broadly speaking, religious experts defined (and redefined) tradition, improving society fell to social reformers, and speaking for the nation became a job for politicians.

Cosmopolitan activities that built national identities always involved mediations between English and other languages. In 1833, English became pre-eminent. But scholars had to document and translate authentic native traditions by using non-English texts. Reformers needed to propagate their ideas in vernaculars, and also to influence government in English. The vast majority of people who wanted their voices heard in government did not know English and needed English interpreters and publicists. Mediators between English and other languages wrote, debated, and interpreted policy, law, tradition, and political programmes. They structured public debate as they constructed nationality within imperial modernity. The regionalism of all the vernaculars gave nationality many languages and many multilingual orientations. In the early days, the old imperial languages, Persian and Sanskrit, held special privilege; and this gave the old Indo-Persian elite special prominence in the formative phases of imperial legislation and Indian national identity.

The first generations of linguistic mediators lived in eighteenth-century Calcutta. Under Company authority, they developed a methodology for writing laws for British India by compiling authentic indigenous traditions from native texts in Sanskrit, Arabic, and Persian. To apply their methodology, which they called Orientalism, they needed classical-language expertise. To write native law, Orientalists and officials established that Hindus and Muslims formed separate legal communities with their own separate laws, cultures, and histories, documented in their separate classical languages. Defining legal canons on religious grounds suited British ideas about the fundamental separation of Christianity from Islam and Hinduism; it provided an imperial template for accommodating cultural difference.

Ideas from European legal history thus underpinned laws and policies which gave old texts and textual expertise a new modern authority. These ideas acquired lasting imperial authority, applied far and wide. In Ceylon, native Christians required special attention. In Nepal, Hindu law became state law with the *Mulk-i-Ain*, in 1854, using elements of law codes from British India to enforce the House of Gurkha's control over labour and taxes. In Kashmir, Raja Ranbir Singh enacted Brahmanical law codes called the *Ain-i-Dharmath* in a native state inhabited mostly by Muslims. In British India, Sanskrit *dharmasastra*s enabled officials to organize Hindu society around a permanent classification of social ranks according to *varna* and *jati*; this principle was applied legally and bureaucratically across British India to reinvent caste as a modern legal and administrative category.

These principles led census enumerators to count Jains, Sikhs, Parsis, Jews, Buddhists, and other religious groups as residual categories, though they counted as many non-Muslims and non-Christians as they could manage under the category of Hindus, assigning groups to caste (*jati*) or 'sub-caste' ranks inside the four *varna*s (Brahman, Kshatriya, Vaisya, and Sudra). Divisions between Hindu and Muslim were most scrupulously maintained in the official mind even after Orientalist methods for writing and interpreting law were abandoned, in the 1820s, in favour of legal methods that gave more weight to local precedent and universal principles of individual rights. The classification of people in society according to religion and caste organized imperial activity to the end of British rule and beyond. Hindu and Muslim personal law remained separate. Hindus and Muslims were treated as statistically separate native communities for many official purposes. After 1871, imperial census enumerators found that many people did not identify themselves as either Hindu or Muslim, but officials insisted that people be assigned to one of these two categories anyway.

Orientalist methods and the modern imperial definition of India as a majority Hindu culture gave British India a distinctly Brahmanical flavour and Sanskrit texts unprecedented authority. This trend had many antecedents and parallels. As we have seen,

Brahman authority had prevailed in Maratha imperial territory under the Peshwas. Religious codes became popular among many eighteenth-century rulers, notably in Hyderabad and Mysore and in the Portuguese and French Catholic colonies. In Portuguese Goa, the Inquisition was extremely harsh. Brahmans became arbiters of law and political power in nineteenth-century Nepal, despite the large population of Buddhists, and in mostly Muslim Kashmir.

After 1833, when English became the language of the empire, cosmopolitan bilingualism abandoned mediations between English and Persian, Arabic, and Sanskrit to focus on mediations between English and the regional languages: Tamil and Sinhala in Colombo, Bengali in Calcutta, Tamil and Telugu in Madras, Marathi and Gujarati in Bombay, Punjabi and Urdu in Punjab, and Hindustani across the Gangetic plains. This shift made language a political issue, because different literati specialized in different regional languages, and thus on different texts defining what native society should be. Schools and printing presses standardized the regional languages, which made them more distinct. In everyday speech, people typically combined elements from various languages, and in non-literate social life, language difference was not sharply marked. But in print, language difference becomes more visible, and when people become literate, script, grammar, and vocabulary separate the languages they learn to read. South Asian scripts are phonetic, so that almost any language can be written in almost any script. In modern printed texts, each language attained its own script. Script thus became an iconic representation of distinctive literate language communities, each with its own literary culture and tradition.

Modern print culture separated vernacular language communities, particularly in urban centres where literacy was most widespread, but also more generally for people who became literate during upward social mobility, which typically led from village to town to city. This separation of social identities along linguistic lines produced conflict over the representation of native society by people in linguistic communities that were coming into existence by diverging from one another.

Hindi and Urdu provide the most glaring case of language separation, with major implications for national identity and politics. These two languages composed one vernacular, called Hindustani, but were typically printed in different scripts: Devanagari and Nastaliq. With mass machine printing, Hindi and Urdu literary cultures generated groups of organized activists who used Hindi and Urdu to propagate different ideas about native society and to lobby for imperial recognition. They strove to separate the languages by using Sanskrit and Persian vocabularies and literary styles respectively. As a result, Hindi and Urdu became associated with Hindu and Muslim 'communities' that were also codified in law and in population statistics. Each population thus acquired popular publicists who composed public print cultures in two separate languages, mutually intelligible in speech, but illegible to one another in print.

POLITICAL INDIA IN CALCUTTA

Bengal Presidency was the original homeland of British India and by far its biggest nineteenth-century province. In 1900, it was more populous than the Austro-Hungarian Empire, Japan, the Ottoman Empire, and the Netherlands with all its colonies, including Indonesia. Bengal contained most of the British population and physical assets of British India until the 1860s, when roads, railways, irrigation, military installations, and other imperial investments up the Ganga basin shifted the empire's centre of gravity into the regions around Delhi. Even then, however, Bengal remained several times larger than other provinces until 1905, when the upheaval caused by its reduction became a watershed moment for the nation, as we will see.

Calcutta was the capital of Bengal and of British India. It stood well above all the other imperial cities, second only to London. When New Delhi became the Indian capital in 1911, Calcutta became merely one more provincial capital, and after 1947, its official hinterland shrank by more than half when East Bengal went to Pakistan, but in the nineteenth century, Calcutta's cosmopolitan stature was supreme.

Calcutta was British India's hometown. On the streets, people spoke Bengali, as did most people in the surrounding Bengal region. Its eighteenth-century elites were Indo-Persian literati, both Hindu and Muslim. As it became a sprawling imperial capital, its urban population came to include a larger proportion than any other imperial city of English-literate Indian professionals and office workers, many from upwardly mobile families arriving in droves over the decades from the countryside, including Zamindars and their employees. In 1911, Calcutta's English-literate population was half again as large as Delhi's and five times that of Madras and Bombay combined. Calcutta was the only regional city that spoke directly to London. Laws were made in Calcutta for all of British India. For the empire's metropolitan elite, Calcutta's English-literate

public activists represented Indian native society. Calcutta intellectuals thus attained a special native status to speak for, about, and
to India. They were mostly high-caste members of the Bengali
bhadralok ('respectable people'), a creative cosmopolitan construction of native society providing a multi-caste elite counterpoint to
imperial Brahmanism.

Indian native society first took intellectual shape in Calcutta in
the days of Ram Mohun Roy (1772–1833), who is often called the
father of modern India. Ram Mohun grew up in a stronghold of
Indo-Persian intellectualism which included, in his day, a number
of Englishmen, most prominently the great Orientalist William
Jones (1746–94). Jones learnt Latin, Greek, Hebrew, Arabic, and
Persian at Oxford. Called to the bar in 1774, and knighted in 1783,
he came to Calcutta as a Supreme Court judge. There, he studied
Sanskrit and, in 1784, founded the Asiatic Society. Jones pioneered
Orientalism by using classical learning, legal training, linguistic
skill, and the command of local experts to compile Hindu and
Muslim law codes. Another of Ram Mohun Roy's contemporaries,
Mirza Abu Taleb (1752–1806), was born in Lucknow to a family
from Isphahan, and also moved to Calcutta for government work,
but failing to find it, sailed to England with a Scottish friend. He
returned to publish an account of his travels that argued in classic
Persian style that Europe was steeped in materialism, whereas (religious) truth prevailed in India. He agreed with Ram Mohun Roy
and William Jones that Indian and European cultures rested on
distinctive, coherent traditions that could be reconciled by keeping
each in their proper place.

The idea that Indian tradition lay in sacred tenets guided Ram
Mohun's education. He was twenty-two when Jones arrived, and
thirty when Abu Taleb returned from London. At thirty-two, he
published his first book on the essence of monotheism. He wrote in
a Persian style that was indistinguishable to many at the time from
that of Shah Wali Allah (1702–63), a renowned Sufi scholar in
north India who strove to return Islam to Qur'anic essentials. Roy
undertook a similar task for Hinduism. In 1828, he formed the
Brahmo Samaj to promulgate a faithful interpretation of Vedic
truth, congregational worship, and rational discussion. His Vedic
purism rejected idol worship and caste, which are not described in
the Vedas. His religious mission included reforming Brahman social
practices such as child marriage and the prohibition of widow
remarriage. His cultural innovations were designed to make
Brahman ideas more relevant for urbane Bengalis who worked

alongside Europeans in Calcutta to form the beginnings of what would become known as India's modern urban middle class.

In the 1820s, in Ram Mohun Roy's later life, as British national power expanded, imperialists became more nationally self-conscious and aggressive. English missionaries attacked Hinduism, Utilitarians denounced Orientalism, Company taxation broke prominent Zamindars, British tariffs ruined Bengali weavers, and British businessmen excluded Calcutta's merchants from the export trade. Aggressive English ethnic chauvinism fostered a new brand of cosmopolitan society where natives stood squarely on the underside of the racial divide. The separation of Indian and English cultures became more stark. One of the merchants who declined as a result was Ram Mohun's friend, Dwarkanath Tagore, a prominent Zamindar and businessman. Dwarkanath's son, Debendranath (1817–1905) succeeded Roy as leader of the Brahmo Samaj, repudiated the Vedas, and declared reason and intuition to be the basis of true Brahmanism. Keshab Chunder Sen (1838–84) then opened a new branch of the Samaj that sponsored temperance, encouraged the education of women, and campaigned for widow remarriage and laws to prevent child marriage. When Keshab Sen arranged for his young daughter to marry a child prince of Cooch Behar, another new branch of the Samaj formed, in 1878, and embraced Upanishadic mysticism.

Over the years, social reform faded in the Brahmo agenda amid a rising *bhadralok* sense of separation and opposition between Indian and English culture. In this context, Calcutta's growing middle class employed in offices, schools, businesses, professions, and government service flocked to hear a young charismatic preacher, Sri Ramakrishna (1836–86), who led a spiritual revival. Born Gadadhar Chattopadhyaya, Ramakrishna was a poor Brahman with little formal schooling. He spoke only Bengali and knew neither English nor Sanskrit. A talented mystic, he had visions of Muhammad, Jesus, and Krishna. He preached that all religions are one. His large audiences included flocks of Europeans for whom he represented a distinctively Indian spirituality. He never published. He foreshadowed Mohandas Karamchand Gandhi (1869–1948) – India's national *mahatma* (great soul) – in seeing God everywhere. He proclaimed that all religions are different *ghat*s (steps) leading to the same water. 'Hindus call the water *jal*,' he said, 'while Muslims call it *pani* and Christians call it water; but it is all the same substance, no essential difference.' Ramakrishna inspired middle-class individuals who sought to encompass the manifold diversity of their cultural environment, transcending the West's materialism and Christianity, also incorporating Islam into a larger cultural essence in the idiom of the Upanishads.

In Ramakrishna's lifetime, however, *jal* and *pani* were becoming linguistic markers for diverging cultural identities among activist Bengali Hindus and Muslims. Ideas hardened about the separation of religious groups. Decades before Gandhi, Ramakrishna declared that India's essence is the mystical transcendence of all religious difference, while other activists turned religious opposition into a defining feature of Indian society.

Divergence became notable after the 1857 rebellion had raised and crushed the last vestige of Mughal authority. Defensive efforts ensued to revive Muslim culture in India. In 1868, Muhammad 'Abid Husayn founded the Deoband school, to inculcate ideas of Shah Wali Allah and create a modern Indian brand of Islamic puritanism. In 1875, Syed Ahmad Khan founded the Muhammadan Anglo-Oriental College at Aligarh, to foster Western learning among the Muslim intelligentsia. In his long illustrious career, which earned him a knighthood, Sir Syed Ahmad Khan underlined the division of Indian native society into 'two prominent nations, which are distinguished by the names of Hindus and Mussulmans'. He explained that, 'Just as a man has some principal organs, similarly these two nations are like the principal limbs of India'. At the same time, Mīrzā Ghulām Aḥmad travelled from Afghanistan across India engaging in religious debates to revive Islam, founding the Ahmadiyya movement in 1885, as Sikh and British armies conquered Afghanistan and triggered declarations that *jihad* (spiritual struggle) included war against non-believers. These religious pronouncements led Muslim intellectuals and scholars (*ulema*) in India, including Mīrzā Ghulām Aḥmad, to repudiate *jihad* and declare loyalty to British India. Meanwhile, in Punjab, Swami Dayanand Sarasvati founded the aggressively anti-Muslim, anti-Christian Arya Samaj, propagating a *suddhi* ritual of reconversion to Hinduism. In Kashmir, Raja Ranbir Singh enacted the *Ain-i-Dharmath*. Like the Ranas of Nepal, Brahmans in Pune promulgated a new Hindu orthodoxy, harking back to the Peshwas, to counter challenges to Brahmanism by Jotirao Phule (1827–90), whose searing critique, *Priestcraft Exposed*, appeared in 1869. The aggressive reaffirmation of traditional Hindu authority thus targeted perceived threats from Muslims and low-caste Hindus as well.

A new generation of Orientalists, led by Max Mueller, contributed with scholarly work to document the grandeur of the

Hindu 'golden age', and in 1870, H. H. Cole, Superintendent of Archaeology, announced that his department would seek to rediscover India 'before the Mohamedan invasions'. In 1871, when the first all-India census revealed the vast Muslim majority living in eastern Bengal, the Viceroy, Lord Mayo, commissioned a Bengal official, W. W. Hunter, to provide a scholarly answer to this pointed question, based on recent imperial experience in Afghanistan: 'Are Indian Musalmans bound in conscience to rebel against the Queen?' Mayo took this to be 'the burning question of the day'. Hunter's answer – published in London, in 1872, under the title *The Indian Musalmans*, which is still in print and still relevant – was a resounding 'no'. He quotes religious opinions (*fatwa*s) to make his case, including this one by esteemed scholars (Maulvis) in Delhi, dated 17 July 1870, concerning the lawfulness of *jihad* in British India:

> The Musalmans here are protected by Christians, and there is no Jihad in a country where protection is afforded, as the absence of protection and liberty between Musalmans and Infidels is essential in a religious war, and that condition does not exist here. Besides, it is necessary that there should be a probability of victory to Musalmans and glory to the Indians. If there be no such probability, the Jihad is unlawful.

However, Hunter also argued strongly that the government needed to court Muslim support, because most Muslims were poor, uneducated, deprived, defensive, and susceptible to calls to their faith.

The first Bengali novelist, Bankim Chandra Chatterjee (1838–94) deepened and complicated the *bhadralok* Bengali Indian Hindu identity that was emerging in Ramakrishna's Calcutta. Raised in an orthodox Brahman family, educated in English at Presidency College, Bankim Chandra was one of the first graduates of the University of Calcutta. He served the government as a deputy magistrate from 1858 until 1891. His novels are historical fictions. The first, *Durgesh Nandini*, featured a Rajput hero and a Bengali heroine; and Debendranath Tagore recalled that it took 'the Bengali heart by storm'. *Kapalkundala* (1866) described gruesome village Tantric rituals to reinforce the same cultural separation of urbane *bhadralok* Hindu spirituality from the rustic low-caste cults that we see in the Brahmo Samaj and Sri Ramakrishna. *Mrnalini* (1869) depicted a Muslim invasion of Bengal. *Rajsimha* (1881) had Rajput heroes fighting Muslim oppressors. *Anandamath* (1882) showed Hindu ascetics (*sannyasis*) fighting Muslim armies. *Sitaram* (1886) described Hindu struggles against Muslim tyranny.

Bankim Chandra's historical fiction became prophetic. The song 'Bande Mataram' ('Hail to the Mother') – taken from *Anandamath* – became a nationalist hymn in 1905 and inspired national activists with religious fervour. In the 1920s, the anti-Muslim implications of the same song became the focal point for Hindu nationalists who rallied around the Rastriya Sevak Sangh (RSS), founded in 1925, whose members still sing it as their anthem today. Looking back from the vantage point of 1926, one leading Bengali national politician, Bipin Chandra Pal, said that the image of a woman in *pardah* killing a Muslim warrior (in the novel *Durgesh Nandini*) raised the 'larger national or racial issue [of] the contest for supremacy over the Hindu populations of West Bengal between their own king and the Moslem invader'.

If Ram Mohun Roy could have toured Calcutta in 1890, he would have seen a city transformed. The capital of the British Indian Empire then bustled with a literate middle class that thrived on print media. In its English and Bengali books, tracts, magazines, and newspapers, he might have discerned three new kinds of social sentiment that were defining what it meant to be Indian in Calcutta. These were all components of emerging Indian nationality: we can usefully call them religious, linguistic, and political.

He might have been proud – though a little surprised – to see Calcutta's modern style of Hindu religiosity. Like his own, it was not the old-fashioned rustic temple-based mass devotional ritualism, but rather a modern urbane individualist, intellectual, and often reformist spirituality; but unlike his, it was now more mystical and sought a broadly popular following. Like his own, it claimed to represent Indian culture as a whole, excluding Islam. It was self-consciously more advanced and also more purely Hindu than old-fashioned village religion, both modern and true to ancient principles, though its ancient reference point had shifted from the Vedas to the Upanishads.

Swami Vivekananda (1863–1902) had exclaimed this modern Hindu religion to the world. Born Narendranath Datta into a wealthy Kayastha family, and educated in English, he joined the Brahmo Samaj and later became Ramakrishna's leading disciple. In 1893, he represented Hinduism at the Parliament of Religions in Chicago, where one journalist called him 'an orator by divine right and undoubtedly the greatest figure at the Parliament'. In 1897, after a long lecture tour, Vivekananda returned to Calcutta with Western disciples to found the Ramakrishna Mission.

Ram Mohun would have marvelled at the prominence of the Bengali media. Its concern with Bengali regional issues would have been novel for him, and the stature of authors writing in Bengali would have been astounding. The rise of a literate middle class in Bengal represented new modern trends which accelerated with immigration into the city from the upper ranks of rural society. Among writers such as Bankim Chandra, he might have detected a creeping cultural opposition between Hindus and Muslims that paralleled divisions he could have found on many Zamindari estates, where owners and managers were mostly high-caste Hindus and tenants were often low-caste Hindus and Muslims, particularly in the eastern districts. Among the literate classes, however, he would have seen growing pride in Bengali literature, heritage, and culture, crossing religious and caste lines, with high-caste Hindus like Bankim Chandra as leading lights.

He would certainly have been impressed by the small but publicly prominent meeting of the Indian National Congress that occurred in Calcutta in 1896, where Bengali delegates numbered 605 out of 784 delegates overall. This was the twelfth annual meeting of an organization that represented a totally new kind of national sentiment and activity, unimaginable in Ram Mohun's day. The Congress first met in Bombay in 1885, and then met every year in late December in a different city of British India. Delegates came at their own expense to these meetings from all the provinces, to discuss government policy and issue public statements that received wide press coverage. Delegates eschewed topics of religion and social reform, which divided them, and concentrated on political issues concerning government policy on which they agreed as prominent urbane leaders in all the regions. They first came together after famines in the 1870s provoked the imperial Famine Commission to call for more state investments in irrigation to prevent future famines. One major inspiration came in 1879, when Dadabhai Naoroji (1825–1917), a brilliant economist from Bombay, who spent most of his life in England, published his influential *The Poverty of India*, documenting the negative economic impact on India of imperial policies that served to enrich Britain. Naoroji presided over Congress meetings in 1886, 1893, and 1906.

The immediate provocation for the first Congress meeting was public outcry over the Ilbert Bill in 1884. The proposed legislation empowered Indian judges to try Englishmen in court; this met with vocal resistance from British residents in India who heaped racist insults on Indian judges and lawyers in the press. By that time, everyday expressions of white supremacy were standard features of imperial society, visible in rules for Indian Civil Service (ICS) exams and quotas, in clubs and railway carriages 'for whites only', and in countless petty indignities that stung cosmopolitan Indians. Congress came together as a forum to express Indian support for the Ilbert Bill against vehement opposition that inscribed an existing division in cosmopolitan society with new public media visibility. In addition, Congress sought more Indian membership in the ICS at higher ranks. Its annual meetings also argued for reduced land taxes and increased state funding for Indian economic development. Early Congress meetings brought together many Brahmans and lawyers, who each comprised about forty percent of all delegates before 1911.

Major Congress leaders came from Calcutta. Two of the most important were Romesh Chandra Dutt (1848–1909) and Surendranath Banerjea (1848–1925), who travelled together to London as young men to take the ICS exam. R. C. Dutt's father worked as a government surveyor, and he himself rose as high in the ICS as Indians could do in his lifetime to become a divisional commissioner in Orissa. He published the first academic study of peasant poverty in Bengal (1874); one of the first modern textbooks on ancient Indian history (1896), which echoed Max Mueller's account of the Hindu 'golden age'; and the first Indian history of British India (1908), which followed Naoroji's account of the negative impact of imperial policy on Indian industry and agriculture: all were written in English. S. N. Banerjea came from a distinguished Brahman family and served briefly in the ICS in Sylhet before undertaking a long career in education, journalism, and politics. He founded Ripon College in Calcutta, and in 1876 he helped to found the Indian Association, an early Bengali nationalist venture and precursor of the Congress. His newspaper, the *Bengalee*, became a leading nationalist organ. He was twice elected Congress President.

SHAKING THE EMPIRE

Events in Calcutta in 1905 changed imperial society for ever. They produced a new kind of Indian politics that Congress delegates could not have imagined at their small, sedate meeting in Calcutta nine years before. Like the formation of the Congress itself, the new politics expressed public controversy over imperial policy. But now the drama moved into the streets and sometimes became violent.

Calcutta was ground zero and centre stage for this radical innova-tion. India's first national agitation spread out from Calcutta to other Indian cities and even to small towns and villages, mostly in Bengal. The new public agitation combined all three kinds of national sentiment – religious, linguistic, and political – that by the 1890s were prominent among the urban middle classes in Calcutta. The outburst occurred when the Viceroy, Lord Curzon, proposed to reorganize the eastern provinces of British India to unite eastern Bengal with Assam, hence dividing East and West Bengal Presidency in what became known immediately as 'the partition of Bengal'. Curzon then publicly insulted Congress critics of the partition plan, calling them 'effete Bengali Babus'. Events that followed more than proved him wrong.

In 1905, Bengal Presidency included Bihar and Orissa (since 1765) and Assam (since 1865). British administrators had argued for some decades that it was too large to manage effectively and its vast size caused poor regions in the east to be neglected. Curzon designed a plan to redraw the provincial boundaries, separating Orissa and Bihar and uniting Assam with fifteen Muslim-majority districts in eastern Bengal. The new Province of Eastern Bengal and Assam would have thirty-one million people, mostly Muslims, with its capital at Dhaka. When Curzon rejected Congress petitions against the partition of Bengal, public mobilization began. An out-burst of agitation ensued that expressed pent-up hostility against the British ruling elites.

Public meetings, marches, speeches, singing, posters, and pam-phleteering against state policy were not themselves new. Even street violence and state repression had many precedents in British India. Skirmishes between urban protesters and armed police had a long history arising from battles among groups over public space owned by the state but lived in by increasingly diverse popula-tions. In the 1890s, the city streets had seen demonstrations around Congress meetings organized by a younger generation of Congressmen who mobilized support for their leadership with popular festivals and marches. In Maharashtra, Bal Gangadhar Tilak had revitalized an old festival to the god Ganesh and invented a new festival to celebrate the Maratha hero, Shivaji. His political promotion of explicitly Hindu political identity occurred at the same time as anti-Muslim riots erupted in cities in the United Provinces (Uttar Pradesh), as a result of agitations against cow killing. These agitations in Bombay and in Uttar Pradesh were dis-tinctly regional in their tone and scope; and the 1905 agitation against the Bengal partition also had regional origins. Anti-partition agitations mobilized a pre-existing public in Bengali sentiments around an issue that primarily riled people in Calcutta.

But the 1905 agitation against partition in Calcutta spread more widely than any before because Calcutta's stature as the imperial capital and as India's national city made Calcutta's public anger an expression of Indian national outrage. Calcutta's local Indian identities became national as agitation expressed Indian opposition to British domination. Opponents of partition argued that partitioning Bengal hacked apart a Bengali nation that symbolized India. The rallying cry and popular song 'Bande Mataram' hailed a mother goddess who stood for the motherland and was identified with India, Bengal, and the mother goddess Kali. Kali devotion thus acquired a new political meaning. Now the goddess became Bengal and a victim of British atrocities. Bengal became a homeland of Indian tradition, ripped apart by cruel foreigners. Religious fervour combined with political protest in the bombing of government buildings and the assassination of British officers by inspired young patriots.

The movement's missionaries travelled to agitate in many cities and in rural Bengal. Aurobindo Ghosh (1872–1950) inspired youth to mystical revolution. He had studied at Cambridge and returned to official work in Baroda and Calcutta before turning to the study of yoga and Sanskrit. In 1905, his advocacy of terrorism landed him in prison; then he fled to safety in the French colony of Pondicherry, where he spent the rest of his long life teaching philosophy and making his spiritual commune (*ashram*) an international cultural centre. By 1918, his national ideas were serialized in 'A Defence of Indian Culture', published in the journal *Arya*, where he said, 'It is only if we have a just and right appreciation of . . . Indian religion that we can come to a true understanding of the sense and spirit of Indian culture'.

The 1905 movement also popularized economic nationalism, based on the writings of Dadabhai Naoroji and R. C. Dutt. Its radically new Swadeshi movement promoted indigenous (*swadeshi*) products and the boycott of foreign goods. Bonfires of British cloth became festival occasions for chanting anti-British slogans, expressing patriotism, and demonstrating local support for Congress.

Unable to stop the movement, the government agreed to rescind the partition, which it finally did in 1911. Assam became a separate administrative territory, as did Bihar and Orissa. Bengali-speaking districts were reunited. At the same time, the capital of British India was moved to New Delhi. This move was clearly intended to give the empire a firmer political foundation in its capital city. The government also enacted constitutional reforms that demonstrated beyond all denying that Indian national politics were now a potent force. This official recognition was a new departure. Curzon's style of autocratic arrogance became archaic. The Morley-Minto constitutional reforms established provincial electorates and assemblies with limited powers, convened in 1911, providing a template for future reforms to increase future Indian imperial participation.

ACTIVISM AND IDENTITY

The year 1905 was a watershed. When the upheaval ended, official representatives of native society sat in the halls of government. The public expression of collective identity in civil society had become part of imperial politics. This original opening of the modern state to the influence of popular pressure pushed not only towards widening the scope of representative democracy, but also towards the political redefinition of social identities by their public mobilization. Political activism expanded the embrace of national identity.

We have already seen how social entities were well entrenched in eighteenth-century regions, and how medieval identities entered modernity as a new empire gave old groups new status. Rustic patriarchs became modern private-property owners who anchored the evolution of agrarian social identities that we will consider in more detail below. We have also seen, above, that modern empire produced new kinds of official collective identities by defining religious communities, castes, and tribes in native society. Before 1905, government used official identities only as legal categories and treated all subjects as exemplars, experts, petitioners, and pleaders. Many subjects had pleaded for official identity groups before 1905. In eighteenth-century Madras city, leaders of caste groups allied under the label of Left and Right castes had pleaded with the Company to recognize their rights to conduct public festivals in the city. Violence between them posed an official problem. Law and order always dominated the government's handling of such cases; and in this respect, the English government merely modernized Akbar's strategy of ethnic divide and rule by balancing demands from competing groups on the scale of state supremacy. Thus in the 1890s, when riots broke out between caste groups in southern Madras over the exclusion of wealthy but low-caste Nadars from temples controlled by locally dominant Maravas; and when riots broke out between Hindu and Muslim groups in Gangetic cities over their respective rights to conduct public festivities; the government cracked down using police force to quell disturbances, and then endeavoured to balance the respective rights of the official identity groups.

Official collective identities became a legal meeting ground for petitioners, judges, bureaucrats, and legislators; and thus part of social identity in imperial society. Expanding imperial bureaucracy gave more people a stake in the definition of their official identity. Nadars and many other upwardly mobile caste groups petitioned government to have their improved caste rank authorized by official classifications, including aspiring peasants in north India who sought to be listed as Kshatriyas. Tenants petitioned for the status of secure tenure holders. As upwardly mobile groups strove to improve their official identity, established groups sought benefits and protection from the government. State officials strove to balance their distribution of rewards to various officially recognized groups to maintain the state's supreme position as the arbiter of social status.

Until 1905, the government viewed the Indian National Congress as merely one of many petitioning groups in civil society that organized in its case to influence government in favour of elite businessmen, landowners, and professionals. Lord Curzon often said that Congress spoke for 'special interests', while his government represented 'the Indian people'. In 1899, during the famines and plagues that killed countless poor people, Curzon attacked nationalist critics by saying that he did immeasurably more than nationalists to help the poor. He tossed off critics of his 1905 partition plan in the same way. But the prospect of partitioning Bengal aroused more public fervour in and around Calcutta than his Victorian imperial mind could imagine.

The 1905 agitations expressed public identities in civil society with more political vigour than ever before; and their mounting force, despite heavy police repression, compelled the government to acknowledge that times had changed. The bombing of government buildings and assassination of British officers (which coincided with the outbreak of revolution in Russia) helped to convince metropolitan authorities that coercive force was not sufficient to restore law and order in British India. Force needed to be supplemented with institutional change. The plan then emerged to bring official Indian representatives into the halls of imperial power on metropolitan terms. People who officially represented native society would be granted official authority.

The new legislative bodies convened under the Morley-Minto reforms represented official identities in native society, including Hindus and Muslims. This method of representing official constituent identity groups was called 'communal representation'. Congress opposed it and spoke in the name of a united Indian society. The government's determination to divide communities was likened to the partition of Bengal, which itself was decried as British 'divide and rule'. But at the same time, other groups also spoke publicly in the name of native society as it was defined through social, public, and official identity groups, called 'communities'. Native society included countless social identities that were not represented officially, but social identity in general was increasingly influenced by official categories, as they became public identities in the media, in popular mobilization, and in electoral activity.

A cultural shift thus occurred towards the formation of social identities shaped by the force of official categories used by government in its legal, administrative, and electoral operations, combined with that of public categories used in mobilizing support for political causes and in discussing issues in civil society. This shift began in earnest in 1905, when Indian politicians still relied on old tools of petitioning and pleading, but now, in addition, groups mobilized public agitation to demonstrate that they, not the British, represented native society, pushing for official recognition of public identities.

The 1905 agitation generated public identities that influenced social identities first of all in Calcutta, then in other big cities, and to a lesser extent in smaller cities and some parts of rural Bengal. Spreading agitation demonstrated the expanding geographical scope of public activism; it diversified the number and variety of groups involved in politics to include a wider range of people; and it put Congress nationalism into the imperial spotlight. The idea spread that Congress represented all of native society.

The events of 1905 spread national ideas well beyond official and elite circles. Agitation was a formative experience for students and teachers who gave nationalism new populist, idealist, progressive, even revolutionary meanings. News, debates, and lore from 1905 entered public culture in most major urban centres. Police repression produced Indian martyrs, and British demons were portrayed in stories, songs, poems, cartoons, editorials, and public oratory, where Victorian racism merged with British brutality to oppose valiant Indian national aspirations. Nationalism became a political movement, which, though small compared to the vast population of imperial society, moved decisively beyond cosmopolitan petitioning. It even attracted attention overseas. Several million Indians had settled abroad, and some became involved in the movement. In faraway California, activists among Punjabi Sikh farmers launched newspapers and raised funds to support the Indian cause.

1905 also produced a schism in the Congress between Extremists, who promoted public agitation, and Moderates, who opposed it. These factions did not reconcile and join forces until 1916. The activist wildfire of 1905 indicated that Moderates were right to believe that political leaders, however astute and influential, could not control a popular movement that was filled with energetic young people flying unpredictably in many directions. The aftermath of 1905 also showed that Extremists were right to believe that public protest brought pressure on government that legal action could not. Both beliefs remained part of the new political environment that emerged in 1911 when Indian lawyers, educators, and other professionals became a national political force.

The new generation of Indian politicians that emerged to carry the movement forward came primarily from Bengal, Punjab, and Maharashtra. In 1902, one major leader, Gopal Krishna Gokhale (1866–1915) left his chair in history and political economy at Fergusson College, Pune, to enter politics full-time. In 1905 he led the Moderates as Congress President, and like most Moderates, he advocated social reform measures that were lost in the Extremist agenda. He founded the Servants of India Society, whose members took vows of poverty and of service to the poor, especially the poorest 'untouchable' *jati*s in Hindu society, who were excluded from imperial society and national politics. Also from Maharashtra, Bal Gangadhar Tilak (1856–1920) led the Extremists. A Brahman lawyer and teacher, Tilak founded the Deccan Education Society (1884); ran two nationalist newspapers, *Kesari* ('The Lion') in Marathi, and *The Mahratta*, in English; made Ganesh and Shivaji festivals venues for popular politics; and opposed social reform as a distraction from national goals. His ally, Lala Lajpat Rai (1865–1928), also a lawyer, was from Lahore in Punjab. Lajpat Rai followed Dayananda Sarasvati, who was the founder of the Arya Samaj and of Cow Protection Societies that treated Muslims as Hindu adversaries. Lajpat Rai established the Dayananda Anglo-Vedic School and his 1905 radicalism got him deported to Mandalay, without trial, in 1907. On his return, his campaign to become Congress President provoked the split between Moderates and Extremists.

TABLE 5. WATERSHED YEARS: 1905 TO 1918

1905	Partition of Bengal. Anti-partition agitation. Swadeshi movement.
1906	All-India Muslim League founded at Dhaka.
1907	Surat Congress. Moderate–Extremist clash. Tata Iron and Steel Company founded.
1909	Morley-Minto reforms. V. D. Savarkar, *The Indian War of Independence.* M. K. Gandhi, *Hind Swaraj* in Gujarati (English, 1910). Punjab Hindu Sabha.
1911	Delhi *darbar*: Bengal partition revoked. Delhi made capital of British India.
1913	Nobel Prize for Rabindranath Tagore. Annie Besant publishes *Wake Up India.*
1914	Mohandas Gandhi returns from South Africa. World War I, Indian troops overseas.
1916	Lord Chelmsford Viceroy to 1921. Lala Lajpat Rai publishes *Young India.* Lucknow Pact between All-India Muslim League and Indian National Congress.
1917	Tamil non-Brahman movement launched with publication of *The Dravidian.*
1918	*Ghadr* movement. Besant and Tilak Home Rule League.

Though Congress's nationalism spoke for everyone in native society, its public agitation also invoked and provoked other official and unofficial social identities. As we have seen, Curzon lit the 1905 wildfire by torching high-caste *bhadralok* Hindu Congress leaders in Calcutta who spoke to and for the cosmopolitan English-literate youth whose professional prospects would be curtailed by partitioning Bengal. Calcutta's English-educated youth, who had come from villages and towns in Bengal, went home to spread the wildfire in the countryside. The popular appeal of Hindu devotionalism fanned the flames. Cosmopolitan literati invoked the passion of religious devotees who had been excluded from the temple of patriotic love by tyrants who abused their goddess. Their vernacular verse spoke the many languages of the Indian nation.

As the movement spread, it took more distinctly regional forms. In Madras, for example, Aurobindo Ghosh inspired the Brahman poet Subrahmanya Bharathiyar (1882–1921), who had made his living as a translator, became a mystic, made a pilgrimage to Benares, and in 1906 declared that he would never again write in English. Bharathiyar sang his Tamil songs to open public meetings praising Kali and 'the mother (goddess)' with 'Bande Mataram'. He popularized Swadeshi with a song praising Chidambaran Pillai, who founded the short-lived Swadeshi Steamship Company in Madras and became a national hero in Bharathiyar's verse. The Tamil language then became an icon of native identity, like Bengali; but at the same time, in Madras, a regional non-Brahman movement evolved which identified Brahmans and Sanskrit alike as foreign elements in southern India. When the periodical *The Dravidian* appeared in 1917, it announced a new public identity based on traditions among people who spoke Dravidian languages (Tamil, Telugu, Kannada, and Malayalam), which, unlike Hindi and Bengali, did not derive from Sanskrit. It also echoed Phule's legacy in Maharashtra by speaking for the ninety-five percent of Indians who were not Brahman.

Another variegated regional formation of national politics emerged from 1905 in eastern Bengal, where Muslim leaders with various social identities – from differing regions, ethnic groups, and sects – came together to reinvent an old official identity as a new public identity, meeting in Dhaka in 1906 to form the All-India Muslim League. The League supported Curzon's partition in the belief that it would benefit Muslims. At the same time, Zamindari tenant politics had generated a public identity that crossed official community boundaries in eastern Bengal, as expressed in a low-caste Namasudra petition from Bakarganj, in 1906, which sided with Muslims who supported the Province of East Bengal and Assam, saying, '. . . Namasudras and Mohamedans are the predominating communities of Eastern Bengal, and the latter unlike the Hindus possess a good deal of sympathy for the Namasudras'.

By 1905, communal issues had begun to inflect political community more generally. For several decades, Cow Protection Societies had mobilized public support for the government prohibition of beef butchers, almost all Muslim. In the 1890s, violence ensued in cities across the Ganga basin when militant Hindus attacked Muslims who sacrificed cows on important ritual occasions. Hindu militants also took umbrage at Muslim population numbers in the census, and the Arya Samaj organized reconversion campaigns to 'bring Hindus back' to the fold. During the 1905 agitation, B. G. Tilak and Lala Lajpat Rai rose to the Congress leadership and Congress rallied support around devotion to Kali, singing the 'Bande Mataram' anthem.

Religious classifications, populations, and conversions became more problematic when government proposed to calculate 'communal representation' according to census statistics. In 1906, it was also not lost on the Aga Khan (leader of Ismaili Muslims) or on the Nawab of Dhaka (a major Zamindar), who sponsored and hosted the League's first meeting in that city, that the proposed creation of an East Bengal district would directly benefit aspiring Muslims in Bengal and Assam by creating more jobs and electoral opportunities for Muslims. It also seemed to Muslim leaders that Congress opposition derived from the partition's negative implications for high-caste Hindus. Even so, Muslim leaders were not of one mind. Mohammad Ali Jinnah (1876–1948), who became the League's most important leader, did not join until 1913. Until then, he, like many other Muslims, believed that Congress represented Muslim interests. Jinnah was already a prominent lawyer, educated at an Islamic school (*madrassah*) in Sind. He had followed Moderates in Congress and recognized Gokhale as his political guru. His opposition to the 1905 agitation followed the Moderate line.

In the decade of World War I, Indian politics entered a phase of institution building. Congress agreed to support the British war effort in return for British promises to expand Indian control in government after the war. Politicians joined and formed organizations that represented the national movement, and at the same time participated in imperial governance. Jinnah, for example, was elected to the Imperial Legislative Council under the 1909 Morley-Minto reforms; and in 1915, he also joined the Bombay branch of the Indian Home Rule League, which Tilak founded on the model of the Irish Home Rule League; and in that context, in 1916, Jinnah signed the Lucknow Pact which brought Moderates, Extremists, and the Muslim League together in the national cause.

The unification of disparate political identities that were being shaped by public activism now preoccupied national leaders. Calcutta remained a heartland of national sentiment, even as disparate groups in Pune, Bombay, Ahmedabad, Delhi, Lahore,

Lucknow, Allahabad, Madras, and other cities entered national politics. In 1913, Debendranath Tagore's son, Rabindranath (1861–1941), won the Nobel Prize for literature for his *Gitanjali* (1912) – his own English renderings of his Bengali devotional poems – with support from W. B. Yeats and André Gide. Educated in England, Tagore had spent the 1890s in eastern Bengal, managing his family's Zamindar land; and in 1919, he wrote a story that looked back on 1905 with the insight of the next decade.

The story, *Ghore Bhaire* (translated as 'Home and the World') – later made into a film by Calcutta's own Satyajit Ray (1921–92) – reinterpreted 1905 as a trial for the country with lessons for later generations. The story concerns the family of a young Zamindar in eastern Bengal. His old mansion was designed to provide for the seclusion of women in *pardah*, but he had undertaken his own version of domestic social reform by making his wife learn English literature, music, and dance, so that she could become a modern woman. He had also tried his hand at Swadeshi industry with a failed soap-making enterprise. One day, all of a sudden, the young Zamindar's college chum arrives from Calcutta, fired with 1905 enthusiasm. A subtle romance ensues between wife and friend, suggesting that modern women face peril when freed from family discipline, and also indicating that well-meaning social reform can spoil domestic harmony. Tragedy strikes when the Zamindar's friend agitates for a Swadeshi boycott of foreign goods in the local market, provoking local activists to attack Muslim shops. Riots break out and the young patriarch dies trying to bring peace to his Zamindari estate.

The story was intended as a national allegory. The British are missing from the stage. The Indian nation is, in effect, on its own, looking out for itself. Moderates and Extremists have disappeared. The new dilemma is to find common cause among forces pulling the nation in various directions. With this goal in view, Mohandas Karamchand Gandhi (1869–1948) had written *Hind Swaraj* in Gujarati in 1909 (and in English in 1910), but at the same time, V. D. Savarkar's *Indian War of Independence* had projected a more militant Hindu view of nationalism than was followed by the Punjab Hindu Sabha, also founded in 1909. When Gandhi returned to India from South Africa in 1915, Home Rule Leagues were forming in major cities to propagate Indian national culture and independence. Calcutta's premier unifying politician of the day, Chitta Ranjan Das (1870–1925) tackled the dilemma of uniting the nation with vigorous pragmatism. As a lawyer, he defended people accused of political crimes during the 1905 crackdown and he opposed continued British rule. He rejected the idea that India must develop along Western lines, and he advocated a vision of Indian uniqueness based on its distinctive, all-inclusive national culture. Tagore's allegory haunted the end of his life: in the year after his death, in 1941, Hindu–Muslim riots broke out in Calcutta that irreversibly alienated politicians in eastern Bengal from the Indian National Congress.

National Territory

By the early twentieth century, nationalism had become an important feature of modern world history. As the century progressed, nationality and nationhood became ubiquitous, in various changing forms, all around the world. In Africa and Asia, nationalism among peoples living under European imperial authority became increasingly political as nationalists mobilized public support for the epochal project of dismantling empires to create sovereign national states.

Until 1919, national politics in South Asia had been contained within the legal framework of the British Empire. World War I unravelled that framework; it also ended British imperial expansion when the empire embraced a quarter of the world's population in Africa, Australia, Canada, the Middle East, and South and South-East Asia. A new world order began to emerge, as imperial nations met in Versailles to refashion the world of competing empires as a manageable international order. Needless to say, they did not succeed: imperial competition continued for another quarter-century and produced another world war; officially, sovereign national states would not cover the world until the 1970s. National states did emerge, however, during this long transition in the mid-century world of staggering empires. The creation of new nations shaped social identities everywhere.

In 1920, British India acquired fiscal autonomy; the governments of India and Ceylon came to include elected native representatives wielding authority over state budgets; and British India became a founding member of the League of Nations. In that context, nationalists burst forth onto the stage of official imperial politics. In India, they demanded full self-government, and their movement expanded rapidly to include larger, more diverse populations, generating mass support for nationalism as well as for competing visions of what constituted the nation and what independence should mean. Over the next two decades, the Great Depression and World War II accompanied nationalist upheavals that effectively killed the possibility that old-fashioned empires could be sustained. After 1945, new nations threw the old empires into history's dustbin as peoples across Asia, Africa, and the Middle East acquired official national identities and legal authority in a world covered entirely with national states. In that new world, old empires fell apart and imperial pretensions crumbled: Britain even had to suffer defeats in test cricket by teams from the West Indies, Pakistan, India, Sri Lanka, and Australia. Metropolitan imperialists might be able to interpret this new world as the crowning glory of imperial modernization, but for nationalists in South Asia and elsewhere, lowering the Union Jack and raising the national flag signalled a final, hard-won victory over imperialism after long, bitter struggles for independence.

In South Asia, national identities changed during these long struggles, as nationalism expanded its reach to embrace populations larger and more diverse than all of Europe and Russia combined. Before 1920, national movements fought for official recognition; national identity remained a feature of specialized public activism. After 1920, nationalism became a mass movement, filled with diverse social identities expressed in countless media, of agitation, elections, legislation, and institutions. In the 1930s, a major expansion of nationalist activity occurred during the upheavals of the Great Depression, when some specific social identities became official political identities, with constitutional authorization; the conflicts that emerged would have enduring influence on national identities. In the 1940s, more upheaval brought empire to an end; it also brought dramatic political divisions and produced the partition of India and Pakistan, which then sparked the separation of Bangladesh from Pakistan.

This chapter considers the production of eight national states – Afghanistan, Bangladesh, Bhutan, India, the Maldives, Nepal, Pakistan, and Sri Lanka – from the early days of national politics through the consolidation of national state territories in the decades after 1950. People in these countries had lived for many centuries in overlapping spaces, which the national states cut into radically novel, rigidly bounded territories. All these new nations emerged in relation to imperial Britain, and historians typically use political histories in the biggest British-ruled territories – India and Ceylon – to organize the study of nationalism in South Asia as a whole. Many other historical trajectories are important to keep in mind, however. Though they fit the same general chronological pattern, they have many distinctive qualities, and embrace the majority of the population of South Asia as a whole.

- A large collection of territories formally outside British India – native states, non-British European colonies (most notably French Pondicherry and Portuguese Goa), and the Protectorate of Sikkim – were incorporated into India and Pakistan but did not share the same histories of nationalism.
- Frontier Provinces of British India, which became regions of north-west Pakistan and north-east India, included large populations that were barely integrated into the empire and had little connection with Indian nationalism. This discrepancy of histories inside imperial India helps to account for some problems of national integration even today.
- Burma was part of British India but not embraced by Indian nationalism. It was separated from India by the 1935 Government of India Act, and conquered by Japan in 1941. It achieved independence separately from other territories of British India.
- Numerous protectorates of British India and Ceylon – Afghanistan, Bhutan, the Maldives, and Sikkim, and coastal regions around the Indian Ocean, including the Malay States, Brunei, Aden, Yemen, Bahrain, Kuwait, and Qatar – were, like British colonies in East and South Africa, part of British imperial space in South Asia but totally separated from national histories in British India.
- Nepal was never subject to Europeans. Its nationalism thus has a distinctly non-colonial quality, shorn of anti-imperialism, but its importance for histories of nationality, identity politics, and national state territorialism in South Asia has increased dramatically in recent decades, as we will see in the following chapters.

THE 1920s

National identity in British India and Ceylon began its existential evolution in the nineteenth century, but these nations started their long march towards independence in 1919, when the Great Powers

TABLE 6. REGIONS IN SOUTH ASIA, 1947

	Area (sq. miles)	Population
Bengal Presidency	77,442	60,306,525
United Provinces	106,247	55,020,617
Madras Presidency	126,166	49,341,810
Bihar	69,745	36,340,151
Punjab	99,089	28,418,819
Bombay Presidency	76,443	20,849,840
Delhi	574	917,939
Ceylon	25,332	5,312,548
Total:		**256,508,249**
All native states	1,581,419	388,997,955
Central Provinces and Berar	98,575	16,813,584
Hyderabad	82,313	16,338,534
British East Africa	715715	15,055,126
Burma	261610	14,667,146
Rajasthan native states	132,559	13,670,208
Assam	54,951	10,204,733
Orissa	32,198	8,728,544
Mysore	29,458	7,329,140
Travancore	7662	6,070,081
Nepal	54,000	5,600,000
Sind	48,136	4,535,008
Kashmir	82,258	4,021,616
North-West Frontier Province	14,263	3,038,067
British Malaya	50.966	2,839,444

TABLE 6. *CONTINUED*

	Area (sq. miles)	Population
Ajmer-Mewar	2400	583,693
Baluchistan	54,456	501,631
Coorg	1593	168,726
Andaman and Nicobar Islands	3143	33,768
Total:		130,199,049

established the League of Nations. In the same year, the Lucknow Pact united Indian National Congress Moderates and Extremists with the Muslim League. During the war, Home Rule Leagues spread the word widely that Indians should rule their own land. Nationalism entered the political mainstream. Gandhi rose through Congress ranks using peaceful non-co-operation to settle disputes between landlords and tenants in Bihar, and between factory workers and factory owners in Gujarat. Gandhi attracted the support of wealthy businessmen who were becoming Congress financiers, as workers and peasants were joining the ranks of activists. The national movement was growing and forging unity amid diversity.

Then unforeseeable events opened a rocky and riotous road to independence and empire's end. During the war, the Viceroy had promised constitutional reforms to widen Indian power in government, and to reward Congress for its active support of the British during the war. But then the Bolshevik revolution provoked British fear of revolution in India, stoked by memories of 1905. This imperial anxiety made nationalist demands for Home Rule along Irish lines frightening in London. Home Rule Leagues were active in all major Indian cities, where nationalists were also protesting against government restrictions on the press and on public assembly, as well as against new taxes and economic controls imposed by the government to support the war. Unity in the growing national movement added strength to public demands in the press that the government must expand Indian self-government. Troops returning to India appeared to pose a threat to imperial order, particularly in Punjab, because many soldiers were Sikhs, and in distant California, an expatriate Sikh Ghadr revolutionary movement promoted the violent overthrow of the empire.

The international history of Indian politics was under way, as the threat of revolution in India also became more ominous thanks to the activity of Indian communists abroad. One 1905-inspired Calcutta revolutionary, Narendranath Bhattacharya (1887–1954) joined a plot to smuggle arms into India, went abroad to seek arms, travelled to San Francisco (where he changed his name to Manabendra Nath Roy), and helped to establish the Communist Party in Mexico, before joining the executive committee of the Communist International in Moscow.

In 1919, in the face of all this promise, anxiety, and pressure, the British Parliament passed the Montagu–Chelmsford (Montford) Reforms, expanding the power of elected governments in the Indian provinces but keeping power in New Delhi firmly in British hands. At the same time, the Rowlatt Acts were passed, which maintained wartime martial law restrictions on public activity in British India, and suspended *habeas corpus*, allowing police to imprison people without trial. This two-handed imperial strategy – giving Indian politicians more power, but cracking down on dissent and agitation – launched decades of rancorous politics. For the next thirty years, British government would measure out increments of new power for elected governments in India with one half-open hand, and use the other hand as mailed fist to crush all opposition with constitutionally established emergency powers, soldiers, police, censors, and judges; all the while blaming nationalists for any disruptions of law and order. By the time Jawaharlal Nehru (1889–1964) announced independence, at midnight on 15 August 1947, he and most other national leaders had spent many years in jail. Meanwhile London took all the credit for establishing South Asia's democracies, and blamed the rancour and violence on indigenous hatreds, communists, and greedy, recalcitrant native politicians.

Congress judged the Montford Reforms grossly inadequate, and opposed the Rowlatt Acts' blatant violation of civil rights. Mohandas Gandhi led the way. Using techniques of disciplined street action he had developed in South Africa, he launched a *satyagraha* campaign of peaceful, non-violent public gatherings, violating the Rowlatt laws and demanding the restoration of civil liberties. When imperial troops gunned down a peaceful protest at the Jallianwala Bagh in Amritsar, under orders from Punjab's military administrator, Colonel Dyer (who was never brought to book), the enraged Congress rejected the Montford Reforms and refused to stand for provincial elections, calling for immediate complete self-government, or *Swaraj*.

TABLE 7. A CHRONOLOGY OF EMPIRE'S END

1. Nationalism becomes a mass movement

1915	Home Rule Leagues active. Gandhi returns from South Africa and tours Indian cities, gathering support.
1916	Lucknow Pact unifies Extremists, Moderates, and Muslim League.
1919	Montagu–Chelmsford Reforms. Jallianwala Bagh massacre. All-India *satyagraha*. Ceylon National Congress formed. Third Afghan War. India enters League of Nations.
1920	Non-co-operation movement. Khilafat movement. Reorganization of Congress at Nagpur. Gurdwara reform movement, to 1925.
1921	Dyarchy established. Provincial governments formed. Moplah rebellion. Indian fiscal autonomy.
1923	V. D. Savarkar, *Who is a Hindu?*
1925	Death of C. R. Das. Founding of Rashtriya Swayamsevak Sangh (RSS) and Shiromani Akali Dal.
1927	M. K. Gandhi, *An Autobiography*, or *The Story of My Experiments with Truth*.

2. Imperial politics redefines nationality

1928	Simon Commission. The journal *Pukhtun* launched by Abdul Ghaffar Khan.
1929	Depression to 1933. Congress call for Purna *Swaraj*. Jinnah's 'parting of the ways'.
1930	Round Table Conferences 1930 and 1932. Salt *satyagraha*.
1931	Donoughmore constitution in Ceylon. Ceylon State Council elected by universal suffrage.
1932	Second civil disobedience movement. Communal award. Separate representation for Sikhs. Gandhi's Poona Pact with B. R. Ambedkar.
1933	'Pakistan' coined in Rahmat Ali, *Now or Never, are We to Perish or Live for Ever?*

TABLE 7. *CONTINUED*

2. Imperial politics redefines nationality (continued)

1934   Muhammad Iqbal, *The Reconstruction of Religious Thought in Islam*.

1935   Government of India Act.

3. Struggles to shape national governance

1937   Burma separated from India. Indian elections. Congress provincial ministries in seven of the eleven Indian provinces. Muslim League reorganized at Lucknow session. Sinhala Mahasabha founded by S. W. R. D. Bandaranaike.

1939   World War II, to 1945. M. S. Golwalkar, *We, or Our Nationhood Defined*.
Congress ministries resign. Muslim League celebrates 'day of deliverance'.

1940   Muslim League declares for Pakistan in Lahore.

1941   Foundation of Jamaat-I-Islami by Syed Abul Ala Maudoodi.

1942   Quit India movement. Maudoodi's *Tehreek-e-Azadi-e-Hind aur Musalman*.

1943   Bengal famine, to 1944.

1944   Tamil Congress founded in Ceylon by G. G. Ponnambalam.

1946   Cabinet mission. Violence in Bengal and elsewhere. Elections. Muslim League wins Muslim-majority areas. Cabinet mission proposal for federal India. Sikh deputation calls for an independent Punjab. Great Calcutta killing. Lord Mountbatten sent to India.

1947   Independence of India and Pakistan. Punjab massacres. Mass dislocations and forced migrations. Accession of Kashmir to India. Naga secessionist movement. United National Party under D. S. Senanayake forms government in Ceylon.

1948   Ceylon independence. Gandhi assassinated. Telangana war. Indo-Pakistan war over Kashmir. UN truce line in Kashmir. Jinnah dies. Integration of the native Indian states within India.

Gandhi led a mass campaign of complete non-co-operation with all aspects of British governance, citing its illegitimate immorality, played out at Amritsar. In 1920, Congress became a national organization designed for mass mobilization. National leaders formed an All-India Congress Committee (AICC). Provincial Congress committees organized district committees throughout British India. Congress activists travelled the country using regional languages to recruit new members and propagate the Congress platform. They called for a total boycott of Legislative Assembly elections under the Montford 'dyarchy' system. In alliance with the Muslim League, Congress non-co-operation supported the Khilafat Movement's demand that the British reinstate the Caliph in Istanbul.

The Montagu–Chelmsford 'dyarchy' system gave provincial assemblies partial power over regional administration, including public works and education, but gave the Imperial Assembly in New Delhi no power beyond advising the Viceroy. This constraint on national authority remained until the end of empire, because even though the 1935 Government of India Act established a central legislature, the outbreak of war in 1939 interrupted progress towards forming a representative imperial government. Nevertheless, in 1920 and 1935, provincial politicians did gain increasing constitutional control over regional governments. By 1920, India's central administration was autonomous financially; it was, in effect, a national government in British hands. The reality of Indian national self-governance was meanwhile coming into being in the provinces.

CONSTITUTIONAL IDENTITIES

Official and public identities which had guided government thinking and political mobilization during the first decades of the twentieth century merged into constitutional identities in the 1920s. This merger had a powerful impact on social identities and national politics in British India and Ceylon.

In Ceylon, reforms in 1920 gave an elected legislature authority over the whole island, which was the size of a small Indian province (Table 7). The Ceylon legislative assembly was like the Indian provincial assemblies, where legislatures and ministries controlled portfolios and budgets for education, health, and public works, using provincial taxes and imperial allocations. These official responsibilities remained in the hands of provincial governments under the 1935 Government of India Act and state governments under India's 1950 constitution.

In Ceylon, British officials kept more control of the administration after 1931, when the Donoughmore constitution also instituted a universal adult franchise, which never occurred in British India. Regional and minority-group politicians in Ceylon – Tamils, Kandyans, Muslims, and Christians – competed for influence in the one central legislature, representing the whole island, which after 1931 was dominated by Sinhala leaders of the Ceylon National Congress, who demanded a total transfer of power from London to Colombo. In British India, the franchise never included more than ten percent of the adult population before 1947, and electoral competition focused entirely on provincial assemblies. In Ceylon and India alike, debates about constitutional reform revolved around transfers of power from British to native representatives and civil servants. In British India, however, debates also involved the definition of the electorate itself; an issue that was settled in Ceylon by 1931.

In Ceylon, the appointment of the Donoughmore Commission to write a new constitution in 1927 spurred political parties to mobilize their influence on government; in India, the arrival of the Simon Commission in 1928 triggered political efforts to affect official decisions about the constitution of Indian constituencies, which would have lasting influence on the character of government. The Ceylon Congress called for a universal franchise and a unitary central government. The Kandyan National Association (KNA) proposed instead to establish a federal system to better represent Kandyan people, who had lost their separate government in 1833. Ceylon's other minority politicians agreed with the KNA that the British were mistaken to treat all the various peoples of Ceylon as a 'homogeneous Ceylonese race'. But the Ceylon Congress plan prevailed because it meshed with the official mainstream in the Colonial Office.

In India, constitutional reform stumbled on the same problem of how to represent group interests in an electoral system. This problem was immensely complicated in India by the existence of official identity groups such as Hindus and Muslims; by the political mobilization of public identities, including Hindu and Muslim, in various different parties; by provincial differences in the distribution of various groups; and by disputes in and among parties and government about the principle of 'communal representation'. This principle was officially established in 1911 and maintained in Montford Reforms in 1919, and thus became a legitimate basis for political strategy and planning. Like the Ceylon Congress, the

Indian National Congress opposed this principle because it broke the electorate into particularistic ethnic blocks rather than uniting the population under the banner of a single national party, represented by each National Congress. But official tradition in London, New Delhi, and in Indian provincial capitals favoured the communal principle in British India.

Indian elections complicated matters further. In 1921, the Congress–League non-co-operation campaign reduced election turnout to less than a third of the small electorate, but this did not prevent many politicians from standing for elections and forming provincial governments. The result was a two-tiered national system. In New Delhi, a central administration under the Viceroy controlled national policymaking, most of the budget, and the Indian Civil Service. The Congress and the Muslim League spoke to the central administration for national constituencies, and their allied boycott of the 1921 elections enhanced their national stature. Meanwhile, elected provincial governments also represented legitimate Indian national opinion, and they controlled budgets for education, agricultural development, and public works, as well as most civil administration. The politicians and parties that joined Legislative Assemblies and formed provincial ministries in the 1920s were regional parties which had defied the Congress–League call for non-co-operation. They worked inside a constitutional system where separate 'communal' electorates – designated seats allocated in proportion to the population of specified groups – were an established feature of national politics in the provinces. Thus the national political system made the communal principle not only legitimate and officially sanctioned but also intensely important for politically mobilized sectors of the public that exercised influence over popular sentiments. In the provinces, Indian nationality included regional public identities mobilized by politicians committed to their continued constitutional recognition.

PROVINCIAL POLITICS

The provincial public mobilization of national identity around official identities produced strident opposition to Congress calls to end communal representation, most of all in Bengal and Punjab, in each region for its own set of reasons. Bengal had spawned many parties other than Congress. A number of these represented Zamindar tenants, who were mostly Muslims, paying rent to Hindu landlords. Legal struggles for tenant rights took off with the 1859 reform acts and escalated in 1873 when tenants formed the Agrarian League in Pabna District to resist rent increases, illegal cesses (*abwab*s), and threats to occupancy rights. Led by wealthy tenants (*jotedar*s) and social reformers, the Agrarian League fought landlords in court to create perpetual leases that jumped in number in Pabna District alone from 627 to 1633 between 1873 and 1877. A more sweeping tenant reform act appeared in 1885. In the decades that followed, tenant representatives carried their struggles into regional politics; in the 1920s, they sat in government. Communal representation benefited Bengal politicians who struggled to secure tenant rights to land.

In Punjab, activists among the Sikh, Muslim, and Hindu populations also won Assembly seats in the 1920s. Their separate interests combined both religious and secular elements. Old Muslim elites were prominent Zamindars. Muslim Jats were the most numerous farmers, particularly in the west. Muslim Pashto clans controlled the neighbouring North-West Frontier Provinces (NWFP) region between Punjab and Afghanistan. Muslim religious leaders received considerable patronage in Punjab and the NWFP, which they used to run schools and to expand their social influence, which increased as the numerical weight of Muslims gained official recognition. Muslim Kashmiri politicians, banned from expressing their views publicly in Kashmir, made Punjab their base of operations.

Sikh soldiers formed powerful regiments in the Indian army, and Sikhs were prominent commanders. Sikh farmers had the reputation of being the most productive and modern in India. Thus the government policy of giving most land in the newly irrigated Punjab Canal Colonies to Sikh veterans served economic as well as political ends. Because of their position on the north-west border, Punjab and the NWFP played a central role in British military planning; Punjab received the lion's share of military investment in British India. In the 1920s, Sikh religious leaders successfully organized a movement to bring all Gurdwaras under an officially unified Sikh administrative control, which increased their political influence further among Sikhs. Meanwhile, Hindu Banias and Khatris who lived in the major cities had become the financial backbone of Punjab's thriving commercial economy. Many merchants from north India also arrived in urban Punjab during the boom decades after 1880, when Punjab was the most profitable region for agrarian business in British India. Merchants became prominent patrons of Hindu revivalist organizations such as the Arya Samaj, whose influence was greater in Punjab than anywhere else.

This mixture of politics with business and religion proved volatile. Government concern for the productivity of Punjab farmers and for the political stability of the region caused official anxiety as many farmers fell deeply into debt to finance commercial production. Officials feared an explosion of violence like the attacks on Marwari moneylenders by indebted Maratha cotton farmers in 1875. Fearing upheaval in Punjab, and committed by their own official tradition to the people they called the 'martial races' and 'sturdy yeomen', the Punjab government passed the Land Alienation Act in 1900, which prohibited the transfer of land for debt default to what it called 'non-cultivating tribes', who were in fact mostly Hindu Banias. This law expelled merchants from markets in agricultural credit and enriched landed groups who moved into moneylending, mostly Muslims and Sikhs. Landowners large and small rallied around the law. Merchants opposed it. For the far more numerous Sikhs and Muslims, communal electorates thus protected their economic interests. The fact that official ethnic identities coincided with religious identities made religious leaders more influential in election campaigns and in debates about contending constitutional proposals in the 1920s and 1930s.

The distinctiveness of Punjab and Bengal stands out when we compare them to Madras Presidency, where another non-Congress regime came to power under Dyarchy in the 1920s. The Justice Party came together in 1921 as a motley assortment of non-Brahman politicians, mostly Tamil-speakers, who controlled the Legislative Assembly. The Justice Party used its government powers to benefit constituents in the same manner as parties in Punjab and Bengal. But in Madras, there was little unity of interests among its constituents, except that they all sought to displace Brahmans from dominance in higher education and administration. One thing that the Tamils had in common was their passion for the Tamil language as the medium and icon of their native cultural identity. Because Brahmans were most prominent in Congress, the Justice Party became a regional collection of politicians who competed with a nationally dominant imperial elite represented by Brahmans in Congress. With its patronage for Tamil scholarship and education, the Justice Party established an enduring Tamil political culture in Madras. But by the 1930s its organizational powers had dissipated, and when faced with all-out Congress electoral campaigns in Madras, it collapsed. Congress took power in elections in 1937, and held power in the land of Tamil nationality until a stronger Tamil non-Brahman party, the Dravida Munnetra Kazhagam (DMK), won elections in 1967.

By contrast to Madras, Congress never won any provincial election in Bengal or Punjab. That political fact laid the constitutional basis for the partition of India and Pakistan in 1947.

With this in view, it is important to note that it was the administrative partitioning of states along linguistic lines in independent India, in 1956, which made the DMK ascendancy possible, alongside the growth of other regional parties that later challenged Congress dominance successfully in most Indian states. By creating linguistic states throughout India, the Congress government in independent India turned linguistic identities into constitutional identities, and thus, in effect, formed 'communal' electorates for public mobilization along linguistic lines. In the new Tamil political environment that came into being in the new Indian state of Tamil Nadu, carved out from Madras Presidency, the Congress Party steadily lost support to explicitly Tamil political parties, which dominated state politics after 1967. Distinctively state-based ethno-cultural politics became the norm in independent India from the 1960s onward, and in that context, disparate forms of identity politics flourished and fought for dominance inside the formal framework of Indian nationality, as we will see in Chapter Seven.

DESIGNING THE NATION

In 1931, after three years of preliminaries, deliberations for a new constitutional system for British India went into high gear. The Indian National Congress, led by Nehru and Gandhi, vehemently opposed communal electorates. Dividing the electorate by official religious categories violated the Congress ideal of Indian unity. Congress called it a British strategy to 'divide and rule' India for ever. Perhaps it was. But communal electorates were also in place in the provinces, where Indian politicians had embraced them and sought not only to maintain them but to enlarge their political importance by increasing the constitutional powers of provincial government. Congress, by contrast, strove to capture national authority in New Delhi and to expand the power of the central government in independent India.

In national debates, the Muslim League identified itself most prominently with Indian demands for communal representation. The League held but a few seats in provincial assemblies, however, and Congress gained strength in all the regions when its membership abandoned the non-co-operation programme to enter provincial elections. Congress then mobilized to win elections in all the provinces, but lost its best hope for unity with Muslim parties in Bengal with the death of C. R. Das, after which riots broke out, alienating Bengal Muslims from Congress. In 1928, Mohammad Ali Jinnah struggled to have an All Parties National Conference, convened in Calcutta, adopt his constitutional provisions to protect the Muslim minority. He reasoned thus:

> Every country struggling for freedom and desirous of establishing a democratic system of Government has had to face the problem of minorities wherever they existed and no constitution, however idealistic it may be and however perfect from [a] theoretical point of view it may seem will ever receive the support of the minorities unless they can feel that they, as an entity, are secured under the proposed constitution . . . Otherwise no proper constitution will last but [will instead] result in a revolution and a civil war.

After all but one of Jinnah's proposals were rejected, he felt sure that Congress would not write constitutional protections for Muslims into its plan for government reforms. When he left the meeting he told a friend, 'This is the parting of the ways.'

Jinnah's 'parting' with Congress over the issue of minority rights had little political force in the early 1930s, because the League was so weak politically. A major Congress leader, Dr B. R. Ambedkar (1891–1956), who would, twenty years later, write the constitution for independent India, posed a more formidable challenge to the Congress position. As Jinnah argued for increased Muslim representation, based on the 1931 census figures, Ambedkar argued that all of India's so-called 'untouchable' castes should have separate electoral representation to compensate for their poverty, subordination, and exclusion. Gandhi conducted a fast to death to force Ambedkar to drop this idea, and Ambedkar settled instead for reserved legislative seats for 'depressed classes', a principle which he later adapted for writing the Indian constitution.

This conflict within nationalism expressed a political divide over the problem posed by the nation's structural inequities. Congress, led by Gandhi and Nehru, called for the constitution to assert the legal equality of all citizens; it also endorsed special programmes to ameliorate inequity. Gandhi called Ambedkar's caste fellows *harijans* ('children of god') and promoted their uplift by charitable action along the lines of Gokhale's Servants of India Society. Nehru became President of the All-India Congress Committee in 1930, amid the devastation of the early Depression, when conflicts broke out among groups on opposite sides of deep economic schisms: between tenants and landlords, debtors and moneylenders, and workers and factory owners. Inequity now seemed to threaten the nation itself, and radicalism increased with discontent. Nehru announced his own radical turn with these words:

> The great poverty and misery of the Indian People are due, not only to foreign exploitation in India but also to the economic structure of society, which the alien rulers support so that their exploitation may continue. In order therefore to remove this poverty and misery and to ameliorate the condition of the masses, it is essential to make revolutionary changes in the present economic and social structure of society and to remove the gross inequalities.

Jinnah and Ambedkar argued, on the contrary, that the only way to give the weaker sections of the nation an effective voice in politics and thus counteract their structural disabilities would be to write provisions into the constitution to allocate electoral power to them specifically. Ambedkar relented in the face of Gandhi's pressure and settled for a weaker mode of redress, but in principle the Congress did accept his argument that 'gross inequities' posed a national problem that did demand a remedy. Jinnah, however, stuck to the position that Muslims needed separate political representation to safeguard their interests as a numerical minority community amid a majority Hindu electorate. Congress rejected not only this remedy but the League's definition of the inequity problem itself.

In 1932, constitutional debates among lawyers gave way to hard politics. In that year, a determined Congress organized another massive non-co-operation campaign to protest against the British exclusion of Congress from planning for a new government reorganization; also to protest against the British proposal to retain communal representation in the new electoral scheme. In 1933, agitation by various groups amid Depression distress led to riots in the rowdy industrial city of Kanpur. The animosity between the League and Congress increased when the Congress committee that convened to investigate the riots blamed the Muslim League for causing violence and for raising opposition to a unified national struggle in tacit connivance with the British to divide the nation with communal representation.

When the government announced its 'communal award', that is, the legislative seat allocations reserved for elected representatives from officially defined groups, based on the 1931 census returns, these reservations comprised a large majority of seats in the North-West Frontier Provinces (82 percent), Punjab (75 percent), Sind (68 percent), and Bengal (68 percent); and a smaller majority in Assam (59 percent). In the NWFP and Sind, Muslims got most reserved seats (72 percent and 57 percent of total reservations, respectively). In Punjab, Muslims got 49 percent and Sikhs 18 percent of reserved seats. In Bengal and Assam, Muslims got 48 percent and 31 percent of total reservations, respectively; and additional reservations were made for British plantation owners. 'Depressed classes' got small reservations in all the provinces, and other reservations went to representatives of Backward Areas, Indian Christians, Anglo-Indians, Europeans, universities, organized labour, and big business.

In 1932 the second Congress non-co-operation campaign succeeded in raising the national stature of Congress but failed to alter substantially the allocation of reserved seats, let alone to dislodge the principle of communal representation. When elections under the 1935 Government of India Act were held, in 1937, Congress candidates obtained huge majorities in Madras (74 percent), the United Provinces (59 percent), Bihar (63 percent), the Central Provinces (63 percent), and Orissa (60 percent). Congress did well enough to become the most powerful party in Bombay (48 percent), where it also formed a government. .

Congress candidates did not win enough seats to form solo governments in Bengal (24 percent), Sind (13 percent), Punjab (10 percent), and the NWFP (38 percent), where Congress refused to join coalition governments. The League fared worse than Congress in Muslim-majority areas, where it failed even to win most Muslim reserved seats. Congress received many more Muslim votes than the League, but provincial parties got many more votes than both combined and formed coalition governments in Bengal, Punjab, Sind, and the NWFP. Congress controlled all other provinces; among these, the United Provinces had many Muslim-majority areas, mostly in cities.

World War II prevented the full implementation of the 1935 Government of India Act. In 1941, Japan conquered Burma. British India became critically strategic territory for the Allies and was therefore once again dominated politically by military interests. The Congress refused to support the war effort and instead launched a massive Quit India Movement in 1942 to drive the British out. Fears of revolution again haunted the British, and for good reason. As the war justified bloody state brutality and the arrest of all major Congress leaders, the lower rank and file mobilized mass anti-British sentiment to provoke pitched battles on the streets. Meanwhile, a leading Congress figure, Subhas Chandra Bose (1897–1945), formed the Indian National Army (INA) in Japanese-occupied Burma to invade India and fight for liberation. When the war did finally end, Britain kept tight control of the transfer of power and London also set a precipitous 1947 deadline for its escape from the now politically unbearable burden of empire in South Asia. This final rush to end empire after the war would be embittered by the harsh British punishment of treason by nationalists during the war.

War also brought disaster in Bengal. Non-Congress ministries headed provincial government in Calcutta, which was also the centre of Allied operations. When food prices skyrocketed, in 1943, administrative measures to secure provisions for Calcutta deprived villagers of food, and millions of people in rural Bengal died. Congress blamed the British and its political foes in Bengal. Desperate people flooded Calcutta. Under these incendiary conditions, massive riots broke out in 1946, when, as the war ended, the idea of partitioning Bengal came into public view. The plan would again separate West Bengal, where Congress would be in control, from East Bengal, where Congress had no prospect of winning elections. Eastern districts held a largely Muslim electorate, filled with tenant farmers fighting for land rights against Zamindars who backed Congress and prevented Congress from promising land reforms. Riots in 1946 again pitted Hindus against Muslims, for reasons having nothing to do with religion but rather with passions stoked by religious activists.

All the while, constitutional politics continued. The League responded to its election debacle in 1937 with strenuous efforts to attract Muslim voters and form alliances with the provincial parties which had won so many Muslim votes. Jinnah reorganized the League along lines similar to Congress and conducted similar mass campaigns to attract Muslim politicians, who faced the prospect of being swamped by Congress in any head-to-head competition for national political power. The spectre of Hindu majoritarian domination of the Muslim electorate provided the League with a strong argument for Muslim solidarity across regional and ethnic lines, to make the Muslim League the party of Indian Muslims. By 1941, alliances formed among provincial Muslim politicians in Bengal,

Sind, Punjab, the NWFP, and the United Provinces enabled the League to reverse its fortunes in many by-elections to provincial assemblies, though it did not and would never be able to control any provincial government in British India on its own.

In 1941, at a Muslim League meeting in Lahore, the leader of Bengal's Krishak Praja Party (Peasant and Workers Party), Fazlul Haq, joined forces with Jinnah and tabled a resolution calling for the creation of a separate territory, which he named Pakistan, reserved in its entirety for Muslim government. In 1941, this Pakistan represented one territorial part of a federal constitutional scheme, which the League was proposing, to secure maximum Muslim control over regions in which Muslims counted as the numerical majority. Creating Pakistan would require redrawing political boundaries to separate Muslim-majority areas, which were then mixed into Punjab and Bengal, and then uniting them constitutionally with other Muslim-majority areas. Doing so would give Indian Muslims constitutionally secure territorial power in Muslim-majority regions in a national political system where Hindus would form a large overall majority and Congress would be the dominant political party. Muslim provincial politicians such as Fazlul Haq joined with the League for their own provincial reasons to support the demand for Pakistan.

The Muslim League's campaign to become the party of India's Muslims received inadvertent help from Congress. In 1941, Congress called for ministerial resignations to protest Britain's declaration of war in India. Congress resignations led to by-elections won by League supporters; this echoed trends in 1920, when provincial parties benefited from the Congress boycott of Montford assembly elections. In 1942, when Congress declared its all-out Quit India campaign to drive the British from India, the League supported the government to concentrate its attention on winning by-elections and official support for Pakistan. As a result, when the war was over, the League was in a much stronger position than when the war began.

TERRITORIAL NATIONS

In 1945, urgent negotiations began to design an independent India. The League had powerful electoral support in Bengal, Sind, Punjab, the NWFP, and Baluchistan, and also had supporters in cities along the Ganga basin. Congress controlled all the other regions and was in a position to form a central government immediately. Congress had prominent supporters from all national groups, including Muslims. It sought to make its government a bastion of Indian unity and national strength, one that could bring the country out of ruin caused by decades of war, economic depression, famine, and upheaval. With a legitimate claim to represent the Indian nation, Congress stood firm against Jinnah's less credible claim to represent Indian Muslims. Congress appeared to the League to be a domineering party of the Hindu majority bent on reducing minorities to its authoritarian will. The League appeared to Congress as a threat to Indian unity, a divisive communal party of special interests that sought to hobble if not dismember the nation.

Pakistan remained constitutionally ill-defined when Lord Mountbatten arrived in New Delhi in 1946, carrying a precipitous 1947 deadline for ending negotiations, set unilaterally by the British government. In 1947, intransigence on all sides made the partition of India the only solution that all parties could agree upon. No one originally wanted partition, but no option could be found within the short time frame available. On 15 August 1947, the independent states of India and Pakistan were born at the bargaining table, where agreements to transfer imperial power to national governments were signed at the same time as massive dislocations and rioting occurred in cities, towns, and villages, where people fought for property and revenge. A civil war among the peoples of Punjab sent millions of refugees across the new international border. Countless thousands died.

The new national states altered the meaning and substance of nationality. The partition of India and Pakistan produced a new geography of belonging and alienation that had never existed before. Since 1947, the term 'India' has referred ambiguously to a new national state, to a larger territory encompassed by British India, and to a region of culture and history embracing much of South Asia. After partition, national histories obscured the character of nationality before 1947. For example, in India, Muhammad Ali Jinnah came to be known as the founder of Pakistan, and therefore as not Indian, even anti-Indian, by virtue of being a Pakistani, which he was for only one year of his long life. Before 1947, Jinnah was always an Indian and had no desire to be anything else. He was a devoted Indian nationalist who fought for Muslim minority rights. Indian nationality before 1947 embraced peoples who, after 1947, were divided by nationality. Almost one third of all Indians in 1946 had become Pakistanis by 1948. Indians in 1948 lived in a national state territory that was completely unimaginable a decade before. The Pakistan that Fazlul Haq proposed in Lahore in 1941 was not the Pakistan that came into being in 1947.

Partition uprooted ten million people; most were forced to move either to India or to Pakistan. The pain of partition was very unevenly distributed and afflicted a small proportion of the total population in both countries. For most people, partition affected other people far away in other regions. Non-border regions had little disruption, though many Muslims did leave urban areas that became hostile and unsafe in Uttar Pradesh, Gujarat, Bombay, and elsewhere, to live in Pakistan, mostly in Lahore and Karachi. Almost all the pain of partition fell on three historic regions divided between India and Pakistan: Punjab, Bengal, and Kashmir. In each region, the new international borders were unprecedented; their local details were also quite arbitrary. All the regions involved saw expulsions, riots, killings, refugees, and new justifications for more ethnic solidarity and more hatred. But Punjab produced by far the most dislocation and violence. Battles for assets and for revenge became a civil war. Bengal's partition was long, slow, and peaceful by comparison. Unregulated migration and everyday mobility continued for decades across the new borders. Kashmir was divided by a treaty that ended a war which India and Pakistan fought over the territory in 1947.

Kashmir remains disputed national territory. The Raja of the native state of Jammu and Kashmir opted to join India. Opposition groups from his Muslim-majority population argued for joining Pakistan. Pakistan claimed Kashmir because of its Muslim majority. The polarization of the state along Hindu–Muslim lines originated in the Dogra dynasty's nineteenth-century installation of a Brahman and Kashmiri Pandit ruling elite of landlords, bureaucrats, and businessmen, and its institution of state Hindu rituals and law codes. Public Muslim activity in the observance of prayers and festivals was officially imbued with an air of dissent and even outlawed. A Muslim political opposition arose that was banned in Kashmir and exiled to Lahore, where Kashmiris and their supporters entered the fray of Punjabi politics. Political antagonisms among Hindu, Muslim, and Sikh groups in Punjab were thus embroiled in struggles over the rights of Hindus, Muslims, and Sikhs in Kashmir. These external dimensions of Kashmiri politics were well established in 1947, when India and Pakistan went to war. Their peace treaty divided Kashmir to bring the major portion, including the Vale and its capital, Srinagar, into India, and to bring a smaller portion, called Azad Kashmir, into Pakistan. The two countries went to war over Kashmir again in 1965, and simmering hostilities continue. Extricating the people of Kashmir from hostile claims by both countries, and from related internal divisions among Kashmiri politicians, still seems impossible.

Partition's pain also continues to haunt other groups in partitioned regions. Assam was partitioned to put Sylhet into East Pakistan, but everyday livelihoods continued to cross the border. Thousands of Muslim Biharis left to live in East Pakistan, and when East Pakistan became Bangladesh in 1971, they became 'stranded Pakistanis' living on the margins of another new national society. Partition scattered villages in the territories of the old Raja of Cooch Bihar to form tiny enclaves of foreign Bengalis on both sides of the India–East Pakistan border – Indian villages in what became Bangladesh, and Bangladeshi villages in India – hostages in hostile territory. Since 1947, Muslim Bengalis who have continued the long tradition of moving to farm land in Assam and to find work in West Bengal have become suspect and sometimes hated foreigners, subject to local and state violence.

CREATING NATIONAL STATES

The Maldives, Bhutan, Afghanistan, and Nepal continued to be governed by existing ruling dynasties after the great historical divide that marked their independence. India and Pakistan were the only countries whose boundaries changed at independence, creating a distinctive territorial disjuncture in those two countries. National independence nevertheless brought dramatic changes in the social life of nationality everywhere in South Asia.

The new national states defined nationality in strictly territorial terms, and wielded unprecedented political legitimacy in a new post-imperial world order defined by national state sovereignty, and represented by the United Nations. Nationality thus became strictly identified with nations ruled by state governments. In each South Asian country, the new nation was ruled by a single dominant political party or royal elite. National goals became state goals; these merged with the imperatives of dominant party politics, and, above all, the pursuit of national unity, security, law and order, and economic development. Wars nationalized militant patriotism in India, Pakistan, and Sri Lanka. Educational systems blended national identities into social identities everywhere. National boundaries marked people as citizens and as aliens. National maps and national languages became icons of territorial identity. Historical sites became national treasures. History writing, films, songs, holidays, parades, and countless cultural events expressed, embodied, and inculcated national pride and unity, which coloured and shaped social identity and delineated the boundaries of social exclusion, organized and authorized by the state.

After 1947, social change accelerated, as new national states consolidated control over territories and resources, defined citizens' entitlements to all the necessities of life, and became leading investors in economic development. Old nationalist movements had produced a public desire to participate in state activity, and now, after independence, politically active groups mobilized to shape the constitution of their new governments. The result was a rapid shift in the social basis of political order. This shift bears comparison with others in earlier periods following imperial collapse. The end of the Gupta and Mughal Empires had opened the field of opportunity for local and regional elites, who then used powers inherited from old empires to create new political domains. The end of the British Empire likewise accelerated upward mobility for politically active groups who were positioned to establish themselves in a new institutional framework.

India

Partition left the Congress with uncontested national power in the Republic of India, which inherited most of British India's assets and institutions. The All-India Congress Committee quickly formed an elected national government. India's 1950 constitution kept most features of the 1935 Government of India Act: it gave the central government in New Delhi all the power of the old imperial administration under a new universal adult franchise; it maintained the old powers of the regional governments. India's national territory incorporated all the native states, Goa, Pondicherry, and Sikkim. Military force became part of national consolidation. War with Pakistan secured the major portion of Kashmir for India. The army took more than a year to crush a revolution in the Telangana region of the former Hyderabad state. The military secured North-East India against an armed struggle for independence in Nagaland, and India's 1962 war with China marked limits of territorial incorporation along their border.

The Indian constitution produced new official identities. It erased communal electorates and instead established defined 'reservations' in legislatures, government employment, and education for underprivileged groups listed on official 'schedules' of 'backward castes' and 'backward tribes'. Caste disappeared from the Indian census, but official classifications and enumerations of populations by religious categories remained.

Under the universal franchise, social identities did not need to be officially authorized in legal and census operations to become prominent politically. Old regional patterns of ethnic and caste demography expanded their role in government as Congress endorsed the principle it had rejected before 1947, that state territories should follow lines of majority social identities. By 1960, the Indian electorate had been redefined along territorial lines that gave old public identities new official status. The partitioning of Punjab between India and Pakistan was followed by the repartitioning of the Indian Punjab into three states, Himachal Pradesh, Punjab, and Haryana, with substantial Sikh and Hindu Jat majorities in Punjab and Haryana respectively. In 1956, the government partitioned old provinces according to linguistic majorities to give Marathas, Rajputs, Gujaratis, Tamils, Telugus, Oriyas, Kannadigas, and Malayalis their own territories. Assam was partitioned to produce the ethnic-majority states of Meghalaya, Manipur, Nagaland, Mizoram, and Tripura. Struggles for ethno-cultural territorial autonomy along lines followed by the Muslim League before 1947 became the basis for nationalism among Bengalis in Pakistan, who produced Bangladesh in 1971. Tamil identity in Sri Lanka and regional ethnic identities in north-eastern India and Kashmir became the basis for extended struggles to redesign political territory. Identity politics was deeply etched into the political landscape.

Voting 'blocks' also developed in all the regions around social identities mobilized in public to win elections and seek advantages for a growing variety of groups. These groups included workers, peasants, landlords, industrialists, Muslims, Sikhs, and various Hindu sects and caste alliances that formed distinctive patterns in each Indian state. Official religious and unofficial ethnic, class, and family identities remained a major public asset for candidates who represented local and regional identities under the Congress banner.

The Indian National Congress became a vast political umbrella under which many groups mobilized to seek official entitlements and influence. Under Jawaharlal Nehru, who was Prime Minister until his death in 1964, Congress built a national system of political alliances in villages, towns, and districts, based on loyalties inherited from the long independence struggle and on the ability of the ruling party to provide patronage in return for votes. That ability emerged from a vast and rapid increase in the government's power to affect local living conditions. The national state forcefully integrated old territorial frontiers of empire and the erstwhile native states. It invested heavily in transportation and communication, increased economic growth, and reduced economic inequality, as Nehru had promised, with land reforms, public provisioning of food and energy, and subsidies for water, electricity, fertilizer, and high-yielding varieties of wheat and rice. Programmes to foster national integration and unity thus promoted equal citizenship for all Indians, and promoted ideals of socialism inside a thriving market economy, where the rampant inequality of private property ownership became a serious political challenge. On the one hand, major agrarian landlords supported Congress, whose industrial policies also favoured major businesses and urban voters, but at the same time, fostering economic development with Green Revolution technologies favoured upwardly mobile and economically progressive rich farmers who represented an expansive agrarian electoral power base.

Political imperatives thus pulled in opposing directions, and balancing change with stability to win votes in the countryside became the hallmark of Indian party politics. Land reform provides a good example. As we have seen, Zamindari landlordism was a hot political issue during the long independence struggle. Agriculture became a provincial subject in 1920, and remained so in the Indian constitution; so that, after 1950, land reforms were enacted state by state, and their variety reflects the balance of power in each state. As it had before 1947, land reform again opened cracks between regional and national politicians. Prime Minister Nehru supported radical land reforms that would redistribute landed property among small farmers. This was unacceptable for the politically dominant landed castes in the states. Charan Singh was a leader of Nehru's opposition. His strategy of land reform in Uttar Pradesh did end Zamindari tenure, but it also established a two-tier system of land rights favouring locally dominant Jat landed elites in the villages. A Jat himself, from a poor rural background, Charan Singh symbolized and propelled the rise of 'rich peasant' political power in India. In 1957, expressing a political logic that became popular internationally in response to the radicalism of the Chinese revolution, he explained his strategy thus:

The political consequences of the land reforms are . . . far reaching. Much thought was given to this matter since the drafters of the legislation were cognisant of the need to ensure political stability in the countryside. By strengthening the principle of private property where it was weakest, i.e. at the base of the social pyramid, the reformers have created a huge class of strong opponents of the class war ideology. By multiplying the number of independent land-owning peasants there came into being a middle of the road stable rural society and a barrier against political extremism.

Pakistan and Bangladesh

Reconciling social change and state stability proved impossible in Pakistan, which was an improbably shaped state territory composed of two 'wings', East and West, culturally very different and separated by fifteen hundred miles of hostile Indian territory. The new national government immediately came into the conservative hands of major landowners, industrialists, military men, bureaucrats, and business families, mostly from Punjab, but also from Sind, where many immigrants from India would settle in Karachi. By contrast, but at the same time, when formerly eastern districts of Bengal Presidency became East Pakistan, rapid social change was under way. Hindu Zamindars and their retainers left for India in droves and former rich Muslim tenants (*jotedars*) became powerful local politicians. In West Pakistan, powerful landed elites blocked land reform and redistributive social programmes. The West had a strong military legacy; the East had none. In the East, the politics of national independence included a popular tenant struggle for property rights against entrenched landlord interests, and partition had not been violent. In the West, the ruling elites included entrenched landlords, who craved nothing more than order and stability after the massive violence of partition.

The same kind of regional ethnic politics that produced India's reorganization of states in 1956 produced a military coup in Pakistan, where General Ayub Khan became martial law administrator in 1958 to establish Punjabi military power in government as regional politics radicalized East Pakistan, where the capital city, Dhaka, grew rapidly with the creation of a new Bengali middle class.

Many aspiring East Pakistanis came straight from villages. Others came from Calcutta and from towns in West Bengal. Few knew Urdu, Pakistan's national language; more were literate in English. Their common language was Bengali. Elite Muslim Bengali culture closely resembled that of Calcutta's *bhadralok*, with whom aspiring Bengalis in East Pakistan shared tastes, habits, and expectations. When Pakistan's Urdu-speaking state officials arrived in Dhaka, they were foreigners. In 1952, they tried to make Urdu the language of law, education, and administration in East Pakistan. Bengali opposition spilled from the universities into the streets. Bengali activists were killed by soldiers and became martyrs for their language. At the same time, government efforts to requisition grain to end food shortages that lingered from the 1943 famine triggered resentment among the landed elites. The Pakistan government's heavy-handed policies not only failed to improve the food situation, it generated corruption, destabilized local grain markets, and provoked landowners (*jotedars*) to attack Hindu merchants, who fled the country.

By 1954, urban and rural resentments had driven the Muslim League from power in the East Pakistan elections. The Awami League became the party of East Pakistan. Meanwhile, Pakistan government controls over economic development widened disparities between East and West. The Awami League sought more provincial authority in the East to give Bengalis more economic and political opportunity. The military government in the new capital of Islamabad resisted. In 1966, the Awami League leader, Sheikh Mujibur Rahman, published his *Six Points: Our Demand for Survival*, advocating federal autonomy for East Pakistan. In 1970, when Pakistan held elections, the Awami League won an absolute majority by sweeping Bengali constituencies that contained 55 percent of Pakistan's total electorate. Euphoria in Dhaka gave way to horror when Sheikh Mujib was arrested and Pakistani troops arrived to subdue the rebel province. The Awami League declared independence. Poorly armed freedom fighters fought well-equipped Pakistan army battalions from March to December 1971, chanting *Joy Bangla*, 'Victory for Bengali'. Villagers fought soldiers to a stalemate, as Pakistan received support from the United States. In December, the Indian army flew in to expel Pakistan. Bangladesh became independent, and national state unification began again. Five years later, Bangladesh military officers assassinated Sheikh Mujib. The army ruled the country until 1990, when a popular democracy movement forced the return of an elected government and national development began yet again.

Sri Lanka

Ceylon became Sri Lanka in 1975. The name change reflected a continuing drive for national unity which had extensive social repercussions. To consolidate power, the United National Party passed the Citizen Act (1948), the Indian and Pakistani Residents Act (1949), and the Parliamentary Elections Amendment Act (1949), which denied citizenship to most Indian Tamils and then disenfranchised the rest, in the expectation that Indian Tamil plantation workers, who formed a large population in the central highlands, would support the Trotskyist Lanka Sama Samaya Party, which had ten seats in Parliament. Language also became a volatile issue, as it was in India and Pakistan. Parliamentary elections in 1956 triggered national mobilization by Sinhala-speaking rural elites who sought more positions in the Civil Service, which was still dominated by English literates, and also by Buddhist monks who sought more influence in government on the 2500th anniversary of Buddha's enlightenment. In 1956 – the same year that riots erupted in Madras when New Delhi tried to force Hindi into schools – the 'Sinhala Only' election slogan attracted votes from aspiring Sinhala-speakers and Buddhist monks in Sri Lanka.

In 1956, the most prominent public definition of nationality in Sri Lanka became Sinhala Buddhist. English-educated Tamils had been prominent in the Ceylon government, but now they were losing the advantages of English literacy as well as official recognition of their native tongue. The 1956 Official Language Act in effect altered the 1947 constitution, which explicitly forbade language discrimination. In 1972, a new constitution gave Sinhala and Buddhism supreme official status. Anti-government riots ensued in the Tamil-majority areas in the north and east. Tamil demands for regional Tamil authority were opposed in Colombo and increasingly met with Sinhala hostility. In 1981 and 1983, political division and public hostility turned into civil war with the creation of Tamil fighting forces led by the Liberation Tigers of Tamil Eelam (LTTE). Ethnic war continued for twenty-five years and continues today to have a profound effect on the substance of nationality.

Bhutan

Ruled by a hereditary monarch since 1616, and occupying its current Himalayan territory since 1885, when King Ugyen Wangchuck forged close ties with British India, Bhutan has been a formally sovereign state since the Treaty of Punakha with British India in 1910. In 1947, the new government of India recognized Bhutan as a sovereign state. Bhutan became a member of the United Nations in 1971.

Afghanistan

A large and diverse Pashtun ethnic identity pervades the social life of nationality in Afghanistan, where the term 'Afghan' itself often refers to Pashtuns, whose elite families have ruled as kings, and whose population is about half the country's total. Tajiks living mostly in the north comprise about half the remainder, and all other groups are much smaller in size. From the first Anglo-Afghan War in 1838 until 1919, the politics that would shape nationality in Afghanistan comprised an imperial Great Game, pitting Russia against Britain. In the second Anglo-Afghan War in 1878, the British occupied all major Afghan cities, established their own ruler, and made Afghanistan an official protectorate of British India, a status it retained until 1919, when King Amanullah declared independence. Kings officially ruled until 1973, when the king was overthrown and a republic declared by a powerful relative, who became president.

The Maldives

The British made the Maldives an administratively organized collection of islands and a protectorate under the authority of British Ceylon in 1887, to secure British access to natural resources and their strategic location in the Indian Ocean. The Maldives remained under independent Ceylon until an independence agreement was signed with Britain in 1965. A sultanate government was replaced with a republic in 1952, was restored in 1954, and was finally replaced by referendum with a republic after independence in 1968, yielding a series of powerful presidents, the last of which was elected to a sixth five-year term in 2003.

Nepal

An independent state since its king signed a treaty with British India in 1816, Nepal was ruled by Rana kings until 1950, when a revolt

TABLE 8. EVENTS IN THE HISTORIES OF THE NATIONAL
STATES

1950	Constitution of India. Universal adult franchise. Indian National Planning Commission.
1951	Fall of the Rana regime in Nepal. India's First Five Year Plan and general election.
	Jana Sangh Party founded by Dr S. P. Mookerjee, former head of Hindu Mahasabha.
1952	Bengali language movement in East Pakistan. Massacre of students.
1953	First linguistic state, Andhra Pradesh. Akali Dal demands Punjabi Subha.
1954	Muslim League defeated by United Front in East Pakistan; United Front government dismissed.
1956	Indian States Reorganization Act. Pakistan constitution introduces presidential government. Militant Naga insurgency.
1958	Ayub Khan becomes martial law administrator of Pakistan.
1962	Third Indian general election. Indo-Chinese war on Tibetan frontier.
1963	Indian state of Nagaland created.
1964	Death of Jawaharlal Nehru. Vishwa Hindu Parishad (VHP) founded by Swami Chinmayananda.
1965	India–Pakistan war over Kashmir.
1966	Indira Gandhi becomes Indian Prime Minister.
	Sheikh Mujibur Rahman, *Six Points: Our Demand for Survival.*
1966	M. S. Golwalkar, *Bunch of Thoughts.* Militant Mizo insurgency.
1967	Fourth Indian general election. Dravida Munnetra Kazhakam (DMK) victory.
	Congress dominance declines; Pakistan People's Party (PPP) founded.
	Naxalbari revolution begins in north-east India.
1970	Pakistan's first national elections. Zulfiqar Ali Bhutto becomes president. Awami League wins absolute majority.

TABLE 8. *CONTINUED*

1971	Fifth Indian general election. Arrest of Sheikh Mujibur Rahman. Bangladesh Liberation War, Indian war with Pakistan. Janatha Vimukthi Peramuna (JVP) 'People's Liberation Movement' suppressed in Ceylon, where state of emergency declared to 1977.
	Naxalbari revolution suppressed in Calcutta and north-east India.
1972	G. M. Syed heightens Sindhi nationalism with Sindhi culture. Pakistan's third constitution. Riots following Sind Language Bill. Ceylon becomes Sri Lanka.
1973	Insurgency in Baluchistan.
1974	Akali Dal passes Anandpur Sahib Resolution. Police violence at fourth International Tamil Conference in Jaffna.
1975	State of emergency in India, to 1977. Sheikh Mujib assassinated. Military coup in Bangladesh. Chelvanayakam declares for a separate Tamil state in Sri Lanka.
1977	Janata Dal government in India. Zia-ul-Haq martial law regime in Pakistan.
1978	Anandpur Sahib Resolution. Foundation of All-Pakistan Mohajir Students Organization. Liberation Tigers of Tamil Eelam proscribed in Sri Lanka.
1979	Execution of Zulfiqar Ali Bhutto; Tehrik-i-Nifaz-i-Jafria founded by Shias in response to Zia's state-sponsored Sunni Islamic law. Prevention of Terrorism Act in Sri Lanka. Military occupation of Jaffna district.
1980	Indira Gandhi wins general election. Jana Sangh becomes Bharatiya Janata Party (BJP).
1981	Akali Dal launches Dharam Yudh Morcha for Punjab autonomy. Mandal Commission report. Movement for the Restoration of Democracy in Pakistan. Anti-Tamil riots across Sri Lanka; war with Tamil separatists begins.

TABLE 8. *CONTINUED*

1984	Indian army Operation Bluestar at Golden Temple at Amritsar. Indira Gandhi assassinated. Delhi anti-Sikh riots. Rajiv Gandhi elected. Formation of the Mohajir Qaumi Mahaz (MQM) by Altaf Hussain. VHP calls for the liberation of the Ramjanmabhoomi. *Khalistan News* published in the UK; *World Sikh News* and *The Sword* in the US.
1985	Partyless elections in Pakistan. Rajiv Gandhi accord with Sant Harchand Singh Longowal; Longowal assassinated.
1986	Shah Bano case. New social movements arise in India. Babri Masjid Committee formed.
1987	VHP mobilizes liberation of Ramjanmabhoomi. MQM triumphs in Karachi elections. V. P. Singh forms Janata Dal government. Indian Peace Keeping Force (IPKF) in Jaffna.
1988	Zia's death. Elections in Pakistan; Benazir Bhutto leads PPP government.
1989	National Front wins Indian elections. BJP seats leap from two to 85. Mandal Commission report accepted. Ram Shila Pujan programme. Insurgency begins in Kashmir.
1990	L. K. Advani's *rath yatra*. Kar Sevaks killed in Ayodhya. Secessionist movement in Assam. Dismissal of Benazir Bhutto's government. BJP withdraws support from Janata Dal government. Democracy movement changes constitution in Nepal.
1991	Nepal general elections. Nepali Congress wins majority. Elections in Bangladesh. Bangladesh National Party (BNP) wins. Rajiv Gandhi assassinated; P. V. Narasimha Rao minority Congress government; BJP government in Uttar Pradesh. Indian economic liberalization accelerated.
1992	Destruction of Babri Masjid, 6 December. Riots kill 1700, injure 5500 in four months.
1993	Dismissal of Nawaz Sharif. Benazir Bhutto returns to power after elections.

TABLE 8. *CONTINUED*

1994	Karachi MQM violence. Caste violence in Tamil Nadu.
1996	Thirteen-day minority BJP government. Bhutto dismissed. Nawaz Sharif returns. Awami League government in Bangladesh.
1998	Fall of Gujral government. BJP-led coalition government in India.
1999	Fall and re-election of BJP-led coalition government; Indo-Pakistan conflict in Kargil. Parvez Musharaf; military coup removes Nawaz Sharif from power.
2000	War over Tamil Eelam continues in Sri Lanka. Maoists in power in majority of Nepal districts. Caste wars in Bihar.

led by the Congress Party of Nepal brought a new constitution. In 1959, parliamentary elections gave the Nepal Congress a majority, but the constitution also retained the authority of the king, who dissolved Parliament, and, in 1962, proclaimed 'basic democracy' under a Panchayat System, banning all political parties. Crown Prince Birenda became king in 1972 and, like his father, married a member of the Rana family. The Panchayat System remained in place until 1990.

SEVEN

Identity Politics

The new nations in South Asia continued to change after independence in mid-century. Disparate trends occurred in old regions where national states used their new sovereign powers to unify and develop national territory. Influences also moved across national borders, circulating among nations, affecting them all. The meaning and substance of national identity and sovereignty changed more visibly after 1970, as national cultures, politics, and economies became more intricately interwoven by globalization, which we consider in more detail in Chapter Eight.

NATIONAL REGIONS

The national states that emerged after 1947 embraced many old regions, whose languages, cultures, societies, and politics were more deeply entrenched in everyday life than those of any new nation. National identity and governance were entrenched in some regions much more than in others; they had their deepest roots in urban centres and in the old imperial heartlands of agrarian wealth and elite culture. Empires had always embraced spatial and cultural diversity unevenly, elevating core regions and their elites to superior ranks, leaving peripheral, low-status regions weakly integrated into the imperial order. Old empires included motley assortments of officially unequal peoples living in diverse administrative and legal territories, embraced in various ways by state authorities who were but a tiny percentage of the imperial population. In sharp contrast, newly sovereign national states had comprehensive territorial ambitions. Their leaders sought to spread the sovereign power and the legitimate authority of national governments to include everyone and every place in national territory. New states generated increasingly large numbers of politically active citizens, embraced by standardized systems of law, administration, and politics. All citizens became officially equivalent constituent members of national communities that stretched from border to border. Regional cultural diversity was therefore no longer a mere context for state politics, as it had been for the empires: it became a constituent of the nation itself. National diversity would now be organized officially by the national state to produce cultural structures of national unity within state systems of education, art, literature, law, politics, public ritual, and armed force. Social identities in all the old regions would now be fashioned in national terms: people in localities and regions became fragments of the nation.

Identity politics acquired new life in this new world of nations, as regional and local identities became more politically prominent. India exemplifies wider trends. Until the 1970s, the Congress Party provided an all-inclusive political framework for India's diverse national fragments. But each decade increased the number of groups that were mobilized politically. Political parties proliferated, based in the states; they challenged Congress in Assembly elections, with increasing success. In 1975, India's Prime Minister, Indira Gandhi, tried to stem the decline of Congress by declaring a national state of emergency, which had the opposite effect: India's first non-Congress government came to New Delhi with the first post-emergency election. The proliferation of regional parties challenging Congress accelerated. In the 1990s, one-party governments in New Delhi gave way to kaleidoscopic coalitions. Indian nationality acquired disparate political forms. Nationhood became an official container for shifting, temporary alliances, with each political party anchored in its own state-based, ethno-cultural system of territorial power. Since 1990, Congress has continued to provide national leadership for governing coalitions in New Delhi, but only in competition with its national rival, the Bharatiya Janata Party, whose vision of Hindu India contradicts the official Congress vision.

Regions did not all fit neatly into the national mould: regional identities and politics could provoke resistance to dominant forms of national identity and modes of national governance. This kind of conflictual interaction between region and nation had been prominent in the run-up to Partition, in 1947; it also provoked the Bangladesh war of liberation from Pakistan; and it has sparked many analogous struggles, in various registers, over the decades in India, Pakistan, Sri Lanka, and Nepal. Regional struggles to secure state protection and benefits for workers, farmers, hill peoples and many other groups have mobilized ethnic, religious, and linguistic identities against established state structures of privilege and power. Challenges to national authority have also provoked popular movements to enforce national unity with physical force and with ideologies of ethno-cultural majoritarianism, which often deploy religion for national political purposes.

Political movements contesting the substance of national identity have also emerged from efforts to consolidate national power and authority against opposition from regional efforts to resist, revise, and even escape the national order. All this complexity of cultural politics has fed into and also responded to the rapid expansion of global media, migration, and finance. The meanings of religious identities and the politics of religious expression have grown more complicated, very often contradictory, even treacherous. Religion has acquired a new kind of history inside the increasingly global politics of national identity. For Buddhists, Christians, Sikhs, Muslims, and Hindus, the public mobilization of religion is only one part of cultural life: their religions have deep, multiple, intimate, cultural meanings outside of politics altogether. But religion has become ever more prominent in politics, over the last half-century, in much of the world. Recent history in South Asia indicates how the politics of religion has changed the form and substance of nationality in the world of globalization.

A CHANGING WORLD

Conditions affecting social experience, identity, and politics changed more dramatically after 1900 than ever before, and such changes accelerated further after 1950, 1970, and 1990. South Asia had always been thinly populated, but in the twentieth century it became known worldwide for 'overpopulation', so that reducing the number of children born to each woman became a political project, in pursuit of national development. South Asia had always been covered with forests, which disappeared at a quickening pace, as new land for farms also disappeared. Pressure increased to grow more on each plot, which brought a Green Revolution with more productive seeds, mechanized irrigation, and petrochemical fertilizers and pesticides. As land became covered with farming villages, commercial towns, and industrial cities, the very idea of 'open space' – owned by no one – became meaningless. Every inch of land now belonged to someone under the legal authority of the national state. In 2001, people living in South Asia outnumbered its entire cumulative population before 1900; everyone, and every inch of land, had an official identity in the eyes of the state. Politics in some form or other became an everyday necessity.

Urbanism has defined, intensified, and complicated national politics, as we have seen in the case of Calcutta. South Asia is still predominantly rural: officially only 30 percent of 'its people live in urban centres; this compares to 42 percent in South-East Asia and 50 percent in East Asia. This official count is probably low, but the more important fact is that urbanization has been accelerating for more than a century. Moreover, the very big cities are prime locations for elite wealth and power, sustained by networks of mobility running among urban centres around the world; and big cities radiate their influence outward into the surrounding regions, exerting disproportionate historical force. As a general rule, in Asia, higher *rates* of urbanization appear in areas with lower overall *levels* of urbanization, so the least urbanized areas with the most rustic environments experience the greatest proportional urbanization, as village folk migrate to settle in cities, generating the most dramatic transformation in the region.

India exemplifies the overall urbanization trend: its urban population increased by just over one percent (from 11 percent to 12 percent) in the first three decades of the twentieth century; then by six percent during the next three decades (1931–61); and then by eight percent over the next three decades (1961–91). This accelerating upward trend has continued in all regions except Sri Lanka, which started with a relatively large urban population (12 percent in 1901) and had less than twice that figure (22 percent) in 1991, whereas India's 1991 figure (26 percent) was 2.4 times the 1901 level (11 percent). Decades of war in Sri Lanka, which ended only in 2009, featured attacks on cities that may have further reduced the rate of urbanization.

Less urbanized regions have continued to urbanize faster. Pakistan urbanized 70 percent faster than India after 1961, reaching 33 percent in 1991. Since then, Nepal and Afghanistan have urbanized the fastest; their urban populations are now growing at over five percent per annum. Nepal's small urban population (nine percent in 1991) grew as fast as Pakistan's after 1961. Bangladesh urbanized faster still: its 1961 population was only five percent urban, double the 1901 figure; it then quadrupled after 1961 to reach 20 percent in 1991. South Asia as a whole is on average urbanizing twice as fast as East Asia, though it is still less urbanized overall.

In addition, echoing Calcutta's oversized role in the early twentieth century, South Asia has exceptionally large cities, which create dramatic contrasts between huge urban centres and their vast rural surroundings. Delhi and Mumbai compare in size (20 million) with Seoul and Jakarta, and today, Dhaka, with 15 million inhabitants, is the fastest-growing 'mega-city' in the world. Dhaka's population has increased fourfold in the last twenty-five years, and doubled in size (from six to 12 million) between 1990 and 2005, after the return of civilian government. The UN predicts that by 2025, Dhaka will have more than 20 million people and be larger than Mexico City, Beijing, and Shanghai. South Asia has four of the largest cities in Asia (fourth, Delhi; fifth, Mumbai; ninth, Kolkata; tenth, Karachi), and ten out of the top thirty (including Dhaka, Lahore, Chennai, Bangalore, Hyderabad, and Ahmedabad); each of these major hubs has a place in the transnational circuits of capital and labour mobility that now define the geography of globalization.

Urbanization represents a shift in the economic balance of power, favouring industry and services over agriculture. In the first half of the twentieth century, South Asia actually became more agricultural, as cultivators and farm workers in undivided India increased from 69 percent to 73 percent of the male workforce between 1901 and 1951. From the 1950s onward, heavy national state investments in industry and city-centred government institutions and economic infrastructure rapidly reversed that trend. Urbanization accompanied unprecedented economic growth. India's Gross Domestic Product (GDP) had previously declined for more than a century, compared to Britain and America, until 1947, when that negative trend stopped abruptly. Independence allowed India and other post-colonial countries in Asia to keep and create more wealth inside national territory. India remained poor, with per capita GDP hovering at around 10 percent of the US–UK average, and it is still the poorest of the world's five largest national economies, but India's trend of relative impoverishment compared to rich Western countries stopped dead in 1947. From the 1960s, as farms became more productive during the Green Revolution, farming declined as a proportion of the national economy. GDP and employment shifted towards urban industries and services. In the 1990s, farming accounted for only 57 percent of the workforce in Bangladesh, 63 percent in India, 50 percent in Pakistan, and 43 percent in Sri Lanka. Since 1991, cities have housed the rapid growth of the service sector, and, reflecting a larger trend, farms in India today account for only 18 percent of GDP.

The physical landscape has been transformed in the last half-century. During the three decades after 1950, livestock, net cultivation, and built-up land increased as much as they had during the seven previous decades, while forest cover declined at about the same rate and the population grew about 15 percent faster. Vast areas were transformed over a very short time. After 1950, a million people moved from Bihar into the Chhotanagpur jungles to turn tribal farmland into industrial sites and mines. Farmers and miners marched into the mountains to acquire land and minerals; big dams produced vast lakes in the mountains to generate electricity and irrigation in the plains. Lowlanders pursuing state programmes of economic development displaced and incorporated hill peoples across the central and eastern mountain-forest belt in India, in north-east India, and in the Chittagong Hill Tracts of Bangladesh, swelling the ranks of tribal insurgencies. Mountain peoples engaged in struggles for automony in many of these regions, as well as in the west, from Baluchistan to Kashmir.

Urban political upheavals have also been propelled by the transformations of the countryside, sending many poor migrants into the city, who have arrived in tidal waves during seasons of distress and dislocation. Famines brought millions of hungry families into Calcutta, Dhaka, and Patna in the 1940s, 1950s, 1960s, and 1970s. The Calcutta riots in 1946 encouraged the partition of British India, which in turn uprooted Punjabis who poured into Delhi, and Uttar Pradesh Muslims who resettled in Karachi and Lahore. The relative decline of agricultural employment and wealth has attracted impoverished villagers to the city, where their living conditions are typically dire. In 2005, an estimated 50 percent of the total urban population in South Asia lived in slums, with higher proportions in Bangladesh (71 percent) and Nepal (61 percent).

Inequality in the countryside became inequality in the city, as upward mobility in the villages enriched cities by bringing in well-to-do residents, businesses, and professionals. One small but useful example comes from Nellore District, just north of Madras in Andhra Pradesh, where improved irrigation and urban demand for rural products pushed up land rents by a factor of nine between 1850 and 1927, and then doubled rents again from 1927 to 1982. The ratio of rental income to farm output also increased, especially after 1940, and this additional income fed the upward social mobility of the rustic rent receivers, who moved out of farming and into urban business, education, and employment. Families receiving higher rents moved from village to town and to the big city, where rising rents in the village fed urban consumers, and urban expansion raised the value of city real estate. The concentration of wealth and investments in the cities exaggerated urban–rural differences to make cities more attractive places to live and work.

Migration has also led overseas. Many millions have travelled first by sea and then by air to live and work in richer countries for long and short periods of time, and often to settle permanently. They typically cherish their national identities, and actively engage national cultures and politics from abroad. Overseas Indian nationality was famously embodied in Mohandas Gandhi's career in South Africa, where he defended Indian rights in a context marked by legal distinctions among Europeans, Africans, and Indians. On his return to India, Gandhi unified nationalist forces, testifying to the sense of cultural unity that was being cultivated among overseas Indians then, and is still today. After 1947, citizen identities stamped in passports travelled with migrants overseas. The term 'diaspora' came to represent an expansive mobile space of South Asian national identities. Non-resident nationals from all of the South Asian countries became important political partisans and supporters of aspiring groups in their home countries. Nationalism has been international from the very beginning, and India's founding generation included many leaders with a broadly transnational vision. Since independence, every major political and cultural movement in South Asia has involved overseas nationals, and overseas earnings have been heavily invested in many South Asian localities, which became attached economically to widening circuits of migration and business. Thus the world economy also became a mobile space for changing social identities inside South Asia.

TRANSITIONAL DECADES

A transitional period in the politics of nationality began in the 1960s and accelerated in the 1970s, which also launched the age of globalization that we will study in the next chapter. Until 1967, Congress politicians monopolized national leadership, but in that year they lost control of the state governments in Kerala, Tamil Nadu, and West Bengal. In each state, parties came to power with more radical, populist agendas than Congress could muster for constituents who demanded more effective state action to improve social conditions. Decades of popular mobilization and economic development had spawned aspirations that Congress could not satisfy. Activists sought new solutions and rallied support in regional vernacular languages, which became more prominent in politics. Like Sheikh Mujib and the Awami League in East Pakistan, Indian populists worked in social environments marked by severe inequity, and they attracted followers by attacking the established elites. India's Congress system had rested on old national loyalties that legitimized Congress power-brokers who managed patronage flowing from New Delhi. In the early decades of national independence, economic growth in all of the South Asian countries had strengthened national parties, their elite power base, and the politics of national self-sufficiency. The economic downturn during the world oil crisis and recession in the 1970s cost the old political establishment much of its legitimacy. Difficult financial times led national governments to borrow funds from international agencies, which supervised a revision of national sovereignty to reduce government economic controls, increase international trade, boost imports and exports, and improve the market environment for business enterprise.

National politicians had promoted national business enterprise since the days of *swadeshi*: Gandhi had worked closely with big-business families, notably the Birlas, and Nehru's economic development regime featured national plans designed to improve national markets for national products. The Congress embraced and supported Indian industrialists such as the Tatas, and in the 1970s, when Indira Gandhi faced pressure to resign, a group of major businessmen, led by K. K. Birla, encouraged her to stay in power. India's military victory against Pakistan in 1971 had lifted Prime Minister Indira Gandhi's popularity, and in 1975, facing threats from all around, she declared a draconian national emergency, suspending civil rights with constitutional powers retained from the 1935 Government of India Act. The emergency regime was intended to stabilize the political environment in which she supported business groups, who in turn supported a shift in national policies that would increase profits and production.

The 1970s brought a shift towards more open market economies in the South Asian countries, and a shift in national politics that included more popular disruption and more state militarism. This complicated double trend began with Pakistan's repression and war in Bangladesh, which echoed the British Empire's response to nationalist agitation. When the Indian army expelled Pakistan from Bangladesh, in December 1971, it was also crushing a four-year, communist-led peasant revolt in nearby Naxalbari, in the Darjeeling district, in the Himalayan foothills of West Bengal.

At the same time, the army and police suppressed Naxalite supporters in Calcutta. Also in 1971, Sri Lankan armies massacred People's
Liberation Front revolutionaries and suppressed their public supporters. Sri Lanka's 1972 constitution strove to strengthen Sinhala
Buddhist national dominance. In 1975, Sheikh Mujib was killed,
along with most of his family, in a coup that brought army rule to
Bangladesh for fifteen years.

Charan Singh's fear of rustic radicals had proved justified:
revolts broke out in many Indian districts, where poor peasants and
workers and forest peoples attacked elites supported by the army,
the police, and the courts, turning subaltern wrath against the state.
In 1975, India's Home Ministry echoed Nehru's 1930 declaration
by reporting that continued failure to alleviate severe inequalities
'may lead to a situation where the discontented elements are compelled to organize themselves and the extreme tensions building up
within . . . the Indian village may end in an explosion'. In the decades following the emergency, special military powers and martial
law regulations were imposed with increasing regularity to suppress
rebellions in many regions. Personalized Congress power lost its
popular base. After Indira Gandhi's assassination in 1984, in retaliation for the military's attack on Sikh rebels in Amritsar, her son
Rajiv became Prime Minister and effectively signed a death warrant
for the old Congress system of one-party rule in India, at the cele-
bration of the party's 100th anniversary, blasting 'cliques' which
held 'the living body of the Congress in their net of avarice'.

In the 1970s, the everyday social life of nationality came to
include many struggles pitting citizen against citizen and against
national states. New social movements arose among workers,
women, farmers, tribal groups, and other underprivileged people to
fight for new citizen rights. The mobilization of former untouchables and *harijans* produced a new radical social identity for Dalits
('the oppressed'). Ethnic regional autonomy movements erupted.
Indian Sikhs fought for an independent Khalistan in Punjab, supported by Sikhs abroad; they were crushed by the Indian army in
1984, triggering Indira Gandhi's assassination by her Sikh bodyguards and a massacre of Sikhs in Delhi supported by Congress
thugs. Militant Tamils fought for Eelam in Sri Lanka, supported by
overseas Tamils; they warred for two decades, until the Sri Lankan
army finally crushed the rebels in 2009, with widespread civilian
suffering. Kashmiris fought to free Kashmir, erupting in the 1990s
in pitched battles with the Indian army, which produced a massive
Indian military occupation of Kashmir and led to more upheavals

and the alienation of Kashmiri identity from Indian nationality. Mountain peoples fought for autonomy in Assam, Mizoram, and Nagaland. In 1991, as democratic movements brought down autocratic regimes in Nepal and Bangladesh, to establish elected governments, Afghanistan became a battleground for warring citizens against the kings, Russians, the Taliban, and Americans. A Maoist revolution spread across Nepal and then across eastern India.

The changing social character of nationality in South Asia was also influenced by trends in the wider world. As we have seen, South Asia has never been isolated, and before 1970 its new national environments were certainly affected by world capitalism, socialism, and the Cold War; but the wider world had a more pervasive influence from the 1970s onward. Foreign aid donors, the World Bank, and the International Monetary Fund (IMF) supervised a revision of national sovereignty by bringing South Asia governments into programmes of 'structural adjustment' in return for economic development loans. National economic policies were then tuned to the expansion of world markets and to the increasing influence of big business. The result was more rapid economic growth and increasing inequality. Emigration also accelerated as foreign companies, overseas connections, and global media became more influential in national life, and new social movements went global in their struggles for human rights.

This expanding set of global interconnections informed the public reformulation of national identities, as conservative public activists used every means at their disposal to reinforce the nation's eternal unity and stability. Sri Lanka's 1972 constitution was a landmark in its implicit declaration that Sri Lanka belonged to Sinhalese Buddhists. At the same time, Sheikh Mujib declared to a gathering of non-Bengalis in the Bangladesh Chittagong Hill Tracts, 'We are all Bengalis now'. Hindu India, Islamic Pakistan, and Islamic Afghanistan emerged as new formations of national identity, steeped in majoritarian politics, suppressing minority rights and fighting against change in dominant social power relations, using religious formulations that captured the limelight overseas, where political and financial support emerged among the diaspora communities.

Meanwhile, cities spawned a cosmopolitan youth culture that travelled a world of nations that was very different from the one their parents had known. National cultures have been transformed since 1970 by changing social identities among interacting local, regional, international, and global trends. Today's emerging social identities include mixtures of meanings and substance that are unstable and unpredictable. Identities are being reconstructed constantly in ever more diverse cultural idioms. Communications media – cinema, television, and now the internet – are expanding the influence and spreading the ideas of public activists more widely than ever before. More groups than ever before mobilize now to increase their entitlements, secure their rights, and turn their popular support into political power. Public identities, promulgated by public activists, now influence social identity ever more widely.

During the transitional decades, from the 1960s, identity politics in South Asia moved rapidly beyond what now seems to have been the youthful, euphoric simplicity of national independence. Nationality and nationhood became visibly shifting formulations of social identity and political power whose unpredictable histories run across the long twentieth century and into the future. In that context, religion has become an increasingly prominent feature of cultural politics.

BUDDHIST REFORMERS, EXILES, RULERS, AND MAJORITARIANS

By 1900, new Buddhist organizations were being established by social reformers in British India to invent a cultural alternative to the Hindu caste ideology, which some reformers saw as the root of degradation and deprivation for poor people in the lowest Hindu caste groups. In 1900, a prominent Brahman officer in Madras, S. Srivinasa Raghava Aiyangar, submitted an official report saying that untouchable Pariahs in Madras could not make progress without leaving Hinduism.

Fifty years later – and twenty-five years after he relented to Gandhi on the question of separate electorates for Indian untouchables – B. R. Ambedkar converted to Buddhism and led a mass neo-Buddhist conversion movement in Maharashtra. Ambedkar had been the main author of India's constitution, where he secured state recognition for 'scheduled castes', that is, the untouchable *jati*s listed on a constitutional schedule of groups needing special government assistance. By 1956, however, Ambedkar had concluded that government efforts and Gandhian voluntarism would never empower the poorest Hindus. He led several hundred thousand converts to Buddhism in order to provide them with the organization, visibility, and state recognition that came with being members of an officially recognized religious community. The new Buddhists sought to gain political representation that they could not acquire by other means. Today, they number as many as four million, mostly among Mahars in Maharashtra, though their numbers remain hard to assess because of political resistance to their official enumeration.

Also in the 1950s, a very different kind of dissident Buddhist identity came into being when China conquered Tibet. Thousands of Tibetan Buddhist refugees, including leading Lamas and the Dalai Lama himself, settled in exile communities in north India and Nepal. These countries became bases for the international movement to restore the Dalai Lama in a free Tibet, which continues today. New Buddhist visibility in Nepal energized Nepal's own Buddhist cultural identities in a country where the ruling elites were mostly Brahman, the majority population was Hindu, and the law of the land enforced divisions among religions and Hindu castes.

By contrast, in the old Himalayan kingdoms of Sikkim and Bhutan, regional forms of Tibetan Buddhism remained state religions, as under the old Lamas in Tibet. Sikkim was incorporated into India in 1975, when it became a Buddhist state in a vastly diverse, secular, multicultural republic. Bhutan remained an independent nation where state Buddhism sustained a substantial population of influential monks. In Bhutan's southern region, the large national minority of Nepali Hindus became politically suspect. Since 1980, Nepalis have been pressured to repatriate to Nepal or to adopt Bhutan's national dress, customs, religion, and language; as have the fifteen percent of Bhutan's people who are from indigenous and/or migratory tribal groups.

Making Buddhism into a ruling Sinhala state religion became a political project for monks and allied activists in Sri Lanka, who endeavour to use Buddhism to unite the country against threats from Tamils, Marxists, and Western culture. This recent political trend represents a much longer and quite varied tradition of Buddhist activism. Since the nineteenth century, many social movements with multiple political agendas have reinterpreted Buddhism and deployed its cultural authority on the island. As a result, Buddhism today means many things in Sri Lanka, as it does in South Asia more generally. The Siam Nikaya are a conservative, wealthy Buddhist sect in which membership is restricted to high-caste Goigama families. The large Amarapura sect has grown over the years by reaching out to include lower castes. Various social reform sects have also emerged. The most prominent are the Sarvodaya groups that conduct social programmes such as those of the Gandhian Sarvodaya movement in India, using volunteers among the middle classes to serve the rural poor.

After the outbreak of civil war in 1983, when Tamil fighters and Sri Lankan troops in their hundreds started killing each other, Buddhist nationalism attained broader public influence. This occurred at the same time as Hindu nationalism gained ascendancy in India, and the two have much in common. They both endeavour to define and enforce allegiance to a national ethnicity that was described by official religious categories under British rule. Neither has any substantial theological basis, and both gloss over diversity within religious communities and ambiguities at their borders. Both combine a reverence for classical texts and modern language with support from religious activists to forge an ethnic-linguistic support for national cultural unity defined by religious community.

Their nationalization of ethnicity involves an ethnic genealogy of the nation that dominates Sinhala Buddhist as it does Hindu nationalist (Hindutva) historical writing. The *Mahavamsa* is often cited and interpreted by Sinhala Buddhist activists to establish basic articles of faith, which are these: (1) Sinhala identity can be traced genealogically to the arrival of Vijaya in ancient times, when (2) Buddha chose Sri Lanka to be a pure island for his teaching (*dhamma dipa*). Thus (3) the Sinhala have been chosen as pure Aryans from Buddha's home territory to protect his *dhamma* for ever. (4) Sinhala Buddhists had been ruled by their kings, and are today ruled by an elected government that continues the mission to protect *dhamma*. (5) Tamils are intruders from South India who are neither Buddhist nor Aryan. Their language is Dravidian, while Sinhala is Indo-Aryan. Tamils occupy parts of a Sinhala Buddhist motherland (*mawbima*). Such ideas anchor Buddhist nationalism in Sri Lanka.

CHRISTIAN COMMUNITIES, REFORMERS, MINORITIES, AND TARGETS

In 1900, the size and diversity of South Asia's many small Christian societies continued to increase with the influx of Europeans, the spread of English education, the growth of ethnically mixed Anglo-Indian communities, and the expansion of missionary education and medical facilities. As European residents declined in number in South Asia, the Christian population continued to expand. The vast majority of Christians and Christian missionaries in South Asia have always been South Asians, and after 1940, the number of ethnically non-South Asian Christians became insignificant.

Christian societies have ethnic and regional patterns, like others. The oldest Christian communities began in medieval Kerala, where

Syrian Christians remain a majority in the northern districts and a potent cultural and political force in the state as a whole. After 1500, Catholicism spread around the Portuguese and French settlements; Protestantism, around Dutch and English settlements. In Sri Lanka, numerous English-educated urbanites are from upper-caste Sinhala (Goigama) and Tamil (Vellala) families. In the nineteenth and twentieth centuries, Protestant missionaries and churches became part of local society in many urban centres but were most influential among the poor and in marginal areas, where they provided education and medical care. Missionary schools and hospitals provided a public service to many people who were served poorly or not at all by the state. India's poor north-eastern hill states are almost all Protestant.

Christians became most numerous in the scattered localities along the coast from Goa to Madras, in Sri Lanka, and in India's north-eastern mountains. Christian social elites include Catholics, Syrian Christians, and Protestants in Goa, Kerala, Sri Lanka, and India's north-eastern hill states (Meghalaya, Mizoram, Nagaland, and Manipur). But in these regions and in others, the majority of Christians are poor people with low-caste backgrounds, Anglo-Indians, and mountain people. Protestant churches in particular developed a reputation for social reform and local activism. In the nineteenth century, for example, missionaries built schools and communities of converts among the low-caste Shanars in southern Madras Presidency whose English education allowed them to become the most prominent of all non-elite castes in education and government service. Today, Protestant church groups are active in movements to improve living conditions among poor low-caste and tribal peoples in many parts of India.

External perceptions of Christians by people in more powerful social groups have been important for Christian identities. The British government provided support for Christian activities. Though many social reformers in South Asia were influenced by Christianity, and though individual Christians did gain public prominence, particularly in Sri Lanka, Christians never became a national political force anywhere in South Asia. Their respected minority stature in Indian politics was established by national leaders such as Ram Mohun Roy, Sri Ramakrishna, Sri Aurobindo, and Mohandas Gandhi, all of whom saw Christianity as one *dharma* or spiritual path among others inside India's all-inclusive culture.

Hindu nationalists have made Christian conversion a politically rancorous issue. In the early twentieth century, the Arya Samaj and

Hindu Mahasabha began promoting the idea that Christians and Muslims were taking Hindus away from their native faith to bolster alien powers, particularly in Punjab. More anti-Christian activism came with the Rashtriya Swayamsevak Sangh (RSS), formed in 1925. Hindu nationalists kept their distance from national politics before independence, and staked their superior claim to represent the nation on their militant defence of Hindu tradition. They took this to include fierce resistance to all Muslim and Christian influence. The Vishwa Hindu Parishad (VHP), Jana Sangh, and Bharatiya Janata Party (BJP) followed this strategy after independence, with increasing vehemence after 1980. Since the 1950s, politically prominent Buddhist monks in Sri Lanka have also attacked Christian influence in government. Since the 1990s, Indian Christian schools, churches, and clinics have been burnt to the ground in the name of Hindu pride. Hindu nationalist (Hindutva) activists have killed Christian missionaries.

SIKH ELECTORATES, RELIGION, RIGHTS, AND TERRITORY

As we have seen in Chapter Six, the 1932 communal award gave Sikhs separate representation in Punjab. In 1948, Punjab's mountain districts were made into the Indian state of Himachal Pradesh. In 1966, Haryana became a predominantly Hindu, Hindi-speaking state. Indian Punjab then became a primarily Sikh, Punjabi-speaking state.

High levels of public and private investments in agricultural productivity made the three plains regions of old Punjab – Pakistani Punjab, Indian Punjab, and Haryana – the wealthiest agrarian regions in South Asia, and among the most productive in the world. The rising wealth of Punjab came with a combination of state and local investments that enriched Jat farming lineages, and also helps to explain the territorial politics behind Punjab's three partitions. Sikh, Hindu, and Muslim identities in Punjab changed in relation to one another; and state policy combined with lineage power to produce an ethnically and religiously organized agrarian citizenry.

The rivers of Punjab flow down from Afghanistan, Kashmir, and the Himalayas; and the long history of contemporary Punjabi politics has moved up and down these river valleys as well as down roads across the Indus and Ganga plains. In strategic crossroads of empire, solidarity among landed warriors sustained the official imperial idea of 'Indian village republics', which was most rigorously applied in Punjab. After the annexation of Punjab in 1849, the Punjab village became a proprietary body composed of landed lineages. Village culture changed as collective arrangements for local defence became unnecessary and the joint interests of lineages focused on privatizing family control over land and labour. By 1900, Punjab landowners had privatized all the open, common land around their villages. As Jat lineages expanded their control over agricultural territory, their sons became the backbone of the Indian army. The imperial military was organized around ethnic regiments in which the so-called 'martial races' of Punjab were most highly valued, along with Gurkha recruits from Nepal.

A preference for Punjabi soldiers combined with Punjab's location astride routes to Central Asia made Punjab critical territory for imperial military strategists. This paid huge local dividends in Punjab. Road and railway building benefited cities where merchants sent export commodities from Punjab and Kashmir to Karachi, Bombay, and Calcutta. Lahore boomed as the regional capital. Military installations brought lucrative contracts for supplies and construction. From 1880 to 1930, the state built huge systems of irrigation dams and canals in Punjab and in western districts of the United Provinces (Uttar Pradesh), to water the land of Jat farmers adorned with the imperial reputation of being the most productive farmers in India. In Punjab, the Canal Colonies especially benefited military families. Farms were large and provided ample scope for investment at low rents. The Punjab government granted most land to families officially defined as 'peasant', owning one square of about 27 acres each; larger tracts (with up to three squares) to 'yeomen' farmers and 'military' grantees; and huge tracts to 'capitalist' farmers with five to 100 squares.

Heavy government investments in the land of old Punjab continued after 1947. In the 1960s, under the aegis of the Green Revolution, public and private investments accelerated. As a result, the regions of old Punjab became powerful economically in India and in Pakistan. In 1992, Punjab and Haryana together held nine percent of India's population and eight percent of its cultivated acreage, but 17 percent of its food grains. In India, only Punjab and Haryana have routinely had large food-crop surpluses to export to other states: Punjab has proportionately six times as much food as it has people, and Haryana, three times as much. Since 1960, Punjab and Haryana have also had the highest growth rate in the value of agricultural produce. Very substantial farmers own much of this prime farmland. In India as a whole, 73 percent of all farmers work holdings of less than one hectare, but the Punjab and Haryana average is around two-thirds of that figure, meaning that many more land holdings are large. Some of Punjab's very large farmers are truly capitalist tycoons with thousands of acres under potatoes, flowers, rice, and many other crops for sale on world markets.

The individual economic success of Punjab farmers is rooted in a long history of collective action. As we have seen, religious solidarities have been prominent since the foundation of Sikhism. Soon after Punjab became a province of British India, the Brahmo Samaj became active in Punjab, spawning the Arya Samaj to pursue a similar reformist agenda but with stronger commitments to the sanctity of the Vedas and with a harsh critical stance towards other religions. Muslim and Sikh activists responded in kind, as Christian missionaries became the most prominent providers of English education.

Sikh Sabhas were first organized by large landowners and by Sikh native-state rulers but soon came to be led by middle-class activists who organized Sikhs to increase their employment and their influence in government. At the same time, Sikh army regiments gave Singh families rising in the imperial ranks more influence in shaping a Sikh identity; this became a critical feature of the empire's military recruitment and discipline. In 1900, when the Punjab Land Alienation Act set in motion a political opposition between merchants and farmers in Punjab, it also fostered opposed solidarities among Hindu merchants allied with the Congress and Muslim and Sikh landowning groups that were much more successful than Congress in elections.

The Shiromani Akali Dal was founded in 1925 to represent Sikh political interests after the Gurdwara reform movement succeeded in making representatives of the Sikh community official managers of Sikh temples (Gurdwaras). Thus religious institutions became centres of Sikh politics, which became more urbanized and religious in tone. During the partition of Punjab in 1947, violence forced Sikhs out of the Canal Colonies (which fell into Pakistan) and into eastern Punjab and New Delhi, where their numbers and influence increased. In independent India, the electoral success of Sikh parties led Congress politicians to pursue strategies to win Sikh votes and to keep the Akali Dal in check. Green Revolution policies favoured Punjab economically, and a gleaming new capital arose in Chandigarh (after losing Lahore to Pakistan).

After Jawaharlal Nehru's death in 1964, and the creation of a Sikh Punjab in 1966, the Akali Dal faced stiff competition from other parties in Punjab. But now the Congress was also weakening.

National struggles for power would prove momentous for Sikhs in Punjab.

Until 1967, Congress controlled Indian state governments as well as the upper (Raj Sabha) and lower (Lok Sabha) houses of Parliament in New Delhi. But in 1967, regional parties began to beat Congress in state Assembly and Lok Sabha elections, beginning in Tamil Nadu, Kerala, and West Bengal. At this fractious time, Nehru's Oxford-educated daughter, Indira Gandhi (1917–84), ascended to the Congress leadership. She had been primed for the role by her father. She became Minister of Information and Broadcasting under his successor, Lal Bahadur Shastri, and then Prime Minister after Shastri's sudden death in 1966.

Indira Gandhi struggled for the next decade to strengthen herself against Congress rivals, to maintain Congress power in the states against regional parties, and to prevent defections from Congress. Her political strategy centred on cultivating personal loyalties and increasing her personal authority in Congress, and it succeeded for a time. But in 1975, faced with a legal challenge to her own election victory, she instituted a national emergency regime using martial law powers retained from the 1935 Government of India Act. Two years later, she lifted the emergency, held national elections, and lost. A non-Congress coalition government led by the Janata Dal and Jayaprakah Narayan (1902–79), a venerable Gandhian and former Congressman, came to power in Delhi. Under this government, which lasted three years, calls for more regional autonomy became insistent.

The most famous of these calls for more regional autonomy was the Anandpur Sahib Resolution, a landmark in modern Sikhism. It was composed by a committee of the Shiromani Akali Dal, appointed in 1972, and adopted unanimously by its working committee in 1973 at Anandpur Sahib, a town sacred to Guru Gobind Singh and revered as the birthplace of the *khalsa*. The resolution was proclaimed in 1978 by the All-India Akali Conference at Ludhiana. Citing the centralization of national powers 'in the form of the Emergency, when all fundamental rights of all citizens were usurped', and proclaiming support from various non-Congress parties for 'the principle of State autonomy in keeping with the concept of Federalism', the resolution pressed the Janata government 'to take cognizance of the different linguistic and cultural sections, religious minorities as also the voice of millions of people and [to] recast the constitutional structure of the country on real and meaningful federal principles to obviate the possibility of any danger to National unity and the integrity of the Country'.

The Anandpur Sahib Resolution affirmed that 'the Shiromani Akali Dal is the very embodiment of the hopes and aspirations of the Sikh Nation and as such is fully entitled to its representation', and went on to assert that 'basic postulates of this Organization are Human progress and ultimate unity of all human beings with the Spiritual Soul', based on 'the three great principles of Guru Nanak Dev Ji, namely, a Meditation on God's Name, dignity of Labour and sharing of fruits of this Labour'. Authenticated by the Akali Dal leader, Sant Harchand Singh Longowal, the resolution concentrated on an economic programme whose 'chief sources of inspiration . . . [are] the secular, democratic and socialistic concepts of Sri Guru Nanak Dev and Sri Guru Gobind Singh Ji', which are 'Dignity of Labour; An economic and social structure which provides for the uplift of the poor and depressed sections of society; and Unabated opposition to concentration of economic and political power in the hands of the capitalists'. The secular dimensions of the resolution stand out, and it goes on to proclaim 'the need to break the monopolistic hold of the capitalists foisted on the Indian economy by 30 years of Congress rule in India'. It is well worth quoting at length.

> This capitalistic hold enabled the central government to assume all powers in its hands after the manner of Mughal Imperialism. This was bound to thwart the economic progress of the states and injure the social and economic interests of the people. The Shiromani Akali Dal once again reiterates the Sikh way of life by resolving to fulfil the holy words of Guru Nanak Dev: 'He alone realizes the True Path who labours honestly and shares the fruits of that Labour.'

> The Shiromani Akali Dal calls upon the Central and the State Government to eradicate unemployment during the next ten years. While pursuing this aim special emphasis should be laid on ameliorating the lot of the weaker sections, Scheduled and depressed classes, workers, landless and poor farmers and urban poor. Minimum wages should be fixed for them all.

> The Shiromani Akali Dal urges upon the Punjab Government to draw up such an economic plan for the State as would turn it into the leading province during the next ten years, by raising per capita income to Rs. 3,000 and by generating an economic growth rate of 7% per annum as against 4% at National level.

The Shiromani Akali Dal gives first priority to the redrafting of the taxation structure in such a way that the burden of taxation is shifted from the poor to the richer classes and an equitable distribution of National income is ensured. The main plank of the economic programme of the Shiromani Akali Dal is to enable the economically weaker sections of the Society to share the fruits of National income.

In opposition to the secular and constitutional tone of the Akali Dal's resolution, a radical Sikh militant movement arose around a young mystic, Sant Jarnail Singh Bhindranwale, whose following grew after Indira Gandhi returned to become Prime Minister in 1980. Militant calls for an independent Sikh state, Khalistan, inspired Bhindranwale's militant followers to take up arms. A war ensued in Punjab. In 1984, the Indian army trapped the rebels in the Golden Temple, in Amritsar, and killed them all during Operation Bluestar, damaging the Golden Temple in the process. This provoked outrage even among Sikhs such as Longowal who opposed Bhindranwale; it also provoked the riotous murders of Sikhs in Delhi with police complicity. In apparent retaliation, several of her Sikh bodyguards assassinated Indira Gandhi. Massive anti-Sikh riots then broke out in Delhi, where the police and local Congress activists were implicated in atrocities. When her son, Rajiv, became Prime Minister and signed a pact with Sant Longowal, accepting basic Anandapur Sahib demands, Longowal was shot dead by three young Sikhs in the Akal Parkash Gurdwara at Sherpur in Sangrur District, where he had gone to address an Akali Dal conference.

Since 1985, the Akali Dal has pursued a strategy of optimizing its leadership within shifting political coalitions, and the party has splintered into various factions. Since 1998, the Akali Dal has worked in coalition with the BJP, but remains committed to Anandpur Sahib. Its Amritsar Declaration, in 1994, 'reiterates its commitment to pursue a democratic struggle for the creation of a separate region for the Sikhs, where they can enjoy freedom . . . [and] the practice of ideals enshrined in the Guru Granth Sahib of universal brotherhood and unity, humility, corruption-free politics and peaceful coexistence . . . [where] religious, economic, political and social institutions based on the Sikh way of life will uphold moral awareness, and also provide the Sikh people with a place in history, hitherto unavailable'. The Amritsar Declaration concludes thus: 'In case such a new confederal structure is not accepted by

Indian rulers, then the Shiromani Akali Dal has no option but to demand and struggle for an independent and sovereign Sikh state.'

MUSLIM SOCIETIES, POLITICS, MINORITIES, AND NATIONALITY

In 1900, Muslims lived in every region of South Asia. They were part of regional society like any other group. Muslim communities, like others, were organized on ethnic lines within localities where religious institutions and leaders enjoyed prominence and respect. Islam was one feature of Muslim social identity among many others. For most Muslims, belonging to the *umma* or community of believers meant participating in local religious activities, though in theology, it evoked a spiritual community of all Muslims. This theological concept was part of a Muslim cultural ethos that travelled with Muslims across wide migratory circuits in Asia and Africa. Migratory Muslims continued to travel these old circuits in the nineteenth and twentieth centuries, creating social connections and cultural communication among dispersed Muslim communities. Among migratory groups, merchants, artisans, and manual workers were most numerous, though in and around Bengal especially, peasant migrations to settle new land also changed the social composition of local populations. Among migratory cultural activists, learned Muslim religious leaders were important as communicators of ideas about Islam and of information about Muslim societies in distant places.

South Asia has long been historically part of a wider Muslim world. Muslim societies have developed and spread across countless political domains from Africa to the Philippines. Muslim Arabs colonized the Kerala coast in the eighth century. Arab merchant communities later formed coastal enclaves all around the Indian Ocean, from Zanzibar to Indonesia. After 1300, inland migrations brought Turks, Afghans, and Persians into India, where they settled mostly in towns and cities; and local conversion and long-distance migration also produced large Muslim populations across Afghanistan, Baluchistan, Sind, Punjab, and Bengal. Urban Muslim societies spread from Mughal times across the Indian peninsula.

By 1900, primarily pastoral and agrarian Muslim societies covered Baluchistan, Sind, Afghanistan, and Punjab. Stratified village societies with Muslim farmers and landlords covered Sind, western Punjab, and eastern Bengal. Urban Muslim communities composed mostly of merchants, literati, aristocrats, and craftworkers were scattered across the Gangetic Plain, in the Deccan, and in coastal regions, including Sri Lanka. Muslim societies in all these regions have very different histories. Locally, these histories carry ethnic cultures that are often quite loosely attached to religion. For example, Sri Lanka's Muslims are mostly Tamil-speakers. Muslim Tamils in Sri Lanka and India have historically identified with Tamil culture. Muslim Tamil writers have made major contributions to Tamil literature. Muslims in Tamil Nadu became prominent Tamil nationalists in the twentieth century. Similar ethnic and regional affiliations define Muslim identities everywhere.

The British Empire produced a new official environment for South Asia's Muslim societies. The official classification of Muslims as a single religious community in the empire gave all Indian Muslims a common feature they had never had before. Communications among diverse communities came to include public assertions that being Muslim meant being a different kind of Indian. Muslim society became a different kind of native society. Its difference was inscribed with various meanings. The 1857 rebellion made Muslim identity fearsome for imperial authority. In 1871, Muslims became a single population. As we have seen, Lord Mayo commissioned a report from W. W. Hunter to evaluate the political threat that Muslims posed as a population. In Bengal, Bankim Chandra Chatterjee's historical novels imbued Muslim difference with animosity among Bengali Hindus. In Punjab, the Arya Samaj depicted all Muslims as foreigners in a Hindu land.

As Muslim communities became officially distinct from their social surroundings, and as they became officially homogenized into a population of different Indians, Muslims developed a more distinctively Muslim idiom of public activity. Muslim petitioners and representatives stressed the religion that defined their common official identity rather than all the other elements in their diverse social identities. In this context, clerics, Sufis, scholars, missionaries, mystics, poets, and other cultural activists – eventually including professional politicians – used Islamic idioms to address Muslim community issues. Problems that Muslims shared were addressed in Islamic idioms to mobilize people classified as Muslims for public action.

The concept of a Muslim political community thus emerged in the nineteenth century, when Muslims – like Hindus, Sikhs, Buddhists, and Christians – acquired official identities in government courts and administration. Even then, being a Muslim inside Muslim societies still meant belonging to the *umma*, which was not a political community. Islamic theology does not support the idea that Muslims constitute a single political community. In 1930, Muhammad Ali Jinnah indicated that by then, this distinction had been blurred by Muslim political history when he said, 'I have a culture, a polity, an outlook on life – a complete synthesis which is Islam.' Then he clarified what he meant by saying that 'where God commands, I am . . . nothing but a Muslim', but 'where India is concerned . . . I am . . . nothing but an Indian'. On the verge of Pakistan's independence, many orthodox Muslim scholars chided the idea that Islam could be identified with a national state. The relationship between being Muslim and being a citizen of a Muslim-majority state remains a culturally complex issue in many countries today.

By 1930, Muslim politicians in British India had seriously blurred the distinction between religious and political identity. As we have seen, Sir Syed Ahmad Khan and Muhammad Ali Jinnah were adamant that Muslims were a separate community, a nation with its own culture and history, with its own political leaders and needs. The Muslim League underlined this assertion by forming its public alliance among Muslim leaders from various sects, regions, and ethnic groups. In 1920, the Khilafat movement won Congress support for its drive to force the British to reinstate the Caliph in Turkey as the official public leader of all the world's Muslims.

By this time, the mobilization of Muslim tenants to gain land rights in Bengal and Malabar had produced several generations of leaders for whom Islam had fired politics with religious devotion. In 1921, the Khilafat movement inspired as many as 10,000 Malabar Muslim fighters to join a series of 'Moplah' (Mappillai) revolts dating back to the nineteenth century, seeking to regain land rights lost to the British, led by Muslim preachers but including Namboodri and Nayar radicals. Mappillai warriors attacked British installations and liberated two subdivisions (taluks) in south Malabar for a few months. Indian nationalists disavowed the revolt; its violence was indeed one reason why Gandhi called off non-co-operation. To suppress this revolt, police killed 2337, wounded 1652, and took 45,404 prisoners. Sixty-six prisoners were locked in a railway carriage and died from suffocation, recalling the Black Hole of Calcutta (but without provoking similar outrage). Tenancy reforms later followed. The potential fearsomeness of Muslim outrage had received another affirmation.

Political differences between Muslims and others were sketched on a larger canvas in Bengal. As the upper-caste Bengali Hindu *bhadralok* projected their own cultural identity from Calcutta and over all of Bengal, Muslim Bengali tenant leaders opposed Hindu Zamindars. Hindu Zamindar and Muslim tenant supporters rejected each other's claims to represent Bengal. After the death of C. R. Das in 1926, possibilities declined for national alliances among them. Indian National Congress national strategy called for accommodating landlords. In the 1930s, Congress gained strength and Zamindari power weakened during the Great Depression. In 1941, Fazlul Haq, the leader of the Krishak Praja (Peasants and Workers) Party, joined the Muslim League in calling for Pakistan at the League's meeting in Lahore. The partition of India and Pakistan was hailed in Dhaka as the arrival of a peasant utopia, a land free of Zamindars.

New national states put Muslim societies in a totally new political environment. But being Muslim still included all its old ethnic, class, sectarian, local, linguistic, and regional elements. In India, it lost its former electoral substance but retained political meanings derived from decades of public activism. Most people who were Indian Muslims in the 1940s remained Indian Muslims in the 1950s, but now they were officially a minority everywhere in India. Anti-Muslim feelings and hostilities continued in some places, particularly in urban centres disrupted by agitation in the 1940s. Attacks on Muslims occurred periodically in the 1950s, 1960s, and 1970s; as we will see below, they attained new political force in the 1980s and thereafter, as a result of Hindutva politics. In everyday social life, however, Muslims became one of the many ethnic identity groups that formed local community organizations and voting blocks in India's multicultural and constitutionally secular polity.

In 1947, being a Muslim in Pakistan came to include being a citizen in a state defined by its Muslim majority. In 1947, Pakistan included five major cultural regions. Very different regional political histories in old Sindhi, Baluchi, Paxtun, Punjabi, Kashmiri, and Bengali cultural regions had converged unpredictably. Nationalities and societies in each region remained distinct.

- In Sind, elite families owning huge Zamindar estates – including the Bhutto family that would provide Pakistan with two prime ministers, Zulfiqar Ali and his daughter, Benazir – supported Pakistan to maintain their own elite power. This they effectively did by preventing land reform.
- In Punjab, small and large landowners in village communities who were much like those across the border in India fought for valuable farmland such as that in the Canal Colonies.

Business families in Pakistani towns and cities, most prominently Lahore in Punjab and Karachi in Sind, had carved out
new zones of national influence.

- In the hills above Sind and Punjab, Baluchi and Paxtun clan
  leaders had long before established their own distinct domains
  under British rule, which they strove to maintain.

- Kashmir posed a unique problem. Most Kashmiri Muslims
  remained in India after war partitioned Kashmir in 1947. Many
  exiled Kashmiri Muslim political activists were already living and
  working in Lahore, now in Pakistan; while Azad Kashmir, on the
  northern borders of Pakistani Punjab, was and remains a thinly
  populated mountain region. Kashmir remained a burning issue in
  Pakistan because of Kashmiri activists and their supporters in
  Punjab, which is the most powerful region in Pakistan. Over the
  decades, Islam became more identified with Kashmiri nationalism
  in Kashmir.

- In East Pakistan, being Bengali became an increasingly powerful feature of Muslim identity. The elevation of Islam in Pakistan
  strove for Muslim unity in opposition to the regional autonomy
  of Bengal. After 1971, over the decades, being Muslim became
  a more prominent nationalist feature of being Bangladeshi.

After 1971, being Muslim in Bangladesh reinforced national
loyalty, but suspicions remained among Bengali activists who had
fresh memories of how Islamic rhetoric and loyalty had been used
to support Pakistan over Bangladesh. Bengali Jamaat-i-Islami activists fought for Pakistan in 1971. During fifteen years of military
rule after 1975, state-sponsored Islam became more prominent in
Bangladesh. For a small but influential population, Islam represented national unity and cultural strength amid the turmoil of
domestic social change and globalization. Islam became one symbol
of national unity in a Bengali Muslim nation where divisive struggles for national resources pulled Bengalis apart, and where social
activism threatened elites who sought security in public invocations
of traditional moral order backed by the state. For many activists,
however, Islamic politics threatened rights promised in the country's secular constitution, which are still insecurely established in
society, particularly for non-Muslim minorities and women. After
2001, the 'global war on terror' launched by the United States,
which began with the conquest of the Taliban in Afghanistan,
added fuel to the fires of Islamic loyalism and its secular opposition
in Bangladesh.

Islamic traditionalism also emerged more forcefully under military rule in Pakistan, where disorder increased when war erupted in Afghanistan in 1978. Originally the war pitted US-armed Afghan guerrillas against Soviet forces. By 1992, more than a million Afghans had died. After 1992, the war set ethnically diverse Afghan militias against Sunni fundamentalist fighters, the Mujahidin, most prominently the Taliban, who came to control most of the country by the end of the 1990s and who began their career in Pakistan. The war spilled its influence across all the borders around Afghanistan, as it has done again since the US invasion and conquest of the Taliban in 2001. By 1992, five million refugees had fled along old routes into Punjab, Sind, and Kashmir. Warfare in the 1990s brought the Taliban to power but the 2001 US invasion began another decade of war, producing still more refugees inside the 'global war on terror' which has made life increasingly complex and troubled for Muslims whose religion has been stigmatized in a manner which recalls the British imperial fears of Muslim rebels in the 1870s.

During the 1990s, Sindhi activists also began to attack the Punjabi domination of the Pakistan government in Sind. The Muhajir Qaumi Movement, representing immigrants from pre-1947 India, also fought for power in Sind. In 1979, Zia ul Huq had instituted Sunni Islamic state law in an Islamic republic. This triggered a repression of the many minority Muslim communities in Pakistan, where Shia activists formed the Tehrik-i-Nifaz-i-Jafria to gain official recognition. Conflicts ensued between Shias and Sunnis, which have been most violent in Punjab. Drawing on intellectual activity going back to the eighteenth-century Shah Wali Allah, state-sponsored Sunni orthodoxy is intended to unify diverse Muslim societies inside Pakistan and to maintain the orderly state management of elite interests. In addition, however, it has provoked the use of competing Islamic idioms in struggles among contending groups in all the regions. It also produced a new kind of cultural opposition between the idioms of secularism and religion, which has been most pronounced in public efforts to improve the rights of women.

CHANGING HINDU SOCIETIES

Over the centuries, cultural activism and diverse local patronage combined to establish many different kinds of Hindu societies. Though connected, they did not claim a common theological foundation in the manner of Muslims, Christians, Sikhs, and Buddhists. Their many commonalities include the veneration of deities in the *purana*s, above all Siva and Vishnu, whose devotees formed the two major Hindu sectarian groups, Shaiva and Vaishnava. They all conduct *puja* rituals and other ceremonies led by ritual specialists who represent divinity in everyday life. Various kinds of temples house their living deities. Social rituals make spiritual principles a part of community life. Rituals define collective *jati* or caste identities attached to specific regions. Castes constructed internally by rituals of marriage and family are constructed by rituals that define each *jati* in relation to others.

Medieval Hindu kingdoms were complex ritual and political institutions. They were political and also religious domains where rituals of caste ranking focused on dynasties and deities at the same time. In medieval times, temple ceremonialism seems to have been paramount in the definition of social rank, including that of king. Sacred texts and inscriptional records indicate that the ritually purest Brahman *jati*s played a paramount personal role in defining social rank, because their command of sacred texts governed ritual activity in temple, state, and society.

The *varna* ranks of Brahman, Kshatriya, Vaisya, and Sudra provide a cultural template for social order in Hindu cultures. This order is often called 'Brahmanical' because Brahmans have special authority as interpreters of the Sanskrit texts, which prescribe *dharma*, the sanctified way of life that each Hindu should pursue. Rituals of social ranking also provide a cultural template for disputation over social status; thus rituals are basic political institutions in Hindu societies. Because Brahmans uphold moral order, challenges to Brahman authority often attend social change when aspiring groups challenge Brahman rights to determine social ranks in ritual. In the medieval centuries, devotional *bhakti* movements raised the stature of non-Brahman groups in deity worship. Socially mobile groups formed new sects and communities based on spiritual principles and practices that denied, bypassed, or ignored Brahman authority.

One exemplary reformist Shaiva sect arose in the twelfth century in the Deccan, on the borders of Maharashtra and Karnataka. Virashaivas ('heroic Shaivas') worship Siva in the form of the phallic linga. Also called Lingayats, 'bearers of a linga', they wear the Siva image to make each male and female body a temple of god. Lingayats are thus all spiritual equals. They do not recognize Brahman authority. Parents have never married daughters before puberty, to protect their purity. Lingayat widows are freely allowed to remarry. Lingayats also conduct burials rather than cremation.

Each family has a guru or spiritual guide. A distinctive Virashaiva *jati* of Jangama gurus attain personal sanctity based on ascetic detachment. Monasteries (*matha*) for training Jangamas are central Lingayat institutions. Lingayat *ahimsa* (non-violence) and strict vegetarianism also indicate the formative Jain influence among the original Lingayats, who were primarily merchants. Jangama ascetic gurus are teachers and spiritual guides who mediate between Virashaiva communities and the wider world, providing wisdom for changing times.

Virashaivism is one of many innovative religious movements organized historically around dissenting spiritual leaders. Such movements have been pervasive vehicles of social and political change. Their style and influence has overlapped with Muslim, Jain, Buddhist, and Christian spirituality. The Brahmo Samaj, for example, has a Protestant flavour, like the Jain flavour of Virashaivism. Such movements typically emerge around the moral authority of key individuals, typically styled as gurus (spiritual teachers) or *sannyasi*s (ascetic monks). Their followers weave networks of communication and teaching, and build institutions for sectarian learning that constitute social movements. These movements articulate and generate new forms of community and social activism. They have suffused modern political environments, where leaders have often employed idioms of popular devotionalism and ascetic authority. These agents of change have worked in settings of social change to improve the powers of various caste groups to acquire honour, rank, and entitlements.

Hindu cultures have never lived in a vacuum. In medieval times, warrior sultans provided new ways for Hindu groups to acquire honour and ritual status to supplement those available in Hindu royal courts and temples. Expanding commercial economies provided new wealth for families who patronized new sects and invested in rituals to improve their social standing. Commercial wealth became noticeably more prominent in Murshid Quli Khan's Bengal, where new temples built by business families rose to a third of the total as the proportion built by landed *zamindar*s declined to around sixty percent. This change reflects a shift in social power over the honours that were being conferred by deities on pious individuals.

Hindu societies changed more dramatically in the nineteenth century. Most temples that are used today in India were built after 1800 with financial endowments from merchants and landowners. The influence of the educated white-collar middle classes also increased. Modern urban reformulations of Hindu religion followed theological lines such as were present in Calcutta, stressing personal piety and philosophy, downplaying caste and temple ritual. As a result, by the twentieth century there were more different kinds of Hindu societies than ever before. A new kind of cultural division had been established. In the villages, rustic ritualism bolstered the dominant castes in the agrarian power structure. In the cities, urbane spirituality detached itself from rustic localism, absorbed diverse groups from surrounding regions, and became more literate in regional languages. Hinduism thus changed with the increasing influence of urbanism, a trend that continues today. As urbane Hinduism became more separate from village oral cultures, it became more self-consciously and politically Hindu, merging Vaishnava and Shivite sectarian traditions and retuning itself to the formulation of Indian national identity. Similar changes occurred in Muslim and Buddhist societies, which were, however, more urbane from the start.

Conflict often attends upward mobility in Hindu societies. Struggles for status and challenges to old patterns of social ranking are clearly visible in records from medieval times to the present. For example, in eighteenth-century Madras (Chennai), two organized groups of *jati*s formed so-called Left- and Right-hand caste alliances. The Right-hand group had its base in landownership. The Left-hand group featured merchants and artisans. They competed for state recognition of their rights to express their solidarity in public. They came into conflict over the use of city space to build temples and conduct festivals. British officials did not understand why people would fight on the streets and petition governors for exclusive rights to use religious insignia and to carry idols along certain streets at particular times. But even as the English East India Company puzzled over this problem in Madras, Nayaka rulers in Madurai galloped from one town to another to resolve similar disputes, asserting their authority by resolving local conflicts over social and ritual status. Such official activity was part of governance in societies where families achieved status through honours displayed and dispensed in public rituals patronized and authorized by rulers. Imperial Peshwas turned this status-structuring work of the state into an organized legal and bureaucratic system.

The British initially endeavoured to comply with social expectations along these lines, and to inform their decisions they consulted local experts, typically learned Brahmans. The new regime also continued to provide tax relief for temples and monasteries that often owned substantial tracts of land. Centuries of pious endowments had made major temples vastly rich, for example, in Kanchipuram, where five temples owned thousands of acres of prime farmland scattered across all Tamil districts. Temples not only reflected prosperity, they also produced it, increasing their importance for the state. Temple precincts in Kanchipuram were also the site of silk production, and merchants flocked to the city to trade in textiles and to endow temples at the same time. Peasants looked to the state to support rituals that sustained their livelihoods. Living gods and social rituals were understood as fonts of prosperity. In 1811, Tamil peasants in the Tirunelveli District in southern Madras Presidency petitioned the English Collector to fund temple rituals to help prevent famine, which was for them the onset of *Kali Yuga*, the cosmic age of destruction. The Company *sarkar* obliged, because panicky peasants could become lawless or might flee the country. With the advice of trusted Brahmans, the Collector paid for rain-making ceremonies in all the major temples 'with the view of inspiring the people with confidence and encouraging them to proceed with their preparations for cultivation'.

This state policy changed in British India, after 1830, under pressure from English missionaries. The government withdrew from religious patronage and settled into bureaucratic routines of regulating temple finance and management without interfering in temple affairs. Legally, temples became a 'public trust'. In this regulatory capacity, the state established a new relationship with religion, which focused on adjudicating rights to control the assets of religious institutions. Ritual activity became the private business of individual subjects in the modern state. The state could thus influence the institutional structure of religious leadership, as it did in response to the Gurdwara Reform movement in Punjab, where, in the 1920s, the Punjab government established a single Sikh authority to administer Gurdwaras. This administration officially recognized Sikh religious leaders as the leaders of their religious community. Also in the 1920s, government institutionalized official sectarian leadership in Hindu temples across British India. The imperial state thus absented itself from participation in temple rituals, but officially designated religious community leadership, focusing on temples.

As state officials formed new religious institutions, change accelerated in Hindu societies: records abound that express anxiety and even anger in the higher social ranks towards upward mobility from below. For example, in early nineteenth-century Travancore, a public dispute ensued when low-caste women took to wearing saris covering their breasts, because such modesty marked higher status. In southern Tamil districts, high-caste non-Brahman farmers fought on the streets and in courts against insistent Brahman claims to own the land they had farmed for generations. Local caste elites argued that caste ritual ranks should govern official state allocations of rights and privileges. They met mounting public criticism from lower castes and from social reformers. In the 1850s, untouchables in Tirunelveli violated caste traditions that called for them to take their funeral processions through rice fields and irrigation ditches rather than along city streets. They were attacked on city roads by caste elites who claimed that the public space belonged to them. Company troops suppressed the violence with support from social reformers. The untouchables' procession was then allowed to pass through Brahman streets; this change in funeral rituals signalled new state control over public space and changed the rules of public life for everyone in the city.

The government thus became permanently implicated in social conflict over public rights and honours that marked the status quo and secured upward mobility in Hindu societies. After 1850, modern economies provided new avenues for social change, and modern politics produced new means to resist it. State control over public space and private property introduced an important new element into conflicts over social mobility by usurping domains of caste privilege and by making legal rights a matter of public dispute. Old regimes had left property matters and social regulation to local authorities, though eighteenth-century regimes increased the role of the state in everyday social affairs, as we have seen. Under British rule, Brahman influence initially supported conservative interpretations of custom by English judges and British policy-makers. Brahmans became literate in English, assumed official authority, and became lawyers, judges, and politicians with influence far out of proportion to their numbers. Struggles for upward social mobility therefore soon came to include attacks on Brahman authority. Social reformers who worked to abolish *sati* and to legalize widow remarriage criticized 'Brahmanical British laws'. In 1869, in the old heartland of Maratha warrior-peasant power, in Bombay Presidency, Jotirao Phule published his tract *Priestcraft Exposed* to generate dramatic opposition to Brahmanism.

The tension between rising social ambition bubbling up 'from below' and social restraint clamping down 'from above' was not confined to Hindu societies. As we have seen, the cultural politics of social rank and honour embroiled Muslims, Christians, Sikhs, and others. Struggles over upward social mobility sometimes pitted aspiring non-Hindus against high-caste Hindus, especially Brahmans. Such instances became public symbols of religious difference. Mappillai Muslims in Malabar fought for rights against landlords, high-caste elites, and British officials all at once. The Raja of Jammu and Kashmir restricted Muslim public activity to maintain the supremacy of Brahmans and Kashmiri Pandits. As Tagore's story, 'Home and the World' indicates, political activity could easily pit elite Hindus against poor Muslims.

In urban north India, conflicts erupted in the 1890s that resembled those between the Right- and Left-hand castes in Madras of a century before. When upwardly mobile Muslim merchants, workers, and artisans in cities along the Ganga basin sought to display their piety more grandly by sacrificing cows, rather than goats, for their ritual feasts during Eid festivities, Cow Protection Societies led by high-caste landlords attacked them and sought a state ban on 'cow slaughter', which would have included even butcher shops that provided meat for the majority of lower-caste Hindus who were not vegetarians.

The government of British India, which made 'Hindu' and 'Muslim' legal categories, and which gave religious leaders official status, logically interpreted any conflict pitting Hindus against Muslims as a battle between two opposing religious communities. Social conflicts of many sorts were thus homogenized under the single official heading of 'communal conflicts'. 'Communalism' became a modern term for the antagonistic mobilization of 'communal' sentiment by Hindus and Muslims. Thus the concept of the 'communal electorate', which the Indian National Congress opposed in principle, became laced with histories of Hindu–Muslim conflict that Congress sought to transcend in its quest for Indian national unity.

Conflicts within Hindu and Muslim societies were often of the same kind as conflicts across religious borders. Struggles for rights by many different groups produced leaders who sought state support and faced elite opposition. Dr B. R. Ambedkar underlined the political similarity of Muslims and untouchable Hindus in his 1945 book *Pakistan, Or the Partition of India*. In it, he argues that separate electorates are a legitimate constitutional solution to the problem of securing collective rights for peoples who struggle against entrenched elites and electoral majorities. Non-Brahman politicians in Bombay and Madras Presidency made similar claims when they sought regional autonomy to secure power for high-caste non-Brahmans inside an imperial polity that they understood as being controlled by Brahmans in government and in the Congress. The pursuit of upward mobility for lower-caste groups through political mobilization to acquire state power became an increasingly important feature of Indian political life, which by the 1990s had turned governments in New Delhi into shifting coalitions of regional parties, many representing upwardly mobile constituencies.

Political movements for upward mobility have much in common. They typically stress the importance of language in social and political identities that are also often expressed in ethnic and religious idioms. They challenge the cultural legitimacy of dominance by higher-status groups. They often concentrate spatially in particular areas and assert demands for regional autonomy. Dominant social groups often stigmatize political demands for securing social mobility as being separatist, divisive, self-interested, and unpatriotic. Loyalty to the nation can thus become an instrument of status quo conservatism. Facing elite political opposition and state suppression, public movements for social mobility often provoke violence. This pattern has repeated itself countless times, including today in Kashmir, north-east India, Sri Lanka, Nepal, and regions of Maoist rebellion in eastern India. Elements of so-called 'communalism' and 'communal conflict' are dispersed in many contexts where groups fight for rights against established privilege, and where the cultural dimensions of such conflicts are typically religious, political, ethnic, and economic, all at once.

As the modern state grew in size and complexity, its capacity increased to absorb many struggles for social mobility within institutions for accumulating cultural capital where the pursuit of honours and symbols of status, including personal wealth, strengthened government authority. In that respect, the first imperial census, in 1871, was a landmark. It immediately generated disputes over caste definitions and status ranking. Activists representing upwardly mobile castes sought to have their caste names changed to indicate higher status. For example, a group of wealthy cotton merchants in market towns in southern Tamil Nadu petitioned to have their *jati* name changed from Shanar, which denoted low-caste toddy tappers, to the more prestigious name, Nadar, a term used within the *jati* to designate its elite. This change would make the merchant Nadars leaders of the whole caste and also increase Nadar numbers in the census, and therefore their official visibility. Their census campaign was combined with funding for English schools and with petitions to the courts to grant Nadars the right to enter temples from which they were excluded by virtue of their lowly

Shanar status. The court cases and demonstrations that comprised the Nadar temple-entry campaign provoked riotous opposition from the locally dominant Maravas. After riots in the 1890s, 'communal' conflict between Nadars and Maravas simmered for decades. A century later, in the 1990s, Maravas in Tirunelveli attacked upwardly mobile low-caste workers returning from the Persian Gulf with more money to spend on prestige items than Maravas thought appropriate to their lowly status.

Because exclusion from temples most dramatically locked people into low Hindu status ranks, temple entry rose to the top of the low-caste political agenda. The logic was the same as that which secured the Tirunelveli untouchables' rights to use the city streets for funerals: leaders argued that temples are public places that everyone has a right to enter. The radical step was to call the ritual interior of temples 'public' by virtue of the temple's being a 'public trust' under government regulation. Though Nadars won their name change for the 1921 census, the courts upheld the right of temple managers to exclude them.

The drive to make it illegal for elite castes to exclude low-caste people from temples gained force after 1920. In Madras, Mylai Chinna Thambi Pillai Rajah (1883–1943) led an untouchables movement pressing the idea that the low-caste people were Adi Dravidas, that is, the original inhabitants of Dravidian-language regions in southern India. Their combined numbers made India's lowest-caste people a potentially formidable electoral force for any political party. As a consequence, agitation to give them new rights as Indian citizens entered Article 15 of the Indian Constitution, which says, 'No citizen shall, on grounds only of religion, race, caste, sex, place of birth or any of them, be subject to any disability, liability, restriction or condition with regard to (a) access to shops, public restaurants, hotels and places of public entertainment; or (b) the use of wells, tanks, bathing ghats, roads and places of public resort maintained wholly or partly out of State funds or dedicated to the use of the general public.' Struggles to enforce this constitutional right continue in many Indian villages today, where local groups must still mobilize political force against entrenched elites to make the state enforce citizens' rights.

By contrast to lower-caste social mobility movements, the aspiring middle *jati* ranks of Hindu societies embraced classical *varna* categories to improve *jati* social status. This cultural strategy became popular in Bihar and Uttar Pradesh among the Sudra peasant castes of Kurmis, Yadavas, and Kushvahas. Organized under Vaishnava Ramanandi *sannyasi* leadership, the Kshatriya Movement spread all across north India and produced a new warrior style of cultural aspiration among upwardly mobile farming families. Activists invented warrior genealogies and ancestors, re-interpreted ancient texts, embraced Rajput customs, promoted strict Vaishnava social conduct, proclaimed racial equality among all Aryans, and, like Sikh activists, insisted on the dignity of manual labour. Their efforts reinforced solidarity among tenants who were also fighting for land rights against the claims of Rajput, Brahman, and Bhumihar Zamindars. At the same time, the movement promoted strict patriarchal authority over women and fed anti-Muslim activity among Cow Protection Societies in the 1890s.

Other movements initially embraced *varna* ranks but then rejected them as an impediment to mobilizing different groups who shared the same disadvantages. Swami Sahajanand Saraswati led a movement of this kind. An ascetic of the Shaiva Dasnami *sannyasi* order, Swami Sahajanand entered the social reform movement in 1914 and devoted himself to defending the Brahman status of Bhumihar cultivators against denigrations by Maithil Brahmans and other elites. Using Sanskrit texts, he showed that Brahmans did not have a monopoly on receiving charity and doing priestly work. He elevated the spiritual status of the manual labour done by Bhumihars, which Brahmans claimed lowered their status. To promote this work, he founded his Sitaram *ashram* (sanctuary) in Bihar, where he came to the aid of local Goala and other *kisan*s (peasant farmers), who sought his help in their struggles with Zamindars. In 1927, his movement became a broadly peasant rather than a caste movement, and he became the leader of the Kisan Sabha, fighting for 'downtrodden people . . . regardless of their *jati* or religion [in a place where] the question of *jati* does not arise'. This struggle crossed caste lines, because some Bhumihars were Zamindars while others were peasants. Though most Bihar Kisan Sabha leaders in the 1920s and 1930s were Bhumihars, most of its members, like most peasants in the region, were Yadavas, Koeris, and Kurmis.

Kisan Sabha led a broad trend away from caste, religion, and ethnicity as organizing principles in social movements which occurred in the 1920s and 1930s. The disruptions of the Great Depression and mass mobilization by the Congress led many activists to adopt secular socialist democratic ideals that concentrated attention on inequality and justice rather than on caste and religion. All of South Asia's Left parties have followed this approach to politics, which gained strength when Jawaharlal Nehru made his 1930 proclamation (quoted above) that the 'structure of society' in India perpetuated the 'poverty and misery of the Indian People' and demanded 'revolutionary changes . . . to remove the gross inequalities'.

This analysis led Nehru and the Congress to promote state strategies for social improvement and economic development that became official policy with India's first Five Year Plan in 1952. Combined with a constitutional abolition of caste discrimination and with official lists of scheduled castes and tribes, government planning sought to address the poverty problem as a whole, which the Congress platform in 1947 analysed in this way:

> Though poverty is widespread in India, it is essentially a rural problem, caused chiefly by overpressure on land and a lack of other wealth producing occupations. India, under British rule, has been progressively ruralised, many of her avenues of work and employment closed, a vast mass of the population thrown on the land, which has undergone continuous fragmentation, till a very large number of holdings have become uneconomic. It is essential, therefore, that the problem of the land should be dealt with in all its aspects. Agriculture has to be improved on scientific lines and industry has to be developed rapidly in its various forms . . . so as not only to produce wealth but also to absorb people from the land . . . Planning must lead to maximum employment, indeed to the employment of every able bodied person.

The abolition of Zamindar landlordism in independent India eliminated the most politically contentious 'gross inequality'. And as in East Pakistan, also in India: a new class of prosperous farmers emerged as a political force. In India, differences among them became pronounced. Between 1960 and 1990, the proportion of cultivated land in holdings of over 10 hectares shrank from 31 to 17 percent, as holdings of less than one hectare increased by roughly the same proportion, from 19 to 32 percent. A huge number of small landlords and substantial farmers emerged from the ranks of former tenants and Ryotwari peasants. They became the bulwark of the Congress strategy of agrarian patronage announced by Charan Singh. They were a rising rural elite composed of former tenant middle castes who won struggles for land rights and who now aspired to supplant the political power of rural elites. Beneath them in rural society, however, a much larger population of poor people working tiny farms and owning no land at all also developed political aspirations. These two rising forces undid the Congress system in the countryside, where the patronage could not flow fast enough to satisfy a rising middle class that faced political challenges from lower-caste activists representing the lower-caste rural poor.

Agrarian societies differ significantly across regions. Very small farms and relatively poor farmers typify the wetter regions in eastern and southern India, Sri Lanka, and Bangladesh, while larger farms cover drier regions of canal and tube-well irrigation in Pakistan, Punjab, Rajasthan, Haryana, and western Uttar Pradesh. In India, larger land holdings (over 2.6 hectares) comprise the highest percentage of farms in Rajasthan and Punjab (30 percent), and are also prominent in Gujarat, Madhya Pradesh, and Haryana (20 percent). They are least visible in Assam (four percent), Bihar (four percent), Tamil Nadu (three percent), West Bengal (one percent), and Kerala (0.5 percent). Maharashtra, Karnataka, Andhra Pradesh, and Odisha fall in between, averaging 10 percent. Uttar Pradesh resembles Bihar in that only three percent of the total holdings are bigger than 2.6 hectares, and the resemblance increases in the east, which has 49 percent of all the farms in Uttar Pradesh that are smaller than one hectare. In this as in other respects, western Uttar Pradesh more resembles Haryana and contains 40 percent of all Uttar Pradesh land holdings between four and 10 hectares.

Larger farms, where the owners command substantial political and economic power at the local and the state level, account for much of India's agricultural growth. Between 1962 and 1965 and 1992 and 1995, the highest annual rates of growth in farm output came in Punjab (five percent), Rajasthan (four percent), and Haryana (four percent). These are also regions in which dominant farmers, mostly Jats and Rajputs, make the strongest claim to represent their regions politically and culturally. India's north-west quadrant, with the largest farmers and highest per capita state investments in irrigation, had the highest overall growth rate, averaging three percent. Eastern states averaged two percent. Central (2.7 percent) and southern states (2.6 percent) fell in between, while Kerala (1.7 percent), Odisha (1.6 percent), and Bihar (1.0 percent) had the least growth. Everywhere in India, politically well-connected and organized farmers get state subsidies for capital-intensive cultivation, and their local capital accumulation depends on state-managed electrical supplies; on state prices for petrol, pump sets, tractors, pipes, fertilizer, and hybrid seeds; and on state procurement prices, transport costs, bank charges, and credit conditions.

Influential farmers have spurred political movements to represent farming interests. Sugar growers, for instance, led the co-operative movement in Maharashtra from the 1920s, and they also led farmers' movements in Maharashtra and elsewhere from the 1970s. In Uttar Pradesh, under the flag of the Bharatiya Kisan Union, farmer-activists made headlines in 1988, when they stormed Meerut to demand higher sugar-cane prices, lower input prices, a waiver on loan repayments, more rural investment, and lower rates for electricity and water. Whereas the old-style peasant movements focused on land rights, the new farmer movements that arose in Tamil Nadu, Punjab, Maharashtra, Uttar Pradesh, Karnataka, and Gujarat in the 1970s and 1980s have used roadblocks, marches, and votes to demand better prices and to assert village interests against the entrenched urban bias of development policies. As we have seen, the Anandapur Sahib Resolution anchors Sikh cultural politics in Punjab farmers' economic interests.

HINDUTVA AND INDIA

Regional disparities in economic development and regional alliances among urban and rural politicians steadily increased the prominence of regional political parties; this brought the public identities of regionally prominent social groups into the political foreground. Activists organized groups along ethnic, religious, and caste lines in the context of a universal adult franchise, as the national state promised equality for all citizens. By 1975, when India's Home Ministry warned of the 'explosion' in rural India that could result from state failures to tackle rural inequality, the success of high-caste groups in capturing the benefits of national development had become obvious to many observers. One of these was an elderly leader of the untouchables movement in Punjab, Mangoo Ram. Decades before, he had formed a political sect for Chamars, called the Adi Dharm, which struggled to put an end to untouchability. In 1971, Mangoo Ram told a colleague that despite his movement's success and despite government help, 'our people . . . are still treated like slaves . . . [by] their superiors and high-caste people'. He proclaimed at an Adi Dharm conference, in 1970, that 'Hinduism is a fraud to us. Adi Dharm is our only true religion'.

Disenchantment in many quarters became politically active as Indira Gandhi's emergency regime of 1975–6 weakened the Congress Party's claim to represent popular aspirations. Movements for regional autonomy and federalism gained strength. New social movements mobilized women, mountain peoples, farmers, and low-caste groups. In this context of disruptive politics – which also spawned aggressive Sinhala Buddhist majoritarianism and state-sponsored Islamic traditionalism – Hindu nationalism (Hindutva) began to mobilize mass support in India.

We have seen that Hindu nationalist parties had local and regional roots in late nineteenth-century India, when Hindu public sentiment (as distinct from religious feeling) acquired an urban middle-class audience. Before 1947, the major Hindu nationalist organizations were the Arya Samaj, Cow Protection Societies, Rashtriya Swayamsevak Sangh (RSS), and Hindu Mahasabha. None had a large following. They all distanced themselves from Congress, though some of their members were individually active in Congress. One fervent Hindu nationalist assassinated Mohandas Gandhi in 1948 to express hatred of Gandhi for 'accepting' partition, for it became an article of faith among Hindu nationalists that Pakistan took away land that belonged to Hindu India. The Hindu Mahasabha turned into an electoral party in independent India, the Jana Sangh. It maintained a separate political identity for Hindu nationalists and consistently won a few seats in the Lok Sabha, mostly in Uttar Pradesh, where it was influential primarily among Brahmans. Led by paramilitary RSS cadres, Hindu nationalists also developed strong local bases among Brahmans in Maharashtra, propagating the idea that Hindu India had been dominated by Muslims for centuries before 1800, ripped apart by Muslims in 1947, and betrayed by the Congress Party, which had given Muslims Pakistan and continued to placate Muslim minorities in India in order to maintain itself, at the expense of the Hindu majority.

Attacking Congress in this way did not win many followers during decades of Congress supremacy in the 1950s and 1960s. Many Congress leaders were nonetheless sympathetic to Hindutva and used its ideas to garner political support. The most influential was Vallabhai 'Sardar' Patel, a major Congress figure from Gujarat, who sponsored the rebuilding of the temple at Somnath, in Saurashtra, which Hindu nationalists claimed Mahmud of Ghazni had destroyed. In the aftermath of Partition and war with Pakistan, and positioned close to the Pakistan border, the Somnath project broadcast Hindu nationalist claims that Muslims had desecrated Hindu India.

By 1980, the number of people looking for political alternatives to Congress had grown substantially. Congress had lost a national election and was losing more seats in state Assemblies with every new poll. In 1980, the Jana Sangh became the Bharatiya Janata

Party and began aggressive national campaigns in alliance with a Hindutva 'family' of organizations, called the Sangh Parivar, led by the RSS. Since then, activists in the Sangh family have concentrated on specific Hindu nationalist (Hindutva) projects. The largest organization, the Vishwa Hindu Parishad (VHP), or World Hindu Council, has propagated Hindutva in a broad range of public endeavours around the world, while the BJP has focused on winning elections in India. BJP strategy focused initially on Gujarat, Rajasthan, Uttar Pradesh, Bihar, Maharashtra, and Madhya Pradesh, where Brahmans were politically important and where no parties were then poised to beat Congress in elections. In southern states, West Bengal, and Punjab, regional parties were already strong and BJP candidates had little chance.

The Sangh Parivar concentrated on generating animosity towards Muslims and Congress. Anti-Muslim agitation propagated Hindutva as attacks on Congress supported BJP opposition. The anti-Muslim campaign centred on Ayodhya, a pilgrimage town in eastern Uttar Pradesh. Here, the Vaishnava god, Rama – the hero of the *Ramayana* – was said to have been born. An old mosque in the town, the Babri Masjid, was said to have been built on the rubble of a temple to Rama destroyed by Babur. The VHP and BJP launched a mass campaign to destroy the mosque and rebuild the Rama temple in Ayodhya.

The Ayodhya campaign was combined with attacks on Congress. In 1984, Operation Blue Star was a national disaster, which the Sangh blamed on Congress Party willingness to accommodate Sikh separatists. Rajiv Gandhi's pact with Sant Longowal, accepting the basic Anandapur Sahib demands, fired more Sangh attacks on Congress for pandering to minorities and weakening the Hindu nation. In 1986, the Sangh's watershed agitation sprang from a Supreme Court decision in favour of Shah Bano, a Muslim widow who sought support from a husband who had divorced her. Prime Minister Rajiv Gandhi pushed through Lok Sabha legislation to nullify the court's ruling that Shah Bano had rights to support. This legislation affirmed the opinion of conservative Muslim clerics, who had argued that the court decision contravened Muslim law. Sangh Parivar agitation sought public support for the credible claim that Rajiv Gandhi had bowed to Muslim conservatives for personal political gain. Hindutva leaders later looked back on the Shah Bano case as a key moment in their political ascendancy.

By 1989, the Congress had lost sufficient public appeal that a coalition government had formed without its support under the

Janata Dal, led by Prime Minister V. P. Singh. The BJP had won enough votes in northern states to allow it to become an external partner of the coalition, in opposition to Congress. This parliamentary position allowed the BJP to launch a major agitation against the Janata Dal's decision to implement the Mandal Commission Report in 1989. The Mandal Commission had proposed a huge increase in reservations in government employment and education to include a very large group of so-called Other Backward Castes. These castes included many aspiring landed groups. Government support for Mandal proposals generated huge opposition from the upper castes whose votes the BJP coveted.

At the same time, the Sangh accelerated its drive to demolish the Babri Masjid to reclaim Ram's birthplace, *Ramjanmabhoomi*, for Hindu India. After the BJP had won elections in Uttar Pradesh and increased its Lok Sabha seats to 185, VHP activists mobilized the attack. Holy men declared 6 December 1992 auspicious. Over 300,000 people gathered in Ayodhya. Most wore saffron cloth, the symbol of the Sangh, adopted from the attire of ascetic monks. At midday, a vanguard broke police barricades around the Babri Masjid. Cheering young men swarmed the domes of the old mosque (built in 1528), and in five hours they had hammered and hacked it to the ground. Video cameras hummed. Reporters took notes for news services around the world. Sangh leaders, who had worked for this day since 1984, watched with satisfaction. Government officials looked on ineffectually. Riots ensued across India, Pakistan, and Bangladesh that killed 1700 people and injured 5500 more in the next four months.

BJP electoral support dipped in the aftermath of the violence. The Sangh became identified with communal hatred and killing. In addition, the BJP's anti-Mandal agitation and its hardcore of high-caste and especially Brahman leaders triggered doubts among many aspiring lower-caste groups that the BJP represented a good political alternative to Congress. Various other opposition parties arose in the north Indian states, representing upwardly mobile landed groups and middle castes of the kind that Mandal had intended to bring to Congress. Congress decline continued. The BJP formed ever larger contingents in the Lok Sabha until, in 1998, it entered a coalition government in alliance with seventeen regional parties. That coalition government fell in 1999 and another version came to power in that year. In 1998, one Sangh leader who looked with satisfaction on the destruction of the Babri mosque, L. K. Advani, became India's Home Minister in charge of law and order for the nation. Hindutva acquired the mantle of a national ideology.

EIGHT

Global South Asia

When the twenty-first century arrived, distant peoples and places were being stitched together globally to form new spaces for history in the new millennium. In the nineteenth century, empires had defined world geography, and in the mid-twentieth century, national state territories had covered the planet. Transitional decades after 1970 opened the age of globalization. By the 1990s, rapid transportation and instant communication were bringing peoples and places closer together with ever-increasing speed and consequence. Localities and regions entered new spaces of global history, less and less defined by national borders. Today, local factories in India and China pollute an atmosphere which has been polluted by Western countries for two centuries, accelerating climate change everywhere, aggravating storms in New York City and drowning the Maldives. Examples are endless of local events with global effects, and of global trends unfolding locally. Like the empires of old, nations no longer seem eternally permanent: they rather seem to be shifting, mobile, and variously durable collections of human activity, engaged in expanding spaces of interaction and interdependence, reflecting and transmitting global trends that are transforming the world of nations.

MONDIALISATION

As we have seen, the peoples of South Asia have always lived in a wider world. Their early settlements concentrated in places where water flows on the land, and people moving among such places, along river valleys and across river basins, formed connections that produced South Asia's ancient geography. Expansive mobility over many centuries made South Asia a vast open land bridge connecting interior Eurasia, Europe, and China with the Indian Ocean, where mobility at sea hugged the coast and sailed with the monsoon. Overland routes – running across west and central Eurasia, and then east and south across South Asia – brought countless millions of migrant settlers within South Asia's frontiers. In these interactive spaces, Gangetic imperial culture spread among regions marked by languages, literatures, and territorial traditions that together formed the mainstream of South Asian history.

In each region, the shape of the wider world has differed according to geographies of mobility affecting localities. Sanskrit and Persian cultures spread along routes of Gangetic imperial power. Dravidian languages marked distinctive cultures in the peninsula, informed by north–south travels but also by mobility along the coast and overseas, which brought Jewish, Christian, and Arab settlers, and also embraced Sri Lanka and South-East Asia. Gujarat became a unique region of connectivity linking the Gangetic empires with the cultures of the Persian Gulf and the Arabian Sea. Mountain regions became distinctive cultural territories where people spoke Sino-Tibetan, Austro-Asiatic, Dravidian, Altaic, and Tai languages, travelled mountain trails, concentrated in valleys, mingled with mountain societies moving in all directions, and interacted with lowland societies, working to preserve mountain environments against lowland expansion.

The wider world of South Asia was transformed dramatically after 1750, 1850, and 1950 by changes in the scale, methods, and trajectories of human mobility. By 1750, seaborne travels had greatly enhanced the influence of Indian Ocean connections, most dramatically near the coast, where fortified port cities made South Asia a dynamic region of the early-modern world economy. After 1750, the British Empire marched inland to form the largest ever political territory in South Asia. The empire also expanded and intensified connections by sea among the coastal regions in and around the Indian Ocean. European migrants further increased the importance of Western Eurasia in the world of South Asia, which had been shaped by Western connections since the days of Alexander, and increasingly with the expansion of Islam. Nineteenth-century industrialization further expanded coastal connections among port cities around the world, including the Americas: steamships, railways, mass printing, the telegraph, telephone, road building, and motor cars brought the interior regions of all continents into closer contact with the coast, and rural regions into closer contact with major cities, which grew and prospered disproportionately as we have seen in the example of Calcutta.

By 1900, travels by sea and rail had woven urban South Asia into the world of English cultures. English became a South Asian language, expressed in many English books that defined Indian nationalism, and in Tagore's Nobel Prize in 1913. His prize-winning *Gitanjali* was originally composed in Bengali. This reflects a broad pattern: anglophone South Asia is multilingual, speaking to the wider world in English, communicating across its own regions in English, and also living inside distinctively regional linguistic cultures with countless local dialects. Modern South Asian histories and cultures thus appear in many forms at many interacting spatial levels of scale, from the global to the local.

Until 1920, global connections focused primarily on London, whose relative importance then declined rapidly. When India entered the League of Nations, Indian nationalists began to enclose their nation more rigorously, in cultural terms; and as the empire became weaker and more oppressive, the ports of Calcutta, Bombay, Madras, Karachi, and Rangoon did more business with other parts of Europe, as well as with China, Japan, the Middle East, and the United States. The Great Depression collapsed the world economy, cutting many economic ties, and for the next three decades, nationalists around the world focused their work on generating self-sufficient economic development within their own national territories. After 1945, decolonization freed nations from empire by dividing peoples from one another with new national borders that demolished old cultural spaces. The partition of British India dramatized a broad demolition of old cultural spaces including South Asia, the Indian Ocean coastal regions, and West, Central, and South-East Asia. Carving up these old spaces of shared human history into separate national state territories redefined culture in national terms and separated the Muslim world from South Asia, whose history now focused primarily on the largest country, India.

National histories became separated from one another everywhere in the world, but at the same time, citizens also acquired a new kind of common cultural ground in a world of nations voiced at the United Nations organization. South Asia became a collection of nations in a world where people everywhere could engage with one another in national terms. UN member states increased from 51 in 1945, to 127 in 1970, and to 193 in 2011, as the nation became the first truly global institution. The term 'global' came to mean a world space embracing all nations, whose standard practices, institutions, and ideas formed a 'global society' organized around citizenship.

South Asia also became a post-colonial region of the Third World, which was another new kind of world space, composed of poor countries with low Gross Domestic Product (GDP) seeking to develop their economies and to improve living conditions in the frame of global Cold War competition between the United States and the Soviet Union. Third World space included Latin America, Africa, and Asia, where national states engaged in programmes of economic development that depended on technological, scientific, and financial resources controlled by rich Western countries and the multilateral institutions they organized, notably the World Bank and the International Monetary Fund (IMF). South Asia's wider world thus continued to focus on the West, and orientation towards socialism and capitalism in South Asia became identified with ideological leanings towards the USSR and the US respectively. The main defining feature of South Asia, in both perspectives, was poverty, which was now expressed in global statistics, with every country ranked according to the size of its GDP. All South Asian countries have pursued national policies of economic development within this global framework as Third World countries, also labelled variously as part of the Global South and as 'developing countries'.

The pace and scale of human mobility increased rapidly in the world of nations. People began flying at high altitudes, and air travel transformed human space. The Boeing 707 took off in 1954. The USSR launched the first satellite with a radio transmitter in 1957. The following year, the US president delivered 'a Christmas greeting to the world' transmitted from a US satellite. Communications satellites took geosynchronous orbits in 1963. The earth became visible from outer space, and in 1968, Apollo 8 astronauts filmed 'earthrise' from the moon. The Boeing 747 took off in 1970; the Airbus in 1972, and the cost and time of long-distance travel fell quickly. In 1945, it took a week to cross the Atlantic by ship; three decades later, it took four hours on the supersonic Concorde. In 2000, aeroplanes flew non-stop from New York to Singapore in eighteen hours.

In 1960, air travel served the elites, but in 2011, nine hundred million passengers flew on the world's top ten airlines. South Asia's social space flew all over the world, focusing on urban areas of opportunity. The word 'diaspora' came into common usage, though as we have seen, significant migration overseas began in the nineteenth century, and migration into South Asia surpassed migration out of the region until 1920. Since the 1980s, flights have carried many thousands of workers annually from South Asia to work in the Persian Gulf and in South-East Asia; they typically return home after a few years. This pattern of circular migration has also been followed by hundreds of thousands of students who fly abroad to study and then return home. Many who fly overseas for work and study do not come back, however, and the rapid accumulation of this South Asian overseas settler population in richer, mostly anglophone countries has reproduced South Asia on all continents. In 1965 the US changed its immigration laws, enabling a huge increase in its South Asian settlers, who now number over three million, the fastest-growing Asian-American ethnic group. Over a million people with South Asia family ties live in Canada, forming about three percent of the Canadian population, most of whom were born outside of Canada.

Global communications have also created new kinds of social space, connecting people who are physically distant. New computer technologies have arrived with each decade since 1945: commercial computing in the 1980s, the internet soon after that, and the world-wide web in the 1990s. There were 13 million internet hosts in 1995, and 20 million by 1998. In 2000, 400 million people used the internet, roughly a third of that number in the US, Europe, and Asia, but by 2008 there were 1700 million users, and Asia's proportion (43 percent) surpassed North America's (14 percent) and Europe's (24 percent) combined, reflecting 'the rise of Asia' in the world economy. Wireless mobile telephone devices using radio transmitters were in military use in automobiles and aeroplanes in the 1940s, and AT&T offered mobile telephone service from automobiles commercially in 1946, but handheld mobile phones arrived only in the 1970s and their commercial success led to innovations in cellular technology over the next two decades. The 2G system with SMS generated a massive explosion in their usage in the 1990s. The UN counted 4.6 billion mobile-phone subscriptions in 2012, and predicts five billion in 2013.

GLOBALIZATION

South Asia's wider world has thus been expanding and changing for centuries, but it has become truly global in a new sense very quickly in the last few decades. I use the French term *mondialisation* to refer to the long-term process of spatial transformation, and to changing human spaces produced by mobility, settlement, communication, culture, politics, and social organization. These spaces get bigger and bigger over time, and today they are vast, covering the planet entirely, so that now the term 'globalization' is often used to translate *mondialisation*. It is more useful, I think, to reserve 'globalization' for a more specific process of historical change, which began in the late twentieth century uniquely inside the world of nations (though it did have its precursors in the late nineteenth-century empires). From the 1970s, as transportation and communication were speeding up, flying faster and higher through the frontiers of space, bringing peoples and places together ever more expansively, intensively, and inexpensively, nations were also changing with the creation of a global market economy, where the self-sufficient style of national development that typified the world as late as the 1970s is no longer possible. National states have been steadily losing autonomous control over national economies, politics, and cultures. National boundaries thus no longer enclose national histories, which are spilling out in all directions and being composed increasingly of elements in global circulation. An emerging global market economy is creating new forms of social life and generating many struggles that are gripping South Asia, where regional trends now reflect trends in the world of globalization.

Early impetus for globalization came from the United States. After World War II, dramatic overseas expansion of US corporate activity focused initially on Europe and Japan, boosted by World Bank and US foreign aid funds for the purchase of US goods, and underpinned by the value of the US dollar as a world currency established at Bretton Woods in 1945. The strength of the dollar improved US corporate buying power overseas, and by the 1970s, US companies owned global assets equal to the entire Japanese economy, making the US multinational corporate sector the third- or fourth-largest economy in the world after the US and USSR. Business interests propelled American political commitments to the global expansion of what became known as 'the free-market economy', a Cold War phrase that became more useful in 1971 when US President Richard Nixon launched the age of global money markets by abandoning the gold standard.

Globalization acquired a truly global dynamic in the 1970s. In 1973, OPEC (Organization of the Petroleum Exporting Countries) raised an oil embargo that sent world oil prices to unprecedented levels and flooded the US Treasury with petrodollars, boosting the dollar's market value. Postwar decades of economic growth and stability gave way to recession and then to cycles of recovery, boom, and recession, which continue today. Governments fought recession with budget cuts and loans, putting poor countries into cycles of debt finance to support political fortunes and economic development. Meanwhile, corporate investors sought to expand globally, and debt finance became an attractive source of profit. Poor countries became financial frontiers. The World Bank, led by Robert McNamara, raised massive private and public funds for loans to poor countries that the Bank promised would boost economic growth, end recession, stabilize currencies, expand business opportunity, and fight poverty. All this would hopefully also reduce popular support for communist revolution. The Bank thus supported Charan Singh's effort to create 'a huge class of strong opponents of the class war ideology . . . a middle of the road stable rural society and a barrier against political extremism'.

National strategies for self-sufficient economic development inside national state territory became dependent on global finance. Funding and technical expertise from the Bank, from donor countries, and from private foundations such as Ford, Carnegie, and Rockefeller enabled Third World governments, and financed every kind of development programme, including expensive infrastructure projects such as dams, roads, railways, ports, and electrification, and costly technology programmes such as the Green Revolution. Investments like these made South Asian countries self-sufficient in food and produced a population of wealthy small landowners, as Charan Singh had hoped. External funding became essential for national development and political careers, so that financiers became more influential in national politics and policy-making. Political success in poor countries required financial support to maintain the flow of development loans. For example, Bangladesh, having won independence in 1971, immediately sought financial solutions to pressing development problems, and soon depended heavily on foreign aid and loans. The year 1974 brought famine to Africa and Bangladesh and serious drought and starvation to India and other countries. In 1975, a military coup launched fifteen years of military rule in Bangladesh, supported by external finance. Sri Lanka's government also became dependent on World Bank loans in 1977.

Debt dependency made the World Bank, the IMF, and donor countries part of national politics in most Third World countries, where national state sovereignty required increasing financial support. The need for international finance became part of domestic political life. This change was gradual and silent; it never appeared in the headlines, but it altered the substance of national sovereignty. Financiers, public and private, could now shift national policy to benefit global investors: their basic strategy was to reduce the role of government in provisioning basic goods and services, to increase the role of private business enterprise, and to have governments secure advantageous conditions for investors in world markets.

South Asian countries had originally defined national sovereignty as self-sufficient national development. As independent countries, they had sought to end the outflow of wealth, which had previously enriched the imperial treasury, so as to keep more wealth to invest inside national territory to benefit national citizens. To that end, governments had variously restricted imports and exports, nationalized essential enterprises (ranging from public utilities to banks and plantations), and subsidized consumer necessities (through government food distribution) and key agricultural inputs (seeds, fertilizer, and pesticides). The result was economic stability with increasing but slow rates of economic growth, and increasing economic equality; but these came with the hidden cost of high vulnerability to price shocks on state treasuries, which hit hard with the 1970s oil shock and recession. All South Asian governments, except Bhutan, then came under the influence of Structural Adjustment Programs (SAP) of economic policy reform, first Sri Lanka (1977) and finally India (1991, Table 9). The SAP process was altered in the 1990s, when Poverty Reduction Strategy Papers secured SAP-style policy commitments, monitored by the World Bank. In return for loans, countries had to become more creditworthy: they had to stabilize currencies by tightening the money supply; they had to reduce deficits by cutting state spending; and they had to privatize state enterprises and liberalize markets, opening up their economies to free enterprise, all of which promised to increase national wealth, improve living standards, and pay back loans. This combination of loan conditions has been at work since the 1970s, under various names. The result has been a shift and standardization of national state economic policies around the world, increasing imports and exports, privatizing public enterprise, using state power to support business, integrating national economies into world markets, and accelerating rates of economic growth and accentuating economic inequality.

This new global institutional regime is not just economic. Between 1990 and 1995, international organizations of all kinds multiplied by more than half to number 41,722. International meetings increased in size and ambition. In 1995, the Fourth World

Conference on Women met in Beijing, the largest ever; it still sets the standard for global advocacy on women's rights. International organizations promoting business interests have also become increasingly powerful. The World Trade Organization (WTO) emerged from the General Agreement on Tariffs and Trade (GATT) in 1994, turning a restrictive club of trading partners into a world-embracing, rule-making and enforcing body, with 153 member nations covering almost all world trade. Like the WTO, the World Economic Forum in Davos became a media event, filled like WTO meetings with transnational glamour and protest. In 1995, the European Union and US government worked with major corporations to form a new public–private policy partnership, the Trans-Atlantic Business Dialogue, to shape global economic governance.

Governments in all South Asian countries have revised their understanding of national leadership and economic nationalism by stressing the importance of economic growth inside the world market economy, by shrinking the state public sector relative to the private sector, and by giving more social leadership and political influence to business, making government more of a business promoter, facilitator, and guarantor, particularly favouring big businesses in growth sectors such as ready-made garments (RMG) in Bangladesh and information technology (IT) in India. Being a late-comer to the new global regime, India has had the most vociferous public debates about globalization, and the Indian government has made the biggest public display of marketing the country as 'the world's largest free market democracy'. Other countries have had less success in making the nation a global brand. But all have followed the same policy path. They have shelved state redistributive programmes, most notably land reform. They have cut state expenditures that subsidize everyday consumption of food, health, and other public goods, as well as for productive inputs such as water, electricity, fertilizer, and high-yielding varieties of wheat and rice. They have exerted influence and force to benefit domestic and foreign business interests, which have become increasingly visible in government policymaking.

REGIONAL TRENDS

Present-day history is unfolding amid globalization, and identity politics are increasingly inflected by global connections, most dramatically since 2001. On 11 September 2001, teams of men from the Middle East hijacked commercial planes to blow up the

World Trade Center twin towers in New York City and attack the Pentagon in Washington, DC as part of the struggle against the US wars in the Middle East, since 1990, when the US fought Iraq's invasion of Kuwait. On 16 October 2001, the US invaded Afghanistan to overthrow the Taliban government that was believed to have supported the 9/11 attacks. The US military succeeded quickly in establishing a new regime, but the US and its allies still struggle today to control the country, facing Taliban and other rebel fighters, who also cross the border in Pakistan, where unmanned US drone bombers strike enemy targets and also kill civilians. Since the 1990s, *jihad* has been declared many times in many ways, and since 2001, the 'global war on terror' has mostly targeted Muslims, justifying attacks and counterattacks in many countries, inflecting Muslim identity in every country with global implications.

The worst civilian attack on Muslims to date occurred in Gujarat in 2002, and this violence also indicates how Hindutva has been inflected by globalization. In 1999, the BJP led the National Democratic Alliance (NDA) and won national elections in India, and the NDA held power in New Delhi until 2004. The Sangh Parivar came centre stage in national life; it captured the Indian Council of Historical Research and Ministry of Education, and set about rewriting school books so that students would learn that Hinduism is indigenously Indian and Islam and Christianity are alien. Government schools enforced the idea that Muslims and Christians had conquered and exploited Hindu India. The Sangh revived the campaign to build a Ram temple in Ayodhya, and on the morning of 27 February, a train filled with Kar Sevaks returning from Ayodhya arrived on the Sabarmati Express at the Godhra railway station in Gujarat. A fire broke out in two bogeys, killing fifty-eight people. Gujarat BJP Chief Minister Narendra Modi came to Godhra to declare that the fire was a Muslim conspiracy, blaming the deaths on Muslims who had gathered at the station to protest the Kar Sevaks' arrival. The next day, well-armed, organized gangs began killing and raping Muslims across Gujarat. Several thousand Muslims died; many thousands lost homes and livelihoods. BJP governments in Gujarat and New Delhi did little to stop the violence, and local officials colluded in attacks on Muslims. Police, lawyers, judges, and thugs then stymied efforts to prosecute rapists, arsonists, and murderers. In the famous case of the Best Bakery murders, the Supreme Court observed, on 12 April 2004 that: 'When a large number of witnesses have turned hostile it should have raised a reasonable suspicion that the witnesses were being threatened or coerced . . . [and yet] . . . public prosecutors did not take any steps to protect the star witness'. The BJP romped to electoral victory in 2003 state assembly elections under Narendra Modi's campaign slogan, 'Gujarat Unlimited', promising law and order and investment opportunities for jubilant business supporters. At a Bombay gala celebrating 'Gujarat Unlimited', one tycoon reportedly dismissed the Gujarat killings as 'a storm in a teacup'.

Human Rights Watch researchers had concluded, however, that 'what happened in Gujarat was not a spontaneous uprising', but rather, 'a carefully orchestrated attack . . . planned in advance and organized with extensive participation of the police and state government officials'. Narendra Modi had protected Hindus during the violence, and this made him a model of good governance. He became a BJP celebrity, and in December 2012 he won his fourth successive term as Chief Minister of Gujarat, largely on the basis of popular support for his government's ability to secure his state's India's superior economic growth rate. Global business connections have made this rapid growth possible, and globalization has also popularized a discourse of market freedom and consumerism, which has further bolstered Mr Modi's popularity. In 2013, he is poised to become the BJP's next candidate for Prime Minister.

India's rise to the ranks of the global economic powerhouses began in the 1990s and has continued since then, carrying political fortunes with it. Economic issues embedded in global markets have become integral features of culture, politics, and social life in South Asia. The underside of globalization has been equally influential. In 2002, hard times for poor people in Gujarat provided opportunities for the Hindutva activists who organized the killings. Free-market policies drove old textile mills out of business, throwing 100,000 workers onto the streets in Ahmedabad alone. At least a million people lost subsistence security. The government curtailed union activity in order to boost profits and growth. Upward social mobility for aspiring Dalits depleted the assets of the Dalit Panthers' social service organizations. Adivasis in the countryside, facing destitution and struggling to repay usurious loans – at 120 percent annual interest – fell into petty crime, including liquor smuggling in India's only prohibition state. In that context, Hindutva organizations attracted poor families from low-status groups with calls for Hindu unity. Many of these organizations embraced the RSS, helped the BJP win elections, and won state patronage in return. Free-market insecurity, fear, ambition, poverty, class anger, criminality, patriarchy, and communalism joined hands when Sangh Parivar recruiters gave Dalits and Adivasis jobs, loans, and other assistance, and then pushed them into violence. Adivasis killed Muslim moneylenders, eliminating Hindu Bania business competitors. Dalits looted Muslim shops and homes to reap the plunder of class war and also to liberate real estate for Hindu investors. High-caste women in high heels followed mobs into vandalized Muslim shops for riot bargain hunting, while most of the middle classes stayed at home with their doors locked. Even Mahatma Gandhi's Sabarmati Ashram closed its gates to Muslims fleeing the killer mobs.

Gujarat is unique. The 2002 killings in Gujarat do not typify India, where every state and many regions in them have unique collections of local and regional elements, as well as various connections to wider worlds. Gujarat has for centuries been uniquely connected to cultures in the Indo-Gangetic basin and around the Arabian Sea; after 1947, it became uniquely possessed by the politics of communal violence, with 3000 incidents in the 1960s alone. It does seem, however, that Gujarat is like India in the importance of economic inequality for cultural politics, and in South Asia generally, it can be said, ideology alone does not seem to bind people's loyalty to any party very strongly or for long. Most BJP voters seem to ignore Hindutva, and many Congress voters could implicitly embrace it. Electoral politics and collective action organized around it, like the 2002 killings, appear to be based mostly on the mobilization of people around ideas of what will improve their well-being, leading over time to some enduring formations of collective identity, with traditions of memory and experience. In Gujarat, the mobilization of economic self-interest seems more important for explaining the 2002 killings and Narendra Modi's celebrity than do ideological commitments to Hindutva.

Gujarat is also telling in other ways. In 2006, a committee headed by Justice Rajinder Sachar released a report showing that India's 150 million Muslims have suffered systematic deprivation to make them one of the poorest groups in the country, amounting to 14 percent of the total population. The Sachar Committee Report describes the structural inequity that is shaping the human impact of globalization, and which underlies headline events like the 2002 killings. Another telling headline event occurred in Dhaka on 25 November 2012, when 112 garment-factory workers, mostly young women, died in a fire, in a building which had been condemned as being unsafe, but where work continued to supply stitched clothing for Wal-Mart and other overseas buyers. Wal-Mart had reportedly stalled efforts to improve fire safety, citing added cost for consumers, who thus unknowingly resembled those high-heeled ladies who plucked clothes from burning Muslim shops in Ahmedabad. These headlines and many others provide a window into the structural inequity of globalization.

Opening South Asian economies to global market flows of investment, labour, culture, and communication has transformed societies and improved living conditions for many people. Educated urban elites have been the major beneficiaries, forming islands of prosperity connected to one another globally. In South Asia, the glamour of 'Asia rising' stands out in any big city, where huge shopping malls and multiplex cinemas attract well-dressed consumers driving luxury cars who send their children to the best schools both at home and abroad. At the same time, and in the same countries, economic disparities are increasing, as they are between rich and poor around the world. India is indicative. In 2004, National Sample Survey data showed that after 1991, new wealth went mostly to the richer classes with privileged access to government and new market opportunities. The urban rich benefited the most: the top quintile of income groups in cities increased their per capita consumption by 40 percent, but in rural areas, by just 20 percent. The rural rich therefore got richer compared to their village neighbours, but got poorer compared to the urban rich, a comparison that politicians took seriously and which helps to explain the change in Indian governments in 2004, when the BJP's 'India Shining' campaign flopped and the new Prime Minister had to face the fact that 600 million Indians, in the bottom 80 percent of rural income groups, had suffered a steady decline in per capita consumption under reforms he introduced as Finance Minister in 1991, which he vowed to accelerate after 2004. Manmohan Singh could, however, feel good that 300 million Indian citizens did get richer under liberalization, after 1991, and that the richest among them became media stars for his aggressive ad campaign promoting India as 'the world's fastest-growing free-market democracy'.

In the poor, dry farming regions of Maharashtra and the Deccan, it is estimated that 250,000 farmers have committed suicide since 1997; that is a rate of two farmers per day, one every twelve hours, for the last fifteen years. For these farmers, swallowing pesticide has proved the only way to escape insurmountable debt in the context of a declining income and rising costs. Family traditions of landownership can also translate into education, business, and employment opportunities, which are not available to the landless, highlighting again the significance of land reform. Upward trajectories of social

mobility typically begin with good landed property. The vast majority of people with no property or with tiny bits of poor farmland
benefit from globalization mostly by migrating to the towns to join
the rapidly growing informal economy. In India, where a CEO's
income can be 30,000 times greater than a typical worker's wage,
real wages have been declining, most of all in agriculture.

Less urbanized regions which depend on agriculture have seen
their prosperity decline, even Punjab, India's richest farming region,
because of declining water tables, increasing input costs, lower soil
fertility, and low support prices for crops. Since the 1990s, annual
growth in agriculture and allied services has dipped to less than half
the rate of growth in India's average per capita GDP, and the ratio
of rural-to-urban poverty has increased. Rural poverty moves to the
city to live in growing slums, which are also out of the loop of capital accumulation that concentrates wealth in affluent neighbour-
hoods protected by high walls and security guards.

Globalization has thus produced a shifting geography of economic and political power, which is invisible in the news. In India,
recent growth has favoured states in the south and west, distressing
states in the north and north-east. The relative poverty of the eastern
Gangetic basin, compared to the west and Punjab, goes back to the
nineteenth century, and continued after independence, but the rise
of south and west India is new, resulting clearly from market-driven
economic growth which has most benefited tightly integrated
urban–rural economic regions in the peninsula and on the Indian
Ocean coast – including Gujarat – where circular migration to the
Persian Gulf and South-East Asia has raised incomes for workers.
Whole regions of South Asia remain out of the loop of capital accumulation under globalization, however, particularly the mountain
regions spanning Nepal, north-east India, and the Chittagong Hill
Tracts. Farmers in rural Afghanistan, always at the centre of east–
west overland trades, and now racked by war, have managed to
reap profits by growing opium for world markets.

Gender inequality indicates that economic growth is necessary
but insufficient by itself for improving social well-being. In 2003, a
study of gender disparity in India concluded in line with earlier
research that the poorest Indian states (with about half the total
population, mostly in the eastern Gangetic Plain) had not improved
conditions for women, while the worst gender disparity continued to
prevail in the richer and faster-growing states, above all Punjab and
Haryana. Globalization has produced a very large female urban
labour force, in industry and services, but wages and working

conditions have not improved in proportion to the profitability of urban businesses for investors. Dangerous sweatshop conditions prevail in many localities, as indicated by the 2012 Dhaka factory fire and even deadlier collapse of the Rana Plaza garment factories in April 2013, which killed over 1100 young people. Women have been targeted as beneficiaries in many development programmes, particularly as recipients for microcredit loans, which have produced huge profits for loan providers but less clear-cut benefits for recipients, whose major measure of 'empowerment' is their ability to repay the loans.

Many minority ethnic groups are trapped in the structural inequity of globalization. India's Muslims are one among many. Where minority ethnic groups concentrate in specific regions, rebellions are more common, and states often respond with force, increasingly, it seems, since the 1990s, in part because many mountain regions are rich in minerals, and in part to secure orderly conditions for global investors. As economic growth rates have increased along with economic inequity, national and international security regimes have become increasingly well-funded and well-armed. Financing security is ever more profitable. Spaces of globalization now include high walls with armed guards around gated urban communities and at national borders, for example, at India's border with Bangladesh, as well as heavy security at airports, and military garrisons in ethnic-minority regions of rebellion. The Chittagong Hill Tracts – the only non-Muslim region of Bangladesh – have been occupied by the military for decades. Kashmir is the only Muslim-majority region of India, and has been under military occupation since the 1990s. India's Armed Forces (Special Powers) Act of 1958 (AFSPA) gives security forces unrestricted power in an area that is declared 'disturbed', where soldiers can shoot to kill on suspicion of threats to public order. AFSPA was first applied to the north-eastern states of Assam and Manipur and was amended in 1972 to extend to all seven states in north-east India: Assam, Manipur, Tripura, Meghalaya, Arunachal Pradesh, Mizoram, and Nagaland. In the mountain-forest regions of eastern India, a Maoist rebellion emerged among minority groups threatened by land grabbing and mining operations after economic reforms in the 1990s. The government of India banned Maoist groups in 2004, with amendments to the 1967 Unlawful Activities (Prevention) Act; and the Chhattisgarh state government passed the Special Public Security Act in 2005, which allows police to arrest people who have a 'tendency to pose an obstacle to the administration of law', stating that any actions to 'encourage the disobedience of the established law' will be considered 'unlawful'.

TABLE 9. EVENTS IN THE HISTORICAL PRESENT

Year   Event

Year	Event
1985	Afghanistan: Mujahidin from Afghanistan come together in Pakistan to form alliance against Soviet forces.
	Nepal: Nepal Congress Party (NCP) begins civil disobedience campaign for restoration of multi-party system.
	Pakistan: martial law and political parties ban lifted.
	Sri Lanka: first attempt at peace talks between Sri Lankan government and LTTE fails.
1986	World Bank issues first Structural Adjustment credit to Nepal, but policies not strictly enforced until 1991, under Nepali Congress Party.
	Bangladesh: military ruler General Muhammad Ershad elected to a five-year term; he lifts martial law and reinstates the constitution.
1987	Structural Adjustment Program (SAP) approved for Bangladesh.
	Pakistan: state of emergency declared after opposition demonstrations and strikes.
1988	Pakistan agrees to SAP under IMF and World Bank.
	Afghanistan: US, USSR, and Pakistan sign peace accords and Soviet Union begins pulling out troops.
	Bangladesh suffers worst flood in 20 years. Ershad pushes constitutional amendment establishing the 'Islamic way of life' as state principle. This is retained under later elected governments.
	Benazir Bhutto's PPP wins general election.
1989	Sri Lanka progresses towards SAP under World Bank, following economic policies initiated in 1977. Trade and transit dispute with India leads to border blockade by Delhi resulting in worsening economic situation.

TABLE 9. *CONTINUED*

Year   Event

1990   Bangladesh: Ershad steps down following mass protests.

Nepal becomes parliamentary monarchy.

Bhutan People's Party begins campaign of violence, causing thousands of ethnic Nepalis to flee to Nepal.

Sri Lanka: Indian troops leave.

India: military operations begin against the United Liberation Front of Assam (ULFA). In Kashmir, Farooq Abdullah resigns as Chief Minister, troops kill unarmed protesters, millions protest, and more killed in police firing. Militant groups, violence, and threats lead to exodus of most Hindus and entire Kashmiri Pandit community. Indian military occupation, repression, upheaval, human rights violations, and civilian casualties begin.

1991   Nepal: first elections held, won by NCP.

Bangladesh: first elections after 15 years of military rule. Bangladesh National Party (BNP) wins in close race with Awami League.

India participates in SAP through World Bank economic reform.

Pakistan: Prime Minister Nawaz Sharif begins economic liberalization programme and Islamic Shariah law formally incorporated into legal code.

1992   Afghanistan: Najibullah's government is toppled; civil war follows.

India: 6 December destruction of Babri Masjid.

1993   Pakistan: general election brings Benazir Bhutto back to power.

1994   Sri Lanka: President Kumaratunga elected, after Premadasa assassinated by LTTE, pledging to end war; peace talks open with LTTE.

Nepal: NCP government falls in no confidence vote. Communists take power.

TABLE 9. *CONTINUED*

Year	Event
1995	Nepal: start of rapid succession of elected governments.
	Sri Lanka: 'Third Eelam War' begins.
1996	Afghanistan: Taliban seize control of Kabul and introduce Islamic rule.
	Bangladesh: Awami League wins elections.
	Nepal: start of Maoist People's War.
	Pakistan: president dismisses Bhutto government amid corruption allegations.
1997	Bhutan: Amnesty International raises concern over human rights.
	Pakistan: Nawaz Sharif returns as Prime Minister after his Pakistan Muslim League Party wins elections.
1998	India: BJP heads the coalition National Democratic Alliance (NDA), wins election, and rules until 2004. India carries out nuclear tests.
	Pakistan conducts nuclear tests.
1999	Bhutan: limited television and internet services allowed.
	India–Pakistan military conflict at Kargil.
	Pakistan: General Pervez Musharraf seizes power in coup.
2001	Pakistan: World Bank approves Interim-Poverty Reduction Strategy Paper (I-PRSP).
	Afghanistan: US invasion and bombing begins. Taliban overthrown and Hamid Karzai sworn in as head of an interim power-sharing government.
	Bangladesh: BNP and its three coalition partners win power.
	India–Pakistan troops confront each other at the Line of Control
	Nepal: King Birendra and most of his family killed in shooting by Crown Prince Dipendra, who shoots himself; Prince Gayendra crowned king.
	Pakistan: Pervez Musharraf names himself President while remaining head of the army; expresses support of US invasion of Afghanistan.

TABLE 9. *CONTINUED*

Year	Event
2002	Nepal: tenth national economic plan in the form of Poverty Reduction Strategy Paper (PRSP) initiated under World Bank and IMF as successor to SAP.
	India: organized killings ensue in Gujarat after Hindutva activists die in train fire.
	Maldives: concern over vulnerability to rising sea levels prompts government to announce decision to take legal action against the US for refusing to sign Kyoto Protocols.
	Nepal: Parliament is dissolved; king indefinitely postpones elections.
	Pakistan: President Musharraf grants himself sweeping new powers, including the right to dismiss an elected parliament.
2003	Bangladesh: change in economic focus to poverty alleviation, following Pakistan and Nepal, under guidance of World Bank and IMF.
	Afghanistan: NATO takes control of security in Kabul, its first-ever operational commitment outside Europe.
	Maldives: Amnesty International accuses Maldives government of political repression and torture.
2004	Bangladesh: opposition calls 21 general strikes in one year; 45 Parliament seats reserved for women.
	India: 'India Shining' slogan launches government marketing of 'world's largest free market democracy', but fails to win NDA victory. Congress-led coalition United Progressive Alliance (UPA) wins national election. India launches an application for a permanent seat on the UN Security Council.
	Maldives: pro-democracy demonstrations; state of emergency imposed.
	Nepal joins the World Trade Organization (WTO).
	Pakistan: military offensive against suspected Al-Qaeda units in north-west tribal areas near Afghan border; readmitted to Commonwealth.

TABLE 9. *CONTINUED*

Year	Event

2005   Afghanistan: parliamentary elections; warlords and strongmen take most seats.

Maldives: Parliament votes unanimously to allow multi-party politics.

Sri Lanka: foreign minister killed; state of emergency.

2006   Bhutan: king abdicates; crown prince assumes the throne.

India: launch of largest-ever rural employment programme.

Nepal: Parliament votes unanimously to curtail the king's political powers; government and Maoists sign a peace accord; Comprehensive Peace Agreement (CPA) declares formal end to a 10-year rebel insurgency.

Pakistan: government signs peace accord with pro-Al-Qaeda militants in Waziristan tribal areas near Afghan border.

Sri Lanka: Tamil Tiger rebels and government forces resume fighting in worst clashes since 2002 ceasefire; peace talks fail in Geneva.

2007   Afghanistan: opium production at record high, according to UN reports.

Bangladesh: state of emergency declared under military, officially for the purpose of securing fair elections; lasts from January 2007 to December 2008.

Bhutan: signs a landmark agreement with India, giving Bhutan more say over its foreign and defence policies.

Nepal: Maoists quit interim government to press demand for monarchy to be scrapped; Parliament approves abolition of monarchy as part of peace deal with Maoists.

Pakistan: President Musharraf wins presidential election; challenged by Supreme Court; declares emergency rule, dismisses Chief Justice and appoints new Supreme Court, which confirms his re-election. Benazir Bhutto assassinated at political rally. President Musharraf resigns; MPs elect Pakistan People's Party's (PPP) Asif Ali Zardari – the widower of Benazir Bhutto – president.

TABLE 9. *CONTINUED*

Year	Event

2008   Afghanistan: National Development Strategy (NDS) drawn from Poverty Reduction Strategy Papers (PRSP), SAP successor.

Bangladesh: Awami League takes Parliament and Sheikh Hasina becomes Prime Minister.

Bhutan: pro-monarchy Bhutan Harmony Party wins 44 out of the 47 seats in the country's first parliamentary elections.

Maldives: President Gayoom of Maldives ratifies new constitution that paves the way for first multi-party presidential elections.

Nepal: monarchy formally abolished; republic formed; writing of new constitution begins.

Pakistan: huge loan from IMF to overcome debt crisis.

Sri Lanka: government pulls out of 2002 ceasefire agreement, launches massive offensive against Tamil Tigers.

2009   Afghanistan: presidential and provincial elections, widespread Taliban attacks, patchy turnout; Karzai becomes president again.

Bangladesh: High Court rules that Sheik Mujib first proclaimed independence from Pakistan in 1971.

India: deal with Russia to supply uranium to Delhi; government approves idea for a new state, Telangana, to be carved out of Andhra Pradesh, violence follows.

Pakistan: government agrees to implement Sharia law in north-western Swat Valley to persuade Islamist militants to agree to permanent ceasefire.

Sri Lanka: government rejects conditions for IMF $1.9 billion emergency loan; Tamil Tigers declared defeated after massive military assault; their leader, Velupillai Prabhakaran, killed; state human-rights abuse charged.

TABLE 9. *CONTINUED*

Year	Event
2010	Afghanistan: government reforms.
	Sri Lanka: Mahinda Rajapaksa re-elected; rival Fonseka is jailed. European Union suspends Sri Lanka's preferential trade status because of concerns over human rights record; Parliament approves a constitutional change allowing President Rajapaksa to seek unlimited number of terms.
2011	Afghanistan: strategic partnership signed with India to expand co-operation in security and development; President Karzai wins the endorsement of tribal elders to negotiate a 10-year military partnership with the US. 2014 deadline set for US troops to leave.
	India: telecom corruption scandal rocks government. Anna Hazare stages hunger strike in protest.
	Pakistan: campaign to reform Pakistan's blasphemy law leads to the killing of two prominent supporters, Punjab Governor Salman Taseer in January, and Minorities Minister Shahbaz Bhatti in March. Pakistan shuts down NATO supply routes after NATO attack kills 25 Pakistani soldiers.
	Sri Lanka: expiration of emergency laws; critics accuse continuation in new guise.
2012	Afghanistan: Tokyo donor conference pledges $16 billion in civilian aid.
	Maldives: President Nasheed of Maldives announces his resignation after a mutiny by police and demonstrations over the arrest of the chief justice.
	Nepal: three political parties resign from the Nepali government over failure to agree on a new constitution.
	Pakistan: US Senate panel cuts $33 million in aid over the jailing of Pakistani doctor Shakil Afridi who helped the CIA find Osama bin Laden. Pakistan agrees to reopen NATO supply routes to Afghanistan after the US apologizes for killing 24 Pakistani soldiers in November.

TABLE 9. *CONTINUED*

Year *Event*

India: Indian government and Lok Sabha vote in support of increasing Foreign Direct Investment (FDI) in retail; Wal-Mart accused of bribery in its effort to enter the Indian (and Mexican) retail markets; corruption scandals and weak economy undermine support for UPA as elections loom.

Bangladesh: 112 workers die in garment factory fire near Dhaka; thousands of workers protest; Wal-Mart implicated in efforts to block measures to improve fire safety in this, among other suppliers of cheap clothing for US markets.

Ethnic-minority rebellions have dominated national politics in Sri Lanka and Nepal, with opposite outcomes. In Sri Lanka, the Tamil rebellion led by the LTTE was finally crushed by government forces in 2009, with heavy civilian casualties. In Nepal, a Maoist rebellion that spread throughout the country from the late 1990s finally led to the inclusion of the Maoists in the national political system; they were victorious in the 2008 elections, and dissolved the monarchy; but the new political system has yet to produce a new constitution which can successfully include all of Nepal's ethnic minorities in democratic governance.

Global South Asia is expanding its presence and significance in the world of nations, where globalization is increasing economic growth, enabling many people to improve their lives, but also increasing economic volatility and inequality, dragging many people down. Current history in South Asia indicates the spatial and social diversity of globalization, and also the role of political and cultural activism in distributing its benefits.

Selected Readings

The New Cambridge History of India (23 vols. Cambridge: Cambridge University Press, 1987–2005) is a vast resource. The internet is increasingly essential: the University of Chicago has a quality reference page (http://www.lib.uchicago.edu/e/su/southasia/reference.html) and its Digital South Asia Library (http://dsal.uchicago.edu/) includes the most critical reference work for historians, Joseph E. Schwartzberg's *Historical Atlas of South Asia* (2nd edition. New York: Oxford University Press, 1992; http://dsal.uchicago.edu/reference/schwartzberg/). For broad surveys, see Burton Stein, *A History of India* (London: Blackwell, 1998); K. M. De Silva, *A History of Sri Lanka* (New York: Penguin Books, 2005); Thomas Barfield, *Afghanistan: A Cultural and Political History* (Princeton: Princeton University Press, 2010); John Whelpton, *A History of Nepal* (Cambridge: Cambridge University Press, 2005); and Willem van Schendel, *A History of Bangladesh* (Cambridge: Cambridge University Press, 2009). Christopher V. Hill, *South Asia: An Environmental History* (Santa Barbara: ABC-CLIO, 2008) and Tirthankar Roy, *India in the World Economy: from Antiquity to the Present* (Cambridge: Cambridge University Press, 2012) provide timely thematic approaches to history in the very long–term.

The Indus Valley civilization unfolds visually in http://www.harappa.com/har/har0.html and historically in Gregory L. Possehl, *The Indus Civilization: a Contemporary Perspective* (Walnut Creek: AltaMira Press, 2002). Transitions from prehistory to ancient history are most accessible in Jonathan Kenoyer and Kimberly Heuston, *The Ancient South Asian World* (New York: Oxford University Press, 2005). Books by Romila Thapar anchor the reading list in ancient history: *Ashoka and the Decline of the*

Mauryas (New Delhi: Oxford University Press, 2012); *From Lineage to State: Social Formation in the Mid-First Millennium BC in the Ganges Valley* (Delhi: Oxford University Press, 1996); *The Aryan: Recasting Constructs* (Gurgaon: Three Essays Collective, 2008); and *India: Historical Beginnings and the Concept of the Aryan* (New Delhi: National Book Trust, 2006).

Transitions across ancient and medieval epochs appear in Romila Thapar's *Early India: from the Origins to AD 1300* (London: Penguin, 2002) and *Somanatha: the Many Voices of a History* (London: Verso, 2005); Brajadulal Chattopadhyaya, *The Making of Early Medieval India* (Delhi: Oxford University Press, 1994); R. A. H. L. Gunawardana, *Robe and Plough: Monastacism and Economic Interest in Early Medieval Sri Lanka* (Tucson: University of Arizona Press, 1979); D. R. Regmi, *Medieval Nepal* (4 vols. Calcutta: Firma K. L. Mukhopadhyaya, 1965–6); Johannes Bronkhorst, *Buddhism in the Shadow of Brahmanism* (Leiden: E. J. Brill 2011); *Monasteries, Shrines, and Society: Buddhist and Brahmanical Religious Institutions in India in their Socio-Economic Context*, edited by Birendranath Prasad (New Delhi: Manak Publishers, 2011); Sheldon Pollock, *The Language of the Gods in the World of Men: Sanskrit, Culture, and Power in Premodern India* (Berkeley: University of California Press, 2006); *Literary Cultures in History: Reconstructions from South Asia*, edited by Sheldon Pollock (Berkeley: University of California Press, 2003); and Burjor Avari, *India, the Ancient Past: a History of the Indian Sub-continent from c. 7000 BC to AD 1200* (London: Routledge, 2007).

Expansive pre-modern historical spaces affecting local histories in South Asia became visible with Janet L. Abu-Lughod, *Before European Hegemony: the World System AD 1250–1350* (New York: Oxford University Press, 1989); K. N. Chaudhuri, *Asia before Europe: Economy and Civilisation of the Indian Ocean from the Rise of Islam to 1750* (Cambridge: Cambridge University Press, 1990); and Richard M. Eaton, *The Rise of Islam and the Bengal Frontier, 1204–1760* (Berkeley: University of California Press, 1993). To these we can now add Liu Xin Ru, *The Silk Road in World History* (New York: Oxford University Press, 2010); Jason Emmanuel Neelis, *Early Buddhist Transmission and Trade Networks: Mobility and Exchange within and beyond the Northwestern Borderlands of South Asia* (Leiden: Brill, 2011); *Society and Circulation: Mobile People and Itinerant Cultures in South Asia, 1750–1950*, edited by Claude Markovits, Jacques Pouchepadass, and Sanjay

Subrahmanyam (Delhi: Permanent Black, 2003); Michael Pearson, *The Indian Ocean* (London: Routledge, 2003); and Milo Kearney, *The Indian Ocean in World History* (London: Routledge, 2004).

Foundations for Mughal historical studies remain Irfan Habib, *The Agrarian System of Mughal India* (New York: Columbia University Press, 1964), and (editor) *An Atlas of Mughal Empire* (Delhi: Oxford University Press, 1982), along with *The Cambridge Economic History of India*, Volume I, edited by Tapan Raychaudhuri and Irfan Habib (Cambridge: Cambridge University Press, 1982), and M. Athar Ali, *Mughal India: Studies in Polity, Ideas, Society, and Culture* (New Delhi: Oxford University Press, 2006). More expansive Mughal spaces come to light in Stephen Dale, *The Muslim Empires of the Ottomans, Safavids, and Mughals* (Cambridge: Cambridge University Press, 2010); Lisa Balabanlilar, *Imperial Identity in the Mughal Empire: Memory and Dynastic Politics in Early Modern South and Central Asia* (London: I. B. Tauris, 2012); Muzaffar Alam and Sanjay Subrahmanyam, *Writing the Mughal World: Studies on Culture and Politics* (New York: Columbia University Press, 2012); *Universal Empire: A Comparative Approach to Imperial Culture and Representation in Eurasian History*, edited by Peter Filbiger Bang and Dariusz Kolodziejczyk (Cambridge: Cambridge University Press, 2012); Andre Wink, *Al-Hind, the Making of the Indo-Islamic World* (Leiden: E. J. Brill, 1990); S. M. Ikram, *Muslim Civilization in India* (New York: Columbia University Press, 1964); and Burjor Avari, *Islamic Civilization in South Asia: a History of Muslim Power and Presence in the Indian Subcontinent* (New York: Routledge, 2012).

The study of modernity has now been complicated by exposing early-modern transitions and questioning national boundaries as containers of history: see *After the Imperial Turn: Thinking with and through the Nation*, edited by Antoinette Burton (Durham: Duke University Press, 2003). C. A. Bayly's books open up studies of early-modern South Asia: *Imperial Meridian: the British Empire and the World, 1780–1830* (London: Longman, 1989), *Indian Society and the Making of the British Empire* (Cambridge: Cambridge University Press, 1988), and *Empire and Information: Intelligence Gathering and Social Communication in India, 1780–1870* (Cambridge: Cambridge University Press, 1996). The early-modern Indian Ocean comes to life in books by Pearson and Kearney, cited above, and British Empire's Indian Ocean expanse appears in Thomas R. Metcalf, *Imperial Connections: India in the Indian Ocean Arena, 1860–1920* (Berkeley: University of California

Press, 2007) and Sugata Bose, *A Hundred Horizons: the Indian Ocean in the Age of Global Empire* (Cambridge: Harvard University Press, 2006). Thomas R. Metcalf explores imperial ideologies with lasting modern impact in *Ideologies of the Raj* (Cambridge: Cambridge University Press, 1994). Peter Perdue and Huri Islamoglu provide comparative perspectives on modernity in their edited volume, *Shared Histories of Modernity: China, India and the Ottoman Empire* (New York: Routledge, 2009).

For economic history, Tirthankar Roy, *The Economic History of India, 1857–1947* (Cambridge: Cambridge University Press, 1998) provides a useful survey. Basic sources remain Dharma Kumar and Meghnad Desai, *The Cambridge Economic History of India, Volume II, c. 1750–c. 1970* (Cambridge: Cambridge University Press, 1983), and B. R. Tomlinson, *The Economy of Modern India* (Cambridge: Cambridge University Press, 1998). Recent economic trends appear in Moazzem Hossain, Rajat Kathuria, and Iyanatul Islam, *South Asian Economic Development* (2nd edition, London: Routledge, 2010), and A. S. Bhalla, *Globalization, Growth and Marginalization* (New York: St Martin's Press, 1998), and for details on India, see *Indian Economy since Independence*, edited by Uma Kapila (21st edition, New Delhi: Academic Foundation, 2011).

Nationality and nationalism are ever-expanding historical subjects. Their co-creation in the imperial context unfolds in C. A. Bayly, *Origins of Nationality in South Asia: Patriotism and Ethical Government in the Making of Modern India* (Oxford: Oxford University Press, 1998) and Manu Goswami, *Producing India: from Colonial Economy to National Space* (Chicago: University of Chicago Press, 2004). Intellectuals take centre stage in Partha Chatterjee, *Nationalist Thought and the Colonial World: a Derivative Discourse?* (London: Zed Books, 1986); Ananya Vajpeyi, *Righteous Republic: the Political Foundations of Modern India* (Cambridge: Harvard University Press, 2012); and Pankaj Mishra, *From the Ruins of Empire: The Intellectuals who Remade Asia* (New York: Strauss and Giroux, 2012). Judith Brown, *Modern India: The Origins of an Asian Democracy* (Oxford: Oxford University Press, 1985) remains the best institutional account of national politics in British India. Bipan Chandra, *The Rise and Growth of Economic Nationalism in India: Economic Policies of the Indian National Leadership* (New Delhi: People's Publishing House, 1966) explains the origins of *swadeshi*, still a potent force in Indian politics. On the politics of nationalism, Bipan Chandra, *Nationalism and*

Colonialism in Modern India (Delhi: Longman, 1979) and Sumit Sarkar, *Modern India, 1885–1947* (Delhi: Macmillan, 1983) focus on India, and Sugata Bose and Ayesha Jalal provide somewhat broader coverage in *Modern South Asia: History, Culture, and Political Economy* (3rd edition. New York: Routledge, 2011). Bipan Chandra, Aditya Mukherjee, and Mridula Mukherjee, *India after Independence* (New Delhi: Penguin Books, 1999) and Ramachandra Guha, *India after Gandhi: the History of the World's Largest Democracy* (London: Macmillan, 2007) bring Indian national history down to the present.

A great diversity of historical trajectories tangle together to create and transform national environments. G. Aloysius, *Nationalism without a Nation in India* (Oxford University Press, 1997) provides an introduction. Religious diversity is prominent – see *Making India Hindu: Religion, Community, and the Politics of Democracy*, edited by David Ludden (2nd edition. Delhi: Oxford University Press, 2005) – and in that context, Muslim political histories have become prominent: see Peter Hardy, *The Muslims of British India* (Cambridge: Cambridge University Press, 1972); David Gilmartin, *Empire and Islam: Punjab and the Making of Pakistan* (Berkeley: University of California Press, 1988); Taj ul-Islam Hashmi, *Pakistan as Peasant Utopia: The Communalization of Class Politics in East Bengal, 1920–1947* (Boulder: Westview, 1992); Ayesha Jalal, *The Sole Spokesman: Jinnah, the Muslim League, and the Demand for Pakistan* (Cambridge: Cambridge University Press, 1994); and Mushirul Hasan, *Making Sense of History: Society, Culture and Politics* (New Delhi: Manohar, 2003) and *A Moral Reckoning: Muslim Intellectuals in Nineteenth-Century Delhi* (New Delhi: Oxford University Press, 2005). Mushirul Hasan has also edited *India's Partition: Process, Strategy and Mobilization* (Delhi: Oxford University Press, 1993), and *India Partitioned: the Other Face of Freedom* (New Delhi: Lotus Collection, 1995).

Many other vectors of difference defining spaces that challenge national territorialism have also become prominent subjects of study, enabling history to illuminate present-day issues inside and crossing national boundaries. *Peasant Struggles in India*, edited by A. R. Desai (Bombay: Oxford University Press, 1979) casts new light on rebels outside national politics, as foreshadowed by A. R. Desai, *Social Background of Indian Nationalism* (Bombay: Oxford University Press, 1948). Subaltern Studies then developed the theme of subordinate resistance to elite authority in great detail – see *Reading Subaltern Studies: Critical History, Contested Meaning, and the Globalisation of South Asia* (New Delhi: Permanent Black, 2002) edited by David Ludden – led by Ranajit Guha, whose books include *Elementary Aspects of Peasant Insurgency in Colonial India* (Delhi: Oxford, 1983), *Selected Subaltern Studies,* edited with Gayatri Chakravorty Spivak (New York: Oxford University Press, 1988), *The Small Voice of History: Collected Essays,* edited with introduction by Partha Chatterjee (Ranikhet: Permanent Black, 2009), and *Dominance without Hegemony: History and Power in Colonial India* (Cambridge: Harvard University Press, 1997).

Gendered histories add further complications. *From Gender to Nation,* edited by Rada Ivekovic and Julie Mostov (Ravenna: Longo, 2002) provides a comparative perspective on gender themes that trouble national history and are explored further in Bina D'Costa, *Nation-Building, Gender and War Crimes in South Asia* (New York: Routledge, 2011). Radha Kumar, *A History of Doing: An Illustrated Account of Movements for Women's Rights and Feminism in India, 1800–1990* (London: Verso, 1997) and *South Asian Feminisms,* edited by Ania Loomba and Ritty A. Lukose (Durham: Duke University Press, 2012) are invaluable guides to the entangling of feminist with national histories.

Ethnic-minority territorialism has most of all troubled national states in the post-colonial world. *Ethnonationalism in India: a Reader,* edited by Sanjib Baruah (New Delhi: Oxford University Press, 2010) surveys ethno-cultural politics explored further for India in Sanjib Baruah, *Durable Disorder: Understanding the Politics of Northeast India* (New York: Oxford University Press, 2005); Shail Mayaram, *Against History, Against State: Counter-perspectives from the Margins* (New York: Columbia University Press, 2003); and Marcus Franke, *War and Nationalism in South Asia: The Indian State and the Nagas* (London: Routledge, 2009). For Bangladesh, see Shapan Adnan, *Migration, Land Alienation and Ethnic Conflict: Causes of Poverty in the Chittagong Hill Tracts of Bangladesh* (Dhaka: Research and Advisory Services, 2004). For Kashmir, see Mridu Rai, *Hindu Rulers, Muslim Subjects: Islam, Rights, and the History of Kashmir* (Princeton: Princeton University Press, 2004); and *The Parchment of Kashmir: History, Society, and Polity,* edited by Nyla Ali Khan (New York: Palgrave Macmillan, 2012). In Sri Lanka, the long, recently ended civil war, officially called an 'ethnic conflict', remains a major theme for history-in-the-present, in personal histories such as Sarika Thiranagama, *In My Mother's House: Civil War in Sri Lanka* (Philadelphia: University of Pennsylvania Press, 2011), and in many political studies, such as M. R. Narayan Swamy, *The Tiger Vanquished: LTTE's story* (New Delhi: Sage, 2010).

Globalization is also defining spaces that challenge national territorialism by changing the substance of national community: see Benedict Anderson, *Imagined Communities: Reflections on the Origin and Spread of Nationalism* (London: Verso, 2006). In *Sri Lanka: Biography of an Island: Between Local and Global* (Paris: Aviator Books, 2006), Eric Meyer notably argues that states accelerate globalization by reducing government provisioning of goods and services; this reduces the nation's ability to sustain the livelihoods, aspirations, and loyalties of disadvantaged minorities; so that increasing economic inequality that favours privileged groups may encourage the use of military force and populist cultural majoritarianism to enforce national unity, as elites and subalterns alike become more expansively networked globally. Globalization is thus making national territorialism a historical problem: see Vazira Fazila-Yacoobali Zamindar, *The Long Partition and the Making of Modern South Asia: Refugees, Boundaries, Histories* (New York: Columbia University Press, 2007); Willem van Schendel, *The Bengal Borderland: Beyond State and Nation in South Asia* (London: Anthem, 2005); Deepak Singh, *Stateless in South Asia: the Chakmas between Bangladesh and India* (Los Angeles: Sage, 2010); and *Refugees and the State: Practices of Asylum and Care in India, 1947–2000*, edited by Ranabir Samaddar (New Delhi: Sage Publications, 2003).

In every country, scholars are rethinking the historical entanglements of states, nations, economies, societies, and cultures. For India, see notably Sumit Sarkar, *Beyond Nationalist Frames: Postmodernism, Hindu Fundamentalism, History* (Bloomington: Indiana University Press, 2002); Nivedita Menon and Sanjay Nigam, *Power and Contestation: India since 1989* (London: Zed, 2007); *Violence and Democracy in India,* edited by Amrita Basu and Srirupa Roy (New York: Seagull Books, 2007); Partha Chatterjee, *Empire and Nation: Selected Essays* (New York: Columbia University Press, 2010); and Atul Kohli, *Poverty amid Plenty in the New India* (New York: Cambridge University Press, 2012). For Pakistan, see Saadia Toor, *The State of Islam: Culture and Cold War Politics in Pakistan* (London: Pluto Press, 2011); and four books by Ayesha Jalal: *The State of Martial Rule: the Origins of Pakistan's Political Economy of Defence* (Cambridge: Cambridge University Press, 1990), *Democracy and Authoritarianism in South Asia: a Comparative and Historical Perspective* (New York: Cambridge University Press,

1995), *Self and Sovereignty: Individual and Community in South Asian Islam since 1850* (London: Routledge, 2000), and *Partisans of Allah: Jihad in South Asia* (Cambridge: Harvard University Press, 2008). For Afghanistan, see *Globalizing Afghanistan: Terrorism, War, and the Rhetoric of Nation Building*, edited by Zubeda Jalalzai and David Jefferess (Durham: Duke University Press, 2011); Shah Mahmoud Hanifi, *Connecting Histories in Afghanistan: Market Relations and State Formation on a Colonial Frontier* (Stanford: Stanford University Press, 2011); and Robert Nichols, *Settling the Frontier: Land, Law and Society in the Peshawar Valley, 1500–1900* (Karachi: Oxford University Press, 2001), and *A History of Pashtun Migration, 1775–2006* (New York: Oxford University Press, 2008).

Nepal includes all the vectors of difference which challenge national territorialism in South Asia, and its contemporary history is in that respect a crucible for the production of new national possibilities in the world of globalization. Useful readings include David Seddon, *Nepal: A State of Poverty* (Delhi: Vikas, 1987); David N. Gellner, Joanna Pfaff-Czarnecka, and John Whelpton, *Nationalism and Ethnicity in a Hindu Kingdom: the Politics of Culture in Contemporary Nepal* (Amsterdam: Harwood, 1997); Deepak Thapa, *Understanding the Maoist Movement of Nepal* (Kathmandu: Centre for Social Research and Development; 2003); Susan I. Hangen, *The Rise of Ethnic Politics in Nepal: Democracy in the Margins* (London: Routledge, 2010); *Nepal in Transition: from People's War to Fragile Peace*, edited by Sebastian von Einsiedel, David Malone, and Suman Pradhan (New York: Cambridge University Press, 2012); and Mahendra Lawoti and Susan Hangen, *Nationalism and Ethnic Conflict in Nepal: Identities and Mobilization after 1990* (London: Routledge, 2013).

Index